# Modern Speech

# Modern Speech

**JOHN V. IRWIN**
Professor of Speech, University of Wisconsin, Madison, Wisconsin

**MARJORIE ROSENBERGER**
Director of Speech, Withrow High School, Cincinnati, Ohio

With editorial assistance from RALPH G. McGEE
Director of Forensics, New Trier High School, Winnetka, Illinois

1866

HOLT, RINEHART AND WINSTON, INC. • NEW YORK

Library of Congress Catalog Card Number: 61-6490

Printed in the United States of America
14324-0111

64A9

Grateful acknowledgment for permission to use material is made to the following authors and publishers:

American Book Company for "The Wind and the Sun" from *McGuffey Readers.*

Brandt & Brandt for "Nancy Hanks" by Rosemary Carr Benét from *A Book of Americans,* Rinehart & Company, Inc., Copyright 1933, by Rosemary and Stephen Vincent Benét.

Doubleday & Company, Inc. for "Experience" from *Candles That Burn* by Aline Kilmer, Copyright 1919, by George H. Doran Company. Reprinted by permission of Doubleday & Company, Inc.

Droke House for quotation from *The Speaker's Special Occasion Book* by Herbert V. Prochnow.

Duell, Sloane & Pearce, Inc. for "Casey Jones" from *Folk Songs U.S.A.* by John A. Lomax and Alan Lomax, Copyright 1947. By permission of the publisher.

E. P. Dutton & Co., Inc. for "Vespers" from *When We Were Very Young* by A. A. Milne, Copyright 1924, by E. P. Dutton & Co., Inc. Renewal by A. A. Milne. Also for "Habits of the Hippopotamus" from *Gaily the Troubador* by Arthur Guiterman, Copyright 1936, by E. P. Dutton & Co., Inc.; and "America the Beautiful" from *The Retinue & Other Poems* by Bates. All reprinted by permission of the publisher.

Frank Music Corp. for "The White Magnolia Tree" by Helen Deutsch, Copyright 1957, by Frank Music Corp., 119 West 57th Street, New York 19, N. Y.

Guideposts Associates, Inc. for "What Prayer Can Do" by Fulton Oursler, Copyright 1951, by Guideposts Associates, Inc., Carmel, New York.

Mrs. Arthur Guiterman for "The Superstitious Ghost" by Arthur Guiterman.

Harcourt, Brace and Company, Inc. for "Jazz Fantasia" from *Smoke and Steel* by Carl Sandburg, Copyright 1920, by Harcourt, Brace and Company, Inc., and renewed by Carl Sandburg. Used by permission of the publisher. Also for a quotation from *Dwight Morrow,* Copyright 1935, by Harold Nicolson. Reprinted by permission of Harcourt, Brace, & World, Inc.

Harper & Brothers for permission to quote material from *Speaker's Handbook of Epigrams and Witticisms* by Herbert V. Prochnow.

Holt, Rinehart and Winston, Inc. for "Mending Wall" by Robert Frost from *You Come Too: Favorite Poems for Young Readers,* Copyright 1959, 1947, by Henry Holt and Company, Inc.

Edith C. List for her story, "Joy Ride."

Little, Brown & Company for "Very Like a Whale," Copyright 1934, The Curtis Publishing Company; and for "The Panther," Copyright 1940, The Curtis Publishing Company. Used by permission of Little, Brown & Company.

The Macmillan Company for "Barter" from Sara Teasdale, *Collected Poems,* Copyright 1917, by The Macmillan Company, renewed 1945; for "Sea-Fever" from John Masefield, *Salt-Water Poems & Ballads,* Copyright 1912, by The Macmillan Company, renewed 1940; and for "The Broncho That Would Not Be Broken" from Vachel Lindsay, *Collected Poems,* Copyright 1917, by The Macmillan Company, renewed 1945. All used with permission of the publisher.

McGraw-Hill Book Company, Inc. for quotations from *Are You Listening?* by Nichols and Stevens; *A Man Called Peter* by Catherine Marshall; and *The Stage and the School* by Ommanney and Ommanney.

G. & C. Merriam Company for material from *A Pronouncing Dictionary of American English,* by John S. Kenyon and Thomas A. Knott, Copyright 1953, by G. & C. Merriam Company, Publishers of the Merriam-Webster Dictionaries. By permission. Also for material from Webster's *New International Dictionary,* Second Edition, Copyright 1959, by G. & C. Merriam Company.

Oxford University Press, Inc., for quotations from *Road to Persuasion* by William Muehl.

The Platt & Munk Co., Inc. for adaptation from *The Little Engine That Could,* edited by Watty Piper, published and copyrighted by The Platt & Munk Co., Inc.

Prentice-Hall, Inc. for quotation from *Effective Speaking for Every Occasion* by W. H. Yeager.

Rand McNally & Company for "The Winds of Fate" by Ella Wheeler Wilcox; and for the Speaker's Kit selection by Ella Wheeler Wilcox.

Fleming H. Revell Company for quotation adapted from *It Will Be Daybreak Soon* by Archibald Rutledge.

The Ronald Press Company for speech regions from Charles K. Thomas—*An Introduction to The Phonetics of American English,* Second Edition, Copyright 1958, by The Ronald Press Company.

Mrs. Lew Sarett for "The Four Little Foxes" from *Covenant With Earth: A Selection from the Poems of Lew Sarett,* edited and copyrighted, 1956, by Alma Johnson Sarett. University of Florida Press, 1956. Reprinted by permission of Mrs. Sarett and the University of Florida Press.

Scholastic Magazines, Inc. for "How to Warm a Bench" by Lee Kennedy, Copyright, © 1955. Reprinted by permission of the editors.

Charles Scribners' Sons for "Little Boy Blue" and "Seein' Things" by Eugene Field from *Poems of Childhood.*

The H. W. Wilson Company for material reproduced from *Readers' Guide to Periodical Literature.*

Mrs. Merlin D. Yoder for "The Touch of the Master's Hand" by Myra Brooks Welch.

For permission to use other quoted materials, cartoons, and photographs, the authors are indebted to the companies and individuals to whom credit is given with each excerpt or illustration.

# Contents

## 4
## *Speaking in More Formal Groups*



## 5
## *Interpreting and Broadcasting*

the crew cuts

UNIT

# I

# *Speaking in Informal Groups*

CHAPTER

# 1 Communicating

> A speaker noticed an elderly lady seated in the front row of the audience with her hand cupped to her ear. Meeting her afterward he asked, "Could you hear me all right?" She replied, "Oh yes, I could *hear* you, but I couldn't *understand* you!"
>
> —*Anonymous*

COMPLETE understanding is the goal of all communication whether you are speaking to a friend or to a large audience.

*The power of the spoken word!* Have you ever stopped to think about the great force that words exert upon your life and the lives of those around you? Words influence your life every day. Words spoken in anger can change friends into enemies; words of apology can regain friends. Words of wisdom arouse respect in business, in school, and in social contacts. Persuasive words win elections and sometimes shape the destiny of nations. Successful individuals, regardless of their careers, will tell you that the one characteristic which has helped them to reach the top is the ability to communicate effectively with others.

You can observe many examples around you of people who have mastered the art of successful communication. In almost any typical community you will recognize some of the people described below.

Mr. A. owns a neighborhood store which everyone likes to patronize because the proprietor is friendly, courteous, and anxious to please his customers. He shows a personal interest in them, calling them by name and inquiring about other members of their families. When you stop in his store, his manner of speaking generates warmth and sincerity, and you can actually feel the glow of friendliness which his words convey. Even if you don't find what you want to buy, you will probably wait for him to get it, rather than go to the new store across the street. The new store may be modern and inviting, but the owner *fails to communicate* with you because of his impersonal, aloof speech and his lack of interest in you as an individual.

Then there is Miss B., a teacher in your school, who is a favorite because her explanations are so easy to understand and so interestingly presented. You never miss a word or an idea because she has learned the secret of successful communication.

Mr. C. just won an important promotion because he could represent his company with poise and speak with confidence to clients on any occasion. Mr. D. failed to get that promotion, even though his technical knowledge surpassed that of anybody else. Why? He could not communicate his thoughts either in conference or in front of an audience. At sales meetings and even at social gatherings he was visibly uncomfortable. Executives appraised him as a valuable worker in the plant but a poor representative in public.

Look around you at school for typical examples in your own

This teacher knows how to communicate effectively with his students. *(Pogue's Portrait Studio)*

age group. Who represents your school on special occasions? Whom do you choose as class president or student council president? Who presides at assemblies? Who leads class discussions or becomes a member of the debating team? Who gives the most intelligent answers in class? Whom do you choose to act as toastmaster or to give speeches at your club banquets? The answer in most cases is the student who can express his thoughts clearly in an interesting manner. He has earned the reputation of being an effective speaker.

Words influence not only your individual life but the lives of men throughout the world. In fact the spoken word is fast becoming the greatest force for good or evil in world relationships. Today world leaders practice the saying, "With words we govern men," as they compete verbally on radio and television programs to win personal favor and to advance their particular political beliefs. Personal visits and summit conferences which promote understanding through spoken communication are replacing lengthy written messages.

Among nations, successful communication of the leaders in face-to-face conversation may mean the difference between war and peace. A better understanding among the peoples of various countries occurs also when nations encourage exchange visits of students, farmers, and scientists. As travel time is shortened, people are

World leaders find verbal communication invaluable. *(U.P.I. Photo)*

brought closer together. When you are only twenty-four hours away from almost any point on the earth's surface, you have a speaking acquaintance with your neighbors of the world. Even though you may not now be speaking the same language, you will more and more be speaking and listening to people from hitherto remote places. The age of jets and electronics has conquered distance and has sent the human voice around the world in a matter of seconds.

You are living in a "one-world" era when the power of speech is taking its place beside the other great powers which are shaping human destiny . . . atomic power, scientific power, and electronic power. Just as these last-mentioned powers can provide peace or total destruction, so can the power of speech bring nations closer together or force them farther apart. It is no longer a question of whether or not you *can* communicate with far-distant places; it is only a question of how well you can communicate.

It is probably true that few of you will ever attend an international summit conference or even speak on the floor of Congress. Although you may never occupy an important public position in which you need to communicate in a top-level capacity, speech is still of utmost importance to you. In nearly every situation a person is measured by his manner of speaking. Among your classmates, your ability to communicate may determine whether you are accepted or rejected. In other situations it may mean the difference between success or failure or between sadness and happiness. Your speech goes with you wherever you go and, furthermore, it tells on you all along the way. One maxim puts it: "Every time you speak, your mind is on parade."

Effective communication is the ultimate goal of any speech course. Many of you, however, have no way of knowing how your speech habits affect others and are unaware, therefore, of your own speech inadequacies. Thus far you have been learning speech through imitation, and for better or worse, your speech reflects the models you have been imitating. Because of the great variety of examples, it is almost inevitable that you have developed some undesirable speech habits. Some of the disturbing habits which appear most frequently are faulty pronunciation of common words, careless enunciation, and speaking too softly or too rapidly. These qualities in speaking interfere with easy understanding. Poor posture, failure to look at your audience, and repetition of "er," "uh," "anduh," "you know," "I mean," "see?" and similar expressions also interfere with enjoyable communication.

Since you are seldom aware of your own faulty habits, your first objective in this course should be to determine wherein you can begin making improvements. One of the most progressive steps that you can take toward improving your speech is simply deciding to become speech-conscious. Listen to yourself with a critical ear; ask others to make constructive suggestions; apply all worthwhile helps that are offered; and, finally, work hard to replace any poor habits with good ones. Follow the suggestions given in this text, solicit help from your teacher and classmates, and use your class periods for persistent experimenting with ways to improve your speaking power. Only through speech awareness and speech consciousness can you eliminate old habits and establish new ones.

As you become more speech-conscious, you will become more aware of the fact that speaking is usually an attempt to win an appropriate response from the listener. Whether you have only one listener or many, there is no reason to speak unless you have a specific purpose and are seeking a definite response. Your goal in trying to develop your maximum speaking powers is to always win a satisfactory reaction from your listeners.

But where should you begin? The successful speaker reaches his goal because he observes many principles of speech training and masters many techniques. As a logical starting point, it would be wise to begin with a few of the general principles involved in the process of communication. The word COMMUNICATE itself suggests a number of guides toward increased speech effectiveness:

**C—CONFIDENCE.** Confidence in yourself is perhaps the most important element in developing successful communication. Without self-confidence a person finds it difficult to inspire confidence and trust in others. Such a person often fails to establish contact with his audience because of nervousness and stage fright. You can achieve poise and self-confidence through careful preparation of your speeches and practicing them before you face an audience. Nothing gives you more confidence than feeling sure of your subject and having a real desire to talk to your audience about it.

**O—OCCASION.** Where, when, and with whom you speak will greatly affect what you say and how you say it. Can you imagine speaking the same way before an adult audience as you would with your friends at a football game? Your ideas, your choice of words, and your method of delivery will always depend upon the place, the time, and the audience.

M—METHODS. The methods used by speakers in preparing and presenting their ideas vary with the individual and the occasion. Later in this book you will read about certain speech skills and techniques, but you should be aware that there is no *one* method of preparation and delivery that can be recommended for all people. For example, some of you may utilize your own experiences in preparing speeches, whereas others will do extensive research. In delivering your speeches, you may prefer to memorize, but others may speak best if they extemporize. In a few rare cases, some may even speak impromptu in an effective manner. There will be variation also in platform behavior, with some speaking without any gestures and others using the entire body to help communicate. The speech class is a laboratory for you to experiment in various methods until you determine which enable you to communicate best.

M—MANNER. Your manner is essentially your attitude toward your subject and your audience. No matter how well prepared your speech is, your attitude will greatly influence the audience's acceptance of your message. An audience quickly senses how the speaker feels toward them, his subject, and himself. For instance, a speaker who seems to be self-satisfied or smug and who gives the impression of speaking only because he has been engaged to do so will get a cool reception from his audience. In place of a bond between the speaker and the audience, there is a barrier. On the other hand, a speaker who radiates friendliness, warmth, and enthusiasm captures an audience instantly and wins their respect. The second type of speaker succeeds in communicating; the first usually ends with a closed circuit.

U—UNDERSTANDING. The ability to communicate requires considerable understanding. First, you need to understand your purpose in speaking and your subject matter before you can expect your audience to understand your message. Communication has broken down many times because an audience could not grasp the meaning behind the speaker's words. By understanding people and becoming more aware of their likes, dislikes, and emotions, you can learn to talk more successfully with them. You will know what subjects to choose and which to avoid as you learn to speak their language. It is necessary, too, to understand your own feelings and limitations. By recognizing some of your own weaknesses or "power failures," you can then mend and strengthen your lines of communication.

N—NATURALNESS. Naturalness and sincerity are two characteristics to which audiences respond most favorably. Effective communication is rarely achieved by artificial poses or by showing off. The speaker who enjoys being an exhibitionist usually has only one admirer—himself. If you are sincere and really believe in what you say, you won't have to worry about being natural. An audience instinctively responds warmly to the speaker who is genuine and without pretense.

I—IDEAS. People's minds meet through the exchange of ideas. The letter "I" can indicate *information* and *interests* as well as ideas. People listen when you have interesting information to communicate. The effective speaker broadens the scope of his interests daily and collects information from every source available. Obviously, to be an "idea-I" speaker, you should devote a considerable amount of time to reading, observing people and things around you, participating in various activities, and listening to any source which will increase your knowledge. Increasing your fund of ideas will improve your background and give you a decided advantage over those whose information is limited. Another important "I" word in improving communication is *imagination,* a quality which enables you to present your information in an entertaining and unusual manner.

C—COMPOSITION. Audience acceptance of ideas depends in part on good composition. You want your speech to be specific, vivid, and clear in its phrasing. You want to express your ideas in a forceful style which will leave a lasting impression upon the audience. A powerful speech is not an accidental occurrence but rather the result of careful planning and meticulous preparation. The polished speaker will tell you that he spends long hours finding just the right words to express his meaning and that his finished speech has been revised perhaps a dozen times. The average speaker is satisfied with the first or second draft—that's the reason he is average; the above-average speaker, however, is rarely satisfied even with the revised speech that he delivers because he realizes there are always chances for further improvement. One of the essentials of composition is orderly organization or careful arrangement of your ideas so that the audience can follow you easily, a fact often overlooked by the beginning speaker. Later in this book you will discover how to organize your thoughts in the most effective pattern and how to prepare an attractive introduction and conclusion to your remarks.

A—ANALYSIS. Critical analysis is an essential in speech training. Analysis implies an alertness to situations and people surrounding you. Do you observe the responses that you receive from your audience? Do you notice if they like or dislike your speeches? Are you aware of their being bored or uncomfortable? Do you know what embarrasses people or what makes them laugh? What do *you* like in the speeches of others? What techniques seem to be especially popular with audiences? These are a few of the questions which you should try to answer if you wish to improve your speaking ability. In addition to self-analysis, you will find valuable help from the critical analysis offered by your teacher and classmates. Welcome such suggestions and apply them to your speaking.

T—TRAINING. Outstanding speakers are not born with the ability to speak well. Speaking is a skill which comes from training and experience just as reading, writing, and singing are skills which must be learned and developed. A scientist, a jet pilot, a teacher, a doctor, a lawyer—all must have careful training to become proficient. In using this book you will learn many ways to make your speaking more dynamic. You will be able to pinpoint some of your problems and you will get help in overcoming them. There will be numerous opportunities for you to present different types of speeches before the class and to have them evaluated. If you make the most of this laboratory situation, your training will stand you in good stead on or off the speaker's platform.

E—ETHICS. Speech was described earlier as a power. As you know, any power can be used for good or evil and this is certainly true of the power of speech. Speech can and should be used to bring comfort, satisfaction, joy, understanding, and progress. On the other hand, dictators and irresponsible leaders can misuse speech to hurt other people, to distort the truth, and to undermine democratic values. This should not be the objective of speech in our civilization. The skills, the techniques, and the power of speech can be yours to command. *It is your responsibility to use them wisely.*

The importance of exercising good judgment and observing ethical standards in the use of speech power has been emphasized by many educators as one of the chief goals for speech students to keep in mind. Mr. Francis Horn, President of the University of Rhode Island, in addressing The New England Speech Association stated, "With the mass means of communication today, never before has it been so essential to learn to separate the true from the false, the objectively presented material from that which is biased or colored." After stressing the fact that our "scientifically dominated world" is requiring more and more training in oral communication, Mr. Horn concluded with these challenging thoughts, ". . . we have come to put great emphasis upon education in science and engineering. But speech rather than science and engineering may actually hold the key to the future of the world. . . . Science makes George Orwell's 1984 a possibility. Effective speaking may prevent its becoming a reality."

You are living in an exciting age of electronic miracles, an age of tape recorders, microphones, trans-oceanic telephones, shortwave radio sets, and every conceivable method of recording and sending the human voice into millions of homes. You have already witnessed the breaking of the sound barrier as well as the outer space barrier. Perhaps you will live to see the breaking of the language barrier. Why not make a beginning by breaking through the barriers of everyday communication to utilize your power of speech to the utmost? It will be one of the most rewarding efforts of your life.

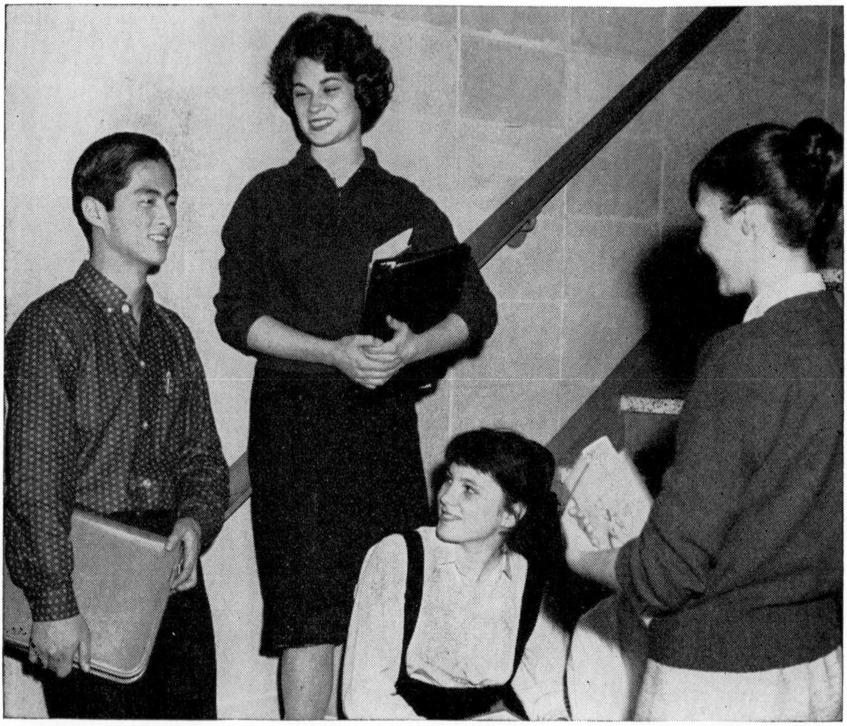

These students have broken the language barrier. *(U.P.I. Photo)*

"If this doesn't work, men, we're cooked!"

THE SATURDAY EVENING POST



## ACTIVITIES

1. What do you first observe in a speaker? What leaves a lasting impression on you?
2. Develop and discuss each of the first ten principles of effective speaking cited in this chapter so as to show their importance.
3. Discuss the relationship between the power of speech and the need for ethics in a democracy. Cite several speakers of local, national, or international importance who have contributed to civilization by the ethical use of their abilities to communicate. What speakers have endangered civilization with their misuse of communicative skills?
4. Discuss how speech rather than science may "hold the key to the future of the world."
5. What is the "George Orwell's 1984" referred to by Mr. Horn? How could speaking prevent its becoming a reality?
6. Discuss your own responsibilities in observing ethical ideals. Why is it important for you to recognize falsehood and bias?

CHAPTER

# 2 Getting Acquainted

> If a man does not make new acquaintances, as he advances through life, he will soon find himself left alone. A man, Sir, should keep his friendships in constant repair.
>
> —*Samuel Johnson*

## Introducing Yourself and Your Interests

IF you have ever watched children at play, you know that it doesn't take them long to get acquainted. They merely say, "What's your name?" The quick response is, "Susie. What's yours?" "Sally," the other will reply. And a friendship is soon on its way.

It is true that with older people friendships are not formed quite as quickly or easily. But even in a classroom any feeling of strangeness that you may feel will dissolve into a spirit of friendliness as you learn to call each other by name and know a little of what's behind the name.

In a speech class a feeling of friendliness and comradeship is especially desirable. It is more meaningful to talk and listen to people you know and like than to try to communicate with strangers. You will find more to do and say with friends.

There is another advantage to participating in a class that knows each other. A big part of the increased skill and confidence that you will get from your speech class will come from the reactions and comments of your classmates. You will find it easier to follow suggestions for improvement if they come from friends. You will treasure the favorable comments that come from people you know.

Probably you already know some of the members of your class. Usually you will not know all of them and, sometimes, even you

This imitator has gotten off to a good start in introducing himself and his favorite pastime. *(Pogue's Portrait Studio)*

and the students you know by name actually know very little about each other. Your first opportunity to talk to your class, therefore, should give you a chance to introduce yourself. You may want to do this either by talking directly about yourself or about one of your hobbies or interests. Either of these two types of talks, which need not be over a minute or two long, will tell your classmates a great deal about you. These talks should serve to get you and your class off to an interesting start.

## Planning the introductory talk

Careful planning will help as you prepare to present your introductory speech to your classmates. Study the suggestions listed below, look over the possible ideas to include, then read the sample speech provided for your help. Keep in mind that talking about yourself should be an enjoyable experience for both you and your audience. Put your best foot forward and introduce yourself in such a way that others will like what they see and hear, will want to know you better, and will look forward to hearing from you again. Here are some specific suggestions:

Be well groomed so as to make a pleasing appearance.

Stand straight and speak clearly so you can easily be seen and heard.

Speak in a friendly and an enthusiastic manner. Talk as if you are enjoying the experience.

Include something humorous. Nothing breaks the ice as quickly as sharing a laugh. Don't overdo this, or it may boomerang!

Select facts that others will want to know.

What are some of the facts and ideas that others will want to know about you? You may find it helpful to group these into ideas about yourself and ideas about your interests and hobbies. Some of the more important items about yourself are:

Your name
Your place of birth
Your address and interesting details about your community
Members of your family
Your pets
The school or schools you have attended prior to your present one.

Possible ideas to develop about your main interest are:

What it is
How you got started
What equipment is required and how much it costs
Whether you pursue this hobby by yourself or with a group
What there is to read about this subject
Famous people who are or have been interested in the same hobby
Practical applications.

Here is a sample speech given by a high-spirited student about herself. She couldn't resist having some fun with everything that had ever happened to her, including her name. Probably you will like this speech, but you may not want to give one just like it. You may want to be more serious, to give more facts about yourself, or even to be briefer. Besides, you may like your name.

## ME

by Clarinda Olster

My name is Clarinda Olster. I'm willing to trade it for a new one if anyone is willing to trade. That is not a hint to the boys, however!

Some people dislike their first names. Some dislike their last ones. But I'm unhappy about both of mine. Why shouldn't I be? Nobody knows how to spell either of them. When I enroll in a class, I have to spell both of them for the teacher. Besides, everyone looks at me in astonishment, wondering, I suppose, why anybody would give me such a name. I wonder, too. I think children should not be named until they're old enough to pick their favorite name. Don't you agree? Just for fun, let's see how many in this class have names they don't like. See? Over half of the class agree! Well, that makes me feel better already. I have a lot of fellow-sufferers. Maybe we could start a club—the Pick Your Own Name Club—!

I was officially christened Clarinda Olster in St. Paul, Minnesota, where I was born fourteen years ago in the midst of a violent electrical storm. Storms have been part of my life ever since. The day I started school, it rained so hard that I looked like a rag doll fresh out of a washing machine. When we moved from St. Paul to Boston, it rained so hard it was a constant downpour. Nearly every move we've made has been a wet one. Daddy claims he could make money as a professional rainmaker. He's sure the dry areas in the country would be glad to hire him to move from one dry spot to another.

You may be wondering why we move so often. My father is with the Bell Telephone System, which means that he has to travel a lot. So far, we've lived in St. Paul, Boston, New York, Cleveland, and now Atlanta. We've been here two years. But every time a big storm occurs, we all make a dash for our suitcases!

I hope we can stay here long enough for me to finish high school. I like the school, and I now have some wonderful friends here.

Here is another sample speech, this time given by a boy about his hobby. This speech is not as gay and humorous as the first. Yet, like the first, it helps you to know the speaker.

## THE LENS AND I

by George Shipman

My name is George Shipman. Perhaps the best way to introduce myself is to tell you about my favorite hobby, photography.

I have been a photographer for over three years. My first camera was a Kodak Brownie which had a flash attachment and which would take both black and white and color pictures. I do most of my shooting in color. Since I do not have a darkroom of my own, I find my fun in taking and showing pictures, not in processing them.

I now own a new 35 mm. camera. It is a single lens reflex with interchangeable lenses and has an automatic meter that sets the exposure for me. I paid for this camera partly from money earned by my paper route and partly from taking pictures at children's parties.

Photography is my hobby because it is fun. Any member of my camera club would tell you that. But to me photography is also more than fun. It has helped me to learn about optics and chemistry; to see people, places, and things with a new eye; and to make money in my spare time.

You are all invited to the next meeting of our Shutter Club here at school this coming Thursday. See you there!

## ACTIVITIES

You have just read a sample of two types of introductory talks. Now answer a few questions before you prepare your own introductory speech.

1. Did you enjoy either or both?
2. If so, what features did you find pleasing?
3. Would you like to know more about either speaker?
4. Why would you enjoy or not enjoy knowing either speaker better?
5. Would you like to hear more speeches from these students?

## Getting started

It may sometimes seem very hard to sit at your desk at school or in your room at home and try to figure how to start and organize your own introduction. You will find it helpful now to look back at the two speeches by Clarinda and George.

In the first talk notice how Clarinda built her introduction around her name, bad weather, and frequent moves. Thus she gave unity to her speech and, perhaps more important in this type of speech, provided an interesting pattern for weaving in all of the interesting details. George, on the other hand, organized his introduction around his cameras, the kinds of pictures he takes, and the advantages of photography as a hobby. As you plan your own introduction, try to find some pattern in your life or a hobby that you can use to tie your speech together.

Now that you have some idea about how to develop your own introduction, it is time to consider ways of actually getting your talk started. Here are some samples of ways in which other students have started their speeches. Use these samples to help you make up a beginning of your own. Note the suggestions that follow each sample.

### SELF-STARTERS

1. I'm known among my friends as Ham. To most of you, the word "ham" is associated with eggs. But in my case, Ham is strongly tied up with amateur radio. In fact, I'm so used to being called Ham that I sometimes don't even respond to my real name, Harry Barnes.

**Suggestions:** Emphasize your hobby. Tell about interesting experiences connected with it and tie in facts about your family, friends, clubs, ambitions, studies, and other interests.

2. If you happen to be the only boy surrounded by four sisters—all older than you—you can appreciate the life that was mapped out for me when I was christened James Woods. And speaking of being a babe in the woods, I was really one! If I had had the sense I have now and I could have found my way out, I should have left the woods right then and there.

**Suggestions:** Emphasize the advantages or disadvantages of being the only boy in the family. Work in other facts about yourself by associating them with your being the only boy. (Try the same procedure if you happen to be the only girl in a family of boys.)

3. I have had many ambitions in my short life. Most boys start out by wanting to be a fireman, but I started my long list of ambitions by hoping to be one of the first astronauts to reach a planet.

**Suggestions:** Give your name and tell about your ambitions. Explain how your family, friends, studies, and other factors have played a part in your list of ambitions.

4. Have you ever thought of the cruel fate faced by all those innocent babies born on Christmas Day? I happen to be one of them and I can tell you it's no fun. At first, it didn't make much difference because for the first few years toys were toys and I didn't care when I got them. Besides, I was such a novelty that everyone was anxious to spend money on me. That was, of course, when I was the first and only child. Now there are four of us. I'm no longer "that sweet darling child who came to brighten our home on Christmas Day." I'm simply Mary White about whom the entire relationship wails, "Why did she have to be born on Christmas Day! A birthday present and a Christmas present both! Oh well, we'll just buy two cheap ones—or maybe pay a little more for one and it can do for both."

**Suggestions:** Continue with facts about your family and some of the gifts or interesting incidents connected with combined birthday and Christmas celebrations. Bring hobbies, interests, and other events into your speech. The same method can be followed if you were born on any special day such as April Fool's Day, Groundhog Day, or July 4. You can tie many facts around birth dates.

# Performing Social Introductions

In addition to introducing yourself, you should be just as familiar with introducing others. Making such introductions is a frequent speech activity which can bring you pleasure and satisfaction if you are familiar with the correct procedure. If you are not familiar with the socially accepted forms of introductions, you probably try to avoid this situation whenever you can. When it becomes impossible to escape from the necessity of introducing someone or being introduced yourself, you may fumble for words and mutter something unintelligible. Such awkward and embarrassing moments need never recur once you have learned and practiced the right rules.

## Performing introductions properly

The problems of introducing others will disappear if you will observe the following simple rules of etiquette:

1. Stand when you make an introduction.
2. Be friendly and poised. Avoid any display of embarrassment.
3. Be sure of the correct pronunciation of the names of the persons being introduced.
4. Pronounce names audibly and distinctly. Mumbling or slurring names is one of the greatest faults in introductions and usually indicates that you may not be sure of the proper phrasing or procedure to follow.

5. Know how to phrase an introduction. Some of the most acceptable forms are:

Miss Dewitt, may I introduce Mrs. Taylor?
Mrs. Taylor, may I present Mr. Green?
Mrs. Taylor, have you met Miss Dewitt?
Mrs. Martin, I'd like you to meet Mrs. Taylor.
Mr. Smith, this is my son, John.
Professor Hall, do you know Mr. Baker?
Miss Dewitt, I want to introduce Mr. Timm.

All of the above are acceptable in both formal and informal situations. An even simpler method can be used by mentioning the names in the right order and saying the first name as if it were followed by a question mark. The rising inflection *implies* the usual questions, "May I introduce?" or "May I present?" Try it below:

Mrs. Martin? Mrs. Taylor.
Mrs. Taylor? Mr. Green.
Mr. Anderson? My son, John.
Professor Hall? Mr. Baker.

Introductions are fun when you know the rules. *(Monkmeyer)*

You will be correct in using any of the above phrases. Stay away, however, from expressions that sound too abrupt, too elaborate, or somewhat crude such as:

Mr. Smith, meet Mr. Brown.
Mr. Smith, I want to make you acquainted with Mr. Brown.
Mr. Smith, shake hands with Mr. Brown.

6. Know who is to be introduced to whom. Although even books on etiquette differ on some of the precise rules of procedure, certain general principles do apply. Thus the name of the person receiving the introduction always comes *first.* For instance, older persons, women, dignitaries, the clergy, and others deserving special consideration usually receive the introduction. Persons presented to such individuals have their names mentioned *last.*

**Examples:**

Mother (receiver), I want you to meet Joan Smith (one presented).

Miss Jones (receiver), may I present my father, Mr. Brown (one presented).

For practical purposes you can feel safe if you observe the following:

Present younger people to older ones.

Present men and boys to women and girls unless the man is the President of the United States, a royal personage, or a dignitary of the church.

Present persons of ordinary rank to those of higher rank.

Present all persons except notables to a hostess or to a clergyman.

Present your school friends to your parents and older members of your family.

Present your parents to the principal of your school.

At school, present your parents to your teacher. In your home, present your teacher to your parents.

7. Always try to provide enough information in your introduction to get a conversation started.

**Examples:**

Introduction of your father to your teacher at school:

"Miss Dewitt, may I present my father, Mr. Brown? He used to be a math teacher, too, before he went into engineering."

"How do you do, Mr. Brown? How did you happen to decide to give up teaching?"

Introduction of two of your school friends to each other:

"Sally, this is Joe Brown. Joe, Sally Smith."

"Hello, Joe."

"Hello, Sally."

"Joe, Sally is new at school this year and is especially interested in music. Can you tell her whom to see about try-outs for orchestra?"

"Of course. They're having try-outs next week. I'll be glad to tell you about them."

## Receiving introductions properly

Knowing how to respond to an introduction is equally important. Here are some suggestions which will help you to be at ease in any situation:

1. Listen carefully to the name. People are vain about their names. By remembering a person's name and using it often, you will win great favor. If you are unable to hear a name when receiving an introduction, ask to have it repeated. Then use it immediately in the conversation to help you remember it.

2. Word your responses properly. The following are acceptable:

How do you do? (Especially for formal situations)
How do you do, Miss Young?
I am very glad to meet you, Miss Smith. (Be sure that it sounds sincere.)

A prompt and gracious response to an introduction is a mark of social poise. *(Ewing Galloway)*

In very informal situations involving young people of school age, the response, "Hello" or "Hello, Mary" is popular.

Avoid using such expressions as "Charmed!" "Delighted!" "I'm pleased to make your acquaintance" or "Pleased to meet you."

3. Observe the usual courtesies. The most important are:

Regardless of age, a gentleman always stands when he meets a lady.
Men stand to meet each other and usually shake hands.
A man should wait for a woman to offer her hand first.
Young girls always rise when meeting older women.

4. Try to avoid awkward silences by starting a conversation yourself. Be quick to respond to any conversation started by others, or to pick up any lead given in the introduction.

5. Display genuine interest in the person being introduced. Be friendly, poised, and comfortable rather than abrupt or bored. Every new acquaintance is a potential friend.

## ACTIVITY

Have you ever wondered how you could get some practice in making and receiving introductions? Of course, most of you get a certain amount of experience in your daily life, but frequently you are too engrossed in the situation to realize exactly what you may have said or done. Moreover, in real life introductions your errors and awkwardness usually go uncorrected. For these reasons, many of you, even those of you who make many introductions, go right on making these introductions with considerable discomfort and without improvement.

In this activity you or a classmate must play one of the roles indicated. Observe the suggestions given previously as to the order of introduction, clarity of pronunciation, and general courtesy. Try to furnish and respond to conversational leads. If you have trouble with any of the situations suggested, try them again. (Incidentally, as you work on this activity, take advantage of every chance to introduce members of the class who are not acquainted.)

Now, working in pairs or in groups with others of your classmates, make and receive the introductions listed below:

1. Your father and a friend of yours
2. At school, your mother and a man teacher
3. In your home, your parents and a teacher
4. A young girl and your grandmother
5. A girl and four boys
6. A friend of yours and an assembly speaker
7. A boy and three girls
8. A friend of yours and a bishop
9. At school, your younger sister and a man teacher
10. A woman guest and four other women attending a luncheon
11. Your father and the superintendent of schools

CHAPTER

# 3 Improving Conversation

Half the world is composed of people who have something to say and can't; and the other half, who have nothing to say and keep on saying it.

—*Robert Frost*

CONVERSATION is the most common form of speech activity. You spend a good portion of each day taking part in one kind of conversation or another. Perhaps because it seems so easy to talk to your close friends, you sometimes forget that it takes real skill to converse effectively and successfully whether with friends, family, or strangers.

This chapter will help you to create a favorable impression in these three types of conversation: (1) person-to-person conversations, (2) group conversations, and (3) telephone conversations. Person-to-person conversations are ones in which two or at the most three or four people converse about a subject of mutual interest. The purpose of such conversations may be purely one of entertainment or social pleasure, or there may be more serious purposes such as learning about a new project or trying to decide which of two plans is better. In person-to-person conversations, the roles of listener and speaker are usually freely interchanged. Group conversations are very like person-to-person conversations in intent; they differ primarily in that the number of persons involved may be much greater and that the distinction between the speaker and listener becomes more sharply defined. Sometimes in group conversations, one or two of the members emerge as speakers and the remainder of the group become listeners. The term telephone conversation as used in this chapter will refer primarily to such conversations as held between only two individuals.

An enjoyable person-to-person conversation between friends. *(WKRC-TV, Cincinnati, Ohio)*

## Person-to-Person Conversations

Of all forms of conversation, person-to-person is the most frequently used. You will find that such conversations can be among the most pleasing and stimulating activities of your daily life and can provide you with many opportunities for developing friendships and increasing your popularity within your group. Such conversations can also enlarge your area of knowledge through an interchange of views and interests.

A young man who knew a great deal about baseball but nothing about music found himself seated next to a lady at a dinner party. She knew nothing about baseball, but a great deal about music. While he played with the silverware trying vainly to think of something to say, she decided to give the young man a wide opening by mentioning an approaching musical event.

Turning to him with a smile, she commented, "I suppose you're excited too, that they're playing the St. Louis Blues here tomorrow night."

Delighted that she evidently spoke his language (even though not too accurately!), he replied, "You bet I am! I sure hope we'll win."

This might have been the end of the conversation if the lady of our story had not been an expert in conversation as well as in music. Instead of laughing at his mistake or turning her attention to the person on the other side of her, she realized that he must be familiar with sports. Trying again, she asked a safe question, "What's your favorite sport?"

"Baseball," he answered eagerly, "and I think we're going to win the pennant this year."

"Is that so? No wonder my husband takes his transistor radio with him to the concerts so that he can listen to the games! What makes you so sure we're going to win the pennant?"

Immediately they were both conversing eagerly because she, who knew nothing about baseball, gave him, who knew nothing about music, the chance to open up on his favorite topic. Besides, they both enjoyed the conversation. He felt at ease beside a woman who had at first unnerved him. She had the opportunity to listen to an enthusiastic account of a sport which she had always ignored. In fact, having shared his enthusiasm, she began to suspect that she had been missing a great deal. It might be fun to attend a night baseball game with her husband and listen to the concert on her radio if necessary; it might even be more fun not to take the radio!

One of the most rewarding features of conversation is that it not only helps you to make friends but it opens up areas of knowledge and interest you never knew or cared about before.

## Preparing for conversation

Good conversationalists are not born that way. They acquire their skill through patience, practice, and preparation over a long period of time. Some people find it easier to talk than others, but do not confuse talk with conversation—that is, *good* conversation. There are all kinds of conversation, ranging from poor to excellent. Unfortunately, some of the worst conversation comes from those who find it the easiest to talk. Perhaps the very ease with which some people talk may make them indifferent to what they say and unaware that they may say too much.

It lies within the power of each one of you to develop quality in your conversational ability. By following the suggestions listed below, you can prepare yourself to take your place confidently in any group regardless of age, social background, or educational level.

1. Force yourself to take part in conversations, even though you have little to contribute at first. If you can't talk, listen. If you don't understand, ask questions. This will help you to gain poise.

2. Enlarge your storehouse of knowledge every day. Never let a day go by without learning something new: talk more with

people; read; listen to the radio; watch television; be more observing of everything and everybody around you; travel as much as you can; start a hobby or two; develop common interests with friends and classmates. For conversational purposes, it is far better to know a little about a lot of subjects than to know a lot about only one.

3. Develop a genuine interest in other people. Discard any ideas that people don't like you. Begin building up others in your mind, and you will soon discover the magic in thinking of others—you forget all about yourself.

4. Build an adequate vocabulary. Throw away trite expressions that you and your friends have abused. Add new and useful words that will make your conversation more expressive.

5. Work hard to improve your grammar and speaking habits. If you are sure of your grammar, you will not be self-conscious about it. Avoid excessive use of slang, vulgarisms, and "off color" remarks and stories.

6. Learn to use pleasing speech. For your purpose at present that includes:

Speaking loudly enough to be plainly heard, but no louder than necessary

Speaking distinctly and clearly—avoiding mumbling, slurring, and swallowing words

Speaking in an alert, enthusiastic manner, avoiding a bored, flat tone or monotone

Speaking at a moderate rate of speed instead of racing or crawling through your thoughts

Speaking on a pleasing voice level, avoiding the extremely shrill, high-pitched level

Speaking without annoying mannerisms such as a nasal twang, a whining or complaining style, or in a bossy or surly fashion

## Starting a conversation

You have probably found by now that the most difficult part of any conversation seems to be getting started. When you get into your car, you step on the starter or push a button and away you go. That is, you start right off unless you have a dead battery or some other mechanical difficulty. Operate on the same principle when you meet a stranger—step on the starter. Even if you know absolutely nothing about him or his background, it should not prove too difficult. Most people enjoy telling you about themselves as long as you are not too personal and do not try to cross-examine them.

In Chapter 2 ways and means of providing conversational leads following an introduction were discussed. You may not always be fortunate enough to have this help, so be prepared to help yourself if necessary. Here are some effective starters which should help you to think of others:

1. Is this your first trip to our city?
2. I enjoyed your speech (or performance). I imagine you find a vast difference among audiences, don't you?
3. Where are you going to school?
4. A friend of mine told me that you are on the basketball team. Is that your favorite sport?
5. Have you had a chance to meet everybody here? (If not, you can tell the person about some of the others present as you get him into a group conversation.)
6. Which team do you think will win the pennant this year?

If you run into "battery trouble" with your first opening remark, try another one. Both persons meeting for the first time usually share a feeling of uneasiness. For that reason, they will probably both try to help each other find a topic of mutual interest. Thus, if your first "conversation starter" doesn't work, the person with whom you are beginning to talk will usually try to be more responsive to your second attempt.

## Continuing a conversation

Once you have a conversation started, whether with a stranger or with a friend, you will want to keep it moving in a way that will be of mutual interest. You will find that in any conversation, the person with whom you are talking will greatly affect the direction

*"Anybody home?"*

Drawing by F. B. Modell, © 1959 *The New Yorker* Magazine, Inc.

in which the conversation moves. Here are a few simple suggestions that will help you to improve your skill in keeping a conversation going smoothly:

1. Cooperate. Conversation is an exchange of views, not a monologue. Stated simply, each of you has an obligation in every conversation, regardless of the number of people involved. You should have something to contribute and you should listen to what others have to say, for the one who never allows anyone else to say anything brands himself as a conversational boor.

Imagine, if you can, eleven persons on a football team all fighting among themselves to grab the ball and carry it across the goal line! This is the same picture you get of a group fighting to grab the ball in conversation. Then picture the one who holds on to the ball all of the time, who hates to relinquish it even for a brief moment, and who fights to get it back again even if he has to step on everyone else.

Conversation has been described as a bridge by which we reach the minds of others. Not only must you travel across the conversational bridge, but you must also allow others the same privilege. The conversational bridge must be regarded as a two-way structure with plenty of room for all to travel back and forth. When only one person has the right of way, cooperation is lost.

2. Select topics of mutual interest. Obviously, talking with others is difficult when a topic holds little interest for both or even for one. Either take turns talking on your favorite topic or find one you both enjoy.

3. Select pleasant topics. Your ailments and family problems are of little interest to others. Conversation should be cheerful, informal, and relaxing. Even though serious problems may be discussed, conversation can still be enjoyable. As long as everyone in the group is vitally interested in a topic, it is a good one. Some of the most stimulating conversations you will ever have will be on topics which present a difference of opinion. To exchange views in a friendly, enthusiastic manner is both healthy and worthwhile, for everyone enjoys a good argument which is congenial and intelligent. To introduce topics, however, which are highly controversial and apt to stir up heated feelings, is in extremely bad taste.

4. Know what you are talking about. Don't bluff if you know nothing about a topic, for only "windbags" and "gushers" rave on about nothing. Simply say that the subject is not "your line" and ask intelligent questions about it.

5. Be a good listener. It is rude to ask anyone to repeat something simply because you have not been paying attention. Listening does not mean waiting for a chance to take the conversation away from someone. It means listening all over—not just with your ears, but with your eyes, with your face and body, and with your heart and brain to get the full meaning of words, to understand ideas, to evaluate what is said, and to react appropriately. Often the best listener is considered the best conversationalist. If you can keep the other person talking on his favorite subject, you will be his favorite listener.

6. Be courteous. Your speech quickly reveals whether you have good manners or bad ones. Even though you may know little about the subject being discussed, you can listen and learn something. On the other hand, if you know a great deal about the subject, you need to be especially careful in showing consideration for others. Examine the conversational courtesies listed below. How many do you follow? How many others could you add?

### THE ABC'S OF CONVERSATIONAL COURTESY

A—ALLOW people to finish sentences and to give full expression to their ideas without interrupting to add, contradict, or correct.

B—BE considerate of the other person's views, his right to express them, and his equality as a free-thinking individual. You need not agree with another's opinions, but courtesy demands that you give him a fair chance to express them without putting obstacles in his way. Appearing bored, making sarcastic remarks, or trying to "show him up" by your own superior knowledge of the subject is inexcusable.

C—CALM your temper and any temptations to shout, issue flat contradictions, or to indulge in personal bickering.

D—DENY yourself any display of self-love. Overusing *I*, boasting about your accomplishments, displaying snobbery, attempting to be the "life of the party," exhibiting a holier-than-thou attitude, or showing any similar symptom of self-devotion is a sure way to lose friends.

## Ending a conversation

A common situation that occurs as two or more people converse is that one or more of the persons will feel that the particular subject of conversation has been exhausted. If you develop this feeling yourself or sense that your conversational partner is developing it, you should begin to look for a natural way of changing the topic.

In a sense, this is very much like starting a new conversation, although in general it is easier to do because the parties concerned will have been together long enough to have overcome their initial uneasiness. If at all possible, try to find a bridge from what you have been saying to the new topic you have in mind. It should not be too difficult to think of a remark which will serve as a springboard to the new subject. If this does not seem possible, try a more open transition such as, "Well, we seem to have just about covered this. What do you think of . . . ?" In rare instances, you may wish to use this lag in the conversation as an opportunity actually to stop the conversation.

## CLASS DISCUSSION

Here are some subjects to talk about:

1. What are the chief advantages of being able to converse well?
2. Find an interesting quotation, or relate an anecdote or personal experience connected with conversation. Share it with your class and decide what principles of conversation it illustrates.
3. What are some good ways of starting a conversation with a person you have met for the first time? Illustrate with examples, using another class member.

It is easy to keep a conversation going that is of mutual interest.

4. What are some topics you consider unpleasant or unsuitable for conversation? What topics do you consider especially suitable?

5. Express your frank opinion of the following types:

   a. Someone who tries to be the "life of the party"

   b. Someone who speaks in an affected manner or who acquires an accent in a few weeks away from home

   c. Someone who insists upon telling every small detail

   d. Someone whose voice is too loud and penetrating

6. What is an intellectual snob? Do you know any? How do you feel about them?

7. Is there such a thing as being too frank? What are your views? Have you had any experiences of this kind that you would like to tell?

8. What do you consider the most desirable trait of conversation?

## Group Conversations

Group conversation is a close relative of person-to-person conversation and frequently grows out of it. For example, you may be attending a party and talking about your family's New York trip when somebody in another conversation across the room mentions going to college. If most of you are interested in college, the several small or private conversations blend easily and naturally into one conversation about college education. Soon you are seeking answers to questions: Do you need a college education in the field you intend to enter? Are small colleges better than large ones? How can you get scholarships? Is it advisable to work your way through college? Which colleges have the strongest football teams? Is it wise to attend a coeducational college? Group conversations of this type are frequently called discussions.

One of the most familiar types of group conversation occurs in your classroom when you encounter problems and challenging ideas in your textbook. Such ideas frequently spark lively discussions in which you are eager to express your views. At times your teacher or a member of your class may act as a leader. At other times, the conversation proceeds in a more informal manner with no leader to steer the group. Actually, if the subject of a group conversation is of genuine interest to the group, any kind of recognized leader may be undesirable since he or she may slow down the spontaneous flow of ideas by imposing an atmosphere of formality.

There are many other ways in which you may suddenly find yourself joining in a group conversation. As a matter of fact, nearly any group of people engages at some time or other in this type of conversing. Your family may talk as a group about finances, use of

Group conversations often grow out of person-to-person conversations. *(Monkmeyer)*

the family car, dating, school problems, or a new recreation room. If you belong to any school or church organization, topics of general group concern are almost certain to turn up, even in those portions of your activities that are almost purely social.

How satisfactory are group conversations both to the individual members of the group and to the group itself? The answer depends, of course, on how well the individuals cooperate as a group. Earlier in this chapter you learned of the importance of cooperation, courtesy, and consideration in person-to-person conversations. What you learned then is also basic to group conversation. The interests of the group must be placed first. Certain restraints, as discussed in person-to-person conversation, must be exercised by every individual. You must know how and when to apply the brakes. The absence of a leader does not mean that you can talk whenever you please. In group conversation you must wait for recognition by the group and then have something worthwhile to contribute. Can you give others your complete attention? Are you interested in what others have to say? Do you only want to say something yourself? Can you wait for others to finish? Unless you can answer these questions in the affirmative, you have little chance of being either a happy or popular member of a group conversation.

## ◄ POINTERS THAT PAY OFF ►

1. Present only your most worthwhile ideas. Particularly if you are not really familiar with the general subject of the conversation, give considerable thought in advance to what you say.
2. Ask only one question at a time. Don't try to ask a question and express an opinion at the same time.
3. Condense your statements in order to avoid a waste of valuable time, and state them as clearly as possible.
4. Listen attentively and courteously to the views of others.
5. Avoid personal bickering and making sarcastic or heated remarks.
6. Regard the discussion process as an opportunity to learn.
7. Speak out clearly and loudly enough for all to hear.
8. Encourage others, especially shy ones, to talk. Instead of trying to keep the spotlight on yourself, turn it on others.
9. Forego any temptation to switch topics as long as others in the group seem interested in the subject, even if you are not.

## ACTIVITIES

In each of the activities that follow, conduct a group conversation about the topic suggested. Do not use an appointed leader. Keep your discussion orderly and interesting.

1. Going steady
2. Money matters such as allowances, earning your own money, working part time
3. College—importance, type of college, size of college, scholarships available, working during college
4. Choice of a career—nursing, engineering, art, teaching, medicine, or any other
5. Best methods of studying

# Telephone Conversations

If a stranger rings your doorbell by mistake, do you snarl at him and slam the door in his face? Do you pay social visits when you know people are eating or preparing to retire? Do you insist upon talking if you know people are busy? Or do you wear a mask and demand that people guess who you are before talking to them?

Of course not! You are ashamed to exhibit such poor manners when you can be seen. Yet every day many people are guilty of this when they use the telephone. Following the ABC's of Courtesy is especially important in telephone conversation. When people can't see you, their impressions depend entirely upon your voice and your manners. With strangers, your voice is you; they can only visualize you on the basis of what they hear. Even friends are quick to detect your mood and emotions from the sound of your voice.

Even your moods and emotions are revealed by your telephone voice. *(Charles Harbutt/Scope)*

## Cultivating a pleasing telephone voice

What special efforts should you make in cultivating a pleasing telephone voice? Here are several important things for you to watch:

1. The telephone, not you, should provide the power to carry your voice. Speaking in a low, distinct manner makes your voice not only more pleasing but also makes it more intelligible.

2. Unpleasant qualities in your voice are exaggerated by the telephone. Try to eliminate shrillness, raspiness, nasality, and all signs of abruptness, irritation, or impatience. One sure method to make your voice pleasant is to feel pleasant and to act pleasant. Do not, of course, go to the extreme of permitting your voice to drip with superficial sweetness.

3. Speak directly into the mouthpiece, keeping the lips about an inch from it so that what you say will be clear and undistorted.

4. Telephone speaking should be a little slower than regular conversation. The person to whom you are speaking does not have the advantage of watching your face and hands for expressions which help convey your meaning, but must concentrate solely on your voice.

## Telephone manners

Every time you use the telephone, you are actually projecting your presence into somebody's home or office. While you are not there in person, you are a part of the group scene which you interrupted when you placed the call. Before using the phone, stop and ask yourself, "Am I interrupting a meal, a party, or sleep?" "Is my call necessary, or am I simply bored and want to kill some time?" A telephone call is as much an invasion of a person's time and privacy as a personal call at his home or office; so consider this thoughtfully before picking up the telephone.

## How to make social calls

Most of the calls that you make come under the heading of social calls. Here are some suggestions on how to make such calls:

1. Call at a time likely to be convenient.
2. Ask for your friend instead of saying, "Who is this?"
3. Identify yourself instead of saying, "Guess who this is."
4. If your friend is out, ask if you may leave a message.
5. If you have a definite reason for calling, state it as soon as possible instead of being vague and general.
6. If you are issuing an invitation, give all details clearly.
7. Converse briefly. Lengthy and frequent calls to another person monopolize his time and deprive others of the chance to call him. This also ties up your own phone and is unfair to others who must share it.
8. Conclude courteously instead of hanging up abruptly. The person who calls usually concludes the conversation.
9. A pad and pencil should always be kept beside the telephone to plan questions or points to be covered in a forthcoming telephone call and to record messages and information received over the telephone.
10. Repeat all important information received over the telephone. This procedure insures accuracy. For example, repeat the time and place of a proposed meeting to be certain that you and the other person understand each other.
11. Be sure you have the right number before you dial. Don't rely on your memory if you are at all uncertain. If you should happen to dial the wrong number, however, be sure to apologize for such an intrusion. Incidentally, let the phone ring long enough (ten rings according to the telephone company) to permit any person who is busy to drop whatever he is doing and get to the phone.

## How to receive social calls

Knowing how to receive social calls is just as important as knowing how to make them. The following suggestions will help you handle more effectively your own calls and those for others.

**Your calls.**

Answer the telephone promptly and pleasantly.

Listen attentively.

Avoid interrupting or showing impatience.

If it is impossible for you to talk at the time you are called, explain very pleasantly the reason and ask if you may return the call.

Be as courteous as you would if you were speaking face to face with the person. It is poor manners to reply in monosyllables and grunts.

Thank the person for calling.

Permit the person who originated the call to terminate it.

**Calls for others.**

Be tactful and polite.

Offer to take a message or to have the call returned.

Avoid asking unnecessary questions. In particular, do not ask bluntly, "Who is this?" or "What do you want?"

**Wrong numbers.** If your number is called by mistake, be pleasant in accepting apologies.

## How to make business calls

All of you have occasion to call busy people and many of you will some day be the busy people receiving such calls. In making business calls, you also want to create a favorable impression. All the rules of courtesy that apply to social calls apply to business ones as well—only more so. Time means money with business firms. For that reason you should observe these courtesies:

1. Call only when necessary.
2. Identify yourself at once and state your reason for calling.
3. Have your thoughts well organized so that you can proceed in a direct, orderly manner. Jot down all ideas in advance so that you will not forget something important.
4. In placing orders, have all specifications written out so that there will be no uncertainty or delay.
5. Be brief and concise but not abrupt.
6. If your purpose is to make a complaint, explain your problem calmly and courteously. You will be more effective and receive better attention if you avoid accusations, irritation, and impatience.
7. Conclude all business calls with a warm and courteous "Thank you."

## How to receive business calls

Since nearly all of you will be called upon to receive business calls also, you should know the correct procedure. In answering a business call, it is especially important for you to create a favorable impression. You and the firm which you represent are both being judged by your telephone personality. You want to make friends for your firm.

1. Identify yourself and the firm at once in a helpful, pleasant tone. For example: "Jones and Company. Miss Smith speaking."

2. Give every call a personal touch by being friendly and interested.

"May I take a message?"

THE SATURDAY EVENING POST

3. Give courteous attention to the request of any caller. Let him tell his own story in his own way instead of hurrying him or trying to tell him what he wants.

4. In getting additional information, be tactful and avoid asking needless questions.

5. In case of complaints, be willing to admit an error, express regret that it occurred, and assure the caller that it will be corrected.

6. Record definite and complete information concerning the request and tell the customer what will be done about it.

7. When necessary for you to leave the phone, ask for permission and give the reason for leaving. Return promptly and thank the customer for waiting.

8. Express appreciation for the call and close it courteously.

## ACTIVITIES

1. Have a party-line discussion in class. Listen in on everyone's remarks and add your own on the following:
   - Telephone habits which are irritating
   - Rules of etiquette to use if your phone is on a party line
   - Examples from your experience of bad telephone manners
2. Get booklets from your local telephone company. Discuss the rules and suggestions offered in them. Try some of the experiments given.
3. Illustrate in a brief telephone conversation the following familiar types of voices:
   - The voice with the smile
   - The whining voice
   - The nasal voice
   - The shrill voice
   - The boisterous voice
   - The bored voice
4. Illustrate proper procedures in placing a long-distance call. It may be wise to check with your local telephone company concerning any new procedures that are now recommended.
5. Below are four situations. Select a partner or partners and carry out the directions given in each situation. Judge yourselves on observing the rules given in this chapter.
   a. The sweater you ordered from a store came in the wrong size and color. Call the store to make the necessary adjustment.
   b. You ordered a gift to be sent to a friend for his birthday. Ten days later you discovered that the gift had not arrived. Call the store, find out to whom you should talk about the situation, make the proper contact, and arrive at a satisfactory agreement.
   c. You wish to take a trip requiring considerable information about fares, schedules, and reservations. Call for the necessary information. Because you are undecided as to whether you are going by plane or train, it will be necessary for you to make several calls before you find out what you want to know.
   d. You are eating dinner. A person has dialed your number by mistake. Handle the situation properly.

UNIT

# 2

# *Being Speech Conscious*

CHAPTER

CHAPTER

# 4 Listening to Others

His thoughts were slow, his words were few
And never formed to glisten,
But he was joy to all the clan—
You should have heard him listen!

—Prochnow: *Speaker's Treasury of Stories for All Occasions*

A HUSBAND who arrived home during his wife's bridge club meeting asked his wife after the guests had departed, "Please answer me just one question: Who listens?"

"Who listens?" is a question which might well be asked more frequently wherever the spoken word is practiced. Learning to talk is only one half of any speech activity; the other half is listening. Generally, it takes at least two to communicate orally—one to talk and one to listen, since there is no reason to speak if nobody listens! In your speech class you will be a listener more often than a speaker. In conversations too you frequently listen more than you talk. A recent survey revealed that on the average people in business spend 75 percent of each day in verbal communication—30 percent in talking and 45 percent in listening. Furthermore, the survey shows that the average listener retains only about 50 percent of what he hears right after he hears it.

If the *average* business person spends a greater percentage of his time in listening than in talking and only remembers half of what he hears, you can become a *better*-than-average listener by learning early in your speech course *how* to listen. There is an old saying, "We have two ears to one mouth. We should use them in that ratio." There is a great deal more to listening, however, than meets the ear, just as there is a great deal more to talking than using the mouth.

# What Is Listening?

Alice Duer Miller described listening in this manner:

"People love to talk but hate to listen. Listening is not merely not talking, though even that is beyond most of our powers; it means taking a vigorous, human interest in what is being told us. We can listen like a blank wall or like a splendid auditorium where every sound comes back fuller and richer.

"The best listener I ever knew was the late Clarence Day, author of *Life With Father.* He did not listen in silence. He laughed, he groaned, he roared; his eyes shone with surprise and delight. However mild the anecdote you might be relating, it became significant through his exciting interest."

What kind of listener are you? Are you a "blank wall" or a "splendid auditorium?" You will be able to answer this question more accurately after you understand the real meaning of listening.

The full process of listening includes four steps: (1) hearing, (2) understanding, (3) evaluating, and (4) responding.

First, you *hear* a series of sounds which you call words. Second, you *understand* the meaning of those words in the context in which you hear them. Third, you *evaluate* (or judge) the meaning to decide whether you accept or reject the idea expressed. Fourth, you *respond*—that is, you convey your reaction to the meaning by bodily movement, facial expression, or audible response, to a great or small degree, as the occasion warrants.

"You think *you* had a close call!"

Reprinted by courtesy of *Field & Stream* Magazine

Have you ever stood in a telegraph office and listened to the sound of a series of dots and dashes? Unless you have studied the Morse code, you do not understand what you hear and your listening stops with the first step. The telegraph operator, on the other hand, understands what he hears because he decodes the sounds into words having meaning. His listening goes a step beyond yours for it includes the second step. When you listen to Morse code, you are an example of a blank wall listener, because you did not carry all four steps to completion. The telegraph operator may also have been a blank wall listener; although he understood the message, he did not have to evaluate the meaning in order to make a decision to accept or reject the idea expressed, nor did he have to respond.

When you listen to speakers whose language is not clear enough for you to decode the message, you are prevented from completing the third and fourth steps to become a complete listener. Listening failures often occur also when you, the receiver, make no attempt to *understand, evaluate,* and *react* to the signals transmitted by the sender. This is your fault. You are a passive and an indifferent listener.

Listening well is an active process, not a passive one. To listen fully requires that you receive a message intact, understand its full meaning, bounce it back and forth in your mind before deciding whether to hold on to it or throw it away, and convey to the speaker some suggestion of your response. You have to listen intently for voice tones, voice inflections, pauses, and words which are emphasized. You must watch the speaker's gestures and facial expressions, for they too are sending you important signals.

The chief difference between the blank wall and the splendid auditorium type of listener seems to lie in the amount of mental activity displayed and in a willingness to take all the steps. The complete listener is on the alert constantly to see, hear, interpret, and react to every possible signal. This is no simple process, especially when you realize that you have few chances in a speech to re-listen. You must hear it, understand it, weigh it, and respond to it accurately the *first* time, for listening is not like reading in which you can go back and re-read any passages that may not be clear. The secret of a good listener becoming a splendid auditorium is in taking that final step: being *responsive.* You can see him listening because, like Clarence Day, he listens all over. He leans forward to hear every word; his body shifts right along with his mind; and his face registers his responses. If he likes what you are saying, he will let you know by visible or even audible response. If he dislikes your message, you will be able to detect that fact, too!

Good listeners watch every movement, listen to every word, and react to every idea. *(Jules Alexander)*

## ACTIVITIES

1. Bring to class a one-minute statement which will arouse difference of opinion. Read it to the class. How many heard it correctly, understood it completely, evaluated it intelligently, and responded fully?
2. Read a brief selection of any type to the class. Ask several persons to restate the meaning in their own words.
3. Read a short selection to the class. Stop several times during your reading to ask your audience to repeat your last few words or last sentence.
4. Prepare a series of ten directions for the class to follow in writing. Make the directions unusual in order that close attention will be required. Collect the papers and report on the number of errors.

   *Examples of possible directions:*

   Write your last name in the lower right hand corner.
   In the upper right hand corner, print your first name.
   In the center of the page, give the date of your birth in number form.
   On the third line from the top, print your homeroom teacher's name.
5. Read an entertaining selection to the class. How many registered active pleasure?

## Why Listen?

You might say that you listen so that you can hear; that you hear so that you can understand; and that you understand so that you can decide. To be more specific, you might say that you listen to increase your knowledge. Here are some additional benefits which should encourage you to improve your listening habits:

1. *Active listening aids in self-advancement.* This begins early and continues throughout your life. You have probably noticed in school that the students with the best listening habits receive the highest grades. The fully alert listener is usually a superior student, whereas the occasional listener is either average or failing in his grades. This mental alertness is valuable not only in school, but it is essential for efficiency and progress in any type of occupation you pursue. Imagine what would happen if doctors didn't listen carefully to your symptoms, or nurses didn't listen to the doctor's orders, or teachers didn't listen to your answers!

2. *Active listening aids your understanding of good speaking.* As you listen to speeches and conversation in class and elsewhere, you can profit by example. Learn to listen with a critical mind—not to tear down the efforts of others, but to build up your own capabilities. You can acquire much valuable training in speaking by paying attention to methods used by other people to make their speaking interesting, worthwhile, and pleasing. Do they use examples, illustrations, anecdotes, humor, vivid language style, personal experiences, quotations, and similar devices to capture and hold attention? If so, observe how they use them and then follow their example in your own talking.

Your opportunities to observe are as numerous as there are speakers in your class, your church, your assembly programs, and on all radio and television programs. Listen to all of them from an analytical viewpoint. Which speakers are most popular? Why? What makes some talking dull and ineffective? Does the difference between interesting and dull communication lie within the speech, the speaker, or both? What makes some speakers easier to follow than others? What mannerisms of speakers bother you?

You represent one typical listener. You know what appeals to you and what does not. Some speeches and conversations will be outstanding in your mind while others will seem weak by comparison. Separate in your mind the qualities responsible for this difference. Apply the good qualities to your speaking and eliminate the undesirable ones. When you focus full attention on analyzing the communication habits of others and applying the same standards of judgment to your own, your improvement will amaze you.

3. *Active listening stimulates other speakers.* Active listening on the part of your audience spurs you on to exhibit your best speech efforts. When you feel that listeners are reaching out to grasp your meaning, you reciprocate by extending yourself to get even closer to them. This ideal speaker-listener relationship occurs only when both speaker and listener cooperate in a lively give-and-take process. As the speaker gives ideas, the listener hears them, understands them, evaluates them, and responds to them. When speaking, you need this active, overt response to provide incentive to speak forcefully; when listening, you should provide this incentive to speakers.

Have you discovered how difficult and discouraging it is to speak when your classmates are talking or writing notes to each other, reading, daydreaming, staring out of the window, or slumping lazily in their seats? Do you ever have the feeling, "What's the use?" How different it is to speak to a group when all are watching your every movement, listening eagerly to every word, and reacting bodily and mentally to every idea!

You must do your part in creating the ideal attentive atmosphere. As a speaker, you must make people *want to listen* by speaking and conversing in ways that capture attention immediately and hold it to the last word. As a listener, you should also make others *want to speak well* by giving active and responsive attention. By working together in this manner, you will improve both your listening and your speaking habits.

4. *Active listening is vital to your best interests.* This refers to *protecting* your interests as an individual and as a public citizen.

Newspapers, radio, and television daily bring a flood of propaganda into your home. These may be in the nature of "hard sell" commercials or speeches for political campaigns. A sponsor pays for time on most broadcasts and he wants to get his money's worth whether he sells you a product, an idea, or a person. Remember this when a smooth-talking person "high-pressures" you to buy a certain brand of dog food or a certain kind of food for thought.

The Better Business Bureau works hard to protect you from fraudulent advertising in print and in door-to-door solicitation. It urges you to read between the lines and the fine print when buying insurance policies from strangers or signing your name to any paper which commits you to legal prosecution in case you fail to pay. The Government also protects you from fraudulent use of the mails.

Your listening powers should be keen enough to detect the "speech to confuse." *(Ewing Galloway)*

But who protects you from the dangers of the spoken word? Only you can provide that kind of protection through sharpening your listening powers. Many of the messages that you hear are honestly and genuinely presented by speakers who believe sincerely in what they say. Many others, however, are slanted, shaded, or sugar-coated in some fashion to capture your attention and motivate you to respond favorably. Indeed, in today's political speaking, the "speech to confuse" has become a recognized, if dangerous, type. You must be the one to judge which you can believe, which you must actively reject, and which you must label as worthless propaganda.

When your own interests are at stake, you can suffer physical, mental, spiritual, and economic loss by failing to listen critically to the wrong ideas. When the interests of your country are at stake, it is even more vital that you evaluate correctly what you hear before accepting it. It is your duty and responsibility to listen critically. Your life and welfare are at stake. The welfare and destiny of your country are even more at stake. Hitlers and Mussolinis cannot seize control when people can see through their idle promises. Communism and similar types of government hold little appeal to listeners who compare facts with promises and who judge on the basis of known existing conditions instead of extravagant misrepresentation.

There is no doubt regarding the importance of listening in speech training or of its value to you personally. It is as untrue to assume, however, that you know how to listen because you have been listening all of your life as it is to think that you know how to speak because you have been speaking most of your life. As you recall, the average person is a "half-listener." Listening and speaking are both habits which you have been forming since you were old enough to do both. Since you are not born with good or bad habits, you acquire them through repeated usage. "Practice makes perfect" is true only when you are practicing in the right direction. You may become a perfect non-listener or a perfect full-time listener depending upon *what* you are practicing!

## How to Improve Listening

Experiments in teaching listening show that you can improve your listening skill through training. One of the most convincing proofs of this appears in *Are You Listening?* Here Nichols and Stevens state that ". . . listening is a mental skill that can be developed through training and practice. We now give listening courses at the University of Minnesota, and every group we have ever trained has averaged better than a 25 percent gain in proficiency." The book goes on to point out that poor listening seems to develop when listeners have thinking time to spare. The average rate of speaking is close to 125 words per minute, but you think four times that fast—which gives you about 400 words of thinking time to spare. The poor listener becomes impatient and lets his mind wander more and more during this spare time, whereas the good listener uses this time in evaluating the speaker and weighing his words carefully.

You have undoubtedly observed how easy it is to let your mind wander off on side excursions even during an interesting speech. The ability to concentrate steadily and to resist distractions is one of the secrets of complete listening. From your own experience, you know that you usually listen in proportion to your desire to listen. For example, it is easy to listen to your favorite television program, to conversations with friends, or to entertaining stories. In these cases, you *want* to listen; so you resist distractions.

Listening becomes difficult only when you feel that you *ought* to listen. On such occasions, you need to exercise strong will power in disciplining your mind. You cannot be trained to listen merely by taking a series of listening tests no matter how sound the tests are or how scientifically they are administered. You must *want* to improve and you must be willing to work and concentrate on it. Your easiest and simplest method is probably self-training.

A golf pro will teach you the fundamentals of golf and will demonstrate such things as the proper grip and stance, but your proficiency in the game depends upon your practicing the rules laid down in your lessons. The pro doesn't play the game for you; he explains the principles and shows you how to apply those principles. Acquiring the skill is up to you. You learn to play golf better and better by practicing the right rules. You learn to listen better and better, too, by practicing the right rules.

Here are the rules that a "listening pro" would teach you. They are arranged according to *the four steps of listening: hearing, understanding, evaluating, and responding.* "Follow through" on all of them and you will notice improvement in your listening.

## How to improve hearing:

1. Be ready to listen. Stop talking to others. Make a habit of having paper and pencil handy in case you wish to record important facts, figures, and ideas. Don't waste time, however, trying to write down every detail. Trying to write everything may keep you from hearing anything.
2. Begin listening at once. Many people state their central idea at the beginning. Don't miss it.
3. Concentrate on the person talking and on what he is saying. Pay no attention to your neighbors or to any distracting elements. Switch off any personal worries or plans which might interfere with your listening. Move closer to the speaker if you cannot hear easily.
4. Hear the words and ideas exactly as they are expressed. Be careful that you are not guessing about what was said or hearing it as you want to hear it.
5. Keep listening all the way through a speech or conversation, regardless of how it impresses you. Unless you have heard everything, you cannot understand, evaluate, or respond wisely.

## How to improve understanding:

1. Improve your vocabulary daily. Choose a new word from the dictionary each day and use it three times that day in conversation. In order to understand the meaning of words, you must be familiar with them. The larger your word comprehension is, the better your chances of understanding will be.
2. Listen for the main ideas and concentrate on their meaning.
3. Listen for supporting ideas and be sure to get them in their true relationship to the main ideas. They will help you to understand the whole meaning.

In listening to a golf pro or a speech pro, you must "follow through" with the same four steps: hearing, understanding, evaluating, and responding. *(Pogue's Portrait Studio)*

4. Try to keep out prejudices or convictions that you might have regarding the speaker or his subject. Listen to understand rather than to misunderstand.

5. Watch the speaker for visual as well as auditory signals. Listen, too, for voice tones, inflections, and emphases.

## How to improve evaluation:

1. Listen for all facts before arriving at a decision. Realize that there are many facts which you do not know. Poor listeners stop listening to disagree or to plan replies, but good listeners keep right on listening. You are really a member of a jury as you judge a speaker or speakers. Be a fair jury member and reserve final judgment until all of the evidence has been presented.

2. Be extremely fair and careful as you weigh ideas. This is one of the most difficult principles to teach, since fair judgment depends largely upon your own attitudes and your ability to reason logically and objectively. If speakers present views which conflict with yours, do your best to avoid feeling that you are always right.

3. Adopt as your listening code the one given by Francis Bacon for reading: "Read not to contradict or confute; not to believe and take for granted; nor to find talk and discourse; but to weigh and consider." Substitute "listen" for "read" and you will have an excellent standard for judging oral communication.

4. Welcome new viewpoints instead of resisting them. Studies in heredity prove that a family degenerates when there are no new blood lines. You can degenerate mentally, too, when you refuse to consider new points of view.

5. Apply fair tests to the speaker but give him no unfair advantages. Speakers as well as listeners may be prejudiced, misinformed, or uninformed. Do not be misled by any of the following:

Personal friendships or antagonisms
A glittering personality or a striking appearance
False reasoning or a distorting of the truth
Smooth talking or irrelevance to the subject
Emotional appeals without sincerity of purpose
Authority, or the lack of it, on the subject

## How to improve responsiveness:

1. Let the person speaking know that you are listening to him. Do this by meeting his glance squarely when he glances at you, by sitting or standing in a posture of comfortable attention, and by avoiding extraneous behavior such as talking to one side, dozing, or following some other activity.

2. Within the bounds of good manners, convey to the person speaking your agreement or disagreement by facial expressions, bodily movements, gestures, and, when appropriate, what you say.

3. Do not react so openly or conspicuously as to embarrass the person speaking or distract your fellow listeners.

The above principles are fundamental in training yourself to listen. You cannot practice them as easily, perhaps, as you can the game of golf. All that you can do is to realize the full responsibility involved in listening and then try to measure up to the standards. In case you feel overwhelmed by the standards, you may enjoy a story which illustrates how easily they work in practice:

> A naturalist and a banker were walking together along a busy, noisy street. Suddenly the naturalist stopped to remark, "Listen, I hear a sparrow." The banker was amazed that, on a busy street, the naturalist could hear a sparrow, but he was willing to investigate. A few moments later, they discovered the sparrow chirping away beside a fire hydrant. They continued their walk until the banker stopped suddenly, and said, "Listen, somebody just dropped a dime on the sidewalk." It was the naturalist's turn to be amazed. After progressing a few steps, the banker stooped and picked up a dime.

The moral of this story is that you hear what you are trained to hear. To have a perfect ending to the story, add a third person as the perfect listener who heard both the sparrow and the dime!

**ACTIVITY**

## ARE YOU A GOOD LISTENER?

*(Please do not write in this book)*

| ATTITUDES | ALMOST ALWAYS | USUALLY | OCCASIONALLY | SELDOM | ALMOST NEVER |
|---|---|---|---|---|---|
| 1. Do you like to listen to other people talk? | 5 | 4 | 3 | 2 | 1 |
| 2. Do you encourage others to talk? | 5 | 4 | 3 | 2 | 1 |
| 3. Do you listen even if you do not like the person who is talking? | 5 | 4 | 3 | 2 | 1 |
| 4. Do you listen equally well whether the person talking is man or woman, young or old? | 5 | 4 | 3 | 2 | 1 |
| 5. Do you listen equally well to friend, acquaintance, stranger? | 5 | 4 | 3 | 2 | 1 |
| **ACTIONS** | | | | | |
| 6. Do you put what you have been doing out of sight and out of mind? | 5 | 4 | 3 | 2 | 1 |
| 7. Do you look at the speaker? | 5 | 4 | 3 | 2 | 1 |
| 8. Do you ignore distractions? | 5 | 4 | 3 | 2 | 1 |
| 9. Do you smile, nod your head, and otherwise encourage him to talk? | 5 | 4 | 3 | 2 | 1 |
| 10. Do you think about what he is saying? | 5 | 4 | 3 | 2 | 1 |
| 11. Do you try to figure out what he means? | 5 | 4 | 3 | 2 | 1 |
| 12. Do you try to figure out why he is saying it? | 5 | 4 | 3 | 2 | 1 |
| 13. Do you let him finish what he is trying to say? | 5 | 4 | 3 | 2 | 1 |
| 14. If he hesitates, do you encourage him to go on? | 5 | 4 | 3 | 2 | 1 |
| 15. Do you re-state what he has said and ask him if you got it right? | 5 | 4 | 3 | 2 | 1 |
| 16. Do you withhold judgment about his idea until he has finished? | 5 | 4 | 3 | 2 | 1 |
| 17. Do you listen regardless of his manner of speaking and choice of words? | 5 | 4 | 3 | 2 | 1 |
| 18. Do you listen even though you anticipate what he is going to say? | 5 | 4 | 3 | 2 | 1 |
| 19. Do you question him in order to get him to explain his idea more fully? | 5 | 4 | 3 | 2 | 1 |
| 20. Do you ask him what the words mean as he uses them? | 5 | 4 | 3 | 2 | 1 |

If your score is 75 or better, you are a GOOD LISTENER.

If your score is 50-75, you are an AVERAGE LISTENER.

If your score is below 50, you are a POOR LISTENER.

CHAPTER

# 5 Listening to Yourself

Speech finely framed delighteth the ears.

—*The Apocrypha,*
*2 Maccabees XV, 39*

WHEN you meet people for the first time, you are likely to judge them on the basis of their personal appearance and their speech, that is, to judge them on how they look and how they sound. Since first impressions may be lasting, you want the first impressions you make to be pleasing to others. In this fast-moving world, you must learn to gain the attention of your listeners effectively and quickly through the skillful use of speech.

What impressions do you stimulate in others when they listen to you in person, over the telephone, on a tape recording, or even on radio? How do you react to your own speech and to that of others?

## ACTIVITY

Listen to several radio announcers or performers of your choice and keep a record of your reactions to their voices. Record your name, the date, name and time of program together with the name of the speaker or announcer. You may wish to evaluate your reactions according to the following very simple check list, or you may wish to make out your own. (*Please do not write in this book.*)

| | | | COMMENT |
|---|---|---|---|
| 1. Voice | Pleasing | ☐ | |
| | Annoying | ☐ | |
| 2. Articulation | Clear | ☐ | |
| | Not clear | ☐ | |
| 3. Personality | Likable | ☐ | |
| | Not likable | ☐ | |

Now try to explain why you checked the items you did on your reaction record. Is it not true that you probably found it easier to react to these speech samples than to explain your reactions? One purpose of this activity is to show you that while you may react strongly to speech and to people who speak, you may not know exactly why you do so.

## The Speech Mechanism

In one very real sense, you have no special speech mechanism. The parts of your body that you use for speech have more primary *biological* functions. Thus your tongue, although certainly useful in

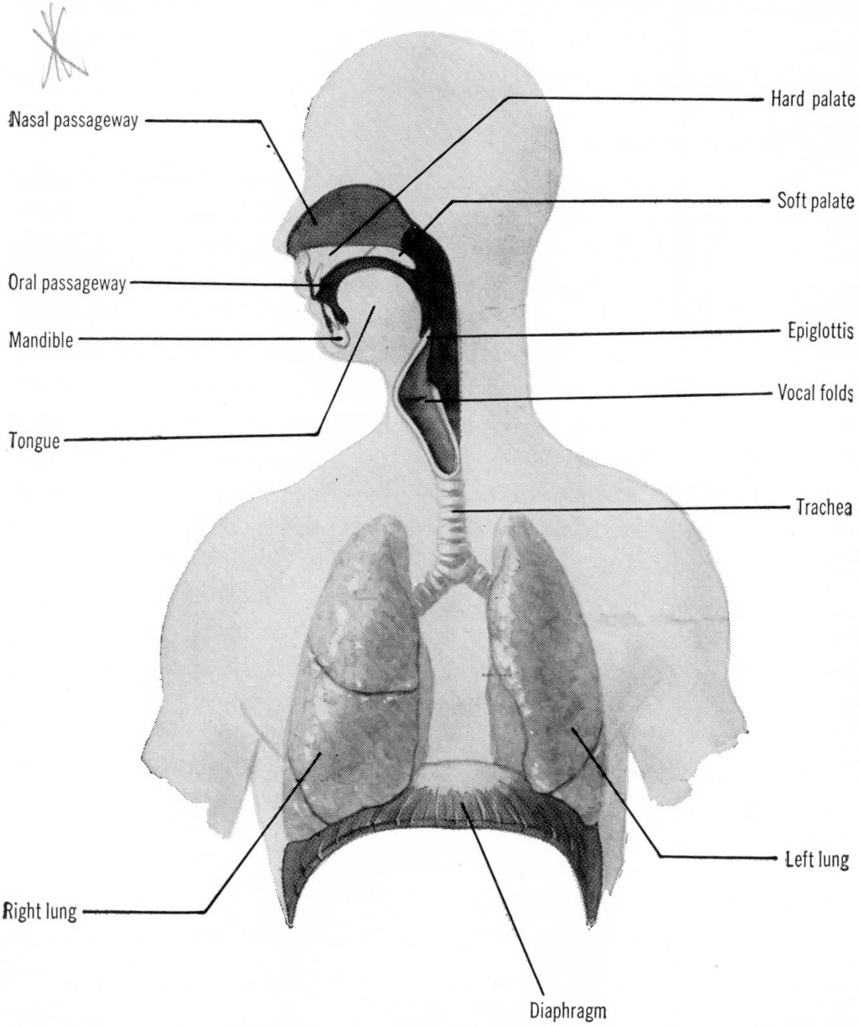


FIG. 1. The Speech Mechanism

talking, is biologically used to shift food in the mouth while you are chewing and swallowing. The larynx, although the source of your voice, acts biologically as a very important valve to control the flow of air in and out of the lungs and as a protective mechanism to keep foreign objects out of the lungs. And even the lungs, although they provide the outgoing air stream used in speech, serve also the more basic function of maintaining respiration.

Nevertheless, because certain parts of your body are used regularly in speech, it is convenient to speak of a speech mechanism. You may wish to think of this speech mechanism as being divided into three parts: the power source, the voice box, and the articulators. In addition, the resonating function is served by the laryngeal, throat, oral, and nasal cavities. Fig. 1, a diagram of the speech mechanism, shows each of these three parts.

## The power source

The lungs, the rib cage, and certain associated muscles make up the power source. Your lungs are two relatively large sacs. They are not muscular. Their size and shape vary with the size and shape of the rib cage and diaphragm which, together, completely enclose them.

From each lung a tube (the bronchus) emerges to join with its counterpart from the other lung to form the trachea or windpipe. This windpipe leads up through the larynx (voice producing organ) to the pharynx, the cavity back of the mouth and nose when the head is in an upright position. The pharynx is connected to the outside air through the mouth and nose. In quiet inspiration, air moves through the nose and pharynx down through the larynx, the trachea, and the two bronchi, and finally enters the lungs. In quiet expiration, the flow of air is reversed. In heavy breathing, air may enter and leave through the mouth as well as nose. In speech, much of the outgoing air stream is directed through the mouth.

The power source (lungs and associated muscles) is adequate for your speech if it can (a) deliver sufficient air to produce the voice you need and (b) control the air flow with sufficient flexibility for your needs.

## The larynx or voice box

Your voice is produced in your larynx. The larynx is an air valve between the top of the trachea and the pharynx. Your larynx has a framework of nine cartilages, three of which are single and six of which are paired. The larynx is shown in Fig. 2. The

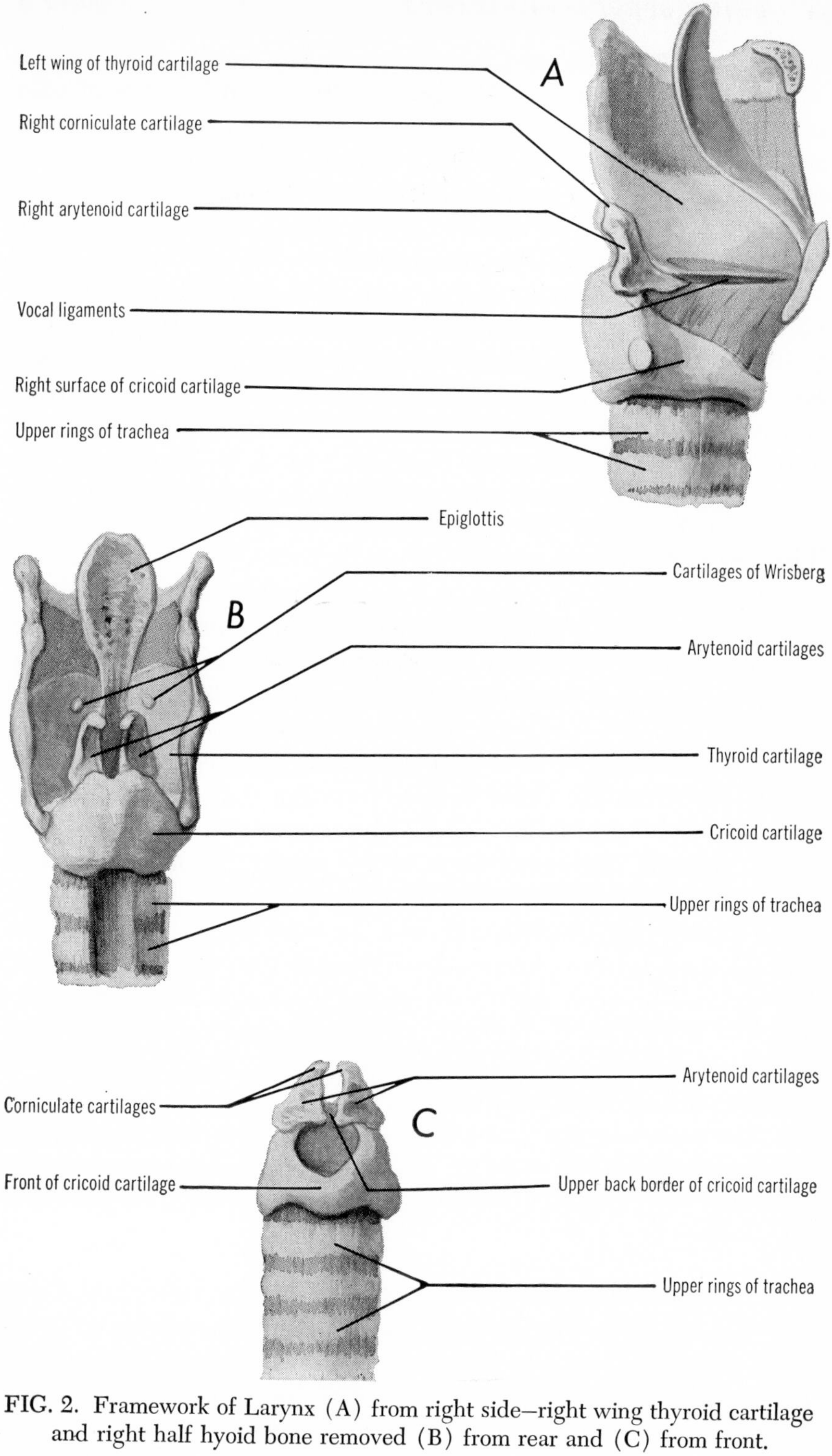


FIG. 2. Framework of Larynx (A) from right side–right wing thyroid cartilage and right half hyoid bone removed (B) from rear and (C) from front.

largest laryngeal cartilage is the thyroid; this is a butterfly-shaped cartilage located so that the body of the butterfly lies vertically along the front midline of the throat with its wings flaring backwards. The lower point of each wing is attached to the outside surface of the cricoid cartilage, which is a ring-shaped cartilage at the top of the trachea. On the upper back surface of the cricoid cartilage are mounted two paired cartilages, the arytenoids. These can tip forward and back, pivot in and out, and slide to and from each other. Your two vocal cords, which are basically muscular folds, run from front to back across the throat, with the front attachments at the butterfly's head and the back attachments to the right and left arytenoids respectively. Depending, then, upon the position of the arytenoids, your vocal folds may open for breathing, may close to block the flow of air completely, or may close just tightly enough so that they will vibrate if air is forced out between them. These positions are shown in Fig. 3. It is this vibration that produces your voice.

You may wonder how the fluttering of two muscular folds can produce your voice. As you exhale with the vocal folds in a voicing position, the air pressure beneath the vocal folds builds up until suddenly the folds snap outward and upward. A puff of air escapes, the pressure beneath the folds drops, and the folds snap back together. The number of times this opening and closing takes place per second determines the pitch of the voice. In a very low bass singer, the rate of this vibration may be as slow as sixty-four times per second; in a high soprano, it may be as rapid as a thousand times or more per second.

### ACTIVITY

Place your forefinger in the front midline of your throat just beneath the level of the jaw. Slowly slide your finger down this soft midline area until you feel a hard, v-shaped notch. This notch is the front of the thyroid cartilage. The vocal folds lie immediately behind this notch in a horizontal plane, that is, they run from front to back. With your finger still on the notch, keep repeating "ah, ah, ah." You will feel the vibration of the vocal folds.

## The articulators

Your articulators may be divided into the bony and fleshy articulators. The bony articulators consist of the upper and lower teeth, the lower jaw, and the upper jaw including the hard or bony palate. The fleshy articulators consist of the lips, tongue, and soft palate. These articulators are shown in a mid-line view in Fig. 4.

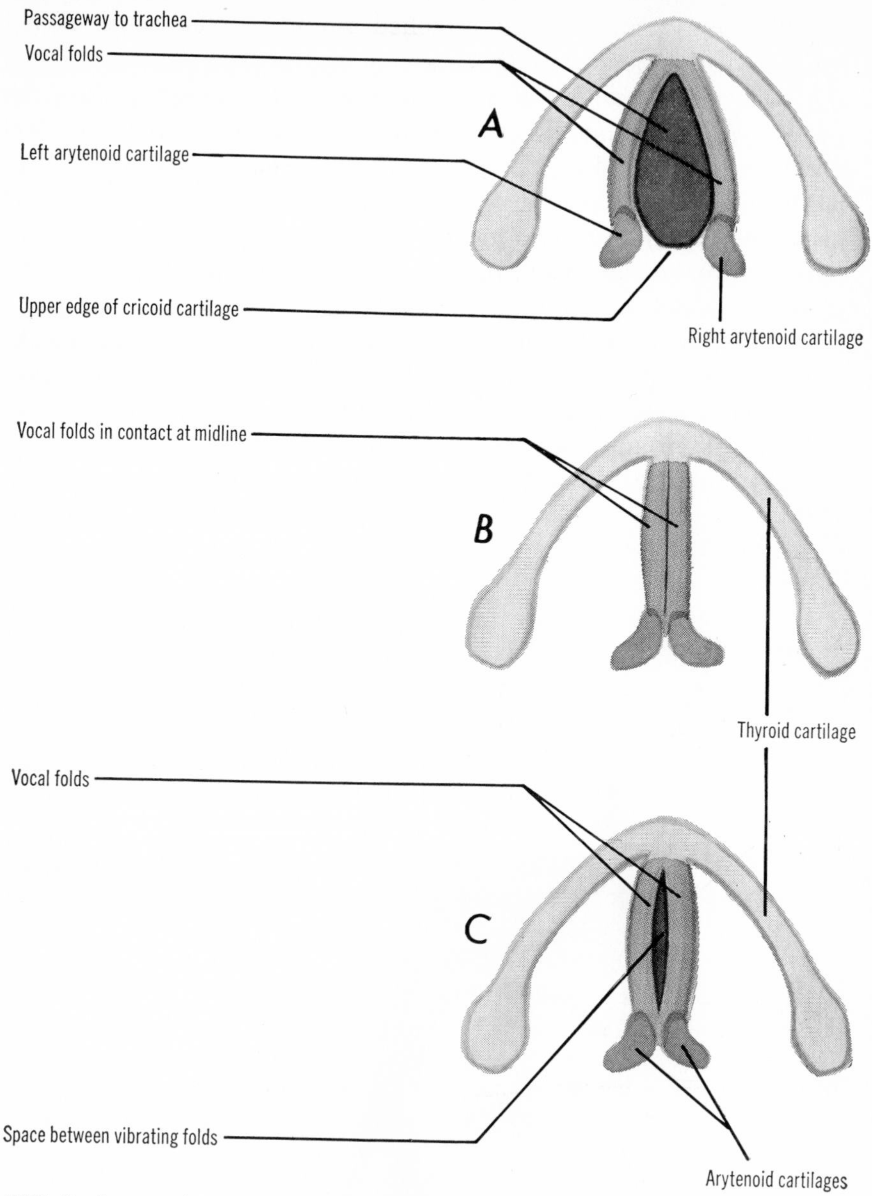


FIG. 3. Larynx from above (A) open for inspiration (B) closed (C) vibrating.

The function of the articulators is threefold: (1) to modify the voice by changing the shape of the oral, nasal, and pharyngeal cavities in making such vowels as *o* and *u*; (2) to modify the outgoing air stream in such a way as to produce friction noises in the mouth area in such sounds as *s* and *f*; and (3) to stop and start the outgoing air stream in such sounds as *p* or *t*.

The upper jaw, being attached rigidly to the skull, is not capable of independent movement. A part of the upper jaw forms the bony palate, which is the thin plate of bone that bridges the upper teeth and thus forms the bony roof of the mouth. To feel your hard palate, put your tongue tip up behind your upper front teeth and then sweep the tip of your tongue backward along the center of the roof of your mouth. In so doing, you are feeling the hard palate. At the back of the hard or bony palate is a fleshy extension which terminates in the little flap that you see when you examine your mouth with a mirror. This muscular or fleshy extension is the soft palate. The extreme back tip of this muscular extension is known as the uvula. By the action of various muscles, you can raise it up and back and block off your nasal passageways, or you can drop it down and forward and open these passageways.

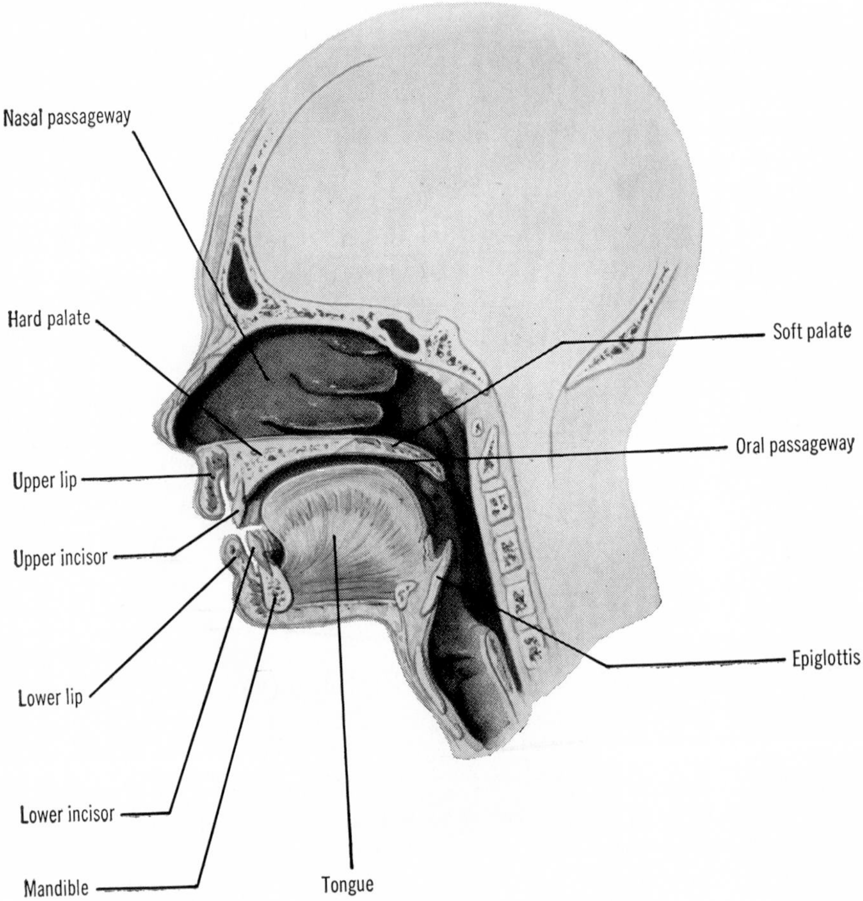


FIG. 4. Mid-Line View of the Articulators.

The lower jaw is a horseshoe-shaped structure; the closed end of the horseshoe makes up your chin. At the open end of the horseshoe are two projections which run up and attach to the skull below the ear. As you know, you can move your jaw up and down, you can slide it forward into a bulldog-like position, and you can slide it from side to side, a little like the movement of a cow chewing a cud. These movements help to control the relative adjustments of the upper and lower teeth to each other and also largely determine the potential size of the mouth passage.

The tongue, a massive muscular organ, is much larger than it looks from in front. The attachments of the tongue are shown in Fig. 5. Because its fibers basically radiate from a point behind the chin, movements of the lower jaw pull the body of the tongue around. In addition, the body of the tongue is attached deep in the throat, so that the tongue can be pulled backwards and downwards in the mouth. Finally, the tongue is also attached to the base of the skull up close to the ears, so that the tongue can be pulled upward and backward. Because your tongue has this complex system of external attachments (front chin, deep throat, and upper throat), you can put it in almost any position you wish. It also has internal fibers that make it possible for you to shape your tongue.

The position and action of the lips are easy to understand if you just make faces at yourself in front of a mirror. Because the lips consist basically of a ring of muscular fibers, and because several

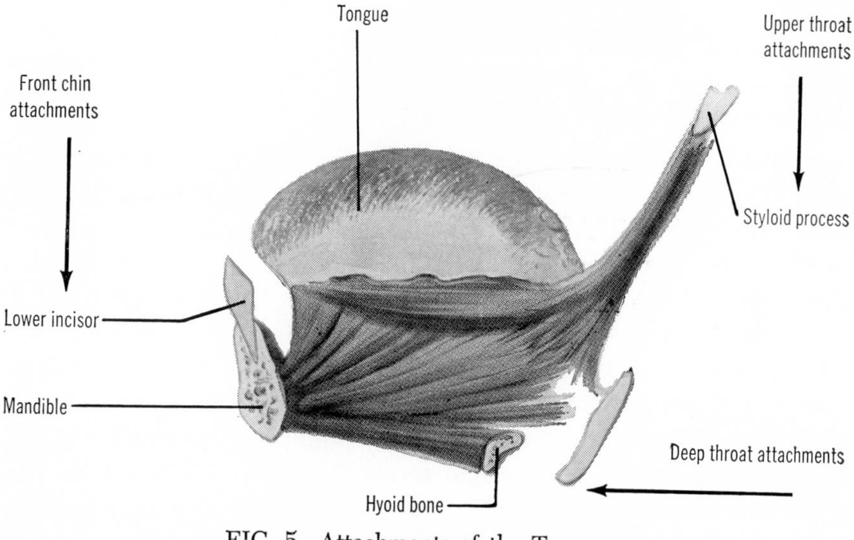


FIG. 5. Attachments of the Tongue.

INTERESTING SOUND PATTERNS

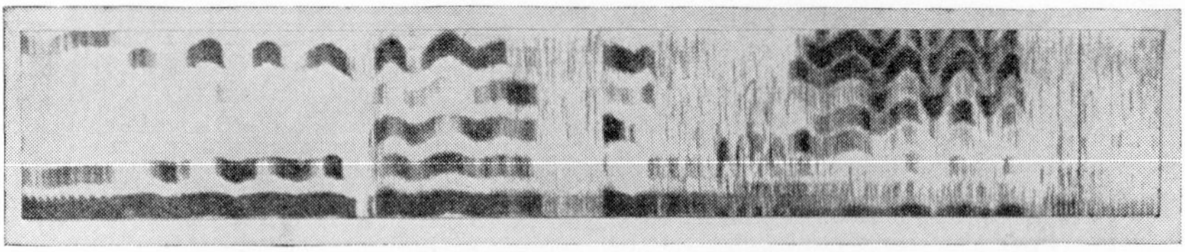

Song — Trained Soprano Voice

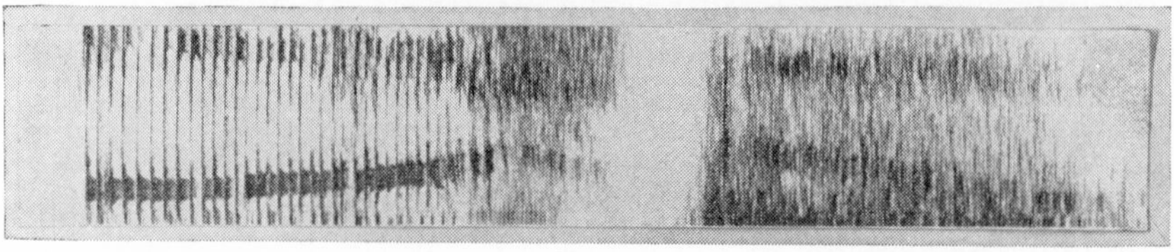

Snore

The diagrams of visible speech shown on these two pages are sound spectrograms, recording the energy used by a person in different forms of speech and speech-like sounds.

paired muscles run away from this ring upwards, backwards, and downwards into the face, the lips can be opened and closed in many ways.

Finally, the nasal passageways are two small tubes that lead from each of your nostrils back into the nasal pharynx above the soft palate. Depending upon the position of the soft palate, these passages may or may not transmit all or portions of the air sound stream.

# *You and Your Voice*

## Problems of pitch

The pitch of your voice, as mentioned earlier, is determined by the rate at which your vocal folds vibrate as the air from the lungs sets the edges of the folds to fluttering. Your pitch range and the pitches you use most frequently in speaking are determined to a large extent by your age and sex. If you are a boy, your vocal bands may open and close between 100 and 150 times per second as you talk; if you are a girl, your rate will be somewhat faster, perhaps around 200 or more times per second.

Some terms that refer to unusually high pitch are shrill, whistle-like, piping, and falsetto; some terms that refer to unusually low pitch are deep, full, sepulchral, bass, and heavy. You may be able to think of other terms for both these extremes of pitch.

INTERESTING SPEECH PATTERNS

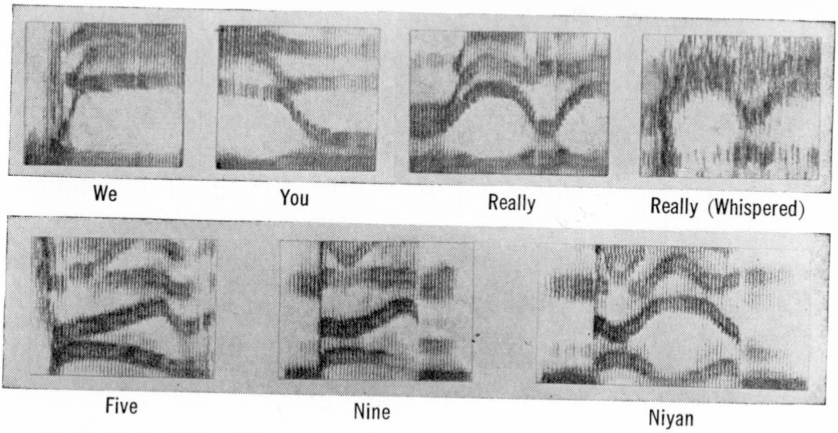


Each of the fifty different sounds of English makes a characteristic pattern in light and shade. The blacker the line, the more energy is expended. *(Bell Telephone)*

**Pitch breaks during adolescence.** Some of you may be going through the "voice change" period and may be experiencing pitch breaks. These pitch changes or breaks are usually not under your control and may cause you mild embarrassment, but will usually occur less frequently as you grow older. These voice breaks result primarily from the rapid growth in the size of the larynx during the early teens. The so-called "change of voice" that comes about during the period of from ten to fourteen years of age need not be a prelude to trouble, despite the fact that in the boy the drop in pitch is likely to be about one octave. Indeed, it has been reported that only 5 percent of over 4,000 subjects interviewed reported that they had ever experienced frequent voice breaks and that only 2 percent reported much embarrassment.

During this period of the rapid growth of the larynx, both boys and girls should be encouraged to use their voices in ways that will not strain their vocal folds. For example, do not yell yourselves hoarse at sports events two or three times a week. Again, if you are experiencing a good many pitch breaks, drop out of the glee club until your voice becomes more stable. When you do return to the chorus, make certain that you are re-tested and placed in the appropriate section according to your new, not your old, voice. Perhaps you should also avoid playing the lead in the school play or singing the lead in the school operetta.

More serious problems can result if this change of voice occurs in your case either at an earlier or a later date than it does with any of your friends. If the change is earlier, you may attempt to maintain your former high pitch, even though your larynx is now too large for such a pitch. And if the change is late, you may attempt to use a low pitch before your larynx is large enough. Either of these alternatives can lead to serious consequences.

**Other factors in unusual pitch.** Under ordinary circumstances you should adopt a basic pitch that feels and sounds right for you and that is in keeping with your age and sex. It is when you attempt to conform to the wishes of your friends or to emulate others with a pitch level which is not right for you, that serious trouble is likely to occur.

Inappropriate pitch may occur when a person tries to use a particular basic pitch in order to sound like someone else. Suppose for instance that a boy actually has a high tenor voice, but his close friend speaks in a low baritone or bass voice. Despite the fact that his larynx is well suited to produce a high tenor voice, the boy attempts to sound exactly like his friend. As a result this tenor may imitate a basic pitch that is far too low for his larynx. Not only will this boy sound somewhat husky, but he may also damage his vocal folds by forcing them into producing a pitch that is not suited to their development.

**Analyzing your voice pitch.** Frequently the first hint that you will receive that something is unusual about your pitch will be that some teacher or other friend will tell you that you are talking either too high or too low. If this does happen to you, don't immediately change or try to change your pitch to the level which sounds best either to you or to your friend. Your own listening preferences will for the most part be based on what you hear; thus you will tend to prefer the average pitch of boys or girls of your own age. But your larynx may not be average in size or function. An average pitch may be much too high or too low for you. Before you change, take the brief test described in the activities that follow:

## ACTIVITIES

1. Sing down the scale until you reach the lowest note you can produce and sustain. Compare this pitch with your average talking pitch. Unless your average talking pitch is higher than your lowest tone, you are talking too near the bottom of your range.
2. Next sing up the scale from your lowest tone to your highest tone. Include your falsetto. Count the number of tones you can sing.
3. Your optimum talking pitch should be roughly one fourth the way up this range. Compare the average pitch that you actually use with the pitch determined by this method.

## Problems of loudness

What are the common loudness problems? It is possible, of course, for you to talk either so softly that no one hears you or so loudly that no one wants to hear you. But the most common problem of loudness, particularly in group communication, is that of not talking loudly enough. A related problem, that of using loudness variation in order to strengthen communication, will be discussed in Chapter 14.

Words commonly used to describe voices that are too loud are blatant, powerful, piercing, deafening, thundering, pealing, swelling, booming, roaring, resounding, ringing, shouting, and bellowing. Terms similarly used to describe voices that are too weak are faint, inaudible, low, dull, muffled, stifled, gentle, soft, and murmured.

**Resonance and loudness.** One way of making yourself heard better is simply to open your mouth adequately while speaking. Your mouth functions as part of the resonating system of your speech mechanism; and adequate resonance may help to increase the basic loudness level of your voice, insofar as the listener is concerned, without requiring any additional effort on your part.

In order to get some idea of the role of resonation in increasing loudness level, you need to perform a very simple experiment. Tap a tuning fork on the desk and hold it up in front of the class. Only

Practice opening your mouth sufficiently to obtain maximum resonance of tone. *(A. M. Rubendunst)*

the people sitting in the front seats will be likely to hear the tone. Now tap the same fork on the desk and hold the fork in front of its resonance box, that is, the box tuned to the frequency of the fork. Now the entire class will be able to hear the tone. Did you add any energy to the fork by placing it in front of a resonance box? Of course the answer is no. Yet the tone became louder. In somewhat the same way your mouth can act to carry the laryngeal tone in a more efficient way to the outside air. This apparent amplification of your voice through proper mouth adjustment occurs only when you open your mouth sufficiently. You wouldn't think of putting a favorite record on your hi-fi set and then putting a large soft pillow over the speaker grille. Yet many people try to speak through their own built-in hi-fi systems without opening their mouths or without keeping their hands away from their mouths.

It will also help you to talk loudly enough if you use a voice pitch that is appropriate to your voice mechanism. The following activity will help you to understand the relationships between voice pitch and loudness:

### ACTIVITY

Talking too near the bottom of your pitch range can contribute to insufficient loudness. To see the relationships between your loudness level and your pitch level, read successively a short selection at three different pitch levels. Do not read in a monotone, but simply work around a relatively high pitch, a relatively low pitch, and one that is relatively centered. At which of these pitch levels did you have the easiest and most flexible loudness? If you record these trials it may help you in your evaluation.

**Respiration and loudness.** It is frequently said that if you do not talk loudly enough, your problem is simply a failure to breathe properly. However, there are several breathing patterns which seem to give satisfactory results. The two important considerations are that you inhale a sufficient amount of air and that you train yourself to *control* the breath system. If you breathe well enough to climb stairs, to dance, or to play basketball, you probably breathe well enough to make yourself heard.

**Habit and loudness.** Again, it is quite possible that if you speak too softly you do so simply because you have formed some bad habits. The original reason for these habits may no longer be important, yet, the habits may continue to bother you. In this case, the obvious remedy is to form some new habits. With the careful help of a friend or teacher, try talking at different loudness levels. Try to be first too loud and then too soft. Experiment freely. Learn

Actors and actresses possess a large repertoire of voice qualities to interpret various emotions and roles. *(UPI Photo)*

what different loudnesses feel and sound like. Find out when your friends think you are talking just about right. Then listen very critically to yourself and try to memorize exactly how you feel and sound.

## Problems of quality

Quality is the characteristic of voice that makes it pleasant or unpleasant to listen to. Subtle differences in quality between voices enable you to tell one person from another, even when they are talking at the same general pitch and loudness level. Acoustically, quality is the result of a combination of the frequencies present in your voice and the relative energy in each frequency. Thus a violin and a trumpet can play the same note at the same pitch and over-all loudness, but because different overtones are present in each instrument and at different strengths, you can tell, sight unseen, which tone is made by a violin and which by a trumpet.

Most people would agree that a pleasant voice quality should be free from undue breathiness, hoarseness, and either too little or too much nasality. Actors and professional speakers use as many variations in voice quality as the situation demands. You, yourself, use a different pattern of qualities in talking with one of your best friends in your own living room than you use when you are asked to give a speech to a large assembly of students.

**Emotions and quality.** The quality of the voice will vary with the emotional response of the speaker to his listener and to his subject matter. More simply, your voice quality reflects your emotional state. Perhaps you recall what happened to your voice the last time you were really angry with someone. Do you remember how your pitch went up and your quality mirrored the tension you were under? Or, to use another type of situation, did your voice waver slightly when you got up to speak for the first time in class? In situations in which you are excited, as when you are called on in class, the autonomic nervous system begins pumping adrenalin through the blood stream in order to condition your body to meet any unforeseen danger. Your voice quality, then, simply responds to your physical and emotional state.

**Common causes of unusual quality.** A particular quality of voice—either good or bad—may result from the way in which a person has become accustomed to speaking; or it may result from a disease, as cerebral palsy; from a physical abnormality, as cleft palate; or even from some psychological need for a distinctive voice, as in the habitual use of a falsetto or other uncommon voice. This discussion will be concerned mainly with those voice quality problems that result from the way in which you use your speech mechanism, as these are the only kinds that can be safely dealt with in a general speech class.

***Nasality.*** One of the most common voice quality problems is nasality. Your voice attracts unfavorable attention when it manifests either too much or too little nasality. You should say the sounds *m, n,* and *ng* through your nose, and make all the other or non-nasal sounds of English through your mouth in order to sound right. That is, in the non-nasal sounds of English, the nose is fairly well shut off from the mouth by the soft palate. True, there may be some carry-over of nasality to the vowels, when *m, n,* or *ng* are near them in a word such as *mammon* or *candy.* In such words the vowel sounds are frequently slightly nasal because of the influence of the nasal sounds on one or both sides. In words where the *m, n,* or *ng* are near vowel sounds, try to keep these vowel sounds from becoming excessively nasal.

Too much nasality may also result from laziness in articulating the sound sequences of our language. Try saying words such as these: cat, cut, keep, court, cab, curb, and cart. Make the initial sounds in these words distinctly, and open your mouth on the vowel sounds to allow for the best oral transmission. Now try to make these same words sound nasal in quality; do this by closing the mouth more, by not exploding the consonant sounds sharply, and by relaxing the soft palate. Do you hear the difference? Do others in your class hear the difference?

Too little nasality may be the result of a cold, some obstruction of the nasal pathway, or even of defective habits of speaking. Adenoids or a crooked septum (center support of nose) frequently contribute to this voice quality problem because they tend to block the nasal passageways. If your nasal sounds are muffled, you should have an examination by a physician to determine the cause.

The production of any sound other than *m, n,* and *ng* with the nasal passageways open is *over-nasality.*

The second type of nasality, *under-nasality,* is a tendency to make *m, n,* and *ng* at least partially through the mouth rather than through the nose. When your nasal passages are blocked with a severe cold, the sentence, "I know I have a nasty cold in my nose," may sound like, "I doe I have a dasty code id by dose."

## ACTIVITY

The following sentences contain many nasal sounds. Say the sentences several times with the nostrils alternately open and pinched together. There should be a pronounced difference in the way the sentences sound. If there is not a difference, you have under-nasality. Here are the sentences:

Come now and meet the man in the moon.
Many minor men made the money.
Elephants and mules make fine work animals.

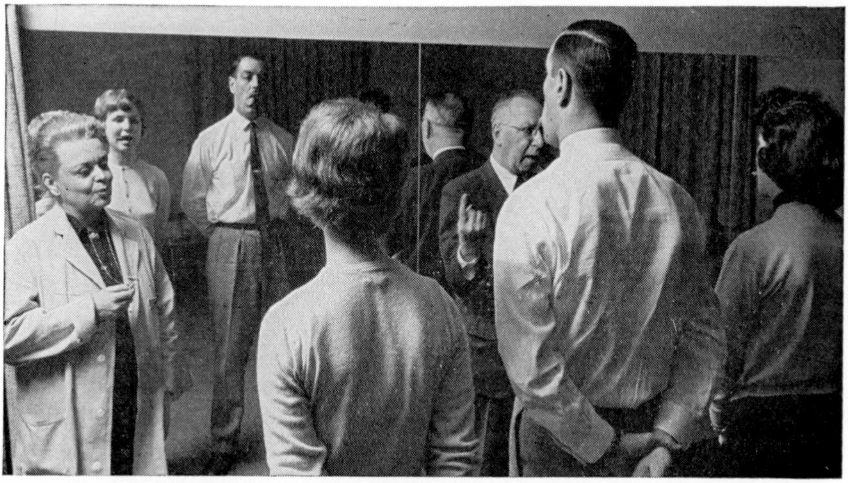

Group drill in slow-rhythm articulation exercises. *(The National Hospital for Speech Disorders)*

Does your voice sound like a bagpipe? *(Pogue's Portrait Studio)*

***Huskiness.*** Another relatively common voice problem among high school students is that of husky voice. The husky voice usually is whisper-like in quality, low in pitch, and somewhat lacking in loudness. Many factors may enter into the use of this type of voice; here are some of the more common:

First of all, attempts to talk at too low a pitch frequently are followed by a chronically husky voice. If your voice is husky, make the pitch test as suggested earlier in this chapter.

Again, if you have frequent colds and throat irritations, you may be prone to develop a husky voice. Throat inflammations (particularly laryngitis) cause your vocal folds to swell and enlarge. This means that as they bump against each other in the act of speaking, they may be further irritated and swollen. The combined effect is to make it impossible to produce a clear tone. This husky quality may become chronic. The most practical procedure to follow in these instances is for you to secure prompt medical treatment for the nasal-throat condition and to do little talking, particularly loud talking, during periods of inflammation.

Another frequent cause of this type of voice is conscious or unconscious imitation of various radio, television, screen, stage, or local celebrities who have made names for themselves and their voices. A little honest self-analysis can help you see if this is your case.

Finally, if the husky quality does not seem to be related to faulty pitch habits, to vocal inflammation, or to imitation, there is always the remote possibility of an unusual laryngeal condition. In this case, you would, of course, consult your family physician.

***Breathiness.*** This quality problem may be caused by speaking around too low a pitch range, or by speaking with insufficient loudness. Combined practice on pitch, volume, and breath control should help.

**Voice quality and personality.** Your voice gives many clues to the kind of person you are. In speech classes you must strive to help yourself toward greater confidence, security, sincerity, and adaptability, so far as speaking situations are concerned. As the training program succeeds, you will develop a speaking voice that reflects these more desirable personality traits. Whenever you deal with the ways in which people react to their environment through speech, you are dealing at least in part with the personality. To this extent then, voice improvement is personality improvement.

# *You and Your Articulation*

## The sounds of English

If you are a typical native-born speaker of English, you probably have little idea of the actual number of sounds used in speaking English. As a matter of fact, even phoneticians disagree somewhat as to the exact number of sounds used in English. If you use *A Pronouncing Dictionary of American English* as your guide, however, you will find that it requires about fifty different sounds to make the common words of English.

You will find it meaningful to divide the sounds of English into two basic types: consonants and vowel-like sounds. Although it is difficult to differentiate these two groups completely, you should think of the vowel-like group as sounds that are made with the mouth passage relatively open and with the lips at least slightly ajar. You should think of consonants, on the other hand, as made with considerable and in some instances complete constriction at some point along the mouth-throat passageway. Thus, as the air escapes from your mouth in the production of a consonant, there is usually considerable friction noise.

The fifty basic sounds of English are presented in the following Articulation Analysis Chart for English Speech Sounds.

## Articulation Analysis Chart for English Speech Sounds

**CONSONANTS**

| NO. | IPA SYMBOL | TEST WORD | TYPE OF SOUND |
|---|---|---|---|
| 1 | f | foot | *fricative* |
| 2 | v | vacuum cleaner | |
| 3 | θ | thumb | |
| 4 | ð | this | |
| 5 | s | soap | |
| 6 | z | zipper | |
| 7 | ʃ | shoe | |
| 8 | ʒ | azure | |
| 9 | p | pie | *plosive* |
| 10 | b | bat | |
| 11 | t | table | |
| 12 | d | dog | |
| 13 | k | can | |
| 14 | g | gun | |
| 15 | tʃ | chair | *affricative* |
| 16 | dʒ | jar | |
| 17 | m | matches | *nasal* |
| 18 | n | nose | |
| 19 | ŋ | ring | |
| 20 | r | records | *glide* |
| 21 | l | ladder | |
| 22 | j | yellow | |
| 23 | w | windows | |
| 24 | m̩ | hold *'em* | *syllabic* |
| 25 | n̩ | mitten | |
| 26 | l̩ | saddle | |
| 27 | h | hat | *aspirate* |
| 28 | hw | white | |

**VOWELS AND VOWEL-LIKE SOUNDS**

| NO. | IPA SYMBOL | TEST WORD | TYPE OF SOUND |
|---|---|---|---|
| 1 | i | feet | *vowel* |
| 2 | ɪ | dishes | |
| 3 | e | cake (1) | |
| 4 | ɛ | pen | |
| 5 | æ | bath (2) | |
| 6 | a | bath (2) | |
| 7 | ɑ | watch (3) | |
| 8 | ɒ | watch (3) | |
| 9 | ɔ | saw | |
| 10 | o | hose (1) | |
| 11 | ʊ | book | |
| 12 | u | boot | |
| 13 | ɝ | bird (4) | |
| 14 | ɜ | bird (5) | |
| 15 | ɚ | mother (4) | |
| 16 | ə | mother (5); alone (6); soda (6) | |
| 17 | ʌ | bug | |
| 18 | aɪ | time | *diphthong* |
| 19 | aʊ | cow | |
| 20 | ju | using | |
| 21 | ɪu | feud (7) | |
| 22 | ɔɪ | boy | |

NOTES

(1) Some phoneticians classify the vowel-like sounds of *cake* and *hose* as diphthongs.

(2) *Bath* is pronounced with different vowels in different sections of the country.

(3) *Watch* is pronounced with different vowels in different sections of the country.

(4) As pronounced in language areas that pronounce their r's.

(5) As pronounced in language areas that do not pronounce their r's.

(6) As pronounced in all dialects.

(7) *Feud* may be pronounced with either (ju) or (ɪu).

## ACTIVITIES

1. Make the "ah" sound of *father*. Note that your mouth-throat passageway is relatively open and that there is little or no air friction noise as you make the sound.
2. Now make the "sh" sound of *show*. Note that this time the mouth-throat passageway is constricted between the tongue and the roof of the mouth just back of the front incisors. Listen carefully to the friction noise created as the air escapes from the mouth.
3. Pronounce the list of words below and classify the italicized consonants according to the types of sounds provided in the Chart.

| | | | | |
|---|---|---|---|---|
| *p*int | *v*ine | *th*em | *sh*ip | *h*im |
| *f*ine | *th*ink | *n*orth | *y*elp | *w*inter |
| *z*inc | *j*aunt | *ch*eer | padd*l*e | *j*ust |
| *b*ite | *l*ap | *d*ig | ki*ng* | *m*int |
| kitte*n* | lad*l*e | *wh*en | mat*ch* | *t*ell |
| *g*ate | *c*amp | *s*ip | sei*z*ure | *r*ent |

**Classifying the sounds of English.** You will see on the Chart that the first eight consonants are called fricatives. Each of these sounds is characterized by a strong friction noise as the air escapes through a constricted aperture. In *f* and *v*, for example, the constriction is between the lower lip and upper teeth. The essential difference between *v* and *f* is that *v* is voiced. This is also true of the other three pairs of fricatives. (On the Chart, in each of the paired consonants the unvoiced member of each pair is always presented first.)

The next group of consonants is the plosives. In the plosives, the constriction is complete. Thus, in *p* and *b*, the lips close tightly and then release a puff of air. As in the fricatives, the plosives consist of voiced and unvoiced pairs.

The next group, in this case only one pair of voiced and unvoiced sounds, combines fricative and plosive elements. Say the first sound of *chair*. Note that you begin with *t* and finish with *sh*.

The next group, the nasals, consists of three sounds, all voiced. They are called nasals because in these sounds the mouth-throat passageway is at some point closed completely, and the air-sound stream escapes through the nose.

The four glides differ from the previous sounds in that the essential element in their production is that of movement; the sound is produced as the articulators move from one relatively open position to another. Put the tip of the tongue against the gum ridge above the front incisors. With the tongue in this position, think and say "uh." Now drop the tongue to the floor of the mouth. You will hear *l* as the tongue drops.

The three syllabic consonants indicated are really very much like vowels. Say each of the words or phrases and you will hear the consonant stand by itself as a syllable. Hence the name syllabic consonant.

The two aspirates are so called because the *h* in particular has a breathy or aspirate sound. In the *wh* combination, a *w* is said with an *h* before it.

In the vowels and vowel-like sounds, you will note that the diphthongs differ from the vowels in that each diphthong is actually two vowels. Thus, to produce the *i* diphthong of *time*, start with the "ah" of *father* and glide to the "ee" of *bee*. When you say "ah-ee," you will hear the *i*.

**Testing your articulation.** Babies usually begin making speech sounds during the first weeks of life, but children are frequently seven or eight years old before they are able to articulate all of the sounds of English. It will probably not surprise you to learn that boys ordinarily take longer to acquire perfect articulation than do girls. In high school and college, it is not too uncommon to find individuals who are still having trouble with some of their sounds. It may be of some interest to you, then, both as a way of learning about English speech sounds and as a check on your own articulation, to test yourself on all the words of the Articulation Chart.

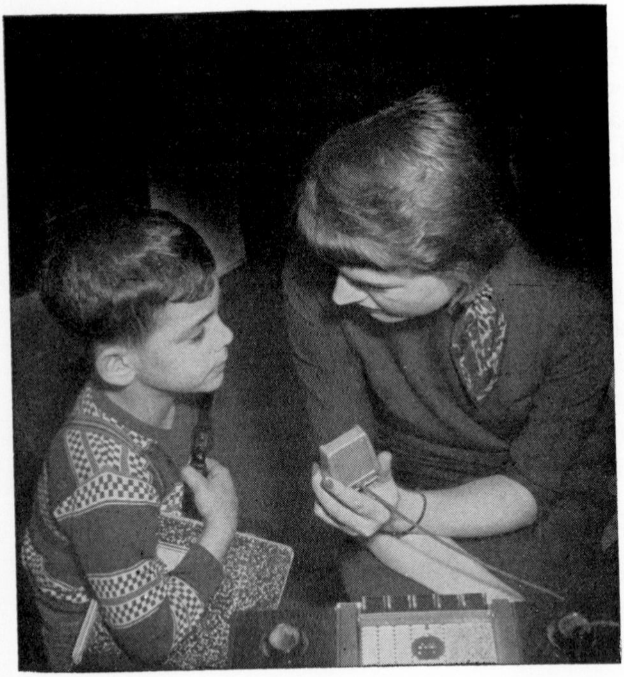

A boy begins early in life to correct articulation difficulties. *(The National Hospital for Speech Disorders)*

## ACTIVITY

Working with a classmate, say each of the fifty words on the Chart. Begin with the consonants and then try the vowel sounds. Your classmate must listen carefully to the italicized portion of each word and decide if you articulate the italicized portion correctly. Using a separate sheet of paper (do not mark in your book), your classmate should note any defective sounds. If you are able to say all of these words correctly, you have essentially normal articulation.

**Problems of articulation.** Slurring words, mumbling, and similar types of indistinct articulation interfere with exact delivery of sound and voice. As you have just learned, the lips, teeth and jaws, tongue, and hard and soft palates are important parts of the voice mechanism in reproducing clear vowels and consonants. If you are careless or lazy in using them, your audience receives only blurred reproductions of words. Your words will sound as fuzzy as pictures look when somebody in them moves.

There are various things you can do to improve articulation. In the first place, it may help to slow down as you speak. All words become blurred when spoken too rapidly. In the second place, start thinking about the sounds at the end of every word. Are you gliding over them, skipping them entirely, or dropping your voice? Distinct articulation of the final sound of a word helps to carry the entire word clearly to the back of the room. Finally, become sound-conscious with all words. How many times do you fail to say clearly speech sounds that may be difficult for you?

The articulation test revealed which sounds, if any, you cannot make in a formal test. Now seek help from your family, your teacher, or your friends in discovering the particular sounds that you do not make or that you say imperfectly when you are talking casually. Perhaps you neglect the *ing* endings, consonant endings such as *s, d,* and *t,* or say *de* instead of *th.* You may have difficulty with *l* or *w.* Usually you are unaware of your inability to articulate sounds accurately, but others notice this. As soon as you know what your special problems are, make a list of them. Study this list at every opportunity, so that you will become conscious of your problems. Read familiar material aloud in front of a mirror and notice how you shape your lips, adjust your tongue, and move your jaw in order to speak correctly. Spend at least ten minutes each day reading aloud before someone who will check you for improvement. Don't be discouraged if this comes slowly the first few weeks. You must not expect to correct overnight a speech habit that you have been doing wrong for most of your life.

***Slurring.*** According to the New York Telephone Company, slurring words is the most common speech fault which interferes with accurate reception. Some familiar examples of slurring are: Whatcha gonna do? Wyncha comover n lemme seem? Weredyu say yu goin?

With your friends who may speak and understand this type of jargon, you may get by. With strangers or people used to distinct articulation, however, you may fail completely to establish contact. Reception of such jumbled sounds is bound to be slower because listeners have to spend time deciphering your code.

***Mumbling.*** Mumbling is similar to slurring as far as accurate reception is concerned. Mumbling poses an additional problem to the listener, since most mumblers speak so low that they sound as if they are talking to themselves. Those who slur words often do so in a loud voice; whereas the mumbler makes little effort to project sound. Mumbling causes an audience to believe that the speaker is lazy, indifferent, or unsure of himself.

Akin to both slurring and mumbling is the habit of dropping letters or entire syllables. Some examples of this are: "cause" (often pronounced "cuz") for "because," "stead of" for "instead of," "for" for "before," "gainst" for "against," "count of" for "on account of."

Sharp, crisp, distinct articulation makes every word clear and insures almost perfect reception when the sound waves reach the ear. For instance, if you mean to say, "A popular writer was the guest speaker at the affair," you don't want your listeners to hear "A poplar rider was the guess speaker at the fair." Careless articulation turns *t*'s into *d*'s, *p*'s into *b*'s, *f*'s into *v*'s, *m*'s into *n*'s.

It requires care to say consonant sounds distinctly whether they occur at the beginning, in the middle, or at the end of words. Be especially careful with the final *s* or *g*. Notice in the list of paired words below how important it is to produce the word you want.

| | | |
|---|---|---|
| wind–win | batch–patch | ghosts–goes |
| latter–ladder | tent–dent | found–pound |
| lost–loss | safe–save | boast–post |
| half–have | life–live | matter–madder |
| bidder–bitter | mist–miss | lease–least |
| wild–whiled | simmer–sinner | bent–bend |
| send–sent | bet–bed | wrap–rapt |
| lest–less | writing–riding | sin–sing |
| pump–bump | gold–goal | gone–gong |
| past–pass | sender–center | bacon–baking |
| last–lass | close–clothes | taken–taking |
| winter–winner | ghost–coast | father-fodder |

These are only a few of the words you use every day which are lost in transit through faulty articulation. Hold on to word endings with all your might. Begin with the right lip consonants. Don't slump in the middle.

## ACTIVITIES

1. Bring to class a list of words containing your own troublesome speech sounds. Say them distinctly in class.
2. What examples of slurring can you give? Translate each example into clear-cut words.
3. Give additional examples of dropping letter sounds.
4. Bring to class some more examples of paired words similar to the ones above. Say them distinctly enough for all to hear. Have your classmates write them as they hear them. Compare their hearing with your speaking!

Drawing by David Langdon, © 1959 *The New Yorker* Magazine, Inc.

CHAPTER

# 6 Improving Pronunciation

Northern youngster just back from a trip to the South: "Those Southern kids certainly talk funny. They say 'you all' instead of 'youse guys.'"

—Prochnow: *Speaker's Treasury of Stories for All Occasions*

## Why Bother with Pronunciation?

Good pronunciation—saying a word with the accepted sounds, syllables, stress, and inflection—improves the acceptability of your speech. Good pronunciation will also improve your own acceptability. Your pronunciation habits reveal many things about you and the people in your home, school, and community who helped you acquire these habits.

You must, at this point, keep clearly in mind the difference between errors of articulation and errors of pronunciation. An articulatory error is the *inability to make* one (or more) of the basic sounds of English. A pronunciation error, on the other hand, so far as the term is restricted to speech sounds, represents the *inability to choose* correctly the usual sound (or sounds) in a particular word. Thus, a speaker who cannot make the initial *r* sound in any word, and who says *wabbit* for *rabbit,* is making an articulatory error. But the speaker who can make the *wh* sound of *whistle* and *whether,* but who says *wisper* for *whisper* is, by usual standards, making a pronunciation error.

### What is accepted and what is not accepted?

A definition of pronunciation in terms of accepted sounds, syllables, stressings, blendings, and inflection patterns, suggests that there are acceptable as well as unacceptable pronunciations. But what determines this acceptance or non-acceptance in pronunciation? In one word, the answer is *usage.* But one-word answers do not always tell the whole story.

It may be well to begin by clearing up certain false notions about pronunciation standards. First, you must learn that there is not always one inherently right (or wrong) pronunciation for every word. Thus, in recognizing that correctness as applied to pronunciation must be a flexible term, John S. Kenyon, an authority on American pronunciation, has said, "It is perhaps as accurate a definition as can be made to say that a pronunciation is correct when it is in actual use by a sufficient number of cultivated speakers." Note that this definition leaves open as matters for judgment (and for disagreement) two questions: (1) What is a sufficient number? and (2) Who are the cultivated speakers?

Furthermore, although there seems to be a widespread popular demand by speakers for a "standard pronunciation," one that could be recognized as better than any other, many famous authorities with respect to language fail to accept this viewpoint. Indeed, it is frequently only the naïve user of American English, whether he be from New York City or Ruston, Louisiana, who looks upon his own pronunciations as right and all others as somehow wrong. The more sophisticated user of English understands and respects many of the differences in regional pronunciations.

Despite any preferences that you may have, the simple facts of the matter are that many pronunciations of the same word may be equally or at least sufficiently acceptable. For example, *A Pronouncing Dictionary of American English* lists no less than six different but acceptable pronunciations of the girl's name, *Naomi.* Here you have an example of differences that are recognized by one dictionary. Another type of difference is that in which the dictionaries themselves disagree. Thus, in the "Guide to Pronunciation" of the 1959 edition of Webster's *New International Dictionary,* some 1100 words are listed whose pronunciations differ according to two or more of seven different English or American dictionaries. So familiar a word as *abdomen* is the first word to appear in this list.

Since there seems to be no standard, it is difficult to argue that one particular pronunciation of a word is to be preferred over another simply for esthetic reasons. In effect, this argument holds that one pronunciation uses sounds of greater natural beauty than another. For example, some speakers say that they pronounce words like *pass* and *dance* with the broad "a" so that the vowel sound is very much like that of *chop,* because the broad "a" is so much prettier than the flat "a." Yet the broad "a" sound itself is not necessarily more pleasing to the ear than is the flat "a" of *cat*. To most ears, *lavender* is a pleasing word to hear, yet it uses the same flat "a" as *cat*. Moreover, many of the very speakers who prefer the broad "a" in *dance* will probably use the flat "a" in *hat* and *cap*. Obviously, therefore, the pronunciation choice is not based on the intrinsic beauty of the sounds themselves.

What then, does make a pronunciation acceptable? The answer again—in one word—is *usage*. Usage influences both *what* you say and *how* you say it. Usage also conditions your reactions to what you hear others say. Your pronunciation patterns will be accepted if they coincide with those of the majority of educated speakers in your community. Yet it is worth stressing that in this day of mass communication media, you must sooner or later realize that there are larger speech communities beyond your own rather limited one. The purpose of this chapter is to help you to understand the pronunciation standards of these various speech communities and to provide you with the information you will need to make your own pronunciations conform to the standards of your listeners. As this chapter indicates, there is, indeed, much variation in American pronunciation. But beneath this variation lie relatively rigid patterns. When measured against the final test of social acceptance, it is surely wrong to assume that any pronunciation is a good pronunciation.

## What about dictionaries?

Dictionaries do not dictate pronunciation standards; they simply represent a carefully compiled record of the way in which educated speakers of the language are actually pronouncing certain words of the language. And, since the pronunciations of a living language, like English, are constantly changing, dictionaries must also change. No dictionary originally fixes what those standards should be. Nor can any dictionary ever be completely up to date.

Should you then throw away your dictionary so far as pronunciation is concerned? By no means! A well-edited dictionary is your most reliable and most convenient guide in cases of troublesome pronunciations. True, the best way to learn how to say a word is to hear it said by someone who uses it in an accepted way. But it is frequently impractical for you to listen until an accepted leader says a particular word at a time when you are interested in hearing it. Fortunately, your dictionary has already done this kind of listening for you. So when you suddenly want to know how to say a particular word, a good dictionary is your best guide.

Don't guess! Use the dictionary. *(Jules Alexander)*

Actually, most of you have learned to say your common words by hearing them rather than by consulting dictionaries. You seldom need to look up the pronunciations of words like *spoon, house,* or *television.* Now these words are not necessarily easier to say than works like *nock* or *mho.* But you have heard people say *house* and *television* since you were a child, probably even before you learned to read. But unless you happen to be an archery fan or an electrical engineer you may never hear *nock* or *mho.* It is for the pronunciation of the unusual or less common words that you most frequently need a dictionary.

## Variation in Pronunciation

The accepted pronunciation of a word may vary with your section of the country, the dictionary that you use, the formality of your speech, and the professional groups to which you speak and listen.

### Why pronunciations vary

Two general types of changes in pronunciation can be recognized. In one type, an existing sound in a word slowly—perhaps over several generations—changes to another sound. Such slow changes really represent a change in the very sound system of a language by which words are kept separate. Thus, as cited by Van Riper, "the number 'feef' by Chaucer became 'five' by Shakespeare's day. . . . 'Down' similarly has descended from a word pronounced as it is today in Scotland, 'doon'." In the second type, the change is very sudden; familiar sounds are used in a new way. This type of change is frequently based on analogy. For example, as cited by Kenyon, the word *friend,* formerly pronounced so as to rhyme with *weaned,* was changed so as to rhyme with *wend* because of the fact that *friendly* and *friendship* were already so pronounced.

Phoneticians (those who study speech sounds) are not certain why pronunciations vary. Until the advent of the phonograph, mankind had no way of preserving oral speech. So our records of pronunciations are really quite fragmentary. But some of the more reasonable explanations that have been advanced for changing pronunciations are: climate; faulty perception; faulty imitation; blending of languages; economy of production; deliberate imitation of the pronunciation of favored groups or individuals; and the effects of placing sounds next to each other in new words or phrases.

## Speech regions in America

If you were to travel around the United States, you would hear a number of different dialects. A dialect is a collective style of pronunciation that is peculiar to a region or to a class of speakers. It distinguishes the class or region from the styles of other regions or classes who use the same language. Phoneticians up to the present time are still not able to agree completely as to the exact number and extent of the speech regions in the United States. Indeed, phoneticians do not agree *completely* about anything! But Kenyon and Knott, in *A Pronouncing Dictionary of American English,* list the major dialects of American English as Eastern, Southern, and Northern. They describe these speech regions as follows:

> Geographically, the East includes New York City (NYC) and its environs and New England east of the Connecticut River. The South includes Virginia, North Carolina, South Carolina, Tennessee, Florida, Georgia, Alabama, Mississippi, Arkansas, Louisiana, Texas, and parts of Maryland, West Virginia, Kentucky, and Oklahoma. The North includes the rest of the U.S.

Other terms frequently substituted for *Northern* in the threefold classification cited above are General American, Western, and Mid-Western. Of these terms, Claude Wise, in *Introduction to Phonetics,* states that General American has been the most widely used.

But many phoneticians believe that any threefold classification of American dialects is inaccurate or, at best, oversimplified. Thomas, in *An Introduction to the Phonetics of American English,* for example, describes the following regional types:

1. Eastern New England
2. New York City Area
3. Middle Atlantic
4. The South
5. The North Central Area
6. Western Pennsylvania
7. The Southern Mountain Area
8. The Central Midland
9. The Northwest
10. The Southwest Coastal Area

The location of each of these is indicated in the map below.

You may wonder if all of these dialects will continue to exist. No one can now give you a completely certain answer to that question. The best present speculation of phoneticians is that the differences in pronunciation within these regions will become less pronounced in years ahead and become more like General American. This belief is held because of the unifying influence of the style of speech heard on radio, television, and in movies, which is predominantly General American, and because of the fact that General American is by far the largest speech region numerically. Nevertheless, it should be noted that the influences of other dialects, as for example Southern, are also acting to change General American. It seems probable, then, that if America ever does become a single speech region, its speech will reflect the present General American

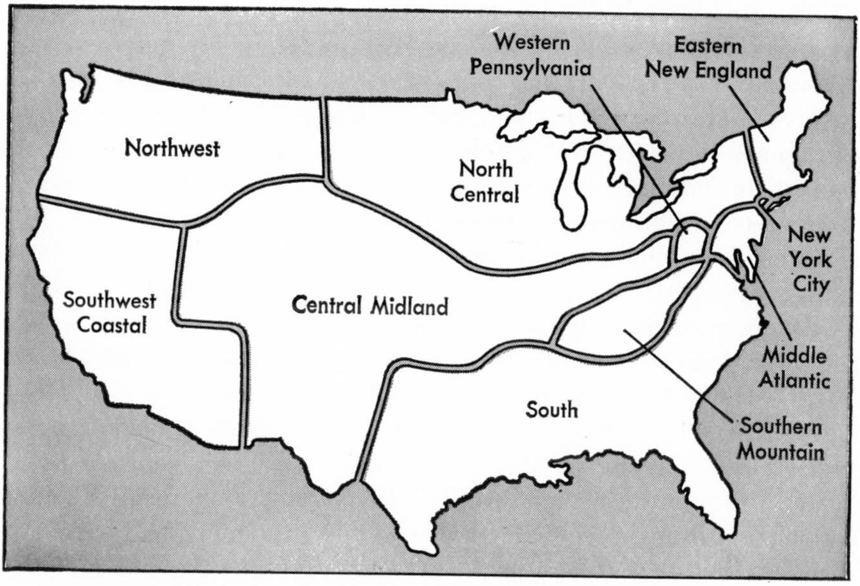


Speech Regions of the United States. *(Adapted from Thomas)*

but not be identical with it. In the meantime, you must remember that mere pluralities do not completely determine the acceptability of a dialect. A speaker from the New England or Southern speech regions may be justifiably as proud of his dialect as a speaker of General American.

## Alternate pronunciations

Even within any one dialect you will frequently hear more than one pronunciation of a particular word. Most dictionaries list the more common pronunciation variants. You should note that the first pronunciation listed is not necessarily the best, although it may be said to represent, so far as possible, the preference of the dictionary consulted. If a pronunciation appears without any specific restriction, you may usually assume that it is acceptable even if it is second or third in order. Both *The New Standard Dictionary* and *The New International* contain sections on disputed pronunciations, that is, words for which no consensus can be said to exist.

## Formal vs. informal pronunciations

Standards of pronunciation vary with the style of speaking. Most of us pronounce a few words in at least two ways: formally and colloquially. But this difference in the two pronunciations has frequently been over-estimated, and the present trend is for even formal speaking to consist more and more of colloquial pronunciations. But both styles are acceptable in the proper circumstance. In using a dictionary, be certain that the style of pronunciation represented is the one that you want. Thus, Funk and Wagnall's *New Standard Dictionary* and Merriam's *New International Dictionary* tend to represent a more formal style of speaking. On the other hand, Merriam's *A Pronouncing Dictionary of American English* represents an informal, conversational style. Oddly enough, the differences in formal vs. informal standards of pronunciation appear most frequently in relatively common words. Truly rare words such as *lycanthropy* are not used frequently enough to acquire a casual pronunciation. The word *diamond* is an interesting example, however, of an informal-formal difference in pronunciation. In Merriam's *New International*, the pronunciation is given as having three syllables: *di-a-mond;* in Merriam's *Pronouncing Dictionary,* a two-syllable pronunciation is also given: *di-mond.* This means that in formal, platform speech the three-syllable pronunciation is recommended, but that in informal, colloquial speech, the two-syllable pronunciation may be used.

## Pronunciations within the professions

Various professional groups have developed somewhat specialized pronunciations. Perhaps the best known of these is so-called stage diction. Actually, stage diction was patterned generally after cultivated, southern British speech, and is not based on any specific American dialect. Radio and television announcers have developed a characteristic speech style. But radio and television pronunciations are not extreme; in general, they are very much like General American speech.

## Is there one style?

The pronunciation of a given word, then, may vary from region to region, within a given region, with different degrees of formality, and with different professional groups. Therefore this book recommends neither a specific style of pronunciation nor a specific dictionary. But this should never be used as an excuse for careless or faulty pronunciation. Rather, with the help of your teacher, select the dictionary or dictionaries that best represent appropriate standards for you and for your class. In Table 1, you will find dictionaries that serve certain specialized pronunciation needs. Other dictionaries could be added to this list.

Today announcers on radio and television tend to use a standardized, conservative speech style which is acceptable throughout the country. (*"Douglas Edwards with the News"—CBS Network*)

# Dictionaries as Pronunciation Guides

Dictionary makers have had to devise many different ways to show readers how to pronounce a word. This is because conventional English spelling represents *different sounds* by the *same alphabetical letter* or combination of letters, and the *same sound* by *different letters* or combination of letters. This unfortunate arrangement grows out of the fact that English is written with a Roman alphabet. Thus, although the Roman alphabet was perfectly adequate for representing the five vowel sounds of classic Latin, since it contained exactly five vowel symbols (a, e, i, o, u), it is completely inadequate for representing all the vowels and diphthongs of contemporary American English. Merriam's *A Pronouncing Dictionary of American English,* for example, recognizes seventeen different vowels and five different diphthongs.

## Representation of the sounds

It follows, then, from the above statements that since English spelling is at best only semi-phonetic, the ordinary alphabet cannot be used by dictionary makers to indicate pronunciation. Either some of the 26 Roman letters must have additional markings to show that they represent more than one sound, or additional letters or symbols must be added so that all of the sounds are included in the pronunciation key. In practice, the major dictionary makers have tended to indicate pronunciation by one or more of the following sets of pronunciation symbols:

1. Diacritical marks
2. A version of the Revised Scientific Alphabet
3. Versions of the International Phonetic Alphabet
4. Respellings intended to suggest preferred pronunciations

**Diacritical marks.** Diacritical marks consist of such symbols as dots, curves, numbers, lines, and other marks placed over or under the conventional letters. As indicated in Table 1, five of the dictionaries cited use their own variations of these diacritical marks. Note that in the case of *The New Standard Dictionary* the diacritical system appears as Key Two.

For a complete explanation of the systems used in each dictionary, you will need to consult the original volume itself. The following examples, however, will give you some impression of the way diacritical marks are used in these different dictionaries. In these examples note that (1) the diacritical marks tend to preserve the original spelling and (2) the systems differ among dictionaries.

TABLE 1.

DICTIONARIES SERVING SPECIALIZED PRONUNCIATION NEEDS.

| *Name* | *Publisher* | *Pronunciation Style* | *Pronunciation Key or Keys* |
|---|---|---|---|
| A Pronouncing Dictionary of American English | G. & C. Merriam | Colloquial American with Regional Variations | International Phonetic Alphabet |
| NBC Handbook of Pronunciation | Thomas Crowell | Broadcast Standard | 1. Suggestive Respelling<br>2. International Phonetic Alphabet |
| New International Dictionary | G. & C. Merriam | Formal American | Diacritical Marks |
| New Standard Dictionary | Funk and Wagnalls | Formal American | 1. Version of Revised Scientific Alphabet<br>2. Diacritical Marks |
| The Winston Dictionary | Holt, Rinehart and Winston, Inc. | Current Educated Usage | Letters and Diacritical Marks |
| The American College Dictionary | Random House | Conservative American | Diacritical Marks |
| Thorndike-Barnhart Comprehensive Desk Dictionary | Scott, Foresman and Company | Current Educated Usage; the commonest acceptable variants | Simplified Diacritical Marks |

TABLE 2.

EXAMPLES OF DIACRITICAL MARKINGS IN FOUR AMERICAN DICTIONARIES

| *Example* | *New Standard* | *American College* | *New International* | *Thorndike-Barnhart* |
|---|---|---|---|---|
| sofa | sō′ fa | (sō′ fə) | (sō′fȧ) | (sō′ fə) |
| ask | ȧsk | (ăsk, äsk) | (ȧsk) | (ask; äsk) |
| artist | ärt′ ĭst | (är′ tĭst) | (är′ tĭst) | (är′ tist) |
| broom | bro͞om | (bro͞om, bro͝om) | (bro͞om) var. | (brüm; bru̇m) |

**The Revised Scientific Alphabet.** *The New Standard,* in addition to its diacritical key, uses its version of the Revised Scientific Alphabet. In this alphabet the essential principle is that each sound is invariably denoted by the same letter. As the following examples indicate, a few modifying symbols are used. In *The New Standard Dictionary,* its version of the Revised Scientific Alphabet appears in every case as Key One.

TABLE 3.

EXAMPLES OF THE REVISED SCIENTIFIC ALPHABET AS USED BY *The New Standard*

| *Example* | *Respelling* |
|---|---|
| sofa | sō′ fə |
| ask | ɑsk |
| artist | ārt′ ist |
| broom | brūm |

**The International Phonetic Alphabet.** In this alphabet each of the 26 letters of the Roman alphabet is used without modification to represent a single sound. The remaining sounds of English are then represented by special symbols devised by phoneticians for this purpose. Thus, in the IPA, the letter [o] is used without modification to represent the first sound in the word *obey;* the special symbol [ɔ] has been devised to represent the vowel sound in the word *cough.* Versions of the IPA are used in *A Pronouncing Dictionary of American English* and *The NBC Handbook of Pronunciation.* Table 4 exemplifies the use of the IPA in these dictionaries.

TABLE 4.

EXAMPLES OF IPA AS USED IN TWO AMERICAN DICTIONARIES

| *Example* | *Pronouncing Dictionary of American English* | *NBC Handbook* |
|---|---|---|
| sofa | ′ sofə | ′so fə |
| ask | æsk; E ask, æsk, ɑsk | æsk |
| artist | ′ɑrtɪst; ES ′ɑːtɪst | ′ɑr tɪst |
| broom | brum, brʊm | brum |

**Respellings intended to suggest preferred pronunciations.** In this technique, which is used in *The NBC Handbook of Pronunciation,* the word is respelled in the conventional letters of the alphabet in such fashion as to suggest the pronunciation. Capital letters indicate syllables that receive primary stress. Table 5 illustrates this.

TABLE 5.

RESPELLING TECHNIQUE AS USED IN NBC HANDBOOK

| *Example* | *NBC Handbook* |
|---|---|
| sofa | SOH fuh |
| ask | ask |
| artist | AHR tist |
| broom | broo:m |

## Representation of syllables and stress

Dictionary makers must also show the number of syllables and the points of syllabic stress in the pronunciations of a given word. In one-syllable words like *jet,* this is no problem. For in one-syllable words, when pronounced alone, the stress must fall on the one syllable. But in two-syllable words like *rock-et,* it is necessary to show how the word is divided in its pronunciation and how its divisions are stressed. Syllabification becomes even more important in many-syllabled words like *ir-ra-di-a-tion.*

Dictionaries usually indicate as closely as possible the relative amount of stress placed on the different syllables of a polysyllabic word. Two degrees of stress are usually all that are indicated: primary (heaviest) and secondary (slightly heavier than average). Thus, in the word *tel-e-vi-sion,* as many Americans pronounce the word, the first syllable is given primary stress (said loudest) and the third syllable is given secondary stress (said louder than either the second or fourth but usually not as loud as the first).

There are two kinds of dictionaries: (1) general and (2) pronouncing. General dictionaries give you both meaning and pronunciation. General dictionaries usually show syllables both in the vocabulary (alphabetical listing of the words in the dictionary) and in the respelling for pronunciation. In these dictionaries, the vocabulary entry usually shows the divisions that would be used in writing if you came to the end of a line in the middle of a word. The divisions in the respelling are for pronunciation. They indicate stress as well. Pronouncing dictionaries do not give the meaning of a word, and syllabification is usually not indicated in the vocabulary section. But the divisions and stresses of pronunciation are shown.

Dictionaries differ in the way they indicate syllabification and stress. The basic techniques of the dictionaries cited in this chapter are shown in Table 6.

## The key-word concept

None of the above systems of representing sounds, syllables, and stress can be effective unless the users of a dictionary agree completely as to the meaning of each symbol. The ideal way to learn any system thoroughly is to work with a competent teacher so that you may be sure of your interpretation.

But in practice you will find that the use of key words can reduce the need for help and instruction. Indeed, most dictionaries treat the key-word technique as a self-teaching device. The sound represented by each symbol is shown in some common word which is presumably pronounced the same by everybody. This identifies the key symbol with a sound that you already know; thus it helps you to use the symbol as it appears in new words.

Here is an example of how a dictionary that uses the IPA might explain its use of the following four symbols: (k), (e), (ʃ), and (ə) by means of the key word technique.

| Symbol | Key Word |
|---|---|
| (k) | *k*ic*k* |
| (e) | *a*te |
| (ʃ) | *sh*ip |
| (ə) | sof*a* |

The italicized letter in each of the key words tells you exactly what sound each symbol represents.

Here is how you use these key words. First, pronounce out loud the entire key word. Next try to make just the key part (*italicized*) of each of the key words. Soon you will be able to make each of these key sounds to your own satisfaction. After you have learned to make the sound that goes with each of the symbols in the above key words, you should be able to use these symbols in pronouncing other words. Try now to pronounce the word *acacia* which is here presented in the above key:

[əkeʃə]

You should be able to say it without difficulty.

Of course, if you mispronounce the key word, you will then carry your mispronunciations over into words in which the key sound appears. So you must work very closely with your teacher in learning the key of any dictionary.

TABLE 6.

SYLLABIFICATION AND STRESS AS INDICATED IN AMERICAN DICTIONARIES

| *Dictionary* | *Syllabification for Spelling* | *Syllabification for Pronunciation*: Division | *Syllabification for Pronunciation*: Stress |
|---|---|---|---|
| Pronouncing Dictionary of American English | Not indicated. Vocabulary entry is not divided. | The only separation is that indicated by stress marks. | In respelling, primary by use of ʹ above and before syllable; secondary stress below and before. |
| | 1. undefeated | 1. ˌʌndɪ ˈfitɪd | |
| NBC Pronunciation Handbook | Not indicated. Vocabulary entry is not divided. | In both respelling and IPA rendering, syllabification is indicated by a space between the syllables. | In respelling, primary stress by use of solid caps; secondary by italics. In IPA, primary stress by mark above and before syllable; secondary, below and before. |
| | 1. unequivocal | 1. *uhn* i KWIV uh k'l<br>2. ˌʌn ɪ ˈkwɪv ə kəl | |
| New International Dictionary | Indicated in vocabulary by the separation of each syllable either by a • or by a stress mark. | Indicated in respelling for pronunciation by separation of syllables either by use of • or by stress mark. | Primary stress by heavy **ʹ** following stressed syllable; secondary stress by light ʹ following syllable. |
| | 1. un′mis • tak**ʹ**a • ble | 1. (ŭn′ mĭs • tāk**ʹ** *ȧ* • b'l) | |
| New Standard Dictionary | Indicated in vocabulary either by separation of each syllable by a - or by a stress mark. | Indicated in respelling for pronunciation by separation of syllables either by use of - or by stress mark. | Primary stress by ′; secondary stress by ″. |
| | 1. un-re″ con-struct**ʹ** ed | 1. ʊn-rī″ kən-strʊkt′ ed<br>2. ŭn-rē″ ɛon-strŭct′ ĕd | |
| The American College Dictionary | Indicated in vocabulary by use of • between orthographic syllables. Stress not indicated. | Indicated in respelling for pronunciation by spatial separation between syllables. | Primary stress by heavy **ʹ** following syllable; secondary stress by light ′ following syllable. |
| | 1. un • fre • quent • ed | 1. (ŭn′ frĭ kwĕn**ʹ** tĭd) | |
| Thorndike-Barnhart Comprehensive Desk Dictionary | Indicated in vocabulary by use of • between orthographic syllables. Stress not indicated. | Indicated in respelling for pronunciation by separation of syllables either by use of • or by a stress mark. | Primary stress by heavy mark **ʹ** after syllable; secondary stress by light ′ following syllable. |
| | 1. un • re • li • a • ble | 1. **(un′ ri • lī′ ə • bəl)** | |

You will be interested to note that the key-word concept makes it possible for dictionary makers to handle problems of regional pronunciation with great ease. As the editors of the *Thorndike-Barnhart* dictionary say, with respect to regional variation:

"A careful use of symbols will make it unnecessary to enter some of these variants separately. For example, speakers from eastern New England and from the North Central states will not pronounce the key word *arm* with the same vowels. But if each pronounces in every word respelled with (ä) the same vowel he uses in the key word, his pronunciation will be correct and appropriate to his own usage."

## Common Types of Pronunciation Errors

As has been suggested before in this chapter, despite the many types of variation in the pronunciation of American English, certain kinds of pronunciations are almost always regarded as wrong. Pronunciations of this type may not only make an unfavorable impression on the listener, but may also confuse him as to what was actually said. Below are given some of the more common types of mispronunciations. Study these examples carefully, and then listen for examples of this type of pronunciation in your own speech and the speech of your friends.

Students working with their teacher to learn correct pronunciation of key words. *(A. M. Rubendunst)*

## Using a wrong basic sound

Some of the most glaring examples of mispronunciation occur when you simply use the wrong vowel, diphthong, or consonant in a word. Some examples of the use of a substitute basic sound are:

*get* to rhyme with *hit*
*been* to rhyme with *hen*
*just* to rhyme with *mist* or *lest*
*wish* to rhyme with *mush*

## Adding syllables

Another type of mispronunciation arises when you say the word with more syllables than are actually present in the spelling of the word. Some examples of this type of addition are:

ath*a*letics for athletics    fil*um* for film    pru*in* for prune

## Omitting syllables

The reverse of the preceding type of error is that of omitting syllables. This is probably even more common than adding syllables, perhaps because in rapid speech the omission is more difficult to detect and hence is not corrected as readily. Examples follow:

his*try* for history    fam*ly* for family    reg*lar* for regular

## Accenting wrong syllables

English is basically an alternate-stress language. That is, except for certain words such as *railroad, baseball,* and *armchair,* in which we give almost equal emphasis to both syllables, we tend to stress—that is, say with greater energy and duration—some syllables in words more than we do other syllables. So characteristic is the stress pattern of English that if the speaker puts the stress on the wrong syllable, he effectively creates a new pronunciation such as:

CIG-ar-ette for cig-ar-ETTE
HO-tel for ho-TEL
DEE-troit for De-TROIT
CEE-ment for ce-MENT

## Confusing spelling with pronunciation

Because English spelling does not accurately reflect its pronunciation, many mispronunciations result from the attempts of speakers to say what they see. As might be expected, this type of mispronunciation is likely to be more common with words that are usually only read than with words that are heard in daily conversation. Among examples of this type of mispronunciation are:

*worsestershire* for woostersheer in Worcestershire sauce
*thime* for time in thyme
*corpse* for core in corps

# Concluding Comments

You should note that this book recommends neither that you must speak in a specific dialect nor that you must use only one dictionary. For, as has been indicated, many variations in pronunciations and pronunciation standards may be perfectly legitimate. Yet, at the same time, it strongly recommends that you should seek to improve your own pronunciation habits. In particular, it recommends that you should try to bring your own pronunciation habits closer to the speech norms of your school and community.

Furthermore, you must recognize that many variations in pronunciation cannot be explained away as legitimate variations. For example, the pronunciation of the word *captain* as *"cap'n"* is not acceptable by any standard. Such pronunciations represent only carelessness on the part of the speaker. Such carelessness tends to have certain elements in common in all parts of the country and with all classes of high school students. Careful study and listening will help you to decide which of your pronunciations are acceptable and which are open to question.

## PRONUNCIATION PROBLEMS

Check your pronunciation of the simple everyday words listed below. If your pronunciation does not agree with the right rhyme word in each case, practice your problem words every day until you have mastered the correct pronunciation.

| WORD | RIGHT RHYME WORD | WRONG RHYME WORD | WORD | RIGHT RHYME WORD | WRONG RHYME WORD |
|---|---|---|---|---|---|
| again | men | tin | figure | your | err |
| any | penny | tinny | for | core | fur |
| attract | act | tack | get | set | sit |
| because | clause | buzz | guess | less | miss |
| beg | keg | vague | if | tiff | clef |
| bury | berry | hurry | instead | head | hid |
| can | ban | bin | just | must | mist or jest |
| catch | latch | ketch | leg | keg | vague |
| chair | wear | cheer | library | prairie | berry |
| corps | core | corpse | maybe | baby | webby |
| deaf | clef | beef | milk | ilk | elk |
| egg | peg | Hague | next | vexed | necks |
| err | purr | pair | our | scour | are |

## READING CHECK-UP

Read aloud the nonsense sentences below to check your pronunciation of any problem words.

Again and again the men in the air corps hurried to bury the corpses of any who had erred in the air. Instead of a hurried burial, every one in the corps was given many tributes due them. Many of the corps had lost legs, a few had been deafened, and some had broken necks. Next to the creek a burial ground for all will attract many visitors who will never forget the valiant men in the air corps.

Can you get some fresh milk at the store for us? Our milk was sour and we are without any milk. You can get milk in the store next to the library just a few blocks past the new burial ground. Maybe you should get some eggs because all of our eggs will be gone if we use them instead of the catch of fish which we figured on using for our supper. I guess you can find my purse on the chair next to the door, or maybe the deaf man just around the corner who was begging for money can pay his dues. Just be sure to hurry because we will just have time to catch the train after our supper. Just a minute before I forget, I want you to get any books reserved for me at the library. I guess that is just about all for now. If I think of any new items or if I have erred in any way, you can get them on the next trip. Run just as fast as your legs can move.

## VOCABULARY BUILD-UP

Use the italicized words in short paragraphs to show that you understand their meanings.

*cliches* in speech
*intimidating* remarks
a *vicarious* experience
a *blatant* voice
a *verbose* individual
*ambiguous* statements
*apropos* questions
*irrelevant* arguments
an *incongruous* situation
a *fatuous* character
*hackneyed* phrases
a *droll* sense of humor
a *feasible* plan
a *sinister* expression
a policy of *reciprocation*
an unforgettable *holocaust*
an example of *alliteration*
a *scintillating* personality
*bigoted* in his opinions
an *orthodox* procedure
an *auspicious* occasion
*beguiling* smile
a *paroxysm* of laughter
a *stipulated* amount
a *glib* speaker
*obsolete* words
a *proxy* vote
*chronic* ailments

CHAPTER

# 7 Believing in Yourself

"What you are speaks so loud that I cannot hear what you say."

—*Ralph Waldo Emerson*

"WHAT you are" is the particular point of interest of this chapter. In Unit I you concentrated on the essentials of being a desirable member of a group. Although you discovered your importance as an individual, top emphasis was placed on helping you to see yourself as part of a group so as to make group activities more satisfying.

In this chapter the spotlight centers on you, and you alone. You are not simply a person. You are a *personality*. Since "what you are" plays such an important part in the success of your speeches, you will want to know how to prepare yourself for public speaking. Indeed, many high school students say that the personal problem of bringing themselves to face the public speaking situation far outweighs such other problems as speech planning, speech construction, or even of finding speech ideas and materials. Too often these students state that their chief worries concern stage fright, gaining poise, and feeling at home or, as some put it, knowing what to do with their hands and feet. Unfortunately, in thus emphasizing their desire to feel more comfortable in front of a group, these students are forgetting both that (a) to experience a considerable degree of excitation in front of an audience is normal and (b) to be fully prepared is one of the best ways of minimizing this reaction.

Nevertheless, it is important that you face squarely up to the problem of overcoming stage fright. Emile Coué, the famous French champion of the power of self-suggestion, who developed his doctrine during the first quarter of the twentieth century, once remarked, "If you persuade yourself that you can do a certain thing, provided that thing is possible to do, you will do it, however difficult it may be."

*Believing in yourself* is the formula for personal success in whatever you do, including speaking. Coué continued with these words, "If, on the contrary, you imagine that you cannot do the simplest thing in the world, it is impossible for you to do it, and molehills become for you unscalable mountains."

As you read this chapter, focus your thinking only on what you *can* do. Forget what you think or imagine you *cannot* do. You can't set fire to wet spaghetti with a match, but neither can anybody else. You can't give a perfect speech the first time you try, but neither can anybody else. The secret of success lies not in expecting to do the impossible, but in picking the possible to do and expecting to do it regardless of how long it takes.

An examination of stage fright will give you a new outlook on this problem. If you let it grow in your mind, it will become an unscalable mountain instead of a molehill. It may even become so magnified that you will convince yourself that you cannot possibly get up in front of an audience. Before that happens, take a sensible look at the facts about stage fright. Understand what it is, why it is, and what you can do about it.

## What Is Stage Fright?

You may best think of stage fright as an emotional state that affects human beings when they stand in front of a class or other audience. You may also think of stage fright as a threefold combination of (1) what you actually do and say, (2) your consciousness of how you feel, and (3) certain physiological changes that go on within your body. Thus, your knees may shake and your words stop; your mind may become a complete but somehow unpleasant vacuum; a lump may appear in your throat; your hands may be either too hot or too cold; your mouth may become dry; and your heart may pound. You may experience other manifestations, too.

Such symptoms appear in stage fright, but they are not peculiar to stage fright alone. Instead, they describe any kind of natural, normal fear. That is exactly what stage fright is—*normal* fear. It is not peculiar to speaking. It is not something you and you, alone, experience.

Suppose you were alone at home at night and you imagined that you heard a prowler attempting to open a window. Or suppose you were swimming and the undercurrent suddenly carried you out into deep water. It would be a normal reaction to feel afraid in any such situation.

Since fear is natural in the presence of danger or strange situations, why be ashamed of or worry about stage fright? If you are normal, you can't help feeling excited the first few times you face an audience. Speaking in public is a new experience for most of you. Although it does not involve the possibility of bodily harm, the element of fear is the same.

Regardless of the cause of fear, your body responds in a certain way to help you meet the fear. Your nervous system is like a large switchboard which sends out danger signals to all parts of the brain and through all branches of your spinal cord. Some of the unpleasant physiological reactions you feel as a result of these danger signals are:

1. Stomach movements stop. The glandular activities of digestion are cut down and saliva stops flowing.
2. The heart beats much more rapidly. Breathing becomes deeper and faster.
3. The sweat glands become more active.
4. The adrenal glands discharge fluids into the blood, stimulating your power to react quickly.

These physical reactions represent an increased state of activity to help you meet an emergency, whether your life is in danger or you are merely facing an audience. Therefore, recognize these internal symptoms as normal and understand that they are both natural and helpful.

## Is Stage Fright Unusual Among Famous Speakers?

Many, if not all, great speakers, actors, and singers have consistently reported an amazing collection of experiences with stage fright. Indeed, although greatness may not be the direct result of stage fright, many of the greatest performers have confessed to a feeling of fear in front of an audience. A look at some of their experiences mentioned below will convince you of this fact. You can draw your own conclusions to this question: Suppose they had given in to their fears?

Chauncey Depew, one of America's greatest speakers, claimed that the best speech he ever gave was given in a taxicab on his way home after he was too frightened to face his audience.

George Washington, in his first inaugural address, was so "visibly perturbed that his hand trembled and his voice shook so that he could scarcely be understood."

Another famous speaker had such a case of stage fright that once he couldn't even remember the beginning of his speech. He finally began, "Ladies and gentlemen, I have nothing to say. It is not my fault I am here."

Madame Schumann-Heink, the famous singer, once said, "I grow so nervous before a performance, I become sick. I want to go home. But after I have been on the stage for a few moments, I am so happy that nobody can drag me off."

Boris Karloff told an interviewer, "I shudder and shake before every scene—after twenty-five years, too." And he is the man who acts so as to make everyone else shudder and shake!

## How Can Stage Fright Help You?

Many great performers, not all of them actors or singers, have commented on the fact that stage fright or nervousness has actually helped them. Bobby Jones, the great golfer, summarized this fact when he said, "I used to think that if I could suppress my feeling of nervousness when starting to play a match, I could then play a better and more thoughtful game. I have since come to think that the man who goes placidly on his way is often the easiest fellow to beat, for it is only the high-strung temperament that rises above its own ability to meet a great occasion."

The same fact has been expressed by speech authorities, one of whom has said, "Nervousness is good for you—it means that your batteries are charged. Don't try to conquer nervousness. Make use of it."

Even the experimental psychologist recognizes that stage fright can be helpful. To many psychologists, an emotion can best be regarded as an activation process. As used in this connection, activate means *to make capable of reacting.* Thus any emotion—including stage fright—may be thought of as a condition that prepares you to react more quickly. In this sense, then, stage fright can actually help you. You will find that your mind and body will be keener, more alert, and ready for action under these circumstances. You will be keyed up to a point where you will work harder to "sell" yourself and your speech because of the extra nervous energy produced by this emotion.

Winning athletes have learned how to use nervousness to beat their opponents. *(Olmedo at Wimbledon—UPI)*

But, in stage fright as in other emotions, you can lose your poise and self-control if you let your feelings get out of hand. It is for this reason that you must learn to control stage fright and turn your fears into extra speaking power.

## How Can You Control Stage Fright?

Before trying to answer this question, examine some of the answers given below by high school students when asked, "What do you worry about before you give a speech?" How many of these reasons would also be yours?

"I'm afraid the audience will make fun of me."

"I feel strange in the class. I don't know anybody."

"I'm naturally shy. I hate to stand up in front of a class."

"If the audience would be more courteous, I wouldn't worry. When they don't pay attention, I think they're bored. When they laugh or whisper, I'm afraid they're laughing or whispering about me."

"I worry about my appearance. Maybe my clothes don't look right or my hair needs combing."

"I feel awkward. I don't know what to do with my hands and feet."

"I'm afraid of making mistakes in grammar. Suppose I use the wrong tense or say 'who' instead of 'whom'?"

"My vocabulary isn't very large. If I use big words, everyone makes fun of me or thinks I'm trying to show off."

"I'm afraid of mispronouncing words. I feel self-conscious when I'm corrected on pronunciation."

"My voice isn't as strong or as pleasant as others'. Some make fun of my voice and my accent."

"I'm afraid I'll forget my speech."

All of the *negative attitudes* listed above defeat the very purpose of speech work which is to establish a friendly relationship through communication. Substitute instead, certain *positive attitudes* and actions which will help you accomplish your goal.

## Basic techniques for controlling stage fright

**Speak as often as possible.** Keep on trying. Can you remember the first time you tried to swim and dive? The first dive into cold water was anything but pleasant. Instead, it was accompanied by a gripping fear, a pounding heart, and chattering teeth. With each succeeding experience, however, the water became pleasanter and more inviting. You felt less fearful and more confident. Why? You kept trying.

The same is true with speaking. Every new experience will give you new confidence. But don't expect perfection or even too much enjoyment at first. Skill in a new activity cannot be achieved in a few attempts but comes only as a result of much practicing.

**Realize that everybody makes mistakes.** How do football players become great heroes? Certainly not by staying in the locker room and worrying! They have to take the fumbles with the touchdowns. They keep playing. The more mistakes they make in one game, the more determined they are to make up for them in the next game.

Follow the same procedure in your speech class. Expect to make mistakes and take them in your stride. You'll soon discover that all of your classmates will make them, too. Some will be far greater than yours, but no single mistake will stand out in anyone's mind.

Realize, also, that a mistake in grammar, pronunciation, or word usage is not a calamity. Regardless of the impression you make on the class in your first or second speech, you can always change that impression in the next one. Keep a list of the suggestions for improvement given to you by your teacher or classmates. Consider each one as a challenge.

**Think of the audience as friends.** Dispel the thought that

If you think of your audience as friends who are rooting for you, your self-confidence will soar. *(Alfred Wertheimer/Scope)*

people are critical. In reality, they are far more sympathetic than you think. Do you enjoy seeing a classmate fail in his speech efforts? Don't you suffer with others if they seem embarrassed and in danger of forgetting their speeches? Audiences feel the same about you. By believing that you have a sympathetic and courteous audience you will overcome timidity and be happier. You are all in a beginning speech class. That means that all of you are on an equal basis as far as making speeches is concerned. If you adopt that attitude you'll find your speech experiences will be both pleasant and profitable.

**Be prepared.** Abraham Lincoln once said, "I believe that I shall never be old enough to speak without embarrassment when I have nothing to say." Careful preparation will eliminate a major amount of nervousness. Not only should you equip yourself with plenty of material but you should also have it in good order if you wish to feel at ease. Much confusion comes through failure to arrange your ideas before you begin speaking.

A pilot makes sure that his plane has been refueled and carefully checked before taking off on a flight. As a speaker, you should take the same precautions to avoid a crash landing. Security comes through knowing, not doubting. An audience will sympathize with you if you try to do your best but not if you fail through your own lack of preparation.

**Practice aloud.** Any vocal activity requires a number of rehearsals. If you are to appear in a play, you rehearse as often as possible before the final production in order to give a smooth performance. The same is true if you are asked to sing a solo. Can you imagine how much stage fright you would experience in either event if you had not practiced? Practicing aloud many times is just as essential in speaking as it is in singing or appearing in plays.

Each time you practice a speech you become more familiar with it and you feel surer of yourself. The sound of your own voice will no longer disconcert you. Allow enough time in your preparation for *at least five* rehearsals. Each time you hear yourself give the speech, draw from your general background and seek to improve either what you say or how you say it. Rehearsing in front of a full-length mirror gives you added confidence because you can see yourself as well as hear yourself.

Perry Como's easy, relaxed manner is simply the result of careful preparation and faithful practice. *(Alfred Wertheimer/Scope)*

## Additional techniques for controlling stage fright

The ideas already mentioned are, of course, the most important techniques for increasing your confidence in yourself and thus controlling stage fright. But, in addition, you should now consider how paying attention to your appearance can also help you to gain self-confidence.

Looking your best helps you feel your best. It also helps you to speak your best. A very important step, therefore, in preparing yourself to speak in public is to take good care of the way you look. This not only gives you more confidence, but it also gives the audience more confidence in you.

An audience forms its first impression of you on the basis of what it sees. Before you speak and all the time that you are speaking, people must look at you. They are quick to notice your posture, your clothes, your grooming. If they like what they see, their first impressions are favorable. If not, they may be so distracted by your appearance as not to listen to your speech.

When you go to church, a dance, the theater, or out for dinner, you are especially careful about your appearance. Even at home when friends arrive unexpectedly, your thoughts fly to your appearance. When caught off guard, you think, "Is my face clean?" "How does my hair look?" or "Why didn't I get dressed instead of wearing these old clothes?" In the presence of friends and strangers alike, you feel uncomfortable and self-conscious if your appearance is below your standard.

Since a favorable appearance is essential in creating a favorable impression, consider now what you can do to improve your own. Many of the fears expressed earlier by the students were concerned with their appearance. The things for you to watch most carefully can best be classified under *grooming* and *posture*.

**Essentials of careful grooming.** In this text, grooming refers to the care you take of your person and of your clothes. The two essentials of good grooming are cleanliness and neatness.

***Care of your person.*** Cleanliness and neatness are within the reach of all. Of course, making yourself unduly conspicuous often destroys the effect of being clean and neat. Boys who wear their hair in extreme or faddish ways, or girls who wear unusual make-up, for instance, seldom win approval from the audience. In taking care of your appearance, you will always gain more by following well-established customs than by attempting to look "different"—and thereby encouraging criticism.

Good platform behavior makes a favorable impression. *(Monkmeyer)*

***The clothes you wear.*** Someone has said that clothes may not make the man, but they help him to make an impression. This is certainly true, but it needs thoughtful understanding. The price you pay does not determine the attractiveness of your clothes. Only you can do that. Here are some of the most important principles involved in choosing and wearing clothes:

1. Dress appropriately for every occasion.
2. Use conservative taste when speaking before an audience.
3. Choose clothes that are becoming to you.
4. Wear only clothes that are spotless and well pressed.

**Essentials of good posture.** What good will it do if you are groomed to perfection—scrubbed and shined—and dressed in attractive and becoming clothes, if you spoil it all by a slouching posture? It is the way you wear your clothes and carry yourself that puts the crowning touch on your appearance. Posture is so definitely a part of the visual impression formed when people look at you, that you should give considerable thought, attention, and correction—if necessary—to your own posture in sitting, standing, and walking.

***How to sit.*** On many occasions you may be one of several speakers seated on a platform waiting your turn. You are in full view of the audience—your every movement watched. This can be disconcerting for you, especially on the first occasion. You may feel nervous and ill at ease. You may even wish you could hide from the audience.

In a high school assembly, a group of nominees for office were required to give their campaign speeches. They had to sit in front of the audience until all of the speeches had been given. One of the speakers complained that having to sit in front of his fellow students for almost an hour was far worse than giving his speech!

If at some time you should have to wait your turn before speaking, think of it as a preview—an advance opportunity to impress your audience in your favor—and make the most of it.

## HELPFUL HINTS.

1. Professional models are taught to sit down in the following manner: With your feet together and your weight evenly distributed, stand so that the backs of your legs touch the front of your chair. Now, keeping the upper part of your body in an upright position, bend your knees and lower your hips in as straight a line as possible, thus seating yourself on the front half of the chair seat. Then, slide back on the seat as far as is comfortable. This two-step method assures a much more graceful descent than does the usual all-in-one movement.
2. In standing up, reverse the procedure. Anticipate your turn to speak. Then slide your hips forward so that you are poised on the front half of your chair with your feet again in position close to the chair, ready to take your weight when you arise. You are then prepared, when called upon, to stand straight up in a graceful manner.
3. While sitting in the chair, keep constantly in mind that you are in view of the audience at all times. Not only can they see your face and hands but your feet and legs as well. Be comfortable and relaxed. But don't sprawl, cross your legs, or tap your feet.
4. Appear alert and interested. Listen courteously to all of the other speeches.
5. Await your turn patiently.
6. Remain quiet and calm instead of fidgeting, talking to your neighbor, or playing with your notes.
7. Rehearse your speech in advance instead of studying it on the platform in full view of the audience.

***How to walk.*** As soon as you are introduced, the audience focuses full attention on you. They watch you carefully as you walk toward the center of the stage. Although you are not talking, your actions are speaking for you. Do you want your actions to say that you don't want to speak, that you are unprepared, that you are indifferent, or that you are "scared stiff?" Or do you want your walk to indicate that you are anxious to speak and that you are prepared and confident?

### HELPFUL HINTS.

1. Walk in a confident, erect, and purposeful manner. Your walk reveals your mental attitude.
2. Approach the stage or speaking position with ease, dignity, and self-control. Avoid hurrying, leaping up on the stage, or other distracting behavior.
3. Walk to the center instead of stopping at the side.
4. *Pause for a moment before starting to speak.*

***How to stand.*** This, perhaps, is the most difficult of all posture problems for the beginner. "If I could only sit down, I'm sure I could speak well," and "I feel so conspicuous standing in front of everybody," are typical remarks of high school students. Such feelings make it difficult for the beginner to stand before an audience with poise and confidence.

### HELPFUL HINTS.

1. Stand up straight and tall in a relaxed manner so as not to look stiff or "at attention." If you are short, standing as tall as possible will add to your height. Tall persons frequently slump in the mistaken belief that they will be less conspicuous. The only time your height is conspicuous, however, is when you call unfavorable attention to it. Compare the tall person who stands up to his full height with the tall one who slouches and slumps like a question mark. The height of the first is not conspicuous, but that of the second is. The first you admire; the second you want to straighten up. Make the most of your height whether you are short or tall.
2. Keep your chin up and your shoulders back. This not only makes you look better, but it helps you in speaking. You breathe easily when your chest can expand, and thus you speak in a more relaxed manner. With a sunken chest, you may cut off easy breathing and hamper smooth speaking.
3. Adjust your feet to give proper balance to your body. Ordinarily, it is easier to stand with one foot slightly ahead of the other and with a little more weight on the forward foot. By shifting weight from time to time from one foot to the other you will be comfortable, relaxed, and poised. Standing with both feet close together makes you look like a top-heavy wooden soldier. Putting your feet too far apart, on the other hand, makes you look "planted." Either position prevents free and smooth bodily movement. Other disturbing foot activities are crossing and uncrossing your feet, standing with one foot on top of the other, keeping your feet in almost constant motion, teetering back and forth, twisting or turning your feet, and slumping on one side so that your weight is constantly on one foot.
4. Keep your arms and hands relaxed and ready for use. For the first few speeches, at least, try to let them do what comes naturally. If you deliberately try to put them out of the way, you call attention to them. If you find yourself able to hold your arms comfortably at your sides, you

are better off keeping them in view. If you must hide one of your hands in your pocket or behind your back, try shifting it now and then from one position to another during your speech partly to avoid monotony, partly for your own physical comfort, and partly to reassure the audience that you still have it! As you become more used to speaking, your hands and arms will serve as more functional parts of your body, and they will automatically go into comfortable action just as they do in conversation. When talking with friends, your hands are no problem. You use them naturally to describe and give meaning to your words. That is the ultimate goal in public speaking, too.

5. Learn how to use a speaker's stand properly. This is actually a posture problem and should be mastered before you finish your speech course—in case you are confronted with a speaker's stand some day. This speaker's device is intended for your convenience if you have notes or wish to have a pitcher of water available. Some teachers do not allow beginners to use one because the frightened student gravitates to it as if it were a magnet. He grasps it to support himself, he wrestles with it throughout his speech, he hides behind it, he practically lies down on it, and consequently he breaks all rules of good posture. Correct procedure is to stand behind it or beside it. You may put one hand or both on it as long as you do not grasp it with force and put your full weight on it. Leaning over it, hanging on to it, slumping along the side of it, and using it for bodily contortions are all abuses of it.

## ACTIVITIES

1. Have you ever had a very frightening experience? Tell about it, including your fear reactions. Would it still terrify you if it happened today?
2. What are some of the physical sensations that you have when called on to speak? Do they disappear after you get into your speech? Are they as great now as they were when you first came into the class?
3. What suggestions have you found helpful in controlling your own stage fright?
4. Did you ever perform in any way in front of an audience when you were a child? Was your fear greater as a child than now? Explain the differences.
5. What is the difference between an overpowering fear and a stimulating one?
6. What can you learn from Gladstone's remark, "No man ever became great or good except through many and great mistakes?"
7. How can an audience (your own class) help you control stage fright? What are the main things an audience does that increase your nervousness?
8. Demonstrate the correct procedure of sitting down and of rising from a chair.
9. Demonstrate correct posture in walking to a speaking position. Show the class several methods of walking which should be avoided.
10. Demonstrate correct posture when standing before an audience. Show the class several posture faults to avoid.

## PRONUNCIATION PROBLEMS

| WORD | RIGHT RHYME WORD | WRONG RHYME WORD |
|---|---|---|
| pen | men | tin |
| pretty | witty | petty |
| rather | lather | other |
| rinse | prince | rents |
| sent | bent | mint |
| since | prince | sense |
| such | much | fetch |
| very | berry | furry |
| wash | josh | harsh |
| went | bent | hint |
| where | share | whirr |
| whole | mole | mull |
| will | mill | wool |
| wish | fish | bush |
| yes | less | miss |
| your | tour | err |

## READING CHECK-UP

Read aloud the nonsense sentences below to check your pronunciation of any problem words.

When you wash your hair, rub very gently, working the suds into a lather. If you wish to have a pretty sheen, rinse your hair several times until you are sure your hair is clean. It is rather hard for some people to rinse their hair after washing it.

Wherever he went he was plagued by pretty girls who wished him to send them his picture. Such popularity was too much.

Men's pens are on sale in the next room. Ten men with ten pens went where they were sent. Their ten pretty, witty wives washed and rinsed their hair.

Yes, yes, yes, yes! Don't plague me with any more such rumors about roomers.

Since the prince went to his room, since the princess went to her room, since the queen went to her room, and since the king went to his room, who will be present to wish the pretty pennant-winner very good wishes?

## VOCABULARY BUILD-UP

Use the italicized words in short paragraphs to show that you understand their meanings.

a *lucrative* position
a *maudlin* display
*histrionic* ability
*stentorian* voice
a *reticent* nature
a *sinister* expression
an enjoyable *respite*
*facetious* remarks
*hypothetical* circumstances
fond of *hyperboles*
an *amenable* person
*chronic* ailments

Commonweal
Ritual and Drama
Segregated Shakespeare

UNIT

# 3

# *Preparing and Presenting a Speech*

CHAPTER

CHAPTER

# 8 Planning With A Purpose

It usually takes more than three weeks to prepare a good impromptu speech!

—*Mark Twain*

"TAKING a trip?" "What are your plans?" "Where are you going?" "What route are you following?" "What are you taking with you?"

You hear such questions each time you start to plan a trip. The same questions arise when you start to plan a speech: You must know your destination, how to get there, what problems you may meet, and what materials you will need.

There is a Chinese proverb about the lack of planning which says, "To talk much and arrive nowhere is the same as climbing a tree to catch a fish." To this you might add, "The speech that has nowhere to go, usually goes nowhere."

In speaking, your destination is your speech *purpose*. It is your reason for giving a speech. It represents the goal that you wish to reach, the *response* that you want from an audience. You do not speak merely for the sake of saying something; you speak with a definite *purpose* in mind. Now you will learn how having a definite speech purpose—how seeking a definite listener response—affects your speech planning.

Depending upon the occasion and the wishes of the people assembled, you may have three objectives or goals for speaking: You may speak (1) to inform, (2) to entertain, or (3) to persuade. You may combine these purposes in any one speech, but you should always emphasize one objective over the others so that there is no doubt about which purpose predominates.

# General Speech Purposes Defined

## The speech to inform

The main purpose of the speech to inform is to increase knowledge by presenting information not already known to your audience. You explain unfamiliar terms, ideas, processes, objects, actions, and so forth. You report. You instruct. You make clear. Your attitude to your listeners is, "I want you to learn." You want them to respond, "We understand you."

## The speech to entertain

To entertain is to provide enjoyment. In this type you aim for pleased attention. You arouse and hold heightened interest throughout your speech. You may use personal experiences, humor, suspense, narration, or any novel treatment as long as it appeals to the interests of the group. In the speech to entertain, you are thinking, "I want you to like my speech." You want your listeners to respond, "We enjoyed every minute of it."

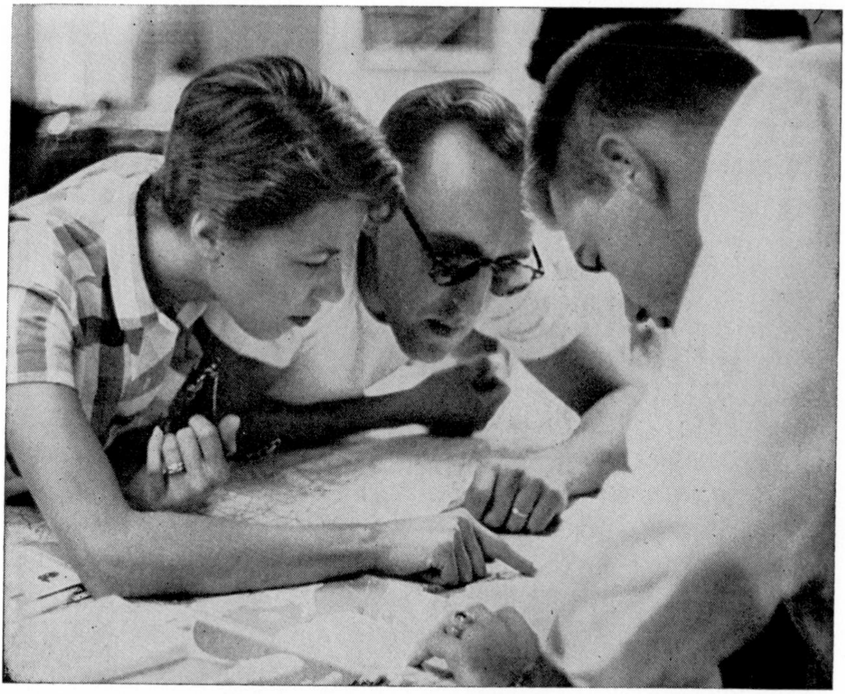

"Where am I going?" is one of the first questions to ask in planning a good trip or a good speech. *(Black Star)*

### The speech to persuade

To persuade is to influence the thought and behavior of others. Thus, in a broad sense, much of the speaking that you do is persuasive speaking, for when you speak you are seeking to affect the beliefs and behavior of another person in some way. In this book the speech to persuade has been limited to include three specific types of speeches: (1) the speech to stimulate, (2) the speech to convince, and (3) the speech to actuate.

**Speaking to stimulate.** Your goal is to inspire, impress, or to arouse your listeners. You can assume that they already agree with certain principles. Unfortunately, many persons become indifferent or lazy about their beliefs and often require "pep" talks to stir them out of their lethargy. In a speech to stimulate, you provide ideas or examples that will dispel attitudes of indifference. Your approach is primarily esthetic and inspirational rather than argumentative. You revive lagging interest and call upon your listeners to renew their old beliefs. You are saying to them, "I want you to give new vigor to your old beliefs." You want them to respond, "We will renew our efforts."

**Speaking to convince.** The response you desire in this type of speaking is to change existing beliefs. You are seeking agreement. You are attempting to overcome disagreement by presenting strong, forceful arguments in your favor. You are saying, "I want you to accept my beliefs." You want them to respond, "We agree with you."

**Speaking to actuate.** Your aim in this type of speech is to induce a specific action. In addition to using strong argument, you will relate your proposed action to the basic and compelling needs of your audience. You are saying, "I want you to act upon my beliefs." You want them to respond, "We will do it."

## Specific Speech Purpose Defined

You cannot speak effectively without limiting your general speech to one specific purpose. A specific purpose is the head of a nail that you keep consciously before you so that you can drive your point home to your audience. You cannot inform in an all-inclusive general way; you must inform in relation to a particular subject. The same limitation applies to speeches to entertain and to persuade.

The difference between general and specific purposes is one of focus. In traveling, your general destination might be New York

"Are you sure we're both going on the same vacation?"

THE SATURDAY EVENING POST



City, but your specific destination might be Rockefeller Center. As in traveling, you must narrow your speech purpose to the amount of territory that you can cover effectively in one speech. Perhaps the following tables and discussion will make this difference clearer.

TABLE 7

GENERALIZED STATEMENT OF SPEAKER'S PURPOSE AND AUDIENCE'S RESPONSE

| *Speaker's General Purpose* | *Speaker's Specific Purpose* | *Desired Audience Response* |
|---|---|---|
| 1. To inform | I want my audience to learn more about my topic. | We understand. |
| 2. To entertain | I want the pleased attention of my audience. | We enjoy this speech. |
| 3. To persuade | | |
| a. To stimulate | I want my audience to strengthen beliefs already held. | We'll renew our faith. |
| b. To convince | I want my audience to accept my views. | We agree with you. |
| c. To actuate | I want my audience to act upon my views. | We'll do it. |

Now assume that you select the topic of "High School Social Organizations." Table 8 shows one of the specific speech purposes that you could develop with this topic for each of the general speech purposes.

TABLE 8

STATEMENT OF POSSIBLE SPECIFIC SPEECH PURPOSES
(Topic: High School Social Organizations)

| *General Purpose* | *Specific Speech Purpose* |
|---|---|
| 1. To inform | You will want to *know* some of the rules that apply to all social groups in our high school. |
| 2. To entertain | You will *enjoy* hearing about some of the funny items that have appeared in the minutes of high school social organizations. |
| 3. To persuade | |
| a. To stimulate | You should *be proud* of the social organization to which you belong. |
| b. To convince | You should *believe* that high school social clubs offer many advantages. |
| c. To actuate | You should *join* a high school social organization this year. |

Notice how each specific purpose limits you to one central idea. This is a definite advantage to both you and your audience. You now know the response you want the audience to make; your audience can follow you clearly and easily.

## Phrasing your specific purpose

In phrasing your specific purpose, keep in mind these essentials:

1. Limit your purpose to only *one* thought or central idea. If you can't reduce it to one thought, you have two or more purposes and should make more than one speech.

2. State your purpose simply and briefly in one complete sentence. Long, involved statements are hard to grasp, cause confusion of meaning, and may easily reflect confusion in your own thinking.

After stating your specific purpose, you must be sure that it will have exactly the effect you want upon your audience. In speeches to inform or to entertain, audiences are inclined to accept your purposes readily and will listen willingly. In speeches to persuade, however, the potential attitudes of the audience may range from favorable, to neutral, to hostile, or, what is perhaps even worse, to indifferent. It is imperative that you anticipate as accurately as possible the reaction of your audience, for this will determine, at least in part, both what you can do and how you can do it. Then you will want to evaluate your specific purpose for (a) exactness and (b) acceptability.

## Testing your specific purpose

**Test for exactness.** This means that your statement must be precise in meaning. It must express no more and no less than your exact intention. For example, in a persuasive speech you might wish to convince a high school audience that the rules of basketball should be changed so as to require a center jump after each basket. Below are three statements of possible specific purposes:

1. You should believe that the present rules for high school basketball need to be changed.
2. You should believe that the present rules concerning the center jump in high school basketball need to be changed.
3. You should believe that the rules concerning the center jump in high school basketball should be changed so that there will be a jump ball after each basket.

Only the last statement expresses your exact meaning by specifying precisely the *kind* of change you want. The first statement commits you to changing all rules; the second one, to changing center jump rules but not specifying the kind of change.

To be successful, both speeches and experiments require exactness. *(Eastman Kodak Co.)*

**Test for acceptability.** This test is especially necessary in speeches to convince or actuate. You should examine your statement of specific purpose carefully in terms of probable audience reaction. Perhaps your greatest danger lies in advocating radical or extreme changes that your audience will reject at once.

For example, a student speaking against cheating used this phrasing of his specific purpose:

> You should believe that any student caught cheating should be expelled immediately from school.

This statement aroused strong resistance among many of his classmates and general disagreement among others. Some refused in effect to listen to the speech whereas others listened only to disagree—with the result that the speech did nothing except stir up a torrent of protest. Even though his audience disapproved of cheating, it did not approve of expulsion and, therefore, refused to accept the speaker's statement of purpose. The speaker failed because he had not thought through the probable audience reaction to his proposal, because he had not evaluated the acceptability of his proposal to his audience.

In the class discussion that followed, the students worked out statements that would permit a firm stand on the subject of cheating and at the same time be acceptable to the audience. The specific statements of purpose agreed on were:

> To convince the audience that the person who cheats must be taught to accept the full consequences of his act.
>
> Or
>
> To convince the audience that the student who cheats does himself a great injustice.
>
> Or
>
> To convince the audience that a student who cheats is forming a habit which will handicap him seriously throughout his school career.

Stating and testing your specific speech purpose are important first steps in accomplishing your general purpose. Take time with these steps. They will help you to develop your speech in a unified manner and to attempt speech goals that are possible.

## ACTIVITIES

1. Below are several informal statements of possible *specific* purposes. Decide under which of the three *general* purposes each belongs.
   You will want to know how a jury is chosen.
   You should support the abolition of the electoral college.
   You will enjoy hearing about my trip to the Grand Canyon.
   You should feel proud of being an American.

2. Below is a list of general topics. Following the example given on page 114, "Statement of Possible Specific Speech Purposes" (High School Social Organizations), select any *five* topics from the list below and phrase a specific speech purpose that could be used for *each* of the three *general* purposes.

| | |
|---|---|
| Safety | Voting |
| College education | Co-curricular activities |
| Juvenile delinquency | Grades |
| Manners | Sports |
| Laws | Patriotism |

3. Test each of your above statements, particularly in your statement of persuasive purposes, for (a) exactness and (b) acceptability.
4. Below is a list of informal statements of specific speech purposes. First decide what is wrong with each statement. Second, correct it to meet the requirements as explained in this chapter. (Ignore the fact that some begin with "I" instead of "You." That is not the error. Some are typical opening sentences which either show or fail to show a specific purpose.)
   I have chosen "horses" as my subject today.
   I want to tell you the main facts about juvenile delinquency.
   You should show good school spirit and should plan to go to college.
   I want you to believe that labor unions should be abolished.
   I believe driving lessons should be taught in high school and the legal driving age should be raised to twenty-one.
   You should believe that all teen-agers caught speeding should have their licenses revoked for three years.
   You should believe that parents are responsible for juvenile delinquency and should be punished if their children get into trouble.
   You should believe that Speech should be compulsory in every curriculum.

# Essentials for Speeches to Inform

## Know your subject thoroughly and accurately

Do not rely on what you already know or what you can pick up in casual inquiry. Using reliable sources, such as are discussed in Chapter 10, "Finding Material," make a real effort to supplement your own knowledge.

## Follow a clear-cut plan

If you are explaining how to do something, present the steps in chronological order. If you are describing a city or region, do it systematically in terms of its area or its products. If you are developing an idea, do it in terms of its features arranged in order of importance.

## Use simple, understandable language

So far as possible, avoid technical or unfamiliar language. If you *must* use technical terms to explain ideas of a scientific, mechanical, or medical nature, define them as you go along.

## Choose words with care

Try to find exactly the right word to convey your meaning. Avoid clumsy explanations. The more you fumble for the right word or say "What I really mean is . . .", the harder it is for others to understand what you *do* mean.

## Be concise

Go over your ideas carefully. Concentrate on the most important facts. Give only the details which are necessary to develop these, weeding out all others.

An experienced gardener spends a great deal of time weeding. Why? He knows that weeds can outgrow flowers and hide them from view, eventually stealing the moisture and nourishment from the soil so that the flowers wither and die. You too must pull out the "weeds" which sap the strength of your main ideas and hide them from view. Some weeds that you need to watch for are (a) trivial details, (b) unnecessary repetition, (c) long, clumsy sentences, (d) unrelated material, and (e) needless expressions such as "as I was saying," "of course," and "you see." Such weeds only lengthen but do not strengthen your speeches.

## Be complete

Although your ideas must be concisely stated, they must provide all necessary information. Even when you must stick to a precise time limit, you must be complete as well as concise. The straight telegram gives you fifteen words; the day or night letter allows you fifty words. If you go beyond the limit, you pay extra. Learning how to compress a complete, understandable message into telegraphic style will help you to prepare informative speeches.

## Use visual aids

Illustrative material is probably the most valuable of all things to pack on a speech trip. You know the old saying, "Seeing is believing," and the Chinese proverb, "A picture is worth a thousand words." Visual aids may be used in nearly all types of speeches and are certainly useful in speeches to inform. You will improve your general speaking skill by learning which aids to use for which purpose and how to present and use each. The ones most frequently employed are:

1. Chalkboards
2. Charts, maps, and diagrams
3. Pictures and photographs
4. Projection devices
5. Miscellaneous objects
6. People

**Chalkboards.** In putting drawings on the board, start with an area that is completely clean and allow ample space so that the completed drawing can be large enough for the entire audience to see your illustrations. Making the lines heavy and using chalk of different colors will also aid visibility. Try not to hide your drawings inadvertently by standing in front of them. Resist turning away from your audience and talking to the board. You can avoid these dangers by standing at one side of the board and using a pointer to explain the area that you are talking about. If it is impossible to prepare your drawings in advance, try to keep talking as you draw in order to prevent periods of silence and loss of interest.

**Charts, maps, and diagrams.** Hang these either on an easel or some other firm object to which they can be safely attached. Circle or outline with dark crayon the points of interest. As with the chalkboard, stand to one side of them and use a pointer as you speak. Watch your local weather man on television; observe how he uses maps, diagrams, and chalkboards.

**Pictures and photographs.** The best method of showing pictures and photographs is to mount them on heavy cardboard or other stiff material and to hold them up in full view. Extremely large pictures may need to be supported by an easel or other object. Use only pictures that can be seen easily. Snapshots are of little value except with extremely small audiences. Do not pass pictures around, as the audience will be looking at them instead of listening to you. Furthermore, by the time the last person has seen each picture, you will have gone on to other ideas and the pictures will have little value.

Use only enough pictures to highlight your main ideas. Too many pictures will detract attention from your speech. In going from one picture to another, avoid such repetitive phrases as, "Here is a picture of . . . " or "This is a picture of . . . . "

**Projection devices.** One of the most effective ways of showing pictures, drawings, charts, and maps is with a slide projector and screen. If it is inconvenient to have slides made, an opaque projector will do a good job on most small pictures, drawings, and printed pages. For sound and silent movies, slides, and filmstrips,

Visual aids are particularly useful in speeches to inform. *(Black Star)*

you will need special projection equipment which you can borrow from your school or a public library.

In using any of these projection devices, follow the same suggestions given above on displaying pictures. That is, use your pictures to supplement rather than to take the place of your speech; bring them into your speech at the right time; and avoid repetitive phrases of introduction.

The arrangement of your pictures and the arrangement of your ideas must fit together in a precise pattern. Prepare a sequence to your speech which will be easy for the audience to follow.

With movies you have an additional problem—the difficulty of synchronizing the pictures with your speaking. In order to overcome this problem, rehearse your speech several times to avoid getting ahead or lagging behind the pictures and having lapses of silence. In any illustrated talk, the pictures must add to the speech instead of taking the place of it.

**Miscellaneous objects.** The use of specific objects is a favorite device with professional speakers which you, too, can use profitably, especially in speeches to inform. When telling about a stamp, coin, or shell collection, for example, bring your own to show the class. This adds greatly to the audience's interest and understanding of your subject. Be sure that the objects can be displayed effectively and be tied in with your speech.

**People.** Have you noticed in your assembly programs how often speakers call on students to assist or to do what they have demonstrated? Have you noticed also the spontaneous enjoyment registered on such occasions?

Your own classmates often furnish the best ways for demonstrating ideas. Explaining methods of artificial respiration, various wrestling holds, and dances are only a few examples in which you can use other people effectively in demonstration. Selecting a cooperative partner and planning your demonstration in advance with him will usually guarantee a smooth performance.

## ◄ POINTERS THAT PAY OFF ►

The use of each type of visual aid requires a slightly different technique; however, certain principles apply to all of them. Observe these general practices:

1. Use only those that are appropriate to your speech and that will fit in with your ideas.
2. Use them to add to your speech instead of taking the place of your speech.
3. Plan the use of your illustrations for your speech at the same time that you plan your speech.
4. Bring in your illustrations at the right time. Using them too early or too late defeats your purpose.
5. Be sure that everyone can see them. Do not block your illustrations by standing between them and your audience.
6. Give the audience plenty of time to see them.
7. Avoid cluttering your speech with too many devices. (This practice is likely to confuse rather than to clarify.)
8. Be sure that illustrations are accurate.
9. Maintain eye contact with your audience instead of watching your illustrations.

## ACTIVITIES

The following speech activities require clear explanations. Prepare several of these for presentation to your class.

GIVING DIRECTIONS

1. Direct a motorist to some place near your school.
2. Select any one of the various cards that you fill out at school. Give directions for filling it out, collect the completed cards, check them for accuracy, and report the number of mistakes you found.

EXPLAINING GAMES AND CONTESTS

Select a radio or television program that is in the form of a contest. Tell the class how the contest is conducted. It will be more effective and enjoyable if you will imagine yourself as a master of ceremonies explaining the game to the audience. Use members of the class to illustrate how it is done.

HOW-TO-DO'S

1. Building a campfire
2. Baking a cake
3. Developing film
4. Changing a tire
5. Making a dress
6. Planting a garden
7. Driving a car
8. Knitting a sweater
9. Making an outline
10. Tying a knot

WHAT'S AND WHY'S

1. What causes cyclones and hurricanes?
2. Why is soil erosion dangerous?
3. What is meant by the Renaissance?
4. What is the City Manager plan of government?
5. Why does milk turn sour?
6. Why does the tide ebb and flow?

USING VISUAL AIDS

(Choose the best illustrative device to use in explaining one of the following, or choose a topic of your own.)

1. How to perform magic tricks or card tricks
2. How to bandage an arm or leg
3. Holds in wrestling
4. Making a block print or another type of art work
5. How to take pictures
6. The techniques of pitching in baseball
7. How to administer artificial respiration

CLASSROOM REPORTS

1. Prepare a report about a person whose life you have studied in one of your classes. Include interesting facts, anecdotes, and human interest stories in addition to statistical facts.
2. Report on an interesting place that is being discussed in one of your classes.
3. Give a report on a current event including necessary background and explanation.

## Essentials for Speeches to Entertain

There are many varieties of speeches which fulfill the purpose of providing entertainment. In all of them, you are aiming for pleased attention and heightened interest. You must know how to capture that interest at the beginning and how to hold it until the very last word. This requires careful planning in choosing attention-getting material and in arranging it in an attractive manner.

W. H. Yeager in *Effective Speaking for Every Occasion* states:

> "It is not the subject which determines success or failure; it is the manner in which the subject is treated . . . no subject is foolproof . . . all subjects, on the other hand, can be made entertaining by speakers who have the proper background and the ingenuity to seek out ways and means of doing it."

What are the ways and means of making a subject entertaining? Setting up such ways and means for you to look at isn't as easy as arranging things in a display window, but here are some suggestions which are sure to help you.

## Be enthusiastic

Begin with an enthusiastic approach to your subject. Keep in mind the goal of entertainment as you prepare and rehearse. Keep saying, "I want them to *like* it." Then keep liking it yourself. Like it as you prepare it; like it as you rehearse it; like it as you deliver it.

## Polish your speech

Give your speech the master touch. Go over it a dozen times if necessary to polish and perfect it. Movie directors who receive "Oscars" earn them on the basis of perfecting every detail even though it may mean shooting certain scenes over and over again at tremendous expense. Successful speakers must do the same, especially in speeches of entertainment. Remember that interest lags quickly in weak spots. There can be no ups and downs in interest;

It is not easy to sustain audience interest and attention at a high school level throughout a speech of entertainment. *(A. M. Rubendunst)*

you must arouse it instantly and keep it up until you sit down. Therefore, do not be satisfied until you are sure your speech represents your very best efforts.

## Match your delivery to the mood of the speech

If the mood is light and gay, use a light, informal style. For suspense and drama, keep your speech moving briskly toward the climax if you want to keep the audience "on the edge of their seats." Animation is an essential element in keeping up interest. Carefully inserted pauses also quicken and intensify interest.

## Be yourself

Closely associated with delivery and mood is the personality factor. Your own personality has much to do in determining audience response. If you are friendly and let the audience know that you like them, they will like you. If they like you, they will, in most cases, enjoy your speech.

Thus far you have been learning how to heighten enjoyment through giving more of yourself in the form of preparation, delivery, and attitudes. Now focus attention on the speech content itself. What can you put into the speeches to make them entertaining? Personal experiences, illustrations, jokes, anecdotes, and witty sayings are all helpful devices for enlivening your speech.

Your final task is putting together all of your material in a pattern that will make listening enjoyable.

### ACTIVITIES

1. Relate an interesting experience you have had.
2. Tell the class about an unusual newspaper or magazine article you enjoyed.
3. Select a commonplace subject such as coal, needles, wood, oil, pins, wheat, rubber, or cattle. Make your subject enjoyable by using anecdotes, jokes, or human interest material. Suggestion: Consult the *Readers' Guide* for magazine articles that have been written on your topic.
4. Entertain with a travelogue about a place you have visited or would like to visit. Use pictures. If possible, show them in one of the projection devices.
5. Tell about an imaginary trip or experience such as a trip to the moon, Mars, or any other place in outer space. Describe your flight and tell about people and their customs or any other imaginary details.
6. Organize your class into the Tall Story Club or the Liars' Club. Have a contest to determine who can tell the most entertaining and far-fetched tall story.

# Essentials for Speeches to Persuade

## Speeches to stimulate

In speeches to stimulate, you make stirring appeals, revive lagging interest, and arouse generous instincts within your listeners. You are dealing with feelings and emotions—an experience which should challenge you to exert your best speech efforts. You will enjoy preparing inspirational speeches since you will have the opportunity to talk about ideas and ideals, beliefs, philosophies, and attitudes that are close to you and your audience. Success in such speaking situations depends largely upon establishing a harmonious relationship and common ground between you and your audience. If you possess the ability to inspire confidence, this will stand you in particularly good stead.

In order to gain favorable response, you will find the following suggestions helpful:

**Be sincere.** Have a strong feeling for your subject. Be stimulated and inspired by it yourself. Impress your audience with your sincerity of purpose.

**Be concrete, vivid, and specific.** Avoid vague generalities. Aim for elegance of simplicity and dignity of expression—an unbeatable combination.

**Use an abundance of illustrations and examples.** These include human interest stories, anecdotes, case histories, proverbs, legends, fables, and quotations.

**Use slogans.** Slogans often help accomplish your purpose in a forceful, unforgettable manner. An example of such is the slogan, "Vote as you please, but please vote."

**Use emotional appeals.** Appeal to memories, emotions, sentiments, sympathies, and to spiritual beliefs. Aim at the heart, soul, and conscience.

**Organize your thoughts.** Build your speech around a definite plan. Decide what ideas you wish to emphasize; make these stand out.

**Use a restrained delivery.** Be forceful in your delivery, but refrain from accusing, belittling, threatening, or displaying maudlin emotion.

## ACTIVITIES

1. Bring to class a quotation that you like. Exchange quotations with a classmate and prepare a stimulating speech on the one you receive.

2. Below is a list of general topics often developed in speeches to stimulate. Select one from the group, work out a specific title, and prepare a speech that will give an inspiring message.

| | | | | |
|---|---|---|---|---|
| Honesty | Democracy | Courage | Loyalty | Parents |
| Thrift | Patriotism | Safety | Gratitude | Love |
| Tolerance | Forgiveness | Youth | Devotion | Animals |
| Peace | Words | Religion | Heroes | Friendship |
| Charity | Brotherhood | Ambition | Memories | Truthfulness |

3. Develop a stimulating speech by using incidents and traits connected with the life of some inspiring person.
4. Prepare a speech suitable for your school assembly during Brotherhood Week.
5. Prepare a speech for a commemorative occasion such as Memorial Day, Independence Day, Veterans' Day, or any similar anniversary.
6. Give a speech to stimulate your classmates to renew pride in your school.

## Speeches to convince

In seeking to change beliefs, you must expect to encounter possible attitudes of indifference, doubt, misunderstanding, and disagreement. Since you cannot expect immediate acceptance of your views (which may clash with long-established ones), anticipate natural resistance and learn to forestall or overcome it. Some suggestions follow.

**Break down resistance to yourself.** Be sure your attitude reflects sincerity, honesty, fairness, tact, and respect for the attitudes of others. Such personality traits can be a strong persuasive factor in winning acceptance of your views.

**Begin with a pleasing approach.** A pleasing introduction to your speech will reveal a friendly attitude even though you let the audience know that you expect many of them to disagree. This friendliness will encourage listening.

**Do not talk down.** In explaining your ideas, be careful not to point out the superiority of your own. Present them in a favorable light without referring unfavorably to opposing views. This method permits your listeners to draw their own conclusions and to feel that they have made their own decisions.

**Know your own position.** In winning belief, it is essential that you develop and present a strong argument. Investigate both sides of your position so that you can point out the strong points as opposed to the weak ones. Furnish facts, statistics, expert opinion, and examples as the basis on which to build your argument. Make your argument clear by the use of illustrative materials. Be fair. Be thorough. Be prepared.

## Speeches to actuate

You may decide that the speech to actuate is the most difficult of the persuasive speeches. Not only may you find it necessary to reinforce beliefs (stimulate) or change beliefs (convince), but you must also motivate your audience to the point of actually doing what you ask. It is for this latter reason that the speech to actuate must make use of psychological appeals.

**A successful pattern of actuation.** A plan that has been used with great success by those engaged in selling and advertising as well as by successful speakers involves these four steps:

**Step 1:** Arouse dissatisfaction with present views or conditions.
**Step 2:** Arouse a desire for something new.
**Step 3:** Prove that the new is better than the old.
**Step 4:** Point out the satisfactions to be derived from the direct course of action suggested.

This is the favorite formula of successful salesmen. You have seen it operate many times. Here is just one example of the above four steps in action: You have an old car in good condition which you have no intention of trading in for a new car since it satisfies you. Notice how you succumb to the car salesman who uses these four steps.

**Step 1:** He arouses your dissatisfaction with your present car.

A salesman drives a new car to your door. He gives you a chance to look at its gleaming exterior and its attractive interior. Mentally, you are already comparing it with your old car with its dented fenders and dull paint. "Just try it out!" he will say.

**Step 2:** He arouses your desire for the new car.

After you have driven the new car, the salesman begins pointing out all the new features which make your car even less attractive. He tells you how easy it is to own the new one—small monthly payments, large trade-in allowance on your car, liberal new-car guarantee. He continues with the argument that you can save money by trading now since your old one is at the stage where repair bills, new tires, battery, and other items will cost more than the down payment. "It's the economical thing to do," he will tell you.

**Step 3:** He proves that the new is better than the old.

He points out that the new car consumes less gasoline, has more power, has greater visibility, is more comfortable, and has all of the newest safety devices and optional equipment.

**Step 4:** He points out the satisfactions to be derived from the action suggested.

He reviews all of the sales points, making each one stand out vividly in your mind. He points out how safe, popular, and admired you will be in your new car. He makes you visualize yourself driving it. As you listen, everything seems reasonable and sensible. In fact, you wonder why you didn't think of all those advantages yourself. By the time he says, "You can't afford NOT to buy a new car," you have your pen in hand and are signing the papers.

At school elections, speakers use persuasive speeches to stimulate interest in candidates and to get out the vote. *(Black Star)*

By following this same pattern in your speeches to actuate, you can be as successful as the car salesman.

**Using the actuation plan.** How can you make this same technique work with speeches? Begin by comparing the new with the old. Give your audience ample opportunity to do their own comparing. This comparison frequently creates dissatisfaction with their present ideas or conditions. This dissatisfaction is an important step to later action. Then begin explaining the advantages of the new and planting the desire for a change as the salesman did. Notice in the above example how the salesman devoted most of his sales talk to stressing the advantages of the new car instead of trying to prove how bad the old one was. He wisely allowed the customer to decide that his old car should be replaced by a new one. This strategy made the customer feel that he had made his own decision on the basis of his own sensible reasoning and he was glad, therefore, to take the final step.

The sales talk is similar to the debate speech which is one form of the speech to actuate. Editorials often are examples of persuasive efforts. The political speech to win your vote, the attorney's plea for a verdict of "Guilty" or "Not Guilty," the Congressman's argument for the passage or defeat of a bill, the Red Cross representative's appeal for contributions, and your school publication's appeal for support are all examples of this type of speech.

Remember that just as you cannot force people to change their ideas, so you cannot force them to act. You can only make your ideas so appealing that others will become dissatisfied with theirs and will accept yours by taking whatever action you suggest to them.

A more detailed treatment of the methods to use in gaining acceptance of your views and in getting action is given in Chapter 18 on debate. Refer to that chapter for specific suggestions. Meanwhile, do your best to accomplish this speech purpose in the activities that follow.

## ACTIVITIES

1. (Time limit: one minute and a half.) Urge your audience to support any one of the following school activities:

| | | |
|---|---|---|
| Concert | Sports Event | Benefit Performance |
| Play | Debate | Recital |

2. (Time limit: two minutes.) Promote interest in one of the following or in one of your choice:

| | |
|---|---|
| Membership in a school club | School yearbook |
| Subscription to the school paper | Tryouts for school play |
| Safety campaign | Season pass to athletic events |

3. Select a subject that is controversial at school. Present your views on *one* side only. Let the class question you at the conclusion of your speech.
4. Pretend that you are a member of your student council. Urge acceptance of a specific idea that would benefit the school.
5. Pretend that you are a member of your state legislature. Advocate the passage of a bill that you sponsor.
6. Campaign for a school (or other) office. Persuade the audience to vote for you by presenting your platform and persuading the group that your platform is both necessary and desirable.
7. Select an issue involving morals, conduct, or ethics. The question to be decided is: Is it right or wrong? Convince the class that your answer is the right one.

## PRONUNCIATION PROBLEMS

Are you careless about contractions? Do you mumble or run words together? Practice distinct enunciation in the words and sentences below.

| | | | |
|---|---|---|---|
| couldn't | didn't | hasn't | doesn't |
| shouldn't | haven't | mustn't | can't |
| wouldn't | hadn't | mightn't | won't |

| SAY | DON'T SAY | SAY | DON'T SAY |
|---|---|---|---|
| could have | could of | want to | wanna |
| might have | might of | have to | hafta |
| must have | must of | ought to | oughta |
| didn't have | didn't of | will you | willya |

| SAY | DON'T SAY |
|---|---|
| What are you going to do? | Whatcha gonna do? |
| Where did you see it? | Wher'dyu see it? |
| How did you find it? | Howdja fineit? |
| Haven't you heard? | Havencha heard? |

## READING CHECK-UP

Read aloud the sentences below to check your pronunciation of any problem words.

How are you going to the party? Oughtn't you to make plans to go with us?

He could have told you the truth, but then he wouldn't have won the prize.

Didn't you know that you have to be honest if you are going to be respected?

Why haven't you told them that you want to go to the party with them, or did you?

He would have made arrangements if he had known that you had to be out of town, but you must have forgotten to tell him.

How are you going to explain to those who might have wanted to see you that you didn't want to go?

Wouldn't you like to try out first, or can't you be there early? Let me know, since I have to arrange the list before going to work.

## VOCABULARY BUILD-UP

Use the italicized words in short paragraphs to show that you understand their meanings.

a *loquacious* person
a noticeable *grimace*
a *macabre* display
a *candid* opinion
a *vapid* speech
a *strident* voice
*fortuitous* circumstances
an attack of *lethargy*

to *misconstrue* a statement
to *indict* a person
an *indigent* individual
a *quixotic* temperament
*dexterous* movements
a *supercilious* air
detecting an *innuendo*
a *novice* in acting

CHAPTER

# 9 Selecting a Subject

> For a speech is not like a Chinese firecracker, to be fired off for the noise which it makes. It is a hunter's gun, and at every discharge he should look to see his game fall.
>
> —*Henry Ward Beecher*

DO you have trouble thinking of any speech subjects? Do you know how to pick the right ones? How can you tell which subjects *are* the right ones?

Sometimes it is easy. You may be asked to speak before your church group, for example, on your experiences at the church camp. In this case, you know who your audience will be and what your topic will be.

But how do you pick the right subject when you are simply called upon to give a speech?

The right subject seldom comes to mind easily and without effort on your part. Choosing a subject requires thorough consideration of the circumstances connected with the speech situation. You must ask yourself such questions as these:

What is the occasion?
What is the purpose of my speech?
Who will be present?
What am I qualified to talk about?
How long should I speak?

Getting the answers to these questions may take a little time, but it is essential for making an intelligent speech selection; otherwise you would simply be "taking a shot in the dark"—without much chance of hitting your speech target. When you can answer these important questions, you are ready to choose speech subjects with confidence and know-how.

In selecting a card for a friend or a speech subject for an audience, you must be sure that it is right for the occasion. *(Monkmeyer)*

## Consider the Occasion

When you are invited to a party, you inquire about it. Is it formal or informal? Is it a dinner party, a picnic, a dance, or a roller skating party? Is it to honor any special person or occasion? Are you expected to take a gift? You want to know what to wear and what to do so that you won't feel out of place.

You don't want to feel out of place, either, when you give a speech. Ask questions, therefore, about the occasion in order to find out what the audience wants and expects from you.

Why are the people assembling? Is it for a football banquet, a class reunion, a Boy Scout meeting, a pep rally, or what?

Where is the meeting being held? Can I be seen and heard easily? Will I be able to use visual aids? Will there be a speaker's stand or table? Can I demonstrate?

How has the program been arranged? Am I the only speaker, or one of several? When on the program do I speak? What are the other speakers going to talk about? Will there be questions?

What will be the mood of the meeting? Informal? Solemn?

These are the kinds of questions to ask before you choose a subject. Giving a speech that is wrong for the occasion will make you feel as out of place as wearing blue jeans to a formal dance.

# Consider Your Speech Purpose

Always ask yourself, "Why am I giving this speech? What is its *purpose?*"

If you are to speak before a pep assembly in your high school, for instance, you would be expected to give a lively, stimulating speech which would arouse enthusiasm. If you were to pay tribute, however, to a departing member of your faculty, your speech should be more dignified and serious. Until you know why you are speaking and what you are to accomplish, you cannot choose a topic or the material for developing it.

You must ask yourself further questions: Does the audience want to be informed about some special topic? Does the audience want primarily to be entertained? Would a speech to inspire or stimulate be more in order? Or would the group be interested in hearing my viewpoints on a controversial subject?

The three basic speech purposes were fully discussed in Chapter 8. Your purpose—whether you intend to inform, entertain, or persuade—will affect your choice of subject. But remember that one speech often combines two or more of these purposes. For example, it is difficult to give *any* speech that does not inform. You inform as you entertain or persuade. In all speeches, however, one purpose should predominate. There should never be any doubt in your mind as to the exact answer to this question: "How do I want to leave my audience—entertained, informed, or persuaded?"

## ACTIVITY

Consider the list below and decide on which occasions you would give a speech to inform. Which may call for a speech of entertainment? Which would stimulate, convince, or actuate? Are there any situations in the list below in which more than one purpose might be suitable? If so, try to select a specific topic that could be used with each.

1. A church dedication
2. A pep rally
3. A football banquet
4. Latin club banquet
5. Mother and daughter banquet
6. Father and son banquet
7. A class reunion
8. A Boy Scout convention
9. A literary club tea
10. A church youth group rally
11. Music club meeting
12. A political rally
13. Girl Scout convention
14. Parent-Teachers meeting
15. Dramatic club banquet
16. Farewell party for a teacher
17. A fund-raising rally
18. A Veterans' Day program
19. A Thanksgiving Day program
20. A meeting to welcome new club members

# Consider Your Audience

When you pick a gift for a friend, you consider what he likes and what would be right for him. You don't pick just anything without caring whether or not your friend will like it. Nor do you select a gift simply because *you* like it, for your friend's tastes may be quite different from yours. Those are facts to remember in selecting speech subjects, too.

Find out the general group of people who will be in the audience and pick a subject that *they* will like. Ask yourself, "What will be right for them?" You are giving your speech to a particular audience—not any audience, but a certain, specific one. What they want and like is of primary importance.

## What do you need to know about your audience?

If you are speaking in front of your class or other members of your own school, most of the interests that are common to all high school students make excellent topics. With other groups, however, you have to consider many additional factors. But how can you be expected to know what strangers would like? Again, it would be wise to ask yourself a series of questions:

The more you learn about your audience, the easier it is to pick a good subject for them. *(Monkmeyer)*

How old are they? Are they adults, children, high school students, college students, or a combination of all? Is it a mixed audience, or all male or all female?

What are their main interests? Do they have anything in common? What is the predominating interest: business, farming, politics, education, flowers, music, model airplanes, art, theater, books, history, sports? Or is there a mixture of interests?

How about their educational backgrounds? Have most of them completed high school, graduated from college, or acquired specialized professional or technical backgrounds? Or do they represent a mixture of backgrounds?

What can you find out about their occupations? Are they laborers, teachers, ministers, office workers, farmers, or businessmen?

Are there any religious, racial, economic, or political barriers to consider? Can you speak freely as one of the group, or must you tread lightly to avoid hurting feelings or creating antagonisms?

If your audience is fairly uniform, your problem is greatly simplified.

### What will almost any audience like?

Suppose that your audience is mixed. How can you find a subject that will be sure to appeal to old and young, male and female, educated and uneducated, and mixed in religious, racial, and political background? Your problem is more difficult, but it is by no means impossible.

Keep in mind a few facts true of all audiences: People are naturally very curious—otherwise they would not be in the audience. They are eager to learn about a subject new to them or to learn something new about a subject with which they are already familiar. Your problem is to choose a specific subject that *you know more about than they do* and that will therefore give them something new to think about.

## Consider Yourself

Naturally, an important factor to consider is yourself—your own knowledge, interests, and limitations. It is very difficult for the average person to talk well on a subject about which he knows or cares little.

After you have carefully considered what the audience wants and likes, consider which of those interests you are best qualified to discuss. The ideal speech subject, of course, is one vitally interesting to *both* you and your audience. Such a subject may not occur to you immediately. You may have to spend valuable time sifting the various possibilities before you hit upon the best one.

When you consider yourself in the selection of a subject, use these three guides: what you know, what you like, and what you represent as an individual.

## What you know

Benjamin Franklin once said, " 'Tis hard for an empty bag to stand upright." You can paraphrase that to read, " 'Tis hard for an empty-headed speaker to speak up." One test of any good speaker is knowledge of his subject. It is easy to see, therefore, that you should consider only those subjects about which you have the best background of knowledge and experience, so that neither your head nor your speech will be empty.

A word of encouragement is in order at this point. Many of you feel that your knowledge is too limited—that you don't know anything new or interesting. You may take for granted that everyone else knows the same things you do. But take a close look at yourself. Although you may never have been on a ship that burned in mid-Atlantic nor have been cited by the President of the United States for heroism, you have probably had less spectacular experiences that have not been shared by your classmates.

As a matter of fact, each of you has a wealth of valuable and interesting information stored away that others know nothing about and would enjoy hearing. Tap that storehouse of knowledge right now. Review your hobbies, your jobs, your trips, your membership in various organizations, the things you like to read about, any unusual happenings or honors you've had, your ambitions, your thoughts about current events, your ideas and notions about right and wrong, your convictions and opinions, and all of the things that interest you most.

Unless you've read nothing, done nothing, and thought nothing, you are bound to have an abundance of knowledge which will make excellent speech material for you to utilize throughout this course.

## What you like

What you like may be as helpful in finding a subject as what you know. Sometimes you fail to consider your likes because they are so much a part of your everyday life and habits that you forget

Try to find a subject that is of lively interest to *both* you and your audience. *(Pogue's Portrait Studio)*

about them. Perhaps, too, even if they come to mind, you instinctively distrust subjects that are so *easy* to talk about.

As stated before, you cannot be sure that an audience will like a subject merely because you do. So there is danger in using this criterion as a final one in selecting a topic. For example, one student in a speech class had a consuming interest in designing aircraft. Because of his talent, he had won three awards from large aircraft companies. You would think that designing aircraft would be the ideal subject for this student by reason of his knowledge and tremendous enthusiasm. It would be, too, if used for speeches in front of audiences with comparable technical knowledge of the subject. When he told the class about the awards he had won, showed pictures of the designs he had submitted, read letters from presidents of aircraft companies, and told about the ways in which he had developed the interest of those companies, the class listened with keen attention. But when he continued to use the same subject for later speeches before his class, going into minute detail concerning the technical phases of aircraft designing, he lost his audience *and* their interest.

Beware, then, of becoming a one-subject speaker, or you may make the same mistake that the irritated housewife made when she said to her husband, "I can't understand you. Monday you liked beans. Tuesday you liked beans. Wednesday you liked beans. Here it is Thursday and suddenly you don't like beans!"

You are safe in choosing subjects you like if you are sure your audience likes them too, or if you can develop them in such a way as to help your audience to like them. This might mean presenting hitherto-unknown facts, or clearing up possible misunderstandings which might have caused lack of interest. In any event, it means presenting your subject on a common plane of understanding and with enthusiasm.

It is very easy to discover when an audience shows no interest in the subjects you like. It is also easy to observe when they begin to tire of the subject. Be on the lookout for any signal from your audience indicating pleasure or displeasure with your choice. Listeners who like what you are saying may nod their heads, smile, and sit well forward in their chairs; listeners who dislike what you are saying may frown, shake their heads in puzzlement, move restlessly, and give you and each other disapproving glances.

Never thrust an unwelcome subject on your audience; never wear them out with too much of one subject.

## What you represent

Your personal standing with your audience—your appearance, your popularity, your reputation, your age, your past successes and failures, and your achievements—should also influence your choice of subjects. What your audience thinks about you affects their reaction to you and your choice of subject.

If you have been considered popular and if you seem to have the good will and respect of your classmates, you will have the confidence of your audience in any subject you know and like. An audience wants to have confidence in a speaker and to feel that he knows what he is talking about. If you are captain of your football team, you can safely choose the subject of sports. Or if you have played in the school orchestra, you can talk about music. On the other hand, it would be presumptuous on your part—because of your inexperience—to attempt to instruct a group of older scientists on the subject of nuclear fission.

As long as you can create and hold confidence and respect on a subject, you may feel free to select it. Most of you have a fair idea of how your classmates feel toward you, what they expect from you, and what they will accept from you. Answering the questions below may help you in making up your mind.

## ACTIVITIES

Here are questions to ask yourself about yourself. If you aren't sure of the answers, ask your teacher or a friend to help you.

1. What sort of person do my classmates think I am? Do they look upon me primarily as a musician, a journalist, a scientist, an honor student, an athlete, an actor, or what?
2. Do they regard me primarily as extremely serious, as moderately so, or as a comedian?
3. With what things have I been credited as doing well?
4. Can I capitalize on any of these in serious speeches?
5. What things have I done poorly?
6. Can I capitalize on any of these in humorous speeches?
7. Can I use any of these failures as topics for serious, thoughtful speeches?
8. On what subjects will my age be an advantage?
9. On what subjects could I be considered an authority?
10. How do I rate in respect to honesty, sincerity, responsibility, integrity, morality, ambition, and leadership?

Don't hesitate to select any subject in which you have confidence in your audience's interest and your own ability to do the subject justice. *(Monkmeyer)*

## Consider Your Time

In addition to knowing about the occasion in general, you must also find out exactly how long you are to talk. If you are to speak for only a few minutes, pick a simple topic that can be handled adequately in a short time. For a three-minute classroom speech, you could not travel far on the subject of outer space! But if you are expected to speak for half an hour, you will need a topic that can be expanded beyond that of how to boil an egg.

After selecting your subject according to an assigned time limit, be careful to stay within that limit. Do not make the mistake of thinking that any audience will be impressed by length alone. If you are ever in doubt about the length of a speech, always try to end your speech just before an audience wants you to stop.

> Eddie Cantor, in his capacity of toastmaster, is credited with reducing the length of after-dinner speeches: "I ask the speakers in advance how much time they want. If a man insists he needs an hour to get his message across, I take out a slip of paper and give it to him with the remark, 'This one can be read in a minute and fifty seconds.' Immediately the speeches get shorter and shorter. On the slip of paper: Lincoln's Gettysburg Address."

### PRONUNCIATION PROBLEMS

Two similar sounds which require careful enunciation are "b" and "p." Do not weaken or confuse them.

Practice clear articulation in the following words:

| | | | | | |
|---|---|---|---|---|---|
| tip | hop | pop | bib | hub-bub | rub |
| top | shop | droop | bob | barb | stub |
| slap | crop | stoop | sob | crib | babble |
| stop | mop | prop | bat | crab | bubble |
| trip | nap | lip | boob | drab | pebble |
| rap | lap | hip | hub | rhubarb | problem |

Avoid confusing the "p" and "b" sounds in these words:

| | | |
|---|---|---|
| pan, ban | pad, bad | roped, robed |
| pin, bin | pack, back | ripped, ribbed |
| pump, bump | prim, brim | disperse, disburse |
| sop, sob | dappled, dabbled | pumper, bumper |
| cup, cub | ample, amble | pumpkin, bumpkin |
| hop, hob | crumpled, crumbled | rumple, rumble |
| maple, Mabel | simple, symbol | limper, limber |
| staple, stable | harper, harbor | slap, slab |

Avoid weakening the "p" or "b" sound in the first word of the following pairs:

| | | |
|---|---|---|
| simper, simmer | lamp, lamb | bumper, bummer |
| primper, primer | hamper, hammer | warping, warring |
| cramping, cramming | barbed, barred | blurb, blur |
| thumping, thumbing | curb, cur | stamper, stammer |
| slumping, slumming | plumper, plumber | slumber, slummer |

## READING CHECK-UP

Read aloud the nonsense sentences below to check your pronunciation of any problem words.

His pay depended primarily upon his capability to mop shops and to read simple symbols.

The superb surprise was a dappled pony for any who dabbled in super prizes in the suburbs.

Bubble-babble-pebble. Babble-bubble-pebble. Pebble-babble-bubble. Rub-a-dub. Rub-a-dub-dub. Bob caused the hub-bub. Bob caused the bub-hub-dub.

The brown bug bit a big brown bear.

The brittle bright stubble broke like chaff and crumpled and crumbled under our feet.

Bluebeard brought back black bric-a-brac while Peter, the pumpkin eater, packed a crop of poppies in a copper coffee pot.

## VOCABULARY BUILD-UP

Use the italicized words in short paragraphs to show that you understand their meanings.

*erratic* in his decisions
to proceed *warily*
to *emulate* your father
*indigenous* to this climate
to *exonerate* a man
a *lackadaisical* manner
an *inopportune* moment
to burn in *effigy*
*plebeian* tastes
a national *panacea*
speaking in *platitudes*
a *tacit* understanding
guilty of *redundancy*

in a *decorous* manner
in *sepulchral* tones
*subtle* hints
*deprecating* remarks
to *usurp* power
to *surmise* an answer
an *affable* person
a *circuitous* route
an *erudite* person
*punitive* methods
an expression of *chagrin*
a person of *discretion*
the *epitome* of success

CHAPTER

# 10 Finding Material

Though a man be born to genius, a natural orator and a natural reasoner, these endowments give him but the outlines of himself. The filling up demands incessant, painstaking, steady work.

*—Henry Ward Beecher*

DETERMINING your purpose and selecting the right subject are only the first steps in presenting a good speech. Your next step is finding the right material to use for your chosen subject. Where can you find that right material?

There are several basic sources available for all types of speeches: (a) yourself, (b) personal contacts, (c) radio, television, and motion pictures, and (d) printed materials.

## Yourself

Your easiest source is right at hand: yourself. In the previous chapter you were advised to pick subjects that are right for you. Such subjects are the ones you can talk about from experience and knowledge. Exploit your own storehouse of material first; nothing is stronger than a speech based upon firsthand information.

Talking about your own experiences, however, requires the exercise of good judgment. You must be careful that you know more than your audience already knows. One student, for instance, spent half an hour telling his classmates about a trip to the slums when all but two had taken the same trip. Instead of wasting time by using his experience as an entire speech, this student should have used it as a *springboard* into such subjects as his own reactions to what he saw and his ideas for improving certain conditions.

# Personal Contacts

The knowledge and experiences of the people around you will often provide stimulating material that you can use. Such material may be obtained through conversations, interviews, and tours.

## Conversations

This is the easiest way to gain information. After you select a speech subject, start talking about it with your friends, parents, teachers, and any others who might give you ideas. These conversations will help you screen your own thoughts more carefully. After you have talked with others, you may change your own ideas and take another point of view. You must be sure, however, that your sources of information are accurate and unbiased, for sometimes in conversation people speak very loosely and do not expect to be quoted or taken too literally. As long as you talk to people whose accuracy can be trusted, you will find such conversation a valuable source of information. Many famous speakers have acknowledged that they owe much of their success to the practice of talking freely with others about their speech interests.

## Interviews

The second personal contact source is the interview. Sometimes it is best to talk to people who are directly connected with the subject of your speech and are in a position to furnish the necessary facts, even if these people are not friends of yours. In every community there are many competent persons who can give you accurate information about almost any local situation. If your topic is about the increase in bus fares, what could be better than a planned interview with an official of the bus company? Judges and police officials will cooperate in providing facts concerning crime problems in your community. City officials can give you information about your local government. Local merchants will be glad to discuss opportunities open to high school students in the merchandising field. Try to think of other interview sources available to you.

In interviewing, as in conversation, you need to exercise good judgment. First, pick an individual who is well informed and fair in his opinions. Next, plan your interview so that you neither waste the time of busy people nor fail to ask important questions. Work out your key questions carefully in advance, then *quote accurately, give correct impressions, and respect any confidences.*

An interview with a qualified specialist in some field is one of the most accurate sources of speech material. *(Monkmeyer)*

If the person best qualified to furnish information is too far away for a personal interview, a letter usually brings a helpful response. This is true especially with state or national congressmen who are happy to send printed material or personal replies upon request. But do not construe this suggestion as an invitation to let other people do your thinking and fact-finding for you. Don't write busy officials for information that you can find yourself, with a little hard work, in your local library.

## Tours

A tour is another good way to get firsthand information. Classes often visit industrial plants, art galleries, courtrooms, museums, city halls, municipal plants, and many other local points of interest. Such tours are especially helpful and stimulating because you have the advantage of making your own observations and evaluations to add to the information given you by the guide.

### ACTIVITIES

1. Make a list of ten places of interest to visit in your community. Visit one of these places and give a speech based on your trip.
2. Interview someone well informed on a subject of general interest. Give a speech to the class based upon the information gathered.
3. Write to your state or national congressman for information on a current topic. Use this material for a speech.

## Radio, Television, and Motion Pictures

These three media constitute increasingly effective ways of presenting information vividly and simultaneously to large numbers of individuals. Many of the programs offered are ideal as sources of basic background for speeches. Moreover, the techniques of presenting information used in these media may help you to visualize for yourself how best to communicate.

The list of educational and informative programs on radio and television is increasing all the time. The motion picture industry is also concentrating on producing outstanding documentaries. Such films reveal facts about people, places, animals, and phenomena of nature that are realistic and authentic. It is difficult, however, to record this material accurately for it is fleeting in nature and you must rely on impressions, general statements, or very short quotations. If the message or occasion is important enough, the words can be recorded on a tape recorder so that you can reproduce them as needed.

## Printed Materials

This category, perhaps the largest and most useful of all so far as source material is concerned, includes newspapers, magazines, bulletins, pamphlets, and books of all types. You may have many of these at home, but, if not, your library can supply almost anything you need. Frequent use of the library gives you a fine background of interesting speech material and enriches your own general background at the same time. In the final analysis, the acquisition of abundant knowledge depends upon reading. If you have not already discovered the pleasure and satisfaction to be derived from reading, perhaps your speech course will help you do so.

### Newspapers

One of your best sources of up-to-the-minute information is the daily newspaper. Since newspapers are published to appeal to all groups of people, their contents cover a wide range of interests. A single copy of a paper may suggest ideas for several speeches.

Have you ever noticed how many human interest stories appear in the daily papers? In order to kindle an enthusiastic response for a cause, newspapers frequently print case histories and show pictures of people who need charitable assistance or who have made unusual contributions. The same methods may be successfully used in preparing your speech material. An audience listens much more attentively to a speech about Mary Smith of 1250 Center Street, Your Town, Your State, than it does to a speech which starts out, "There are some people living in our country who . . . . " In the first speech, Mary Smith is a living person with a name and an address. You can identify yourself with her and rejoice with her or suffer with her. But how can you react much one way or the other with "some people" who are nameless and of no interest to you? You will find much live material of this sort throughout your local papers.

Cultivate the habit of reading the paper every day to give you ideas to spark your conversation and to provide a source of speech material. Clip articles, stories, statistics, and anything which is of particular interest to you. Editorials discuss controversial subjects and are excellent to stimulate worthwhile thinking. Make a habit also of reading two or three columnists.

Although no single newspaper can be named as a "best source" on the national scene, *The New York Times* and *The Christian Science Monitor* have frequently been cited for complete reporting. If you have more than one paper published in your community, compare carefully any opposing points of view. Beware of papers that seem biased or that tend toward being unduly sensational.

Daily reading of a newspaper develops a wide range of interests and keeps you well informed. *(Don Carlos Dunaway)*

## ACTIVITIES

1. Find an item in your newspaper which you consider especially interesting. Read it in class. In what way or ways could it be used in a speech or as an idea for a speech?
2. Bring to class an editorial on a controversial subject. Read part or all of it in class. State your opinions on the views expressed.
3. Which columnists write regularly for your favorite newspaper? Which ones would you recommend as speech sources? Why?

## Magazines

Magazine articles are usually written in a more readable style than general reference books or the encyclopedias. They also offer more up-to-date material on certain topics. You will find it to your advantage, therefore, to explore the magazines in your search for material. If your interests are chiefly along specific lines such as science, current news, aviation, photography, automobiles, mechanics, outdoor life, or fashions, there are specialized magazines in those fields. Or if you desire magazines covering a miscellaneous range of topics, a wide assortment of such publications is available. Your school or public library subscribes to a variety of magazines which enable you to take advantage of this method of enriching your mind and your speeches.

**Readers' Guide to Periodical Literature.** When you want to look for magazine material on a specific topic, consult the *Readers' Guide to Periodical Literature.* It is a very useful timesaver that eliminates many long hours of searching. It offers a current index, as well as a cumulative index of one year or several years, of all articles appearing in the most popular magazines. *Readers' Guide,* which has been in continuous publication since 1902, is indexed both by subject and author. Each reference includes the name of the author, title of the article, name of the magazine, volume number, the pages, and the date of issue.

The *Readers' Guide to Periodical Literature* appears both in a current form and a cumulative form. The current form, which is sent to libraries semi-monthly, contains the most recent references to the subjects listed. The cumulative forms assemble this information for longer periods of time. At present, the *Readers' Guide* is indexing approximately 110 major United States magazines.

A portion of a sample page from *Readers' Guide* is reproduced on page 148. This sample page is to be used for illustrative purposes and will give you all necessary information to understand and use this extremely important publication.

## PERIODICAL LITERATURE

**TACKLE boxes.** See Fishing—Implements and appliances

**TAGGARD** girls; story. See Head, A.

**TAGLIABUE, John Anthony**
Poetry of Juan Ramón Jiménez. Poetry 92: 184-8 Je '58

**TAIWAN**
*See also*
Missions—Taiwan

**TALENT**
*See also*
Genius

**TAPE, Magnetic.** See Magnetic tape

**TAPE recordings**
Working by ear; Audibly instructed manufacturing operations. Bsns W p70+ Je 14 '58

**TARIFF**

**United States**

American trade policy and the lessons of the 1930's. T. C. Mann. U S Dept State Bul 38: 895-9 Je 2 '58

**TARIFF on works of art**
What isn't art? il Time 71:62 Je 9 '58

**TAXATION**

**California**

Trouble in California. T. Le Berthon. Commonweal 68:299-301 Je 20 '58

**United States**

Barrier to tax cuts, will it hold? Newsweek 51:30+ Je 9 '58
Congress considers tax cut proposals. Cong Digest 37:164-92 Je '58
Should the power to tax include the right to censor advertising? Sat Eve Post 230:10 Je 21 '58
Texans on taxes. New Repub 138:7-8 Je 9 '58
Treasury's Anderson. Time 71:14 Je 9 '58
*See also*
Small business—Taxation
Transportation tax

**TAXATION, Exemption from**
Trouble in California. T. Le Berthon. Commonweal 68:299-301 Je 20 '58

**TAYLOR, Edmond**
Democratic parties and the general. Reporter 18:8-11 Je 26 '58
Tragic memories, reminders of hope. Reporter 18:11-13 Je 12 '58

**TAYLOR, Everett G.**
Two-band v.h.f. converter. Radio & Tv N 60:60-1+ Jl '58

**TAYLOR, Gleason**
Polar hunt, old style. por Outdoor Life 122: 42-5+ Jl '58

**TAYLOR, Peter**
Pair of bright-blue eyes; story. New Yorker 34:33-8 Je 7 '58

**TEACHERS**

**Salaries**

Teachers' salaries in Wisconsin. Sch & Soc 86:271 Je 7 '58

**Supply and demand**

Teacher shortage: cause and cure. I. Adler. Nation 186:407-9 My 10 '58; Reply with rejoinder. R. Ashman. 186:inside cover Je 14 '58
We've been asked about army men as schoolteachers. U S News 44:73 Je 20 '58

**TEACHING**
Pursuit of excellence; substance of Rockefeller report. Ladies Home J 75:46-7+ Jl '58
Stuart P. Sherman, master teacher. M. Van Doren. Sch & Soc 86:265-6 Je 7 '58

**TEACHI...** learni... labora...y. See ...ago

Parabolic antenna for u.h.f. tv. H. Harris and P Mattern. il Radio & Tv N 60:50+ Jl '58

**TELEVISION apparatus**
*See also*
Television receiving apparatus

**TELEVISION broadcasting**

**Documentary programs**

Matter of moments; Nightmare at ground zero. G. Seldes. Sat R 41:29 Je 14 '58

**Laws and regulations**

*See* Television laws and regulations

**Music**

Old jump in jazz; Art Ford's jazz party. il Newsweek 51:78 Je 9 '58

**Performers**

*See also* names of television performers, e.g. J. Gleason

**Programs**

Air (cont) J. Lardner. New Yorker 34:123-6 F 22; 85-8 Mr 8; 67-71 Mr 29; 74+ Ap 26; 123-6 My 17; 78-82 Je 7; 96+ Je 14 '58
Good tv shows that don't get seen. R. P. Goldman. Reporter 18:31 Je 12 '58
I call on Lawrence Welk. P. Martin. il Sat Eve Post 230:36-7+ Je 21 '58
Off the deep end; Sea hunt. Time 71:61 Je 9 '58

**Quiz programs**

Lady with the answers. Newsweek 51:78 Je 9 '58

**Subscription programs**

Pay-as-you-see tv; financial failure. New Repub 138:7 Je 9 '58

**Westerns**

Tv western craze; how long will it last? G. Eells. il Look 22:66+ Je 24 '58

**TELEVISION in education**
Communications and education. J. L. Burns. Vital Speeches 24:496-9 Je 1 '58
*See also*
Television stations, Educational

**TELEVISION laws and regulations**
Eaton vs. whom? G. Seldes. Sat R 41:29 Je 21 '58
Monopoly on the air. New Repub 138:8 Je 16 '58

**TELEVISION receiving apparatus**
Tv circuit improvements. W. H. Buchsbaum. il Radio & Tv N 60:39-41+ Jl '58

**Repairing**

Tv's big troublemaker circuit. A. Margolis. il Pop Sci 173:173-6 Jl '58
Test bench puzzler. A. Margolis. Radio & Tv N 60:115 Jl '58

**TELEVISION stations**
Air; WNTA-TV. J. Lardner. New Yorker 34:96+ Je 14 '58

**TELEVISION stations, Educational**
Community chest; San Francisco's KQED-TV. Time 71:76+ Je 16 '58

**TELEVISION tape recording.** See Magnetic recorders and recording—Visual recordings

**TELLER, Edward**
Fact and fable of fallout. L. Pauling. Nation 186:539-41 Je 14 '58

**TEMPEST, Rosalie Claire**
Meet the beardless irises. Flower Grower 45:27-9 Jl '58

**TENNESSEE**

**Description and travel**

New Holiday motor tour: Asheville-TVA-Chatta...ga. M. Morriss. il Holiday 24:13-

First of all, notice that the headings are listed in alphabetical order and are of two kinds: (1) by *subject* and (2) by *author.* These appear in capital letters.

Example of subject listing: TELEVISION in education
Example of author listing: TELLER, Edward

Second, notice that many general subjects are broken down into specific units. For example, TELEVISION broadcasting is subdivided into:

Documentary programs
Laws and regulations
Music
Performers
Programs
Quiz programs
Subscription programs
Westerns

If articles have been written on any of these specific phases, they are listed under the proper headings.

Third, you will observe that the *Readers' Guide* gives you directions to find additional articles on your subject by using the "See also" method.

For example, under TAXATION—United States, note:

*See also*
Small Business—Taxation
Transportation Tax

This useful bit of information helps you to find other articles which may be pertinent to your subject.

Fourth, note how each reference includes this information:

Title of article
Name of author
Name of magazine
Volume number
Number of pages
Date of issue

Certain bits of information are abbreviated in order to condense all of the information necessary in a small amount of space.

To interpret a listing, take as an example one of the difficult ones given under TELEVISION—Programs:

Air (cont) J. Lardner. New Yorker 34:123-6
F 22; 85-8 Mr 8; 67-71 Mr 29; 74 + Ap 26; 123-6 My 17; 78-82 Je 7; 96 + Je 14 '58

Since the listing appears under *Programs*, you know that the title, *Air,* refers to Air Programs; (*cont*) means "continued." In other words, you will find a series of articles on *Air Programs. J. Lardner* is the name of the *author. New Yorker* is the name of the *magazine* containing the series.

The *numbers* following tell a definite story:

"34" is the *volume* number of *The New Yorker.* Since libraries keep magazines over a long period of time, each magazine has its yearly issues bound together, usually in one volume, with a definite number attached to each volume.

The numbers which follow "34" give (1) the page numbers and (2) the date of publication of the articles which appeared in *The New Yorker* on the subject of *Air Programs.*

If you wish to read the entire series, you would ask first for Volume 34 of *The New Yorker.* After obtaining the volume, you would look for the articles in this order:

F 22 (February 22) pages 123-126
Mr 8 (March 8) pages 85-88
Mr 29 (March 29) pages 67-71
Ap 26 (April 26) page 74 + (the plus sign means that the article will be continued on later pages)
My 17 (May 17) pages 123-126
Je 7 (June 7) pages 78-82
Je 14 (June 14 '58) page 96 + (same as 74 + in the Ap 26 issue)

The '58 indicates that all of the above articles were published in 1958.

If you are in doubt regarding any abbreviations, you will find a "Key to Abbreviations" given at the front of every issue of the *Readers' Guide.* You will find also the list of periodicals used in each issue with the symbols used to designate each.

## ACTIVITIES

1. Consult the "Key to Abbreviations" in any one of the issues of *Readers' Guide* in your library to find the meaning of the following abbreviations:

| | | | |
|---|---|---|---|
| + | cond | jr | rev |
| abp | D | jt auth | S |
| abr | ed | Mr | sr |
| Ag | F | My | sup |
| Ap | Hon | N | tr |
| arch | il | no | v |
| arr | bp | Ja | ns |
| assn | inc | Je | O |
| bibliog | introd | Jl | por |

2. Select any five of the listings given on the sample page and interpret all of the information given for each.
3. In the front of each *Readers' Guide* is a list of periodicals from which articles have been selected. Select ten which are *abbreviated.* Give both the abbreviated forms and the full names of the magazines.
4. Select a general topic such as aviation, electronics, or education and find five listings of articles on your topics. Copy all the information for each listing and interpret it for the class.
5. Bring to class one of the magazine articles from your list in No. 4 and tell the class about its contents.
6. Consult your librarian to find out how often the *Readers' Guide* is published. Tell which of the following are correct:
   a. Weekly
   b. Semi-monthly
   c. Monthly
   d. Quarterly
   e. Semi-annually
   f. Annually
   g. Biennially
   h. Every three years
   i. Every five years
   j. Every ten years

**Specific publications on public affairs.** When you wish to speak on controversial topics concerning public affairs, you need the most authentic and up-to-date material available. Newspapers and magazines are good general sources if you can be sure that the material is accurate and not slanted or biased. For particularly reliable data, you can depend on such publications as the following, some of which are not, strictly speaking, periodicals:

*Annals of the American Academy of Political and Social Science*
*Congressional Digest*
*Congressional Record*
*Political Science Quarterly*
*Reference Shelf*
*University Debaters' Annual*
*Vital Speeches of the Day*

How many of the above are available in your library? Select one to explain to the class.

## Bulletins and pamphlets

Some of the most vital current information first appears in these forms. These are now published by many different sources and at different intervals of time. The *Bulletin of Public Affairs Information Service* lists many of the most important bulletins. Your librarian will be able to assist you to find those regularly available in your library. Compile a list of those received and keep it for future use in collecting material.

Your librarian usually knows the answer or knows where to find the answer for you. *(Monkmeyer)*

## General library books

**The card catalog.** Libraries follow a uniform system of grouping books together in order to make it easy for you to find them. Usually, fiction is grouped alphabetically according to the author's last name. For example, all novels written by James Fenimore Cooper will be found together in the section set aside for novelists whose last names begin with *C*. Non-fiction is arranged according to a subject matter basis. If the Dewey Decimal Classification is used, each subject matter group will be assigned to a specific number from **000** to **999.** (Refer to page 157 for the Dewey Decimal Classification.)

Whether you are looking for fiction or non-fiction, the card catalog is your basic key to help you find quickly what you want. Each book in your library is cross-indexed in the card catalog under title, author's last name, and one or more subjects. This gives

The card catalog holds many answers, too; and while looking for one, you may discover a new interest. *(Monkmeyer)*

you three or more chances of finding any book. If you know only the author's name but are not sure of the title, look under the author's name for all books written by him until you recognize the title. If you know the title but not the author's name, look for the title. Titles are grouped alphabetically according to the first word (except for *the, a,* or *an*). If you can't remember either the title or author's name, look under the general subject such as speech, music, or architecture.

The catalog card itself will offer you useful information. In addition to the title and author, this card usually lists date of publication, number of pages, subject headings, classification number, and publisher. Frequently, you will be able to decide from the card whether or not to consult the book.

Using the card catalog is both easy and helpful. As stated above, you have three or more listings to help you find material on any subject. Assume that you wish to find a book containing information about Roman customs. You do not know the name or author of any book. You may find such books by looking for subject cards as illustrated below. Notice that there are *two* possible subjects under which such books might be found: *Rome–Civilization,* and *Rome–Social life and customs.*

913.37 ROME– CIVILIZATION
Jo

Johnston, Mary, 1883-
Roman life. Prepared under the supervision of Eleanore H. Cooper. Scott 1957
478p illus maps

Replaces Private life of the Romans, by H. W. Johnston
A full account of the life of the ancient Romans even to books, libraries, roads and burial customs
Bibliography: p376-89. Glossary: p392-99

1 Rome—Civilization 2 Rome—Social life and customs I Title 913.37

58W170 (W) The H. W. Wilson Company

913.37 ROME– SOCIAL LIFE AND CUSTOMS
Jo

Johnston, Mary, 1883-
Roman life. Prepared under the supervision of Eleanore H. Cooper. Scott 1957
478p illus maps

Replaces Private life of the Romans, by H. W. Johnston
A full account of the life of the ancient Romans even to books, libraries, roads and burial customs
Bibliography: p376-89. Glossary: p392-99

1 Rome—Civilization 2 Rome—Social life and customs I Title 913.37

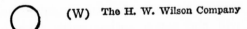

58W170 (W) The H. W. Wilson Company

Each of these subject cards gives you the name of the author and the title of one book. If your library has more than one book on Roman life, you will find all of them listed by *subject* card and arranged alphabetically according to the *last* name of the author. After reading the description about each book, decide which one (or ones) you want to see. Then write down on a slip of paper the classification number (call number) which is at the top left hand corner—in this case, [913.37 Jo]—and look for it yourself in the section containing books with "913.37" listings. If the first one you find is unsuitable, continue your search until you find the book that you can use.

Every book in your library has a *title* card in the card catalog. If you know the title of the book you want, you will find the card for it arranged alphabetically according to the first word of the title. You will find the listing of the title card below in the "Ro" portion of the index.

Roman life

Johnston, Mary, 1883-

Roman life. Prepared under the supervision of Eleanore H. Cooper. Scott 1957

478p illus maps

Replaces Private life of the Romans, by H. W. Johnston

A full account of the life of the ancient Romans even to books, libraries, roads and burial customs

Bibliography: p376-89. Glossary: p392-99

1 Rome—Civilization 2 Rome—Social life and customs I Title 913.37

58W170 (W) The H. W. Wilson Company

Sometimes you know the name of an author who has written books on your chosen subject but you don't know any specific titles of his books. In that case you look for the name of the author arranged alphabetically according to last name. If an author has written seven books, for example, and all are in your library, you will find seven author cards (one for each book) listed in the library's card catalog file. This group of seven cards will itself be arranged alphabetically according to the first word of the *title*. Below is a sample *author* card.

> **Johnston, Mary,** 1883-
> Roman life. Prepared under the supervision of Eleanore H. Cooper. Scott 1957
> 478p illus maps
>
> Replaces Private life of the Romans, by H. W. Johnston
> A full account of the life of the ancient Romans even to books, libraries, roads and burial customs
> Bibliography: p376-89. Glossary: p392-99
>
> 1 Rome—Civilization 2 Rome—Social life and customs I Title 913.37
>
> 58W170 (W) The H. W. Wilson Company

All complete cards (subject, title, and author) contain at least the following information:

1. Classification number at top left
2. Name of author
3. Name of title
4. Publisher and date of publication
5. Number of pages
6. A short description of contents
7. Bibliography (list of references), if one is given
8. Listing of subject cards

## ACTIVITIES

1. Below is a list of *subject* cards. Pick any five from the group and find one *author* card and one *title* card for each in the card catalog of your library.

| | | |
|---|---|---|
| Electronics | Presidents | Vocational education |
| First aid | Missiles | Kentucky |
| Astronomy | Postage stamps | Etiquette |
| Flags | Rockets | Immigration |

2. Select one of your author cards. How many title cards did you find listed for the author?
3. Copy from any one of your cards the complete information given on it.

**Classification Schemes.** Several systems, or "schemes" (to use the library term) have been devised to provide a uniform technique of cataloging books by the type of code number described in the previous section. Of these, the two most familiar are the Dewey Decimal and the Library of Congress.

***The Dewey Decimal Classification.*** This scheme, followed in most libraries, classifies books under ten general divisions ranging from **000** to **999.** Each of these in turn is further subdivided into units of tens: **000** to **010; 011** to **020; 021** to **030;** and so on until **099.** The same applies to the **100** through **900** groups. The general divisions follow:

**000-099**—General works (encyclopedias, periodicals, etc.)
**100-199**—Philosophy (psychology, ethics, etc.)
**200-299**—Religion (Holy Bible, churches, mythology, etc.)
**300-399**—Social Sciences (civics, commerce, economics, education, law, stamps, etc.)
**400-499**—Language (dictionaries, grammars, etc.)
**500-599**—Sciences (mathematics, astronomy, electricity, physics, chemistry, botany, etc.)
**600-699**—Useful Arts (agriculture, home economics, communications, business, aeronautics, manufactures, etc.)
**700-799**—Fine Arts (music, painting, photography, sports, etc.)
**800-899**—Literature (except fiction)
**900-999**—History (geography, travel, biography, etc.)

***The Library of Congress Classification.*** This scheme was developed by the Library of Congress in Washington, D. C. Although it is an extremely workable plan, most high school and city libraries continue to use the Dewey Decimal Classification.

The Library of Congress system of classifying books is similar to that of the Dewey Decimal in that it provides for an arbitrary coded designation of any possible book. Unlike the Dewey classification, the Library of Congress plan uses alphabetical designations to indicate the basic subject matter groupings. Thus the letter **P** indicates the broad heading of Language and Literature. **PN,** followed by a number within the range **4001** to **4321** covers a category of public speaking texts.

## ACTIVITIES

1. What would be the general subject of books whose call numbers are:

| | | | |
|---|---|---|---|
| **652.8** | **507.2** | **394.2** | **150.13** |
| **351.7** | **610.73** | **909.82** | **780.973** |
| **428.3** | **220.8** | **028.5** | **821.08** |

2. For any five *general* Dewey categories, find three book titles, authors' names, and call numbers for each.

"I found it!" is said first and most often by the person who is familiar with the special reference books of the library. *(Monkmeyer)*

## Special reference books

**Books for quick reference.** Often you wish to locate quickly such facts as the population of a state, the chief product of a country, or the date of a significant event. If the information you seek is not too recent, consult any of these sources:

*Collier's Encyclopedia*
*Columbia Encyclopedia*
*Compton's Pictured Encyclopedia*
*Britannica Junior*
*Encyclopedia Americana*
*Encyclopaedia Britannica*
*Lincoln Library of Essential Information*
*World Book Encyclopedia*

If the fact you seek is extremely recent, the following sources should be helpful:

*Americana Annual*
*American Yearbook*
*Britannica Book of the Year*
*Collier's Year Book*

*Information Please Almanac*
*Statesman's Yearbook*
*Statistical Abstract of the United States*
*World Almanac and Book of Facts*

These publications are revised each year. For this reason, they are excellent for current facts.

## ACTIVITIES

1. Using any of the above reference books available in your library, find answers to the following questions and give the source for each:
   a. How old was Abraham Lincoln when he was assassinated?
   b. What was the population of Washington, D. C. in 1960?
   c. How many representatives does your state have in the House of Representatives? What are their names?
   d. Who are the present senators from your state?
   e. What are some of the achievements of Richard E. Byrd? When and where was he born?
   f. Who won the World Series three years ago? Ten years ago?
   g. Who was the heavyweight champion last year?
   h. Who won the Davis Cup last year?
2. Exchange with a classmate a list of reference questions. Did you find all the answers? Give the sources for those you found.

**Books about people.** Although you will find facts about people in many of the sources already cited, the following entries give more detailed and systematic knowledge, particularly if the people are of national or international importance. For living persons, try these sources:

*Current Biography*
*Who's Who in America*
*Who's Who (British)*
*Who's Who in Education*
*International Yearbook and Statesmen's Who's Who*

For persons no longer living or of long-established fame, consult the following:

Biographical dictionaries, such as:
*Chamber's Biographical Dictionary*
*Dictionary of American Biography*
*Lippincott's Biographical Dictionary*
*Webster's Biographical Dictionary*
Any of the standard encyclopedias already mentioned
The basic card catalog (Look under last name of person.)

*Biography Index* (This is a comprehensive, cumulative index of all types of biographical material published in books and magazines, including obituaries from *The New York Times*.)

### ACTIVITIES

1. Try to find the answers to the following questions, giving the source of each answer:
   a. Who is the present Pope? When was he elected? Who was his predecessor?
   b. With what sport is George Mikan identified?
   c. Who was Marconi?
   d. What are some memorable facts about Babe Didrikson Zaharias?
   e. Who were the vice-presidents during the four presidential terms of Franklin D. Roosevelt?
   f. Who was "Bloody Mary" and why was she known by that title?
   g. What are the dates of birth, nationalities, and occupations of: Alfred Hitchcock, J. Edgar Hoover, Orson Welles, Maude Adams, and Werner von Braun?
   h. For what achievements was George Washington Carver famous?
2. Exchange some questions with your classmates about persons of interest. Be prepared to give answers to the questions you received and the sources of your answers.

# How Do You Use Sources?

You are now familiar with the important sources of information. A few general tips on gathering and recording information will help you use the sources to advantage.

## Give yourself plenty of time

Don't start your preparation the night before a speech is due. If rushed for time, you will find it impossible to do an accurate job of gathering information. A good working principle is always to get much more information than you think necessary. This will give you an opportunity to gain a broad perspective of your subject and supply a solid background of facts. You can then sort out the best material so that only the most worthwhile content remains.

Remember that a two-minute speech may sometimes require as much research as a half-hour lecture. A typical example of this is Lincoln's Gettysburg Address. Although it is one of the shortest speeches on record, Lincoln spent many hours in its preparation. According to reliable reports, he was still working on it on his way to deliver it. The result of his ceaseless thinking and his repeated revisions was an address which is generally regarded as one of the most enduring speeches ever made. Americans will cherish it forever, but the main speaker's lengthy speech was soon forgotten.

Lincoln's recipe for his speeches was "Give it another lick." You can't give your speeches that valuable additional "lick" unless you allow plenty of time for preparation.

## Record information systematically

Since you cannot possibly remember all that you hear or read, adopt a suitable plan for recording information. First of all, know what to record. Usually, you write down three general types of information:

Direct quotations from your sources
Condensed or indirect quotations
Impressions or summaries based directly on your sources

Each of the above types is important. You must learn to record only that which fits your material and purpose. Use the direct quotation from your source if it is a brief and compact statement pertinent to your speech. Too many long direct quotations, however, will rob your speech of originality and will make it seem "warmed over." Use the indirect quotation if the statement is too long or detailed to be included verbatim in your speech. Use your own statement if you desire to record only a general summary of what has been said.

The more facts you gather from various sources, the better background you will have when you make your final selections. *(Ewing Galloway)*

Most professional speakers work out note-taking tricks of their own. The system suggested below usually works successfully:

1. Use a separate card for each item of information. The size of the card is not vital, but most speakers use either a 3″ x 5″ or a 4″ x 6″ card of fairly heavy stock. The 4″ x 6″, although small enough to handle easily, is large enough to hold a reasonable amount of information.

2. Put quotation marks around any material directly quoted. If you drop part of a quotation, indicate the omission by a series of dots, thus: . . . . If you add words of your own to a quotation, enclose your own comments in brackets like this: [ ].

3. In addition to quotations, summaries, or impressions, this information about the source should always be included:

For books: Author, title, publisher, city, date, page or pages, and general heading under which information is to be grouped.

For magazines: Author (if any), title of article, name of magazine, volume, date, page or pages, and general heading.

For personal contact sources: It is not possible to specify exactly what should be noted here. Try to include as many as possible of these items: Author, occasion, date, immediate source (movie, radio, TV interview, letter, or other).

The following sample cards will help you prepare your own:

**SAMPLE BOOK CARD**

Eisenhower, personality

Bradley, Omar N. A Soldier's Story, Henry Holt and Co., New York, 1951, p. 343

The COBRA attack [code name for the breakout after the Normandy landing] had been timed for a July 21 jump-off.... But so eager was Eisenhower to get across for a fill-in on our plans that he slipped through the soup in a B-25 [twin engine bomber]. His was the only plane we saw in the air that day.

"You're going to break your neck running around in a B-25 on a day like this," I told him.

Ike snuffed out his cigarette, a tired smile creased his face. "That's one of the privileges that goes with my job," he said, "no one over here can ground me."

As you study these cards notice how well they are organized for quick source reference if necessary and how clearly the selected quotations paint a picture.

SAMPLE MAGAZINE CARD

Labor laws, enforcement

Hazlitt, Henry. "The First Step," Newsweek, LIII, No. 23, June 8, 1959, p. 90

"The hospital strike in New York City threw a brilliant light on what is basically wrong with our labor law and law enforcement.... The situation exposed the absurdity of the slogan, dear to muddleheaded 'liberals,' that one must never pass a picket line."

SAMPLE PERSONAL CONTACT CARD

Needs in Education

Laurence, Frank. Student.
Interview, October 28, 1960

"The gifted student is handicapped under our present system of high school instruction. More emphasis should be placed upon basic subjects such as English, science, mathematics, history, and languages. Gifted students should be placed in classes offering accelerated courses to enable students to work at full capacity. Slow students hold back the entire class. Students who have no interest in academic subjects should be placed in trade schools where they can learn practical subjects which they can use in earning a living."

## ACTIVITY

Select a topic for a speech to inform. Bring to class the following:

1 book card with direct quotations
1 book card with an indirect quotation
1 magazine card with a summary statement based on your reading
1 personal contact card with a direct quotation
1 personal contact card with a summary statement.

## PRONUNCIATION PROBLEMS

In words containing "th," the "th" may be voiced (sounded) or voiceless. Some dictionaries designate voiced "th" with a line drawn through the two letters; voiceless "th" then has no markings. A few words—like "with"—may be pronounced either way. A fairly frequent articulation error occurs when the "th" is given the sound of "d"—for example, "dis," "dese," "dem," and "dose."

| VOICED | | VOICELESS | | COMBINATIONS TO WATCH |
|---|---|---|---|---|
| then | father | thin | thrust | like this |
| that | them | thank | thirst | like that |
| there | gather | thread | thud | asked them |
| breathe | weather | throne | width | like them |
| bathe | whether | three | length | like these |
| bequeath | thy | ether | depth | like those |
| together | thee | heath | thought | saw them |
| this | clothe | theater | thigh | besides these |
| though | clothes | bath | earth | kicked them |
| than | further | beneath | thick | picked these |
| lather | other | thumb | sixth | tried them |
| scythe | rhythm | thunder | hundredth | filled that |
| mother | theirs | thump | fourth | watched them |
| either | heathen | thrush | theorem | told them |

## READING CHECK-UP

Read aloud the nonsense sentences below to check your pronunciation of any problem words.

Theodore Thick Thumb thrust three-thousand thistles through the thick of his thumb. If Theodore Thick Thumb thrust three-thousand thistles through the thick of his thumb, how many unthrust thumbs did Theodore Thick Thumb think he had?

Try twisting ten thin twigs thrice. (repeat fast and often)
Six thick thistles stick. (repeat fast and often)

My father's face was wreathed in smiles when I showed him the wreath that I found like those which were withered in the hot weather. When I saw the wreaths like this, I asked them to pick one that was thick.

The soothsayer was loath to answer whether my father would bequeath his throne to my loathesome brother or my sixth thin sister with the three thick curls.

I picked these clothes for this trip. When I saw them I told the salesgirl that I wanted a sheath like this, a hat like that, shoes like these, and hose like those. I tried them on, bought them, charged them, and carried them home.

## VOCABULARY BUILD-UP

Use the italicized words in short paragraphs to show that you understand their meanings.

*initial* claims
based on the *assumption*
an *ironical* situation
speaking *simultaneously*
*tentative* plans
an *aggressive* labor policy
*compensated* for the loss
a *poignant* story
methods of *retaliation*
*inherent* weaknesses
an *enervating* task
a *perfunctory* remark
an *obsequious* manner
an *unsullied* reputation
a *resplendent* array
an *inveterate* gambler
*adroit* movements
conversational *gambits*
*vociferous* in his speech
*unilateral* agreements
*averse* to change
*peremptory* dismissal
a *predilection* for the truth
a justifiable *tenet*
dwelling on *minutiae*
strange *denizens*
*simulated* moon environment
a *raucous* voice
a *garrulous* person
*grass roots* nature
a *vehement* response
*stereotyped* in his views
*sporadic* attempts
*incorrigible* behavior
*rudimentary* principles
of *nondescript* appearance
an *apathetic* outlook
an *audacious* child
an *ignominious* mistake
a person of *affluence*
the political *incumbent*
unflinching *fortitude*
*epicurean* tastes
*expunged* from his mind
in danger of *atrophy*
*astronomical* proportions
*sanguine* disposition
an *onerous* task
a question of *semantics*
a *conciliatory* attitude
a strange *anomaly*
*gamut* of emotions

CHAPTER

# 11 Outlining the Body of Your Speech

I would never think of speaking without, in some way, ordering my thoughts.

—*Harry Emerson Fosdick*

## Why Outline?

After you have decided on your purpose and subject and have started to collect your speech materials, you should begin at once to think about the arrangement of your speech. Many students, in their haste to prepare their speeches, frequently skip this step entirely and begin at once to compose their speeches. To do this is like trying to bake a cake without a recipe or build a boat without a set of plans. In speech making, too, you need more than good intentions and good materials; you need an organized plan of procedure.

### What is outlining?

A speech outline is a convenient and orderly arrangement of your ideas. Its purpose is to place together all your related thoughts in a meaningful pattern. Its function is to make listening easy, simple to follow, and therefore pleasing for your audience. Your audience becomes annoyed when you throw ideas together in a haphazard manner. When you have mastered the process of arranging your thoughts purposefully, you will have accomplished one of the chief requirements of successful speaking.

In a narrow sense, you may think of outlining as simply a useful tool of arrangement. Arrangement is the process of putting your speech materials together so that they express your specific purpose with both (a) the greatest exactness and (b) the greatest communicative efficiency. Arrangement is the art of aiming your entire speech effort at your goal.

In a broader sense, however, you should think of outlining and arrangement *together* as a *single* process which controls the final structural pattern of your speech. Outlining, as used in this book, includes more than a highly formalized *writing down* of your ideas according to certain rules of indentation and of symbolization; it includes also the *thinking through* of your ideas.

Finally, you should note that this chapter is concerned with the *preparation* outline, that is, the outline that guides you as you work out the best arrangement of your materials. The *delivery* outline is a summary of your finished speech. It is made after you have completely finished the arrangement of your speech and helps you deliver your talk.

## What are the advantages of outlining?

**Orderliness.** The basic advantage of outlining is that it will help you bring orderliness to your speeches. Outlining will assist you to see the relationships among the three major divisions of your speech—the introduction, the body, and the conclusion—and to develop each of these divisions in an orderly fashion.

To realize the importance of orderly arrangement, think of the many examples you find all around you. Offices, libraries, stores, and all kinds of businesses are models of methodical planning.

Offices use an orderly filing system to conserve time and to carry on business efficiently. Without such systematic arrangement, large offices would soon become a hopeless hodgepodge of inquiries, bills, orders, and other mail.

In a library, all books of reference are found in one section; novels are arranged alphabetically by authors in another; books in various subject fields are arranged in numerical order, and so on. Because of the detailed and precise system of arrangement used, you or the librarian can find in a few moments any book or magazine contained in the library.

Another example of orderliness is found in a supermarket where items are shelved according to their general classification. You find cereals in one section, soups in another, canned vegetables in another, and so on. Such groupings make marketing speedy and easy for you.

In just this same way you will group related thoughts together in different sections of your outline, so that your speech will move smoothly and logically from one group to the next.

**Other advantages.** Outlining will also help you to look at your speech as a whole and to judge its total effectiveness. It will help you to see weaknesses in your materials or speech purpose and will guide you in adding necessary additional materials or in modifying your purpose. Finally, the process of outlining will help you in the delivery of your speech, partly as an aid to your memory or as an aid to preparing a delivery outline.

The time you spend in preliminary planning of your speeches will be time well spent. Your speeches will then be compact and easy to follow. Furthermore, after you realize how simple it is to work out an effective grouping of your thoughts, you will discover that you actually *save* time by organizing your thoughts before you start composing a speech.

## When do you outline?

Planning comes *first* in making a model airplane, "customizing" a car, or making a dress. If you were building a house, you would want the blueprint first. There would be no point in asking an architect to draw a blueprint to match the house after it had been built. So it is with a speech. Why make an outline for it *after* you have prepared your speech?

Before a suit or a speech can take form, it is first planned to fit an exact pattern or outline. *(Philip Gendreau, N.Y.)*

Very clearly, you should start your *preparation* outline as soon as you have purpose, subject, and materials in mind. As you will see later, your preparation outline must *reflect* and not *determine* your purpose and your materials.

# Thinking Through Your Speech Outline

## General principles

In any speech you must establish your specific purpose and your main ideas. Your specific purpose determines the response that you want from your audience. Your main ideas are the ways you plan to prove your specific purpose or make it clearer or more interesting. Once you have decided what you intend to do, the job of outlining your speech is already well under way. The *general principles* and *types of speech outlines* you will find in this section will help you to do this work neatly and thoroughly.

**Vary your type of outline with the total speech situation.** Later in this section you will meet specific types of speech outlines. You must recognize at once that no one of these types of outlines is always better than any other. Some speakers become so fond of one

Speech outlines, like house plans, come in a variety of types to suit your particular needs. *(Monkmeyer)*

type of outline—for example, problem solving—that they try to force all of their speeches into this form. This is a dangerous mistake. The *total speech situation*—you, your purpose, your audience, your materials, and the occasion—must control your choice of outline. Choose the mold that fits the total speech situation; don't bend, beat, or disregard the situation to fit your favorite mold.

It follows that you must experiment with all the basic types of speech outlines. Learn at first hand about their advantages and disadvantages. Try them yourself in actual speaking situations. Learn to select the one that best fits your total speech situation. Be master of the outline. Do not let the outline master you.

**Focus on the body of your speech.** Like Caesar's Gaul, all speeches may be divided into three parts: introduction, body, and conclusion. The body of the speech is, ordinarily, the core of the speech. The introduction starts the speech; the conclusion stops the speech; but the body *is* the speech.

This chapter is only concerned with outlining the body of the speech. The next chapter, Chapter 12, is concerned with introductions and conclusions.

The body of a speech should contain the central idea of the speech and the main points that either (a) prove or (b) clarify or (c) intensify the central idea. As you outline, see that your main ideas stand out clearly, that they are up to the task of supporting the central idea, and that they are arranged in the order that will be most effective with your audience. Within limits, the fewer the number of main points, the better. Many experienced speakers feel that as many as four or five main points tax the ability of any audience to follow what is being said.

You can explain, make interesting, or prove your main points with subpoints. However, the fewer subpoints and sub-subpoints under each main point, the better. Two or three levels of subordination are about the practical limit for an audience to follow.

The body of your speech should also contain necessary transitions between your various points. Usually these transitions do not appear in an outline.

**Proceed in this order:** Here is the general order in which the outlining of a speech may be done efficiently. This is not a rigid formula which you *must* follow, for you will find in actual practice that it is often better to "freewheel" from time to time as you go along and your ideas change in their development. Above all, do not hesitate to make a fresh start. The first idea you have is not necessarily your best one.

All the time you spend in studying and thinking through your speech outline will pay off handsomely later. *(Ewing Galloway)*

After you have phrased your specific purpose, and collected your materials, you should decide what your main ideas are going to be. Phrase these carefully. Be certain that they say exactly what you mean. Be certain too that you anticipate, so far as is possible, the audience response to these ideas.

Now, under each main idea assemble the examples, the statistics, the statements from authority, the personal experiences you have had, and the line of reasoning that seems to give you your best chance of winning your specific purpose.

Next choose the type of speech outline that best fits your total speech situation and begin to arrange your ideas in this form. Then, finally, begin to think about your introduction and conclusion.

## Useful types of speech outlines

There are many different types of speech outlines. In this book the topical, sequential, and logical types of outlines will be stressed because you will find them extremely effective in many different kinds of speaking situations. In addition, you will be introduced to the problem-solving outline, the Monroe Motivated Sequence, and the rationalization outline.

**The topical outline.** The topical outline is one in which the several main ideas—or topics—may be selected by the speaker with considerable flexibility and imagination. Typically, there is no causal relation between the topics and the central purpose. In its simplest form, the topical outline is merely a list of ideas. Usually the subheadings explain or intensify the related topic.

Frequently the topics are chosen on the basis of like qualities. This type is illustrated in describing the arrangement used in supermarkets. It is used also to classify literature on page 185. The following groupings give you additional examples of the use of like qualities in speech planning:

AUTOMOBILES

I. Stock cars
II. Customized cars
III. Hot rod cars

SPORTS

I. Football
II. Baseball
III. Basketball

PLAYS

I. Tragedies
II. Comedies
III. Serious dramas

CONVERSATION

I. Difficulties
II. Methods of improvement
III. Pet peeves

Any of the above can be further subdivided into subheads according to like qualities. For example, the subject of SPORTS might be subdivided as follows:

I. Football
   A. Famous football teams
   B. Famous football players
   C. Famous football coaches
II. Baseball
   A. Famous baseball teams
   B. Famous baseball players
   C. Famous baseball managers
III. Basketball
   A. Famous basketball teams
   B. Famous basketball players
   C. Famous basketball coaches

As you can see, such grouping gives your speech unity and enables the audience to remember the main headings or ideas which you developed.

The topical outline is extremely versatile and relatively easy to use. You will find it particularly useful in preparing the speech to inform or the speech to entertain. In general, this is not a strong form to use when you are outlining the persuasive type of speech.

**The sequential outline.** Sequential outlines may almost be thought of as topical outlines in which the topics are arranged in an ordered sequence. But since the effect of the sequence is important, it is convenient to classify them as a separate type. The three most common sequential types are: time order, space order, and order of importance.

***Time order.*** This is often called a *chronological* arrangement. You arrange ideas in the time order in which they happened. It is especially helpful in topics concerning history, biography, travel, and stories. The following groupings will illustrate the time order of a sequential outline.

WARS OF OUR COUNTRY

I. French and Indian War
II. American Revolution
III. War of 1812
IV. Civil War
V. Spanish-American War
VI. World War I

UNITED STATES PRESIDENTS

I. George Washington
II. Abraham Lincoln
III. Theodore Roosevelt
IV. Woodrow Wilson
V. Franklin D. Roosevelt
VI. Dwight D. Eisenhower

BIOGRAPHY
(any person)

I. Early years
II. Middle age
III. Old age

VACATION
(any trip)

I. First week
II. Second week
III. Third week

Any of the main headings in the above examples could be further subdivided on a time basis. For example, in "Wars of Our Country," you could subdivide the main heading of American Revolution as follows:

II. American Revolution
   A. Events leading up to the outbreak of war
   B. The military events
   C. The peace
   D. The post-war period

***Space order.*** You may not recognize the term "space order" on sight, since "space" at the present time is associated with "outer" space. However, this type of grouping has little to do with space travel or outer space. Instead, it refers to the division that can be made within any given area of space such as: from top to bottom, from inside to outside, from left to right, from north to south, from east to west. Space-sequence grouping helps you when you attempt to describe a place, talk about geographical topics, or speak about topics which may be scattered in nature. If you can find a spatial arrangement which will include all of your specific details, you can give unity to your speech. The following examples may help you to understand space sequence:

**GREAT LAKES**
(from east to west)

I. Lake Ontario
II. Lake Erie
III. Lake Huron
IV. Lake Michigan
V. Lake Superior

**PLACES OF INTEREST**
(from west to east)

I. Grand Canyon
II. The Loop in Chicago
III. The Finger Lakes in New York State
IV. Boston

**DESCRIPTION OF SCHOOL**
(from bottom to top)

I. First floor
II. Second floor
III. Third floor

**AUTOMOBILES**
(from inside to outside)

I. Interior arrangement
II. Exterior features

If you wish to describe one room in your school, you could begin at the left and proceed with all items in order from left to right. The same left-to-right sequence can be followed in any limited area.

***Order-of-importance sequence.*** This style of grouping is helpful if you wish to talk about size or quantity when speaking about states, products, and so forth. You use it also in case you wish to progress from the least important to the most important or vice versa. In speeches, you often put the ideas of greatest importance at the beginning or the end. Some examples of such grouping are:

**SIZE OF THE GREAT LAKES**
(largest to smallest)

I. Lake Superior
II. Lake Huron
III. Lake Michigan
IV. Lake Erie
V. Lake Ontario

**FAVORITE HOBBIES**
(last to first)

I. Collecting shells
II. Acting in plays
III. Music
IV. Model trains

## ACTIVITIES

LIKE QUALITIES:

1. Make a list of five names which could be used under the following headings:

| | |
|---|---|
| Jazz | Academy Award winners |
| Foreign cars | Popes |
| Baseball's Hall of Fame | Dictionaries |
| TV programs | Dogs |
| Colleges | Novels |

2. In the list of names below, group all names under general headings that indicate some position, office, or occupation they have in common. For example, Hitler and Mussolini could be classified as **DICTATORS**; Grover Cleveland and George Washington could be classified as **UNITED STATES PRESIDENTS.**

| | |
|---|---|
| King George III | Theodore Roosevelt |
| Lionel Barrymore | Edgar Allan Poe |
| Lou Gehrig | Nathaniel Hawthorne |
| Tyrone Power | Terry Brennan |
| William Saroyan | Katherine Cornell |
| Babe Ruth | Connie Mack |
| Dwight D. Eisenhower | Babe Didrikson Zaharias |
| Queen Elizabeth I | Knute Rockne |
| Helen Hayes | Napoleon Bonaparte |
| Louis XIV | Queen Victoria |

SEQUENTIAL TIME ORDER:

3. In the list of names given in Activity 2, find the dates of birth and arrange the names in order of time sequence.
4. Select one name from the same list and arrange five important events in that person's life according to time sequence.

SEQUENTIAL SPACE ORDER:

5. List from north to south, the states bordering the Atlantic Ocean.
6. Select three countries which could be classified under each of these three headings:

| | | |
|---|---|---|
| Near East | Middle East | Far East |

SEQUENTIAL ORDER-OF-IMPORTANCE:

7. List six continents in (a) order of size and (b) order of population.
8. List four events in your life in order of importance.
9. List four of your favorite television programs in order of preference.

GENERAL SEQUENCE:

10. Arrange the states below (a) in time sequence (according to dates of their admission to the Union); (b) in space sequence (from west to east); and (c) in order of importance (size).

| | | |
|---|---|---|
| Maine | Indiana | Illinois |
| Utah | Vermont | Oklahoma |
| Ohio | Nevada | Missouri |

**Logical order (deductive pattern).** In this method of outlining a speech, you first state your central idea and then proceed to prove it. The central idea is typically supported by two or more main ideas, each of which in turn is usually supported by two or more sub-ideas. Each main head, therefore, ends with the word "because," and all subheads are reasons for the main heads above them. This is an extremely useful type of outline when your purpose is to convince or to actuate. It is called deductive, because it moves from the general to the particular. You will learn more about deductive and inductive reasoning in the chapter on debating.

In order that you may study the organization of this type of outline, here is a sample outline of a speech in which boys and girls are urged to attend camp.

**SAMPLE OF LOGICAL ORDER OUTLINE ON CAMPING**

**Statement of specific purpose:** You should believe that every boy and girl should go to camp.

MAIN ARGUMENT I: Camping helps you physically because
- A. You spend much of your time in the fresh air, and
- B. You acquire skill in sports, and
- C. You develop muscular coordination.

MAIN ARGUMENT II: Camping helps you socially because
- A. You learn to cooperate with others, and
- B. You learn the value of following a code of rules, and
- C. You learn how to meet new people and to adjust to them.

MAIN ARGUMENT III: Camping helps you to develop self-reliance because
- A. You learn to meet emergencies, and
- B. You learn to perform certain tasks, such as:
  1. Building a fire, and
  2. Making a bed, and
  3. Cooking.

The logical outline is particularly useful in total speech situations in which your materials include many solid bits of evidence, in which you can organize your materials around a very few main ideas, and in which your audience is disposed to listen to an argumentative speech. The debate speech frequently follows this pattern.

Interestingly enough, this outline form may also be used in the speech to entertain. In this use, the causal relations are ordinarily so selected as to be humorous.

The major weaknesses of the logical outline are that it is not particularly well adapted to introducing a subject to an audience, it requires ample evidence, and it may antagonize an audience that disagrees strongly with your specific purpose. Despite its wide usage in speeches to persuade, you should not regard it as the only outline form to try.

**Other types.** There are three other types of outline organization with which you should at least be familiar. Briefly they are:

***The problem-solving outline (inductive pattern).*** This type of outline is also effective in speeches to persuade. The approach in this outline is inductive in that it moves from a consideration of specific conditions to a general conclusion. Here are the usual four steps of the problem-solving outline:

I. Definition of the problem
II. Investigation of the nature of the problem in terms of what is wrong and why
III. Examination of possible solutions
IV. Selection of the best solution

***Monroe Motivated Sequence.*** This is a five-step pattern that is particularly useful in speeches to persuade. The five steps are:

I. Getting the *attention* of the audience
II. Describing the situation being considered in such a way as to show that there is a *need* for changing it
III. Presenting a solution that *satisfies* the need
IV. *Visualizing* what will happen (if the suggested solution is adopted) so vividly that the audience can literally see the consequences
V. Requesting that the audience *do,* or *feel,* or *believe* as suggested in the solution

This is an extremely effective type of outline. It is only fair to warn you, however, that this is a difficult pattern to execute well, as each of the steps requires considerable skill. Nevertheless, as Brembeck and Howell say in their book, *Persuasion:* "When logical development of reasoning leading to a course of action must be presented to an initially disinterested and possibly heterogeneous audience, the Monroe Motivated Sequence is excellently suited."

***Rationalization.*** This type of organization is more psychological in its emphasis than logical. The basic premise of this type of outline is that audiences need two types of reasons if they are to be well persuaded. First, they need to be shown that the point of view presented will be helpful to them, even if only in a selfish way. This reason will make your audience *want* to agree with your purpose. Second, they need to be given a reason that they can use to *justify* their agreement.

This outline will work best for you in total speech situations in which your audience will have strong wants and in which logical arguments may not be as plentiful as you would like.

## ACTIVITIES

1. How does a salesman use the rationalization technique? Describe and give examples to your class.
2. How might a teacher use rationalization in making an assignment? Describe and give examples to your class.

# Writing Down Your Outline

After you have thought through your outline and have chosen the outline type that best fits your total speech situation, you will want to put your outline into writing. You will do a better job in preparing this written form if you use the suggestions that follow. Learning to prepare a good written outline is worth all the time it takes. You can apply this information to all types of outlines.

## Make your outline complete

To be effective, an outline should include your complete collection of ideas; otherwise, it is merely a memorandum. This serves two valuable purposes: (1) it avoids the possibility of omission of important ideas, and (2) it forces you to consider carefully the best place to put all of them. Misplacing or omitting ideas in a speech pattern is like misplacing pieces in a jigsaw puzzle or trying to put one together when some of the parts are missing.

A puzzle or an outline is not complete until every part is fitted together. *(Black Star)*

Make certain that your finished outline is always completely clear in meaning to anyone who may read it. Usually, others can understand your outline if (a) you have been consistent in following the rules governing symbols and indentations, (b) you have grouped together the ideas that belong together, and (c) you have expressed your thoughts clearly in complete sentences or well thought out phrases. In general, it is well to avoid the one-word heading in the preparation outline, although this type can be very useful in the delivery outline for quick summarization.

## Divide your outline into Introduction, Body, and Conclusion

The above division applies to all types of speeches, and is particularly applicable in speeches to inform and persuade. This chapter, you will recall, is concerned primarily with the body of your speech.

When, as is usually the case, all three divisions of your speech require a somewhat detailed arrangement, number the main heads of each division separately as shown in the following outline. It is conventional to use Roman Numerals for this purpose.

INTRODUCTION

I.

II.

BODY

I.

II.

III.

CONCLUSION

I.

II.

## Use a consistent system of symbols and indentations

You must learn to use different types of symbols and indentations from the left-hand margin in order to show (a) the subordination and (b) the equivalence of your headings to each other.

The sample outline given will make clear to you the use of symbols, indentation, and punctuation in order to show the relationships among headings. Study these descriptions closely.

BLANK DESCRIPTIVE OUTLINE

I. First main head. Subordinate to central idea or specific purpose, which it must either prove, explain, or intensify. Equal to other main heads, as II, III, or IV.
  A. First level subhead. Subordinate to main head under which it is listed, and which it must either prove, explain, or intensify. Equal in rank to other first level subheads as B, C, or D.
  B. Equal in rank to other first level subheads as A, C, or D.
  C. Equal in rank to other first level subheads as A, B, or D.
    1. Second level subhead. Subordinate to first level under which it is listed, and which it must either prove, explain, or intensify. Equal in rank to other second level subheads as 2, 3, or 4.
    2. Equal in rank to other second level subheads as 1, 3, or 4.
    3. Equal in rank to other second level subheads as 1, 2, or 4.
      a. Third level subhead. Subordinate to second level subhead under which it is listed, and which it must either prove, explain, or intensify. Equal in rank to other third level subheads as b, c, or d.
      b. Equal in rank to other third level subheads as a, c, or d.
      c. Equal in rank to other third level subheads as a, b, or d.
        (1) Fourth level subhead.
        (2)
          (a) Fifth level subhead.
          (b)

II. Second main head. Equal to I above.
  A.
  B.

et cetera . . . .

The set of rules given below summarizes for you the use of symbols, indentations, and punctuation in outlining.

USE OF SYMBOLS, INDENTATION, AND PUNCTUATION

***Symbols.*** The symbols of standard usage in their order of importance are:

Roman numerals for main heads: I, II, III, etc.

Capital letters for the first level of subheads: A, B, C, etc.

Arabic numerals for the second level of subheads: 1, 2, 3, etc.
Small letters for the third level of subheads: a, b, c, etc.
Arabic numerals in parentheses for the fourth level of subheads: (1), (2), (3), etc.
Small letters in parentheses for the fifth level of subheads: (a), (b), (c), etc.

This order *must be uniform* throughout your outline. Observe that the symbols alternate—number, letter, number, letter, etc.

***Indentation.*** The rules governing indentation are as follows:

The amount of indentation varies with each level of headings.
Allow the same amount of indentation for like levels of headings throughout the outline.
Allow the smallest amount for the main heads and the largest amount for the lowest level of subheads.
Keep all symbols clearly visible. Avoid writing any words directly under symbols or to the left of them.

***Punctuation.***

Put a period after each symbol.
In a sentence outline, end each sentence with a period.
Use no punctuation at the end of phrase or word outlines.

***Significance of symbols.*** Since symbols denote *relationship* of your ideas, it is imperative to follow these rules:

Indicate equality of ideas by using the same level of headings for all equal ideas.
Be sure that subheadings relate to the next higher level of heading listed directly *above* them and no others, indicating a specific division of the idea.
Since a heading cannot be divided into *one* part, there must be at least *two* subheads under every heading or *none at all.*
Each heading or subheading should express only one idea.

## ACTIVITIES

1. Check your understanding of the correct use of symbols by correcting the order of those in the three groups below:

| | | |
|---|---|---|
| A. | II. | 1. |
| I. | a. | A. |
| a. | A. | III. |
| 1. | (1). | (1). |
| (a). | 1. | (a). |
| (1). | (a). | a. |

2. Prepare a topical outline on a subject familiar to you. Use three main heads, and carry at least one of the main heads to the third level of subheads.

## Differentiate between main and subordinate ideas

You must also learn to identify your main ideas and your subordinate ideas respectively. Remember that your main heads must actually represent your most important ideas expressed in their broadest sense. Give the selection of your main points very serious thought, because if you miss on your first level of headings, your entire outline will fail.

Think again of the grouping used in the supermarkets. You will find the sign CEREALS used as the general classification in arranging all types of cereals. You will not find the entire cereal section marked BRAN FLAKES or GRANDEE'S CORN FLAKES. Bran flakes is only one kind of cereal. GRANDEE'S Corn Flakes is only one kind of corn flakes among all the kinds of corn flakes to be found under the general heading of cereals. Your main heading must, therefore, be general and inclusive enough to permit further division into subheads. It must also be important enough to warrant further division.

In selecting main headings, as you noted earlier, try to keep them small in number. It is much easier to remember two or three main ideas than ten or twelve. Besides, if you do have ten or twelve main ideas, you probably have chosen unwisely or you should give two or three speeches instead of one! Keeping to a minimum of two and a maximum of five is a practice which most speakers follow.

Supermarkets use the principles of outlining to group items by general classifications and to shelve them in an orderly arrangement. *(Don Carlos Dunaway)*

When you have chosen your main headings to represent your most important ideas, check them to be sure that they meet these requirements: (1) they must be clearly expressed, (2) they must be directly related to your main idea, (3) they must not overlap and, (4) they must represent a logical development of thought.

Here is an example of an outline on the subject of allowing eighteen-year-olds to vote. Your statement of purpose could be: ***To convince the audience that eighteen-year-olds should be allowed to vote.*** Assume that you wish to present these three main reasons in support of your main idea:

I. Eighteen-year-olds have been taught the essentials of intelligent voting.
II. Eighteen-year-olds are considered old enough to handle other responsibilities.
III. Eighteen-year-olds already have the right to vote in some states.

You will notice that each statement is clearly expressed; each is directly related to the main idea; the statements do not overlap in meaning; and there is a logical development of thought.

Now notice what happens when you violate those essentials by using the following statements of possible main arguments:

I. Because all students study about civics and government in high school and read newspapers and listen to news on radio and television, they know as much as their parents who maybe didn't study any of these things in high school.

Such a statement is not only clumsy and difficult to follow, but it also attempts to bring in part of the proof. Clear expression has been lost completely.

II. Voting is a privilege which many people do not appreciate.

Although this is a clear statement, it violates the second essential. It has no direct relationship to the statement of purpose.

I. Eighteen-year-olds are well enough informed to vote.
II. Eighteen-year-olds have sufficient educational background to enable them to vote intelligently.

This arrangement of main ideas violates the principle of keeping your ideas distinct and separate. As you can see, the two statements overlap in meaning. After you have proved the first one, what would you have left to say about the second one?

I. Eighteen-year-olds are intelligent enough to vote.
II. If eighteen-year-olds vote like their parents, it won't make any difference in major elections.
III. Some claim that eighteen-year-olds don't want to vote, but most of them do.

As you can see, in this group there is no logical development of thought and the entire outline falls apart.

## Arrange your supporting details

After you have chosen your main headings with care and have expressed them according to the essentials just given, your next problem is one of sorting out your supporting ideas and placing them under the headings where they rightfully belong. You must be careful to place supporting details under the headings which they support. Each subhead must explain or prove the heading directly above it. Refer to the explanation of this process in *Blank Descriptive Outline*. Be sure to notice again that the subheads explain only the heading above them.

Subheads must also meet the requirements mentioned above for main heads: They must be stated clearly, they must be related to the main idea, they must not overlap, and they should represent a logical development of thought.

You may be wondering how you can be sure that you are placing your subordinate ideas under the proper headings. The process of fitting subheads under the right headings can be explained best by using some common examples of simple classification.

For example, when you have three headings such as Fruits, Vegetables, and Meats, it doesn't take you long to decide where to place the following items: corn, onions, round steak, beets, sausage,

This boy is learning early in life to put things together that belong together. *(Jay-Vee)*

beans, oranges, lemons, wieners, swiss steak, melons, liver, cherries, bacon. Nor does it take you long to decide that you can't classify shampoo, milk, matches, catsup, bread, or gingerale under any one of the main headings above.

You may think that such an example is too easy. You may feel that anyone can group items according to fruit, vegetables, and meat. The principle is the same in all types of grouping. You simply put together the things that belong together. *You must know, however, which are main and which are subordinate ideas.*

Now try the same formula with a speech outline. Below is a list of general topics with only the first level of possible subheads. Study them carefully. Notice how they *belong* together.

| HOBBIES | PETS | LITERATURE |
|---|---|---|
| I. Sports | I. Cats | I. Ancient |
| II. Reading | II. Dogs | II. Medieval |
| III. Theater | III. Horses | III. Modern |

Think of several other possible groupings for any of the above. For instance, literature may be classified in several ways such as:

LITERATURE

| | | | |
|---|---|---|---|
| I. English | I. Romantic | I. Serious | I. Novels |
| II. American | II. Biographical | II. Humorous | II. Poems |
| III. French | III. Historical | III. Mysterious | III. Plays |

You realize quickly that with almost any general topic there are many possibilities for grouping. The important fact to remember is to decide upon one kind and follow through with it consistently. Your first level of subheads is determined largely, of course, by the subject matter which you wish to present. In the above illustrations of possible groupings of literature, you would have to decide if you wanted to talk about literature according to countries, themes, moods, or styles of composition. After you decide how you intend to develop your topic, pick the most general classifications first. Remember these should be ones which will highlight your main thoughts and which will *include all* of your supporting details.

## After your outline—what?

The preparatory outline is an *aid* and not an *end.* Your outline is not a speech. You must still put flesh and blood over the structure you have created. You must still prepare an introduction and a conclusion. And you must still master the delivery of your speech.

## ACTIVITIES

The following activities will give you experience in preparing the various types of outlines. Prepare a complete outline for each, including an introduction and a conclusion. Use complete sentences or phrases.

1. Select one topic for a speech to inform. Prepare four different outlines that could be followed in the development of your topic—(1) topical—like qualities, (2) time sequence, (3) space sequence, and (4) order-of-importance sequence.
2. Plan a speech based on a trip that you have taken. Prepare a spatial sequence and a time sequence type of outline.
3. Read a short story. Arrange the incidents in a time sequence pattern.
4. Describe any building or place. Arrange your ideas in a space sequence order.
5. Prepare topics to exchange with a classmate. Decide upon the purpose of the speech which could be developed from the topic you received and prepare two different types of outlines for it.
6. Select one topic of a controversial nature. Prepare a logical order type of outline using either the deductive or the inductive pattern.

## PRONUNCIATION PROBLEMS

Be particular about the sounds of "f" and "v" which are frequently confused or weakened to the extent that they sound alike.

Practice saying the following words containing the "f" sound:

| | | | | |
|---|---|---|---|---|
| fee | flute | raffle | fifth | calf |
| fie | flown | offer | sphinx | cuff |
| foe | four | muffin | diphthong | off |
| fum | floor | coffin | naphtha | if |
| fact | foxes | affable | diphtheria | proof |

This next list of words contains the "v" sound.

| | | | | |
|---|---|---|---|---|
| vie | villain | savior | striven | stove |
| vow | vocal | devil | shaven | envy |
| valley | volley | rendezvous | shoved | leave |
| verse | vain | carves | wives | live |
| vesper | victim | calves | knives | love |
| volume | vile | shelved | wharves | drive |

Notice what happens to the meaning of words when you confuse the "f" and "v" sounds in the following:

| | | |
|---|---|---|
| fat, vat | luff, love | vast, fast |
| fail, veil | shuffle, shovel | vowel, fowl |
| fine, vine | rifle, rival | loafs, loaves |
| fain, vein or vain | vile, file | veal, feel |
| safe, save | shelf, shelve | few, view |
| strife, strive | folly, volley | vie, fie |

## READING CHECK-UP

Read aloud the nonsense sentences below to check your pronunciation of any problem words.

The fishwives on the wharves were sharpening their carving knives for the fifth time.

Five farmers played five fifes while their wives played five violins.

The villain fled fast to save his life from the volley of shots fired by his foes.

Fifty volumes in vellum filled the bookshelves of the vile villain.

Few can view the lives of rivals with fine and affable vision.

The fancy fanfare of the farm festival was climaxed by a feast consisting of fish, fowl, venison, veal, loaves, and muffins. During the raffle which followed the feast, fifty wives wearing fancy ruffles served waffles on silver trays.

Few frail vocalists have vim and vigor in the strife of diphthongs and vowels.

Fine vines offer full proof of fully-filled fruit.

> The fair breeze blew, the white foam flew,
> The furrow followed free;
> We were the first that ever burst
> Into that silent sea.
>
> —Coleridge

> Fair is foul, and foul is fair,
> Hover through the fog and filthy air.
>
> —Shakespeare

> Full fathom five thy father lies.
>
> —Shakespeare

## VOCABULARY BUILD-UP

Use the italicized words in short paragraphs to show that you understand their meanings.

a *noncommittal* answer
an *insatiable* desire
a *convivial* group
an occasion of *levity*
*vacillating* in his opinions
*oblivious* of the consequences
*obtuse* in his thinking
to *forfeit* the game
a *gruesome* sight
an *insinuating* remark
a *perennial* favorite
a *persistent* rumor
a *fervid* plea
a *caustic* answer
devoted to a *fetish*
*punctilious* in all matters
a *presumptuous* manner
*penurious* habits

CHAPTER

# 12 Introducing and Concluding Your Speech

A good speech has a good beginning and a good ending, both of which are kept close together.

—*Prochnow: Speaker's Handbook of Epigrams and Witticisms*

HAVE you ever watched a new driver try to drive a car for the first time? His first few attempts to get in motion are usually jerky, unsteady, and even dangerous. The driver often feels panicky as he tries to remember all he is supposed to know and do before he starts off. Once he is out on the open road, his driving becomes smoother and he is more relaxed. It is getting started that is hard for him.

Stopping is not easy, either. You have ridden with a driver who steps on the brake so suddenly that his car screeches to an abrupt halt, pitching you forward, and causing the cars behind you to swerve and brake suddenly. Or you know the driver who is afraid of stepping on the brake too hard. Timidly he will reduce speed so slowly that he becomes a hazard to the line of traffic, because no one knows whether or not he's stopping.

Many speakers, especially inexperienced ones, have the same problems in starting and stopping their speeches. When they are unsure of how to begin, they are apt to plunge into their speech wildly or sputter around until they reach the part of the speech where they feel sure of themselves. Uncertainty also causes some speakers to come to a sudden halt as they race toward the finish line. Every sentence goes faster and faster until finally you can feel the speaker thinking, "Whew, I made it." Or right in the middle of a sentence a speaker may stop and leave the platform. There is another type of speaker, too. He resembles the driver who cannot seem to plant his foot firmly on the brake pedal. He doesn't know how to end his speech, he is afraid to stop, and so he goes slower and slower like a car running out of gas until finally the class bell rings, or his audience leaves, or the chairman stops him.

## How to Get Off to a Good Start

The introduction of a speech can decide its success or failure. It is the first impression you make on an audience. If you can capture good will, interest, and understanding at the beginning of your speech, you will have an excellent chance of keeping your audience with you until the end. If you lose your listeners at the very outset, however, when they may *want* to listen, you will have to fight an uphill battle to recapture your audience.

The two goals of introduction are:

1. To gain the favorable attention of your audience
2. To prepare your audience to understand your speech purpose

Would you say that the speaker had gained the favorable attention of this audience? *(Monkmeyer)*

To achieve these goals, always plan your introduction in terms of what your audience now knows, now believes, and now wants. Don't begin in terms of your own knowledge, belief, and desires. Your introduction must always be audience-centered.

## How to gain favorable attention

In your introduction, your first goal is to secure favorable attention for your specific purpose. Ordinarily you will state the main idea of your speech early. It is much easier for your listeners to follow you if they know where you are going. Stating your purpose early is particularly wise if you think your audience is in sympathy with your purpose. If, however, you are afraid that your audience may not agree with your central idea, it may be wiser for you to work into your purpose gradually. One way is to establish areas of agreement with your audience before you turn to the area of difference.

Regardless of whether you reveal your purpose relatively early or relatively late in your speech, you will still need to solve the problem of building favorable attention in the first few sentences of your introduction. Here are ways of beginning a speech that should make an audience like you *and* your speech:

**Refer to your physical surroundings.** In your introduction you might refer to the temperature, the seating, the public address system, or any other physical condition in the total speech situation shared by you and the audience. The more dramatic the condition, the more effective the reference. For example, one high school student spoke to his class on the need for a better building program in his school. He began like this: "As you sit here today behind these scarred, poorly shaped, uncomfortable desks, as you look at these cracked, patched, undecorated walls, and as you breathe this hot, stuffy, and unchanged air, I want you to think with me about the need for a more adequate building program in our Cityville schools."

By calling attention to observable evidence in the room, the speaker gained immediate and favorable attention.

Here is another example: A speaker who wanted to show that Americans like their rooms too warm, began this way, "I have in my hand a thermometer. This particular instrument is guaranteed by its manufacturer to be accurate within plus or minus one degree. What temperature does this instrument record at this moment? Seventy degrees? No! Seventy-five? No! Eighty? Wrong again! This thermometer registers eighty-two degrees!"

This speaker used a magic trick to capture his audience and lead into his speech. *(A. M. Rubendunst)*

This was a dramatic way of capturing attention at the very beginning. Furthermore, the speaker quickly won the audience's approval because he proved his point while winning their attention.

**Refer to other speakers on the program.** This is a friendly and easy way to begin a speech. Sometimes you can plan such references in advance and write them into your speech. At other times, you can take advantage of events as they occur by listening for particular statements made by the speakers who preceded you. Find out ahead of time, if you can, who will be speaking and what aspects of the general subject they are supposed to cover. This will alert you for opportunities to tie in your references.

The president of the student council in a large high school spoke at a meeting to raise funds for new uniforms for the basketball team. He began in this way: "My fellow speakers on this platform are the athletic coach, the president of the PTA, two members of the Board of Education, the principal of our high school, and a classroom teacher. What further proof do you need that this subject is important to all members of our high school community and not just to the players on the squad?"

The prominence of the speakers helped to show the importance of the subject and furnished an easy opening for the talk.

The speaker who can improvise a successful transition from the preceding speech already has a head start. *(Al Currens)*

Now consider this example of a spontaneous reference to something which has just occurred. The previous speaker had given some detailed statistics on the increase in traffic accidents in the country as a whole. Another speaker then arose and said: "You have just heard from Bill Fitzgibbon about what is happening in the nation so far as accidents are concerned. Let me tell you what is happening right here in our own town."

This speaker capitalized on the background provided by the previous speaker to lead directly into his own speech.

**Refer to your audience.** In this type of introduction, the speaker takes advantage of the self-interest of his listeners. A high school debater used this technique in a contest debate on the goals of education. He began, "Tonight, by actual count, there are twenty-seven members in our audience. Look at yourselves carefully, ladies and gentlemen. You represent that important minority in America which is still more interested in public education than in staying home this stormy night."

Although somewhat bitter, this introduction gained the quick attention and approval of the audience. If used properly, reference to the audience is one of the best ways of leading into a speech. The personal element directly involves the audience in the speech.

**Refer to the significance of the occasion.** Don't abuse this method; many events are not really significant.

A city-wide meeting had been called to dedicate a memorial to the former students of the local high school who had lost their lives in the last war. The principal was speaking to an audience that included most of the parents of these students. He began: "We are here tonight to pay tribute to the seventeen former students of our high school who lost their lives while serving in the armed forces of our country."

Certainly such an occasion as this was truly significant. The introduction was forceful because of its obvious directness and commendable simplicity.

## ACTIVITIES

1. Look through *Vital Speeches* or any other publication of speeches. From such a source bring to class examples of introductions using the four methods of beginning listed above.
2. Choose a suitable subject from one of the various speaking occasions listed below and prepare four sample introductions for it, using each method of beginning discussed above:

| | |
|---|---|
| Football pep rally at assembly | Graduation |
| Red Cross donation at school | Political rally |
| Awarding school letters | Senior picnic |

**Use illustrations.** An illustration may be any comparison or example that clarifies or intensifies an idea. Some of the most useful types of illustrations suitable for introductions include quotations, familiar sayings, and short stories or anecdotes. Usually your illustration will be stronger if you show at once how it fits your speech. Note the applications in the following examples:

***The quotation.*** This is the accurate repetition of a statement made by another person. Usually, quotations already well known to an audience are more effective.

*Example:* "What's in a name? A rose by any other name would smell as sweet."

*Application:* "Does it really matter so much what we *name* our paper?"

***The familiar saying.*** This is a brief statement that has wide general familiarity. Frequently it appears in slightly different forms. Often it is not attributed to any one person or source.

*Example:* "A stitch in time saves nine."

*Application:* "Although the burden of defense spending is heavy on our taxpayers, it is only a drop in the bucket in comparison to the taxation we can expect in the event of another war."

***The anecdote.*** This is a brief story or incident, usually of considerable interest. It may be told about either real or imaginary individuals, but it is complete in itself.

*Example:* A farmer had a dog who spent part of his time sitting by the side of the highway waiting for sports cars. When the dog saw one of them come around the corner he would get ready, and as it passed him he would chase it down the road. One day the farmer's neighbor said, "Sam, do you think that hound of yours is ever going to catch a sports car?" "Well, Bill," Sam replied, "that isn't what worries me. What worries me is what he would do with it if he caught one!"

*Application:* "Many of us in life are like that hound. We run madly for things which we could not use even if we caught them. It pays to sit down and think about whether one's objectives are worthwhile."

## ACTIVITIES

1. Develop a personal experience into an anecdote and use it for an introduction to a speech. Have your classmates pick a subject it would fit.
2. Select a familiar saying and use it in an introduction to a speech.
3. Find at least one quotation that could be used to introduce any three of these speech topics:
   The Importance of Education in American Life
   How Good Are Your Manners?
   The Value of a Speech Course
   My Favorite Teacher
   Life's Darkest Moment
   Charity Begins at Home
4. Select an illustration, quotation, anecdote, or one of the other examples from the Sample Speaker's Kit in this book and write an application showing how you would work it into an introduction.

**Use a startling statement or question.** In this kind of introduction, you begin by saying or asking something that will strongly surprise or even shock your audience. This is a dangerous and difficult technique to use well. Unless the kind of shock is appropriate to your subject and situation, you should not try this device.

A speaker on a high school program was a national authority on automobile safety. He began by walking silently to the center of the platform, removing his watch from his wrist, and saying, "Please, will all of you in the audience who are wearing watches kindly help me? I want to time exactly fifteen seconds. When I signal, begin counting. Stop me by shouting, 'Time!' at the end of fifteen seconds."

The audience cooperated. At fifteen seconds, shouts of "Time!" reached the speaker. He refastened his watch and remarked, "Correct. Exactly fifteen seconds." He paused and then added slowly,

"And during each fifteen seconds of each day at least one American has had an automobile accident."

This statement was so startling and specific that the audience was shocked into becoming interested in the speaker's subject.

**Use a series of questions.** Another effective way of pulling your audience into active examination of your purpose is to ask them a series of questions. Sometimes the entire series of questions may be about one point in your talk. Or each of the questions may be keyed to one of the main headings in your speech. In this latter case, the questions serve not only to arouse interest, but also to organize your speech. Among the more useful types of questions are questions of fact, questions of opinion, rhetorical questions, and individualized questions.

***Questions of fact.*** The answer to this type of question contains evidence that is important to your speech. For example, in a talk on injuries in high school football, the speaker asked, "How many high school players in our state received serious injuries this fall?" He used the answer to build his argument.

***Questions of opinion.*** This type of question is aimed at bringing out attitudes that will be helpful to the speaker. The question, "Do you favor the present school cafeteria situation?" was used by a speaker to bring out the resentment he knew to be present.

***Rhetorical questions.*** This is a type of question that actually answers itself, such as, "Do you really want to die in an automobile accident?"

"Do you recognize what I hold in my hand?" *(Don Carlos Dunaway)*

***Individualized questions.*** This is a type of question that seeks to relate your subject to *each* listener. "Can we really not support the team tonight?" was used to introduce a pep rally.

**Use suspense.** With this technique, you seek to arouse curiosity about your speech purpose. Don't try to begin every speech with this device. Be sure that the suspense leads your audience smoothly and directly into the body of your speech.

A classroom speaker used this technique to introduce a speech on transistor hearing aids by stating: "The article that I hold in my hand is less than one inch in its longest dimension. It weighs less than an ounce. It can be purchased at slight cost from several manufacturers. Yet this article—small, light, and inexpensive—has changed the lives of eight million Americans."

Stories are often built on the element of suspense. So are short anecdotes about interesting people. Frequently the name of the person will be withheld until the end to give the "punch" of a surprise ending. Be careful, however, not to overdo a good thing by prolonging the introduction unnecessarily and keeping the audience in suspense when the punch line is not worth it.

**Use the vital as an introductory method.** This refers to the way a speaker makes his speech seem essential to his audience. People will listen to things that matter to them. Sometimes, however, they fail to recognize why a particular subject is of concern to them. In such cases, it is advantageous in gaining attention to point out the relationship at once. Such an introduction may be brief or lengthy. Often one statement will suffice.

Here is an introduction used by a Selective Service officer during the Korean War which caught the attention of a group of high school seniors: "Tonight, I shall try to make clear which of you will probably be drafted into our armed forces and which of you will not."

## ACTIVITIES

1. List ten topics that seem commonplace and unexciting such as "Differences Between Domestic and Imported Wool." Select three from this list and prepare introductions for each, using a startling question or statement.
2. Select a subject for presentation to your speech class. Prepare a series of three *questions of fact* that will (a) interest your listeners and (b) lead into points that you desire to make later in the talk. Now frame a second series of questions, using this time either questions of opinion, individualized questions, or rhetorical questions.
3. Bring to class an anecdote about a sports figure or any prominent person in which the identity of the individual is revealed at the end.

4. Prepare a list of ten obviously exciting subjects such as "Man Visits the Moon." Choose five of these and prepare introductions for them, incorporating startling questions or statements. After delivery before your speech class, ask (a) if your statements *were* startling, (b) if they *were* related to the subject, and (c) if you made a smooth connection between the two.
5. Prepare two introductions with lots of suspense. Deliver them before your speech class and have the class decide which was the more successful.

**Use the direct approach.** Many times it is both effective and easy to begin with an immediate reference to your subject. In fact, this is probably the most frequently used introduction. Thus, in starting a high school banquet, the master of ceremonies might begin by saying: "Here is our program for tonight. You will like every minute of it. Our first feature is . . . . "

**Use humor.** High school students, in particular, like humorous introductions, but to plan for a laugh just for the sake of a laugh is questionable except possibly in the speech to entertain. If you are making an appeal for a contribution to The Heart Fund, for instance, it would be poor taste and poor judgment to use a humorous introduction.

A high school senior speaking to his class on the wonders of science found this bit of humor to give his speech a good send-off with his audience: A cameraman employed by the educational department of a film company met an old farmer at the country store and said, "I've just been taking some moving pictures of life out on your farm."

"Did you get any of my men in action?" asked the old farmer curiously.

"Yes, I did."

The farmer shook his head reflectively, then commented, "Science sure is a wonderful thing!"

Another student speaking on the subject of modern music wanted to clear up some of the misconceptions that people have concerning it. She began her speech thus: Joan asked her father, as the radio ground out the latest popular music, "Did you ever hear anything so wonderful?"

"Can't say I have," answered her father, "although I once heard a collision between a truckload of milk cans and a carload of ducks."

**Use the challenge.** The introductory challenge is an open invitation to the audience to answer the speaker. You will find it a difficult, dangerous, and yet, when successful, a compelling introduction. If you try this type of introduction, use it with great caution.

In an informal classroom debate, the second speaker handled this technique very skillfully. He began by calling attention to a series of statements made by his opponent: "I am going to read to you five statements from the speech you have just heard. In each case I shall read each quotation slowly, distinctly, and accurately. When I have finished the last of these, I shall stop. At that time, I shall challenge anyone in this room to prove that I have in any sense misquoted my opponent."

## ACTIVITIES

1. Select one subject of considerable interest to you. Prepare a speech challenge as an introduction to your subject.
2. Prepare a topic and an introduction using the direct approach.
3. Your subject is "Humor in American Life." Prepare a humorous introduction and try it out on your class.
4. Find examples of humor which would make interesting introductions to five of the following topics:

| | | |
|---|---|---|
| Advertising | Golf | Taxes |
| Success | Fishing | Speech |
| Women Drivers | College Education | Animals |

## How to prepare your audience to understand your speech purpose

You have just been given a number of different keys that will help you to unlock many of the doors that lead to the favorable attention of your audience. Once you have the door open and are about to enter, you must perform the necessary introductions before you go any farther. This is the time and place to present any explanations or background material that may be essential to a clear understanding of your speech.

**Make your use of words and terms clear.** Technical words have specific meanings in particular fields. If you have to use such words in your speech, work out exact definitions for them in your introduction. Even if you use a common word like "democracy," try to help your audience understand *how* you are using it. Sometimes it is the frequently used word that causes the most difficulty, because it is used loosely and does not have the same meaning to all people.

A new crop of words comes into usage every year. They catch on quickly with people who find them expressive for their purposes, but they puzzle others who are not familiar with them and cannot find them as yet in the dictionary. For example, a high school student spoke on the advantages of his city providing "drag strips."

"He certainly knows how to hold an audience."

THE SATURDAY EVENING POST



When he made this speech to his classmates, little explanation was needed in his introduction, for the term had the same meaning for all present. If he had made the speech before an adult audience, however, he would have needed to define the term immediately.

**Include the essential background of your subject.** Some subjects cannot be understood unless your audience knows about previous events. In such cases, your introduction should include whatever summary is necessary to clear and intelligent listening.

A high school audience would require more background information from a speaker talking about our present foreign policy than would an audience composed of newspapermen. A fairly safe guide is: How much background did *you* need to explore before you could speak on the subject?

**Identify your speech purpose.** Try to phrase or imply your speech purpose so clearly that each of your listeners will know exactly what you are trying to say. If you have any reason to suspect that your purpose may be confusing or obscure, take time at once to help your audience. Rephrase your purpose and give examples of it—raising and answering questions.

◄ POINTERS THAT PAY OFF ►

1. Approach your audience with a friendly attitude.
2. Use a strong opening sentence. Memorize it.
3. Use short sentences but avoid a choppy effect.
4. Keep your introduction brief.

## How to Come to a Good Stop

It is just as important to stop smoothly as it is to start that way. You must be in control of your speech all the way from start to finish in order to give your audience the feeling of having had just enough—not too much or too little. "Leave your audience before they want to leave you" is a good warning.

Speeches, like basketball and football games, can be lost or saved in the final moments. Do not overlook the importance of your closing time.

The specific functions of your conclusions will vary from speech to speech. Here, however, are the usual functions of the conclusion. Learn them and use them to greatest advantage:

1. Summarize your main ideas.
2. Reinforce your specific purpose.
3. Secure audience acceptance of your specific purpose.

A speech, like a car, must not be stopped too abruptly. *(ACIR—Cornell University)*

## Conclusions that summarize your main ideas

**Single-sentence summary.** In this method you reduce the entire point of your speech to a single concise sentence.

A junior, speaking on motorcycle racing to a high school club, tied together his whole speech in this one concluding sentence:

"You must now agree that motorcycle racing is an exciting sport for both the spectator and the participant."

**Central-point summary.** This type is a bit more complex than the preceding one. Although you need not review every point, you should try to give an over-all picture of those covered in your speech. Make a clear, forceful restatement of your specific purpose. Brief your audience with a minimum of supporting detail.

Talking on the traffic problem in his city, one student used this summary: "Without question our traffic problem, which is bad now, is actually going to get worse. In the immediate future we are sure to have more cars, faster cars, bigger cars, and smaller cars on our streets. Unless we, as a city, take active steps now to expand our traffic capacity, we shall never unsnarl our streets."

Note the restrained use of supporting detail in the above conclusion.

**Point-by-point summary.** This calls for repeating precisely and in the original order each of the main points of your speech. Frequently you may repeat the exact wording used in the body of your speech. Such a summary leaves a clear-cut impression with your audience when your speech is long and complex. It is particularly forceful in long speeches intended to persuade.

A senior who planned to be a dress designer urged the girls in her class to learn all they could about the design and construction of clothes. Here is her point-by-point summary:

"I urge every feminine member of my audience to learn all she can about clothes. I have suggested many reasons. Here are the most important:

"First, the girl who knows clothes can dress more economically than the girl who simply buys by store name or brand name.

"Second, the girl who knows clothes can be confident that she is dressed in the best of the current style.

"Third, the girl who knows clothes can dress most becomingly.

"Finally, the girl who knows clothes can safely and effectively express her own individuality."

In this conclusion, the speaker very carefully repeated her four main arguments in order to reinforce them in the minds of the audience. Such a summary is almost a necessity in speeches built around several main points.

## Conclusions that reinforce your specific purpose

There are many ways to drive home your message in a forceful conclusion. Some of the best ones follow:

**The quotation.** The right quotation can add great weight and dignity to your speech. Audiences usually are impressed if your message can be restated in the words of a famous person, but unless your quotation expresses exactly the central theme of your speech, it is pointless. Almost any subject, however, lends itself to the use of quotations if you are patient enough to look for the right one. One speaker made use of a familiar quotation in urging that the modern football player use the best of both the T-formation and the single-wing. He concluded by saying:

"In football, as in just about everything else, it is well to follow the ancient and respected advice of Alexander Pope:

> 'Be not the first by whom the new are try'd,
> 'Nor yet the last to lay the old aside.' "

**The incident or example.** An interesting and appropriate incident or example, particularly if drawn from your own experience, makes a strong ending to a speech.

Notice the forceful ending given to a speech advocating compulsory first-aid training in all high schools:

"I have now given you a very detailed explanation of why prominent authorities believe that each of us should have training in the fundamentals of first aid. Now I want to tell you why this means so much to me.

"My little brother, who is now ten years old, got a splinter in his eye while watching my father split wood. Dad, who had no training in first aid, tried to remove the splinter with the corner of his handkerchief. That was three years ago. My brother has been blind in that eye ever since."

Much of the impact of this conclusion comes from its simplicity and obvious authenticity.

**The story or anecdote.** Stories and anecdotes are more forceful if they are somewhat familiar. The following is an illustration: A senior girl, developing the idea that gentleness will frequently persuade when roughness fails, ended her speech with the fable of "The Wind and the Sun." For greater effect, she kept the style of expression used in an older version of the story, from the renowned *McGuffey Readers*.

## THE WIND AND THE SUN

*A Fable*

A dispute once arose between the Wind and the Sun as to which of the two was the stronger.

To decide the matter, they agreed to try their power on a traveler. That party which should strip him of his cloak was to win the day.

The Wind began. He blew a cutting blast which tore up the mountain oaks by their roots and made the whole forest look like a wreck.

But the traveler, though at first he could scarcely keep his cloak on his back, ran under the hill for shelter and buckled his mantle about him more closely than ever.

The Wind, having thus tried his utmost power in vain, the Sun began. Bursting through a thick cloud, he darted his sultry beams so forcibly upon the traveler's head that the poor fellow was almost melted.

"This," said he, "is past all bearing. It is so hot that one might as well be in an oven."

So he quickly threw off his cloak and went under the shade of a tree to cool himself.

*Moral*

This fable teaches us that gentle means will often succeed where force will fail.

**The humorous.** It is difficult to close a speech effectively on a humorous note unless your speech aims solely to entertain. In other types of speeches, the use of humor as a concluding device is either avoided entirely or is mixed liberally with other elements.

A presidential campaign furnished an excellent example of this. The defeated candidate, Adlai Stevenson, well known for his wit, did not use wit alone in concluding his speech conceding defeat. Borrowing from Abraham Lincoln, he sprinkled pathos with his humor: "I am too big to cry, and I feel too bad to laugh."

**Repetition of the introduction.** As previous suggestions have indicated, you may end a speech with almost any of the devices used in that particular speech. Some even use the very same quotation with which they began. Ministers frequently do this for emphasis, repeating the Biblical verse used as a text.

One good technique is to describe in your conclusion the essential proposal of your introduction, then suggest the desirability of accepting your proposal.

For example, in urging contributions to a Thanksgiving Dinner Fund for needy families, one speaker began by describing in detail a family of five seated around an empty table. In his conclusion, he pictured the same family. But this time their table had ample provisions upon it. Would *you* have been able to resist this dramatic and stirring appeal?

## ACTIVITIES

1. You are speaking on the importance of the right to vote. You have stressed the obligation of all citizens of this country to exercise this right. Prepare for classroom delivery the following types of conclusions for your speech:
   The quotation
   The incident or example
   The story or anecdote
   Repetition of an assumed introduction
2. Select a topic of your own in which you use each of the above types of conclusions.
3. In the Speaker's Kit, found later in this book, choose examples of quotations, incidents, stories or anecdotes, and humor which would make forceful conclusions. Suggest specific topics for which these conclusions could be used.

## Conclusions that stimulate acceptance of your specific purpose

Any of the summaries mentioned previously may, of course, stimulate your audience to accept your point of view. But sometimes you will want to make your ending even more compelling. Here are techniques that will do just this:

**Appeal to the emotions.** Many of us will do things while emotionally aroused that we would not do in a calmer mood. It is also true that many of us may later regret actions and decisions made under the spur of emotion. You may choose to arouse your audience to the point that it will accept what you want in a sort of involuntary outburst of feeling. In such cases, however, you must also be willing to accept responsibility for the audience's later reaction.

Appeals to the emotions should be made only in the most serious situations. Otherwise they become ridiculous if the situation does not warrant them. In most of your high school speeches, such strong pleas will not be justified. Nor should you attempt to use them. But sometime, now or later, you will give a speech that you will regard as all important to yourself and to your audience. Then you will need to know exactly how to go about this so that your listeners will be strongly motivated to make a decision favorable to you.

Among the most successful examples of this type of conclusion is that used by Sir Winston Churchill after the fall of Dunkirk. Speaking to the British Parliament on May 14, 1940, Sir Winston concluded his speech with these memorable, defiant, and soul-stirring words:

"We shall go on to the end, we shall fight in France, we shall fight in the seas and oceans, we shall fight with growing confidence and with growing strength in the air, we shall defend our island, whatever the cost may be, we shall fight on the beaches, we shall fight on the landing-grounds, we shall fight in the fields and in the streets, we shall fight in the hills; we shall never surrender, and even if, which I do not for a moment believe, this island or a large part of it were subjugated and starving, then our Empire beyond the seas, armed and guarded by the British Fleet, would carry on the struggle, until, in God's good time, the New World with all its power and might, steps forth to the rescue and liberation of the Old."

**Visualize the future.** This method can well be combined with others that have been presented. You seek belief or action by asking the listener to picture differing futures if the desired course is or is not accepted.

There are two forms of such visualization—positive and negative. In the positive form, you make the listener see what will happen if he follows the recommended course. In the negative, you picture what will happen if he does not follow your proposed course. Either or both may be effective. A high school student in a speech advocating a heavy program of life insurance used both positive and negative visualization in working out a strong conclusion:

"What, then, is actually in store for the average family with two children if the father dies uninsured? Poverty! A small word. But it spells the loss of a full-time mother for these children. It spells the loss of educational opportunities. It spells the loss of recreational opportunities and cultural opportunities. It even spells the loss of adequate medical care.

"But what if the father dies adequately insured? The home is kept. The mother remains a mother. The children can go to college. They can also enjoy normal recreational, cultural, and medical opportunities. What is in store for *your* family?"

**Suggest a definite action.** One of the best ways of concluding a persuasive type of speech is to suggest an immediate and specific action that can be taken by the audience. Even though the speech may have been on a somewhat general theme, the conclusion should suggest a definite course of action.

In a speech on religion, a student stressed the contributions that religion offered his particular community. The speech was meticulously non-denominational. It had been largely informative. But the speaker strengthened his speech by using a persuasive type of ending: "This week attend, at least once, the religious meeting of your choice."

## ◄ POINTERS THAT PAY OFF ►

1. Don't introduce new material in your conclusion.
2. Use short, forceful sentences.
3. Don't threaten or antagonize in trying to be forceful.
4. Avoid the habit of using "In conclusion," "In summary," or "Finally" several times before you actually reach your conclusion.
5. Stay away from weak endings like "Well, I guess that's all."
6. Avoid stopping too abruptly.
7. Have a strong concluding sentence. Memorize it!

## ACTIVITIES

1. Find some well-known speeches that appeal to the emotions such as those given by Patrick Henry, Daniel Webster, or William Jennings Bryan. Copy the conclusions and read them to the class.
2. Bring to class a stirring conclusion to a magazine article.
3. Prepare a conclusion that visualizes the future.
4. Prepare a conclusion that suggests definite action.
5. Assume that you are planning to give a speech urging all seniors in your school to donate blood to the Red Cross. You will discuss these points:

   The need for blood is greater today than ever before.
   The process is not painful.
   The process cannot harm a healthy individual.
   The donation will be made in the office of the school nurse.

For this speech prepare a single conclusion that: (a) appeals to the emotions, (b) makes use of visualization (positive, negative, or both), (c) suggests a specific course of action.

THE SATURDAY EVENING POST

"Well, I see my time is up . . ."

## PRONUNCIATION PROBLEMS

Three difficulties occur in producing distinctly the sound of the tongue consonant "l":

1. It may be weakened before the "y" sound as in "million" and "will you."
2. It may be weakened or dropped before these letters—**b**, p, v, f, g, and k.
3. It may be weakened at the end or in the middle of words.

The lists below will give you words to practice in overcoming each difficulty.

**LIST NO. 1**

| | | | |
|---|---|---|---|
| million | billion | will you | drill you |
| William | trillion | call you | kill you |
| Lillian | cotillion | sell you | fool you |
| stallion | medallion | tell you | pull you |
| dahlia | battalion | bill you | spoil you |
| billiard | cilia | fill you | foil you |

**LIST NO. 2**

| | | | | |
|---|---|---|---|---|
| bulb | help | self | selves | bulk |
| mulberry | pulp | shelf | elves | sulk |
| bulbous | gulp | belfrey | shelves | hulk |
| filbert | culprit | gulf | delve | mulct |
| halberd | pulpit | golf | valves | silk |
| jailbird | scalp | wolf | velvet | milk |

**LIST NO. 3**

| | | | | |
|---|---|---|---|---|
| owl | rule | silly | delicate | lolling |
| all | royal | lullaby | hallelujah | nullify |
| knell | hall | lily | lollipop | roll call |
| school | pale | sullen | billow | roly-poly |
| ball | lull | filthily | dollar | solely |
| goal | pool | doily | collar | Pullman |

## READING CHECK-UP

Read aloud the nonsense sentences below to check your pronunciation of any problem words.

Silly William is lolling in the swimming pool until the knell of the school bell and the roll call of the class are completed and he will be called to the cotillion.

High-wheeled wagons rolled on across the fields where helping hands toiled for daily bread. Mules pulling through the tall grass and deep gullies strained at the pulley until they nearly killed themselves.

Milly and Tilly were two silly elves in the Halloween ballad who crawled into the belfry to toll the bell and then slid hastily into bowls on the shelf to hide themselves.

"This will kill you!" the sullen dullard yelled as he pulled out his revolver from his velvet holster. "Help, help!" the delicate Lillian called, but the callous culprit growled, "You fool, you! Call your silly friends, but I can tell you I'll fill you and drill you full of lead before you can yell 'willy-nilly' or 'lollipop'."

The sullen child sulked over the spilled milk and the spoiled mulberries while her roly-poly poodle went rollicking up and down the hall after the yellow ball.

All of the owls left the belfry to sit in the tall, billowy elm tree and screech at the golfers when the golf balls rolled near the goal at the eighteenth hole.

Millions of yellow dahlia bulbs were sold to help the royal battalion in its battle to win the gold medallion.

## VOCABULARY **BUILD-UP**

Use the italicized words in short paragraphs to show that you understand their meanings.

*mediocre* talents
*potentially* dangerous
to *stagnate* indefinitely
*devoutly* dedicated
*obsessed* with the idea
a part of the *clique*
the *arrogance* of a dictator
a *dynamic* personality
to *liquidate* his holdings
*dire* predictions
insulting *epithets*
crudely *vituperative* quality
*feigning* surprise
a study of *logistics*

an *ebbing* interest
a *provocative* statement
*manifestly* unfair
*obstacle* course
an *arbitrary* ruling
to *jeopardize* the future
*disruption* of the economy
his personal *prestige*
less *obvious* advantage
accept the *status quo*
inclined to *digress*
*sibilant* sounds
a recent *proselyte*
a *benign smile*

CHAPTER

# 13 Speaking on Special Occasions

Most speeches to an hour-glass,
Do some resemblance show,
Because the longer time they run,
The shallower they grow.

—*Prochnow:*
*Speaker's Handbook of*
*Epigrams and Witticisms*

SPECIAL occasions call for special types of speeches which often require individual "recipes." The speeches described in this chapter cannot be classified exclusively as speeches to inform, to entertain, or to persuade. In most of them there is a combination of purpose. For example, telling jokes is usually associated with speeches to entertain, but you may use humorous stories with other speech purposes. The important thing is to know how to tell jokes in any appropriate speech situation.

In this chapter, you will find in capsule form the ingredients for a variety of speeches that you may be called on to give either in school or in situations out of school. You will learn also the special techniques peculiar to the types of speeches included here.

## Telling Jokes

"Have you heard the one about . . . . . ?" Six magic words for capturing attention! The joke *can* be a tonic for lagging conversation and a bright spot in almost any type of public speech *if* you know the kinds of jokes that bring laughs and *if* you know how to tell them. Americans are fun-loving people and they applaud those who can make them laugh. Every year entertainers make millions of dollars in the laugh business. Although you may not make money, there is no doubt that you will make friends if you know how to make people laugh.

Telling a joke requires a special technique. "Getting a laugh" is a somewhat unpredictable business. The same joke told to different audiences will bring different results. Likewise, the same joke told by different people to the same audience often results in various responses. Why? The same type of joke just doesn't appeal to all audiences. And certainly some people can tell jokes much better than others. Success in telling jokes depends upon the joke itself, the audience, and the person telling it.

## How to select a joke

**What kinds of jokes should you choose?** It is impossible to find one type of joke that will please all audiences. Yet you will be fairly certain of getting laughs if you pick one from any of the following categories:

***The ridiculous.*** People will laugh at the utterly ridiculous, the slapstick, or the farcical situation. Red Skelton, Bob Hope and Jerry Lewis have used this technique to achieve great fame.

***The unexpected.*** Jokes with surprise endings are usually surefire laugh-getters.

***The incongruous or out-of-place.*** In this type, the humor is gained by having the people perform out of character. For example, a dignified aristocrat might try to yodel or a country bumpkin might try to impersonate an English butler.

***Misunderstandings or misinterpretations.*** Examples of this are the "Dumb Dora" types. Jokes built around people who always miss the point or manage to get into confusing situations usually bring laughs.

***Accidental slips or unintentional humor.*** Many laughs arise from "fluffs" on radio and TV, slips of the tongue, and "Spoonerisms." You can create laughs either by repeating some of these or by deliberately inserting some of your own that you make up. For example, you might be talking about the habits of the salmon. As you tell about their going up the river every year to spawn, you might say, "Every year the salmon goes up the river to spoon . . . I mean, to spawn."

**What kinds of jokes should you avoid?** Although you may get a few laughs, you will not gain respect if you use any of the following types of jokes:

Obscene or off-color jokes
Jokes that offend by poking fun at people of special groups
Jokes that make fun of physical defects
Sharp, cutting jokes of a sarcastic nature
Dull jokes with no point to them
Creaky, stale jokes that most people have heard
Long, drawn-out jokes which build up to a terrible letdown
Private jokes which concern only two or three persons present
Jokes in which the audience can foresee the ending
Jokes that are not your style. (Dialect types are hard for most of you.)

## How to tell a joke

One discouraged student made this remark, "It doesn't make any difference how funny a joke is. When I tell it, it falls flat. I just can't be funny." Many of you may feel the same way. Actually, there are very few individuals who are naturally skilled in telling jokes or in making humorous remarks. The people you hear on

"He's got the whole thing backward.
I didn't say it like that at all."

television have been telling jokes and tossing off funny lines for years—that's their business and they've made a study of it. So don't feel discouraged. Skill comes through studying the techniques used by people whose style of joke-telling you enjoy. One of the best methods of learning how to tell jokes enjoyably is to practice them several times before attempting to relate them in front of an audience. You will feel more at ease if you are sure of the lines and if you have tried to repeat them often enough to give a smooth style to your delivery.

Some of the best pointers come from the "joke experts" who have been appearing before audiences for a long time. The suggestions that follow include the advice of several comedians and will help you improve your style.

## THE DO'S OF TELLING JOKES

Here are some proven suggestions on how to tell a joke well. Apply these carefully.

Know your joke thoroughly before starting it.

Make no apology for the story or your ability to tell it.

Personalize a joke—tell it as if it happened to you or to somebody in the crowd.

Stick to the original style, especially with dialogue—unless you feel that you can improve upon it.

Watch the length—don't draw out short, quickie types or cut short the ones which require a long build-up for the humor.

Build up carefully to the punch line. Be sure that everyone hears all of the words preceding the punch line.

Throw the punch line with vigor. Usually a slight pause immediately before the punch line will prepare the audience for it.

Stop when you have finished. Explaining or repeating the point is useless and annoying.

Speak out clearly and loudly enough to be heard easily. Lost lines mean lost laughs.

## THE DON'TS OF TELLING JOKES

If you fail to observe the following warnings, you can kill almost any joke.

Don't laugh your way through a joke.

Don't build it up too much at the beginning by saying, "This is positively the funniest joke I've heard in ages—I nearly died laughing—this one will really kill you. . . ."

Don't omit important early details. Having to correct yourself or saying, "Oh, I forgot to tell you . . ." lets the audience down.

Don't give away the point of the joke too soon.

Don't bog down at the end or forget the punch line.

Don't strain too hard to be funny. Over-acting is as bad as under-acting.

Don't be a "chain joker." Give the other person a chance.

Don't speak too fast. This is a primary cause of lost lines.

## How to listen to a joke

Listeners are important to the successful telling of a joke. With certain audiences you may find it almost impossible to tell a joke because some people may attempt to be funny by laughing at the wrong time or by not laughing at all. They often find other ways of interfering with your story. Some of the hazards involved are:

**Interrupting to correct minor details** such as—"No, his name was Frank, not Fred" or "It couldn't have been that year . . . . "

**Grabbing the other person's punch line** by saying it before the speaker has the chance to give it.

**Waiting until the end** and then saying, "Oh, I heard that when I was in the cradle!"

**Trying to outdo the speaker** by giving the same story the way you heard it.

**Daring somebody to make you laugh** by keeping a dead-pan expression.

A good rule for listeners is: **Be cooperative in sharing the laugh.**

## ACTIVITIES

Discuss with your class the following questions:

1. What types of jokes do you consider undesirable?
2. What mannerisms annoy you in joke tellers?
3. What are your opinions regarding excessive amounts of slang in telling a joke?
4. Which comedians on radio or television do you enjoy most? What is the secret of their success?
5. What are some of the devices that you can use in "selling" a joke?
6. What are some of the tricks in throwing a punch line?
7. What are some beginnings that you should avoid in telling a joke?
8. Explain what is wrong with the following remarks:

   "Well, there was this guy who went into this restaurant and there was this waitress who comes up to him andah . . . ."

   "I goes into this joint and I walks up to the man and I says to him, I says . . . ."

   "I saw this friend of mine . . . well, he wasn't exactly a friend . . . he was some guy I met in Florida . . . or was it Georgia? Come to think of it, it musta been in Michigan on account of it was ten years ago . . . the time I went to see my mother who was sick . . . no she wasn't sick that year . . . it musta been the year I went into the Army . . . where was I? Oh yes, that guy I met in the Army . . . what WAS that guy's name . . . ."

# After-Dinner Speeches

Few occasions afford you such an ideal opportunity for winning audience approval as the dinner meeting. Guests have come for the purpose of entertainment. You have a ready-made atmosphere of good will and conviviality. Your only task is to sustain that mood!

You may feel that learning how to give an after-dinner speech is a waste of time—that you will seldom have to give one. One student said, "Only older people and bigwigs give such speeches." That may have been true at one time, but certainly it isn't true now. If you become associated with any social or business group in your life, you will be attending dinner meetings and you will, undoubtedly, be called upon to help in some way as a speaker, a toastmaster, or a member of a committee.

Even in high school, clubs are adopting the custom of arranging banquets at least once a year. Perhaps you already have had experience in giving this type of speech. If not, be ready when the opportunity comes. Unless you are completely inactive socially, few of you will miss this chance. Know what is expected of you when you are invited to preside or to give a toast or an after-dinner speech.

## How to be a good toastmaster

**What is a toast?** The toast originated with the Greeks and Romans when they assembled to pay tribute to the gods or the dead. Later it was enlarged by the English to include kings, ladies, and other famous persons. The English added a piece of toast to the drink used and, thus, the name originated.

A toast is a very brief speech offered as a tribute of respect, honor, or sentiment. It may be offered to one person, a group of persons, an idea, a cause, or an institution. It can be in the form of prose or poetry. The contents may be humorous, serious, or sentimental. But always the toast must be brief, timely, original, and in harmony with the occasion.

**Tips for the toastmaster.** Presiding at any function is a great responsibility and a temptation as well. As master of ceremonies you must set the stage, establish the atmosphere, and "run the show." Therein lies the temptation. The audience expects you to be the central figure but they do not want you to "play center stage." They look to you for management in creating an atmosphere of perfect harmony and congenial fellowship, but this should be accomplished as unobtrusively as possible.

To be chosen toastmaster is a real honor. It indicates that you have poise, speaking ability, and leadership. You would not be chosen unless people respected you and felt that you were more qualified than anyone else to establish the mood and to introduce the speakers.

***Be prepared.*** Know the names of all speakers and the correct pronunciation of their names. Know the exact title of each speech. Find out in advance some facts about the speakers so that you can include any of interest in your introduction. Prepare all of your introductions so that notes will be unnecessary.

***Keep the program moving.*** Limit your own remarks to a few introductory statements concerning the purpose of the occasion. These remarks should establish an attitude of friendliness and companionship. Include a tribute to all who helped with the plans.

***Use good taste in introducing speakers.*** Your responsibility is to make the speakers feel at home—not wish they were there! Give every speaker a pleasant "send-off" and make the audience eager to hear from each. Here are some special points to observe in introducing speakers:

1. Begin with a few well-chosen complimentary remarks, but avoid flowery, fancy, or trite expressions. Be careful not to embarrass with too much praise.
2. *If* the occasion permits and *if* you feel sure that the speaker will not object, use a joke or anecdote. The anecdote may be true or applicable.
3. Let the speaker give his own speech. Don't attempt to express your own views first or to anticipate what you think he is going to say.
4. Avoid being too personal.

***Be courteous.*** Listen to the speeches instead of talking to the person next to you or rehearsing your next introduction. Express appreciation to the speakers at the conclusion of their speeches. Welcome distinguished guests who may be present, but don't ask for a speech without their permission.

In addition to the tips already mentioned, you should observe the good speech habits of speaking clearly and audibly. You will also be successful if you are poised, good-natured, and friendly.

## How to be a good after-dinner speaker

The ideal after-dinner speaker is one who can adapt himself and his speech to any mood or occasion. After-dinner speeches vary in type according to the nature of the meeting. In most cases, the sole purpose is entertainment. With business groups, the purpose

If you can't visualize yourself as toastmaster at this gala dinner at the Waldorf-Astoria, or in the capacity of Jack Benny giving the speech of entertainment, perhaps you can picture yourself as one of the guests. *(UPI Photo)*

may be to inform or to persuade. With some charitable organizations, the dinner meeting may serve as a means of stimulating and actuating those about to embark upon a fund-raising campaign. Or it might follow the conclusion of a campaign when members would be congratulated upon their efforts. Alumni banquets are usually reminiscent in type. Know, and be guided by, the occasion.

Four rules apply to all after-dinner speeches, however, regardless of type. These are:

1. The speech must be prepared carefully and preferably given without notes.
2. The speech must be appropriate for the occasion.
3. The speech must be interesting.
4. The speech should be kept within the time limit. Usually, it must be *brief*.

These rules remind you that your preparation should include finding out about (a) the purpose of the occasion, (b) the type of audience, (c) the general mood—if serious, gay, or sentimental, and (d) the general theme, if any.

After you have discovered these things, apply the essentials of any good speech. These include: (a) finding something to say that will be worthwhile and appropriate to the occasion, (b) arranging your remarks around a central theme—even jokes should be tied together by some relationship to a theme, and (c) using illustrative material such as jokes, quips, anecdotes, or quotations. You will find many helpful examples of illustrative material in the Speaker's Kit later in this book.

In presenting an after-dinner speech, be poised and speak without notes. Above all, observe the time limit. If you are ever tempted to speak too long, remember this thought—"Don't try to be immortal by being eternal." Often the easiest way to entertain people is to allow them to go home!

### ACTIVITIES

1. Find out all you can about the origin of the toast and the customs observed in various countries in connection with it.
2. Bring to class samples of toasts written in prose style, poetry style, and limerick style.
3. Work in groups of six with one as toastmaster and the others as after-dinner speakers. Decide on the type of organization that you will represent and the purpose of your dinner meeting. Present a program for the class.
4. Plan a dinner program for one of the following groups. Limit your plan to (a) a central theme, (b) speeches, readings, and music, and (c) titles for each. If your teacher and class are so inclined, you may want to include skits and novelty numbers.

| | |
|---|---|
| A foreign language club | A science club |
| A speech club | A camera club |
| A football team | A stamp or coin club |
| A Boy Scout group | A literary club |
| A Girl Scout group | A girls' athletic club |
| A dramatic club | A school publication group |

5. Although after-dinner speakers should not be called on without advance warning, some toastmasters violate this rule. Hold one class meeting in which the toastmaster digresses from the program by calling on members of the class to speak impromptu.

## Introducing Speakers

In addition to dinner meetings, you will have numerous opportunities to introduce speakers in assemblies, in club meetings, in church meetings, and in various organizations. Many of the facts that you learned about being a good toastmaster apply to all introductory situations. When you preside at formal meetings, you will be expected to display poise and dignity. These reminders will help you feel at ease in any situations in which you must introduce a speaker:

1. Be extremely cautious about using personal anecdotes or humor in introducing strangers. Sometimes what you intend to use as an "icebreaker" turns out to be an "iceberg." Before using personal references, consider the formality of the occasion and the personality of the speaker. It is wise to ask a speaker in advance if your planned introductory remarks are accurate and satisfactory to him.

2. Give only necessary information. A well-known person needs little more introduction than his name and subject and a few welcoming remarks. With speakers not known by the audience you should include (briefly):

The speaker's background
His present status or position
Qualifications which make him suited to speak on his subject
Any personal facts or interests similar to those of the audience

3. Don't make a production out of a simple speech of introduction. Simplicity of speech by the chairman is particularly appreciated and is always preferable to dramatic or elaborate flights of oratory.

4. Give the name of the speaker and the title of the speech at the *end*. You may wish to mention the name at the beginning *and* at the end. As you mention the speaker's name finally, turn to him while saying it. Pronounce the speaker's name correctly and clearly!

5. Observe the following suggestions so far as your own behavior is concerned:

Be gracious, courteous, friendly, and sincere in your attitude.

Remain standing until the speaker takes his place before the audience. Then seat yourself so that your presence will not be distracting or disturbing to the audience.

## Sample speeches of introduction

### BRIEF INTRODUCTION OF WELL-KNOWN PERSONS

"Members and guests: I wish to express the pleasure and gratitude of all of us in welcoming our distinguished guest, Fire Chief Johnston, who will speak on the subject, 'How to Avoid School Fires.' (Turning to speaker) Chief Johnston."

"Teachers and fellow-students: I am happy to introduce our chief speaker tonight, a person respected by all of us—our own principal, who will speak on the topic, 'Stand Up For Your School.' Mr. Marshall."

### INTRODUCTION OF SPEAKER NOT WELL KNOWN

"Teachers and fellow-students: We are unusually fortunate to have as our assembly speaker, Mr. Rolf Baker, who has served with distinction as a diplomat for our country. For the last twenty-seven years, he has been playing the difficult role of trouble-shooter in some of the most dangerous spots in the world. At present he is touring the United States speaking to high school audiences.

I am happy to present Mr. Baker who will speak on the subject, 'So You Think It Can't Happen Here!' Mr. Baker."

### INTRODUCTION USING HUMOR

"Our next speaker, Dick Roberts, claims that few persons ever listen to what you say at large gatherings. To prove his point, he was telling me about a wedding reception he attended recently. As he moved along the reception line, he purred sweetly, 'My grandmother just died today.'

" 'How nice.' 'Thank you so much.' 'How sweet of you to say so.' were some of the replies. No one had the slightest idea what he said, least of all the groom, who exclaimed jovially, 'It's about time you took the same step, old man!'

"I'm sure you will enjoy hearing what else Dick Roberts has to say about 'Listening, a Lost Art.' "

## A speaker's response to an introduction

Many forms of school, church, and club activities require student speakers. Perhaps you are the guest speaker instead of the person introducing the speaker. Be prepared for such occasions by knowing the correct response to make.

Wherever you may be, remain seated until the chairman has completed his introduction and spoken your name at the end.

After the introduction, walk confidently to the stage, take your place in the center, and begin. First, address the chairman by name and thank him for his remarks. Then address the audience. The simplest and most inclusive phrase is, "Ladies and Gentlemen." When distinguished guests are present, it may seem rude not to give them attention. Your salutation then might be: "Mr. Mayor, members of the city council, parents, teachers, and fellow students."

Under no circumstances should you address the dignitaries first and then refer to all the others as "ladies and gentlemen" or "friends." The reason is quite obvious. Use "ladies and gentlemen" and "friends" only as general greetings including everyone. Never use these as part of another greeting.

### ACTIVITY

Working in pairs with your classmates, prepare speeches of introduction and responses for ten occasions assigned by your teacher.

# Nomination and Acceptance Speeches

## How to nominate a candidate for an office

"I nominate Carol Fox for the president of student council." Sometimes, you make no further remarks. More often, however, you may be expected to give reasons why your candidate should be elected.

The purpose of a nomination speech is to inform and persuade. The nomination speech should balance the specific requirements of the position against the specific qualifications of your candidate. Like an apothecary's scale, one side should balance the other. Because of this balance, the speech should persuade the voters to vote for your nominee in preference to all the others. Therefore, it must be accurate in its details, well organized, and convincing in its presentation. The following criteria will serve as a guide in the preparation of a nominating speech:

1. State the requirements of the office.
2. Explain the type of person needed to fill the position.
3. Explain why your candidate is best fitted to meet all the needs and requirements by telling the following facts:

   Previous training for the position
   Previous experience in the same or similar type of position
   Ability as a leader and ability to get along with others
   Outstanding traits of personality or character
   Reputation among his friends and citizens in the community
   Any other specific facts about his record that should be known

4. Conclude with a convincing appeal to vote for your candidate.

## How to accept an office

The purpose of this type of speech is to inspire confidence and to impress the voters with the fact that you are the right person for the position. Don't make the mistake of thinking, however, that you should devote your speech to telling them how good you are. What should you tell them? Here are some acceptable suggestions:

1. Express your appreciation and gratitude for the honor conferred upon you.
2. Speak about the past record of the organization, its achievements, the principles for which it stands, and its ideals. Pledge your support in continuing this record.
3. Indicate that you realize the responsibility that rests upon you.

## Sample nomination and acceptance speeches

### SAMPLE NOMINATION SPEECH

Fellow students: You should elect Carol Fox president of student council because, to use only four words, *she's the best candidate!* Why is she the best? I'll give you the answer in just four points:

First, She's a great leader whom the students respect. Student council needs a leader!

Second, She was student council president in the 9th grade and has been president of four clubs in the last four years. Student council needs a president with previous experience.

Third, She's trustworthy and conscientious. When teachers and students want something done right, they ask Carol to do it. Student council is a responsible organization and needs a responsible president.

Fourth, She's had an excellent scholarship record, she can speak with poise and certainty in front of a group, she is fair and calm in discussion situations, and she can work with any kind of student without arousing antagonism. Student council needs a president with such ability. Therefore, if you want a president we can be proud of, vote for Carol Fox.

### SAMPLE ACCEPTANCE SPEECH

Fellow students: I want to thank all of you for the honor you've given me. Our student council is well known not only here but in other towns for its many achievements and new ideas that it has put into successful operation. We have an enviable reputation. Other schools model their councils after ours. I know that any president has a real responsibility in living up to past standards. I'm sincerely grateful that you trust me enough to carry on our splendid record. You can be sure that I'll show my true appreciation not only in words, but in deeds. Let's all work together and make the next student council even better than the last one!

### ACTIVITY

Work in pairs with a classmate, with one making the nomination speech and the other giving the acceptance speech for an office.

# Presentation and Acceptance Speeches

"I am pleased to present to Miss Martha Allen a . . . . " There will be times when you may be speaking the above words or will be responding to them. Ceremonies in which gifts and awards are presented occur often in high school and continue to occur after school. Although such occasions call for brief speeches, you may become even too confused or embarrassed to say the few words required unless you know what is expected of you. Learn now a few simple rules to guide you.

## Presenting a gift or award

When you are making the presentation speech, you are giving recognition or paying tribute to one or more individuals for some outstanding quality, act, skill, or service. Simplicity and sincerity are the two essentials of such a speech. Express appreciation, congratulations, and praise as simply and earnestly as possible. An easy and acceptable organization to use is:

1. Refer to the specific occasion.
2. Pay tribute to the recipient.
3. Give the reason for presenting the gift or award.
4. Explain the character or purpose of the award.

## Accepting a gift or award

First of all, find out if you have to make a speech. If you are one in a large group receiving the same honor, merely smile and say "Thank you." If you are the only honored guest or one of a chosen few, you should make a short acceptance speech.

The shortest of all acceptance speeches is probably that of the graduate receiving her diploma. *(Monkmeyer)*

Prepare a short speech in advance, memorize it, and then speak sincerely and modestly. Don't bubble over with enthusiasm or become too sentimental or maudlin. People like to know that you appreciate a gift, but they don't want to see you put on an emotional scene. Select your words wisely. In other words, express your appreciation of the honor, your gratitude for the gift, and your pleasant association with the people present.

### ACTIVITY

Working with your classmates in groups of appropriate size, present and accept a specific gift or award.

## Speeches of Welcome and Response

"Welcome home!" are two of the most appreciated words in our language. Sometimes, you say "We're glad to have you here" when a visitor arrives to spend time at your school or in any one of your organizations. Such a greeting when spoken warmly and sincerely is pleasing to any guest.

Whenever one or more individuals arrive for a visit, move into your community, or come home after an absence, you often arrange a reception in their honor. On such occasions, one person usually gives a speech welcoming the guest or guests and one of the guests so honored responds to the speech of welcome.

### Giving a speech of welcome

If you are selected to give a speech of welcome, think of yourself as a host welcoming a guest at a reception in your own home. What would you say?

First, you would want the honored guest to meet all of your other guests. You would identify him by giving his name and any unusual facts concerning his talents, ability, interests, occupation, and any special achievement. Your first thought, therefore, would be to establish a friendly relationship.

In addition, you would undoubtedly express your pleasure in having the guest present and you would certainly offer any possible assistance that might add to the comfort and enjoyment of your guest.

In welcoming strangers, your speech should contain the same ideas mentioned above. You should speak with warmth, friendliness, and sincerity in order to make your words ring true.

### Responding to a speech of welcome

If you happen to be the guest or a spokesman for several guests, you should be ready with a brief, sincere response expressing appreciation for the hospitality extended to you. You would want to assure your host that you are pleased to be present and that you are looking forward to the opportunity of becoming better acquainted. Acknowledge any special tributes contained in the welcoming speech and voice your gratitude for anything else of special note.

The perfect guest adds warmth and sincerity of voice when he responds. You want everyone to see and hear that you really mean what you are saying.

## Commemoration Speeches

A commemorative speech is one that celebrates a memorable occasion or event. It usually is somewhat solemn in theme and is delivered with formality and dignity. You will probably want to write out such a speech and memorize it verbatim so that your delivery will be easy and graceful.

Events requiring commemorative speeches are those which honor a person, a group of people, or the completion of something worth remembering. Some examples are: dedication of a building or other project, a eulogy to some person or idea, and special anniversaries of all kinds.

The basic element of all speeches of this type is the expression of praise and tribute. You can follow practically the same pattern for all of them. Begin with a reference to the event or person being honored; give the reasons why tribute is due; express your tribute simply and sincerely in a manner that will be impressive; and conclude with an expression of gratitude or appreciation for the memorable deeds or accomplishments.

A perfect example of the commemorative speech is Lincoln's Gettysburg Address, which was cited earlier in Chapter 10. In ten sentences, he paid tribute to the soldiers who had fought on that battlefield. His words, so simply and sincerely spoken, will never be forgotten.

You may never be called upon to prepare a dedication speech, but occasions requiring eulogies or anniversary-type speeches are numerous. Eulogies are speeches which praise either the living or the dead and, on rare occasions, inanimate objects, abstract ideas,

Queen Elizabeth II reads a commemorative speech at the dedication of the St. Lawrence Seaway. *(UPI Photo)*

and even animals. Whenever you offer praise to a person, thing, or idea, you are presenting a eulogy. Sometimes you devote an entire speech to eulogizing, but more often you include remarks of praise in other speeches such as those telling about interesting people or contributions to mankind by scientists, inventors, artists, or members of the clergy.

In your own experience, you often wish to praise a hero at your school or in your community. It may be that a group of athletes, musicians, debaters, or journalists have won recognition and you want to honor them in a formal manner in an assembly program, in your school paper, or at a banquet. Whenever you do so, you prepare a eulogistic type of speech.

Anniversaries also present opportunities for praise. Birth dates of famous people, special holidays, anniversaries of alumni groups, Mother's Day, and Father's Day are a few of the anniversary occasions celebrated with speeches of praise.

## ACTIVITIES

1. Prepare a speech of eulogy for a person either living or dead.
2. Prepare a eulogy for a special group.
3. Present a speech for an anniversary.

# The Graduation Speech

Although the speech which a representative of a class delivers at graduation time is commemorative in type, it differs slightly from the typical commemorative speech. In its broadest interpretation, it is a farewell speech.

A student who was selected to make the graduation speech for her class looked everywhere for a ready-made one in the hope that she could at least use it as a model. Finally she sought help from her speech teacher. "What in the world are you supposed to say in a commencement speech? They all sound alike when I hear them and they don't seem to say anything!"

Her teacher explained that her speech should be a farewell tribute to those who had helped the class during its four years in school. Those receiving tribute would include parents, teachers, school administrators, and any others who had had some part in influencing the lives of the graduates. After praising and expressing appreciation of all these people, she should next mention the pleasant association of the members of the class with each other and

Fortunate is the audience that will listen to this valedictorian's well-planned and thought-out graduation speech. *(Monkmeyer)*

with the faculty, referring to the associations, activities, and outstanding events of their high school career. Then she should turn her attention to the future.

This teacher's advice furnishes a workable recipe for the commencement speech. Look backward to praise, express appreciation, and mention the highlights of your school career. Look forward to speak confidently about the future. The graduation is the ending of a high school career, but more important is the fact that it marks the "commencement" of a new experience. Keep this in mind as you choose the central idea that you are going to develop. Give your audience a speech to remember so that they will go away thinking that you really said something worthwhile. Poetry selections or quotations of an inspirational nature will help to provide such a theme and will make your speech dignified and impressive.

## The Job Interview

The special types of speeches you have been preparing thus far are associated with social or impressive occasions.

Of greater importance to you, however, may be the business occasion such as the interview for a job, a professional appointment, or entrance into a college. This is a real situation in which you wish to appear at your best. You know that you have to sell yourself if you are to succeed. Suddenly, speech becomes an all-important thought in your mind. "What will I say? How can I talk to someone I don't even know?" will be among the questions that will fly around in your mind as you wonder how to impress that important person who will be sitting on the other side of the desk.

Although speech is a large determining factor in creating a favorable impression, there are several ways in which you can lay the groundwork even before you enter an office. Before you start worrying about what to say, take care of these preliminaries: (1) make an appointment in advance, (2) arrive early, (3) prepare yourself, (4) dress appropriately, and (5) watch your manners.

### Make an appointment in advance

Write a letter or telephone the office to see if it will be convenient to have an interview. Give your name and the reason you want the interview. In requesting an appointment, be sure that you let the person you wish to see set up the time for the conference at his convenience.

## Arrive early

Punctuality is an essential in all kinds of work. If you are late, any employer will receive an unfavorable impression before he sees you. The advantages of arriving early are that you have time to relax, organize your thoughts, and become calm while waiting for your name to be called.

When the door opens, you and the employer are face to face. Those first few moments are usually tense ones for you. Who speaks first? What should you say? Ordinarily, most business men rise to greet you, say "Good morning" first, shake hands with you and invite you to sit down. Your interviewer will want to know personal facts such as your age, education, and training. You will want to know many details concerning the position such as the territory to be covered, working arrangements, salary, possibilities of advancement, hours, and many others. Usually, therefore, an interview consists of a series of questions and answers between the employer and the prospective employee. While an employer listens to you, he is also making mental notes about your personality. He judges you by what he hears and sees.

## Prepare yourself

Try to think of some of the questions that you are likely to be asked in your interview and to work out in advance the most appropriate answers. It is also a good idea for you to do some thinking about what you will want to learn in the interview and to work out some questions of your own. Finally, as all interviews are not always all business, you may want to keep some good general topics of conversation in mind.

## Dress appropriately

What does that mean? In the broadest sense, it means wearing clothes suitable for the type of work or the position which you want. If you are to associate with professional people, you will be expected to dress in keeping with others in the same position. If you arrive for an interview dressed according to the standards followed by people in the same category, you will take another step forward in the estimation of the employer.

You are always safe in wearing a neat, clean, and conservative outfit. Discard the fads of high school attire which are associated mainly with your own age group. In business, you are expected to be decorous in appearance and actions.

After these preliminaries are over, a job interviewer must judge your character and personality by what he sees and hears. Say it well! *(Monkmeyer)*

## Watch your manners

During an interview, your manners are always on display. Your behavior toward an interviewer will show how you are likely to behave on the job. After the conversation starts, do your part to keep it moving in a courteous, friendly manner. That implies that you should follow all of the good conversational habits discussed earlier. You should be especially careful about the following ones:

1. Look at your interviewer, listen carefully, and respond to questions in a co-operative manner. Give complete and straightforward answers.
2. Don't interrupt.
3. Use good grammar, your best voice and articulation. You've learned what these are. Now use them to speak well for you!
4. Speak with assurance and self-confidence, but avoid acting over-confident or conceited.
5. Know when to leave. Usually the interviewer will give you the cue by rising or making a conclusive remark such as, "Thank you for stopping in to see us. We'll keep your application on file (or we'll call you)."
6. Thank the interviewer for his time and interest.

7. Leave a typed résumé of your experience and qualifications. This should include at least the following information:

Your name, address, phone number, and social security number

Your educational background, special training, experience, and qualifications for the job

Why you left last job and why you want this particular job

Your ambitions and future plans for a career

Salary expected or willing to accept

Your clubs, interests, hobbies, and activities

Names of references. (You should have permission of those whose names you give as references.)

8. Following your interview, it may be wise to write a thank-you note for the time and consideration shown you. This thoughtfulness on your part may swing the decision in your favor.

## ACTIVITIES

Work in pairs with a classmate as you practice these interviews in class. In each case the person applying for the job should have a résumé ready to present. Prepare a rating sheet including the facts you have learned in this chapter. Judge each other's performance carefully. Offer friendly suggestions for improvement.

1. Select the kind of position you hope to hold eventually. Plan an interview with your would-be employer.
2. Apply for a part-time job that you would like to have.
3. Select a want ad from your paper. Plan an interview for the job.
4. Bring to class a want ad and exchange it with someone else. Take turns with this partner applying for the jobs advertised.

## PRONUNCIATION PROBLEMS

Below is a list of words with troublesome endings. When an "s" is preceded by certain letter combinations, it is hard to pronounce. Use the words below to test your distinctness in articulation. Make up *five tongue twisters* from the list.

| | | | | |
|---|---|---|---|---|
| depths | months | ghosts | nests | husks |
| breadths | lathes | posts | casts | discs |
| widths | mouths | mists | masts | facts |
| lengths | moths | fists | contrasts | expects |
| eighths | clothes | wrists | broadcasts | defects |
| ninths | cloths | frosts | hosts | affects |
| fourths | oaths | boasts | guests | directs |
| elevenths | paths | thrusts | tests | shafts |
| tenths | scythes | insists | pests | lifts |
| fifths | seethes | coasts | tastes | tufts |
| sixths | sheaths | hoists | lists | rifts |

## READING CHECK-UP

Read aloud the nonsense sentences below to check your pronunciation of any problem words.

They used their scythes many months clearing paths for the youths who were hosts to the guests who brought artists' gifts from far-away coasts.

Wasps in their nests frightened the guests, and tests for pests followed lists of requests on broadcasts for the deaths of insects including moths who live for months in clothes before effects of their wastes can be seen.

The youths won many fourths, fifths, and sixths in the tests but never any firsts. Their tasks were to figure widths, lengths, breadths, and depths to hundredths or thousandths.

Four-fifths of the artists and seven-eighths of the casts knew the risks when the mists settled over the gulfs and the masts were lowered.

Amidst the mists and coldest frosts,
With stoutest wrists and loudest boasts,
He thrusts his fists against the posts,
And still insists he sees the ghosts.

## VOCABULARY BUILD-UP

Use the italicized words in short paragraphs to show that you understand their meanings.

a *tranquilizing* effect
a *baleful* look
a woman's *intuition*
an *optimistic* outlook
a *premonition* of danger
attempts to *contrive*
*mutually* acceptable
*illusions* of power
an *anthology* of poetry
a *phenomenal* success
a *sinister* expression
*adept* in dealing with others
in the process of *litigation*
*egregious* nonsense
the press *claque*
a *penchant* for writing
an *ambulatory* patient
to *surmount* all difficulties
a *grueling* experience
a *perilous* undertaking
no other *alternative*
to *retrieve* a loss
greater than his *predecessor*
behaving like a *renegade*
facing *annihilation*
rising *antagonism*
*chronic* ailments
an *altruistic* nature
a *cogent* argument
ready to *capitulate*
a need for *recapitulation*
*salutary* effects

CHAPTER

# 14 Delivering Your Speech

> Isn't it peculiar that the human brain begins to function from the moment you are born, improves as you grow older, then stops completely when you stand up to talk?
>
> —*Anonymous*

WHEN you order a blue cashmere sweater to be delivered as a gift to a friend, you expect your friend to receive a blue cashmere sweater. Unless the saleswoman misunderstood you, your gift should be delivered according to your instructions to her.

Delivering a speech is quite different from delivering a gift. You can never be sure that the message which leaves your lips will be received exactly as you sent it because of the many possibilities that words may be lost in transit or misunderstood if received. Such mishaps occur because of the intricate processes involved in communicating thought. A thought originates first in your mind. You then attempt to put your thought precisely into words. But even after you have the right words, you can't wrap up your words and send them! Instead, you must change your words into a series of lip and tongue movements. What you finally send out to your audience as you start talking is not your idea or even your words, but simply a pattern of sound waves. The sound waves travel through the air and strike the eardrums of those within hearing distance. After the sound waves have been received, then translated by the listener into his words, they are finally given meaning. This series of translations to be effective must produce in the listener's mind the same thought which originated in your mind.

Do you realize now how easily your thoughts can be changed in transit or even be lost completely? Do you understand the importance of speaking in such a manner that listeners *cannot fail* to hear your words exactly as you say them and to interpret your ideas exactly as you mean them? If so, you are ready to consider the elements involved in establishing contact with your listeners or audience. To state these in terms of positive responsibilities on your part, you must (a) impress others audibly, (b) impress others visibly, (c) impress others psychologically, and (d) select and use the type of delivery that is best adapted to the audience, the occasion, and to you.

## How to Impress Others Audibly

A poorly trained violinist can ruin the greatest masterpiece, even though he plays it on a Stradivarius. He has not learned how to use the violin nor has he learned how to interpret music. Different musicians may use the same instrument and play the same selection, but you will enjoy some much more than others. This is also true of speakers.

Think of your vocal mechanism as a sound-producing instrument and of yourself as the musician using it. Are you making the best use of it, or are you "playing" it in a haphazard manner with no attempt to create enjoyment for your listeners? Above all, will your interpretation be such that your audience will receive the exact impression you wish to convey?

After preparing an intelligent expression of your ideas, you naturally want to speak as accurately as possible so that no words will be garbled in transit. Here are some of the best ways you can help your listeners:

### Use variety in voice and speech

Monotony is deadly, but "variety's the very spice of life." You may vary (a) the loudness of your voice, (b) the pitch of your voice, (c) the quality of your voice, (d) the rate of your speaking, and (e) the total pattern in which you combine all these elements to give emphasis to your words.

**Speak with varied loudness.** As you learned in Chapter 5, "Listening to Yourself," two basic faults in controlling loudness are speaking too softly and speaking too loudly.

Obviously, when you speak so softly that others cannot hear you, there seems to be little reason to speak. If you have this problem, try speaking particularly to the last row. Ask those in the back of the room to keep their hands raised until they can hear you. Most of you can talk loudly enough, but until others help you, you may not know how much volume to use. You are like an automatic furnace; if the thermostat is set too low, the house will be cold no matter how big the furnace is. Let your classmates be your thermostat.

Since shouting puts an unpleasant strain on the eardrums, speaking too loudly can interfere with accurate audibility. People may try to listen, but their listening pleasure will be decreased to the point that they may have heard but not remembered much of what you said. To overcome this fault, again ask for certain signals from the audience to warn you when your voice becomes too loud. Because speaking with proper loudness depends upon the size of the room, many of you will have difficulty adjusting your voices unless others feed back to you the information you need.

But once you have established, with the aid of your classmates and teacher, good basic loudness levels for yourself while speaking, you must learn to vary your loudness. Speaking at the same level

"LOUDER!"

THE SATURDAY EVENING POST

of loudness gives a monotonous effect. Trained speakers use degrees of loudness for emphasis and holding attention. Have you noticed how closely you listen when a speaker drops his voice to practically a stage whisper? In the same way that the fine print on a document catches your eye, words spoken at a lower level than usual catch your attention.

**Speak with varied pitch.** Pitch, as the term is used here, refers both to range and inflection. Your pitch range is the difference between your lowest and highest pitches; your inflections are pitch glides that you make on single sounds or syllables. Few untrained speakers realize how effective pitch change can be. The well-known actor, E. H. Sothern, in his famous rendering of Shylock's speech, used a range of over two octaves and single inflections of a full octave and more. Although such changes would be extreme in many speech situations, talking within a pitch range of only a few notes is comparable to picking out a guitar selection using only one string. Use high notes *part* of the time, low notes *part* of the time, and in-between notes *most* of the time.

Changing your pitch gives inflection to your voice. Inflection makes your voice easy to listen to, interesting, and pleasing. In conversation, you probably speak quite naturally with various inflections to express your true feeling. When you say "How exciting!" your voice goes up. Your voice goes down as you say "I'm so sorry." When you are confident, your inflection goes up and down in saying "I know I can do it." There is seldom any monopitch when you express genuine feelings in conversation.

Beware of monopitch when you speak in public. Such delivery lulls an audience to sleep or into a state of indifference. In either case, your meaning is lost in transit. Many well-prepared speeches are labeled dull because the speaker delivered the words but not the meaning.

To overcome monopitch, practice your speech as if you were talking with one or two of your friends. Think how you would say it to them to capture their attention and interest. Your voice range will increase and your inflection will go up and down naturally in your rehearsal. Try to keep similar range and inflection when you deliver the speech in public.

**Speak with varied quality.** Another way to overcome monotony and to add meaning to your speaking is to adjust your voice quality to the *mood* of the words you are speaking. Can you imagine Patrick Henry saying meekly, "I know not what course others may take; but as for me, give me liberty or give me death"? Or can you

Practice on a tape recorder is an excellent way to find out if you need greater variety in your voice and speech. *(Jay-Vee)*

imagine a strong voice booming out these words of Sydney Carton as he went to his death, "It is a far, far better rest that I go to than I have ever known"?

Any one sentence may be said in a variety of moods, but your voice must convey the one intended or the meaning will be lost. The following sentence may be expressed in all the moods indicated.

With scorn: You won the prize!
With happiness: You won the prize!
With affection: You won the prize.
With surprise: You won the prize?
With disappointment: You won the prize.

Obviously, a great deal of your speaking will be done in your normal voice. But you must be prepared to use many variations of your basic voice quality in different speaking situations. Don't try to make your voice throb with emotion when you announce a fifteen-minute change in your homeroom schedule. But don't talk about human rights in the same voice with which you buy tooth paste at the store.

**Speak with varied rate.** Monotony in speaking occurs also when you talk at the same rate of speed. Speaking too slowly or too rapidly throughout a speech makes listening difficult. In conversation, you talk rapidly when you are excited and slowly when you are considering serious problems. It is only natural that your speaking tempo will vary according to your mood. Introduce these same natural changes in your public speaking.

All music is written with changes in tempo. Literature contains countless examples of changes to heighten interest and to build toward a climax. Your speaking should provide the same kind of variety in rate.

**Speak with varied emphasis.** Effective emphasis depends upon a combination of the four vocal elements just discussed: loudness, pitch, quality, and rate. If you emphasize only by talking louder, or by speeding up, or by lowering your pitch, your very pattern of emphasis will become a kind of monotony. You must learn to combine all of these elements in a *flexible* pattern.

As you know, failure to emphasize any words or the wrong words robs your message of meaning. On the other hand, to overemphasize is to give no emphasis. When you prepare a speech, you alone know what meaning you wish to convey to the audience. It is your responsibility to transfer that exact meaning through emphasizing the key words so that your audience correctly interprets your ideas. Beware of drifting into a *voice pattern,* a term used to describe the habit of always emphasizing the first, second, or any other word in the series, so that every sentence has the same rhythm. Such meaningless emphasis is not only monotonous but makes you sound more like a mechanical robot than a human speaker.

To show the importance of emphasis, notice how the meaning changes when you emphasize different words in the same sentence:

*Why* did you blame him?
Why *did* you blame him?
Why did *you* blame him?
Why did you *blame* him?
Why did you blame *him*?

Which words would you emphasize in Lincoln's famous quotation, "government of the people, by the people, and for the people"? What techniques of emphasis would you use? What meaning do you think Lincoln wished to convey? What are the key words—government? people? or the series of prepositions?

Study your own speeches carefully to find the key words that stress your meaning. Practice aloud until you are sure that you are emphasizing flexibly the right words. Not only will audiences understand you better, but they will enjoy listening to you.

You are the sole agent in impressing your audience audibly.

It is not only *what* you say but *how* you say it. If you use all of the suggestions given in this section, you can be sure that the audience will want to hear you and they will be able to understand you.

### Use clear oral language

To ensure better listening, use familiar words that are clear and unmistakable in meaning. Although some of you may be tempted to use long words merely to show off your knowledge of them, the audience would rather hear words that *they* know than words that *you* know.

Some of the most memorable statements in history have contained short, simple, action-packed words. Could any audience fail to understand and respond to the examples below? Could you improve upon any of them?

"I came. I saw. I conquered."
"I only regret that I have but one life to lose for my country."
"Thou shalt not kill."
"There is nothing to fear but fear itself."
"United we stand, divided we fall."

Here are some short but strong words:

*go, join, act, buy, note, do, help, work,* and *give.*

The surest way of obtaining action in words is to use active verbs. For any speech purpose, the best words are those which strike a response clearly and unmistakably.

### ◄ POINTERS THAT PAY OFF ►

1. Speak in complete sentences—avoid sentence fragments unless they contribute to forcefulness and are understandable.
2. Separate sentences by stopping at the end of each one before going on with the next.
3. Eliminate the use of "and" between sentences.
4. Use shorter sentences in preference to long, involved ones in which the audience may forget the beginning before you reach the end.
5. Try to speak fluently with no "er's" and "uh's."

## How to Impress Others Visibly

Have you ever seen inexperienced students trying to conduct a school orchestra? Or have you watched TV programs in which the orchestra leader called upon some members of the audience to conduct? Usually, such acts are for fun, but they illustrate what happens when musicians try to follow meaningless signals.

The expressive gestures of the well-known conductor, Leonard Bernstein, speak eloquently to gain the desired response from his orchestra. *(Inger Abrahamsen)*

The trained conductor provides the right interpretation through visible signals which the orchestra follows. The untrained conductor, unable to read notes and unfamiliar with the visible signals to give to the musicians, makes up a series of meaningless gestures which fail to provide anything but laughter.

How does this apply to speaking? Your audience will respond to your visible signals as automatically as an orchestra does to those of a conductor.

Shakespeare advised, ". . . suit the action to the word." Centuries later, William Norwood Brigance stated: "Every speaker gives two speeches simultaneously, one with words, and one with actions . . . when words say one thing, and actions say another, the listener usually lets the words go by and gives attention to the action." Both of these quotations are another way of saying, "Actions speak louder than words."

Often you will say, "Do you see what I mean?" Although your question implies, "Do you understand what I mean?" you are closer to the truth than you think by using the word "see." For instance, when you travel in countries where you don't know the native language, you can make yourself understood to a certain extent by sign language. Some movements are almost universal in meaning, like nodding your head to mean "Yes," shaking your head to mean "No," shrugging your shoulders to indicate "Who knows?" or "I'm doubtful," or pointing at something to say "This is what I mean." Your hands, head, and eyes speak for you in every language. Make them help in transmitting your exact meaning to an audience.

In conversation, your entire body swings into action as you talk. The same freedom of action should take place as you speak in front of an audience.

Watch a football player telling about an exciting moment in a game; observe an elated student relating how he won a contest; or notice a jubilant father telling about his newborn baby. The entire body registers happiness and excitement. Joy, anger, fear, despair, grief, and all other feelings are almost impossible to conceal entirely.

Since others can see many telltale signs as they watch you deliver a speech, your speech in action must correspond with your speech in words. If not, as Brigance states, people may heed your actions instead of your words.

In considering what others see, pay particular attention to (1) eye contact, (2) facial expression, (3) gesture, (4) platform movement, and (5) posture. Posture, the action of standing, sitting, and walking, has already been discussed in Chapter 7. The others will be explained here.

## Eye contact

Eye contact means that by actually meeting the glances of your audience you can establish and maintain a relationship with them. It is vital that you learn to face your listeners and make eye contact with them. Each listener is important; you make him feel his importance by including him with your eyes. Think how frustrating it is to people if they watch you constantly but you never even glance at them! If you always look above them, watch some inanimate object on the wall, stare at the ceiling, contemplate the floor, gaze out of the window, or concentrate on one portion of the room or even on one person, what possible interest can the audience have in watching you? How can you communicate to them under these circumstances? You can't hit a baseball by staring at the sky or the bleachers. You can't drive home a message, either, by looking at the ceiling.

Looking at your audience serves another useful purpose besides pleasing your listeners. You can gauge reactions, judge responses, and determine how well your audience is following you. If you detect pleased attention you are encouraged. Your enthusiasm will mount and, as a direct result, your entire delivery will be improved. Nothing can be more gratifying to you than watching an audience respond pleasantly.

You should be quick to notice, also, if your listeners appear puzzled or bored. If they do, you are failing to communicate adequately. Your responsibility, in that event, is not to give up but to work harder to "get through" to them. Perhaps, you are speaking too rapidly, in a monotone, or in terms that are not clear. Make a quick appraisal of the situation and try to correct it in the remainder of your speech.

## Facial expression

In trying to impress an audience visibly, don't overlook what the audience sees in your face. "Of all the things you wear, your expression is the most important," is a saying which emphasizes the importance of letting your face reflect your true meaning. Smiling constantly during a serious speech destroys the seriousness of your message. Frowning, looking bored, wearing a dead-pan expression, and looking afraid or uncomfortable will ruin any message.

Cicero is credited with the remark, "The countenance is the portrait of the mind; the eyes are its informers."

The head and the face are two strong informers of your inner thoughts. Each nod, shake, and movement of the head is speaking either for or against you. Each smile, frown, twisting of the mouth, and movement of the eyebrows is also telling on you. What do you want them to tell?

## ACTIVITIES

1. Memorize any one-or-two-minute selection. A short poem, sports story, or brief essay would do admirably. Take turns delivering it in the following ways:
   a. Look at the ceiling during the selection.
   b. Face one wall or window and speak to it.
   c. Look at the floor all the time.
   d. Pick one person and speak only to him.
   e. Pick one small portion of the audience and speak to it.
   f. Look slightly over the heads of everyone.
   g. Look directly into the faces of the audience allowing your gaze to shift naturally from one side of the room to the other.

   After you have tried each of the above, try to answer the following questions:

   In which of the above did you feel most comfortable?
   In which did you feel least comfortable?

2. Choose a serious selection from Chapter 19. Read the entire selection with a smile on your face. Insert laughter at the most serious parts.
3. Choose a humorous selection from Chapter 19 or the Speaker's Kit. Read it with a solemn expression, an angry expression, a bored expression.
4. Choose any selection. Read it with a facial expression that shows you are very ill at ease.
5. Go back to No. 2, No. 3, and No. 4, and read the selections with the proper facial expression for each.
6. Stand before your mirror and recite the alphabet in a neutral, unemphatic manner of speaking. By *facial expression* only, express happiness, anger, love, disappointment, and conceit. Do the same before your class to see how many can guess your emotion.

After performing the above experiments with facial expression, can you now realize the importance of revealing visibly the exact mood of your speech?

## Gesture

In *A Winter's Tale,* Shakespeare wrote "There is a language in every gesture." Even when you are silent, your actions reveal what you are thinking.

Gestures refer primarily to movements of the head, hands, and arms for the purpose of emphasizing ideas and feelings. Gestures arise from natural impulses to reveal visibly as well as audibly what you are thinking. In conversation, gestures follow a natural pattern because most of you talk informally without realizing that you are even using hand, head, or arm movement. Such spontaneous and unrehearsed gesturing produces harmony of speech with movement. This same harmony should exist when you are delivering a prepared speech.

In the old school of elocution, emphasis was placed on training in the mechanics of gestures. Often the teacher would write into the speech definite gestures to use without considering whether the speaker could feel them sincerely or whether they would even fit the speaker. It was as though someone else were selecting a pair of shoes for you in your absence. Just as you need to see for yourself if your shoes fit and look right on you, so do you need to work out your own appropriate gestures. You need to try them on for size and appearance.

You can train your body to make natural gestures if you will forget about training hands and feet separately. Follow the athlete's plan of training your entire body so that when the time comes for you to speak, you can swing into coordinated action. Begin your training period by becoming action-conscious. Watch others conversing and speaking in public. Above all, watch your own actions. Are you making a series of helpless gestures because you do not know what to do with your hands? Are you waving your arms around? Are you constantly shifting your feet? If you discover that you are using many nervous movements that mean nothing, force yourself to sit or stand quietly. Whenever you start going into action, ask yourself, "Is this action really necessary?" Stand in front of a mirror as you rehearse speeches. Ask your classmates to tell you honestly if your gestures express meaning. Remember that your gestures must be timed properly if they are to have value. Making them too soon or too late is worse than not making them at all. It will take some practice to synchronize your words and your actions.

In your first speeches, you may have the impulse to use gestures too often, but this is a common fault with beginning speakers. It is better, however, to use too many gestures than too few in your early speeches. Those who feel no impulse to gesticulate seldom develop into lively, interesting speakers. They remain wooden-Indian or marble-statue types speaking only with words. But, those whose actions are prompted by natural impulses soon learn how to control

This speech student is practicing his delivery before an evaluating audience of teacher, classmates, and tape recorder. *(Al Currens)*

excessive action and become enthusiastic speakers who "speak all over." Only you know whether or not you feel an impulse to use your head, hands, or arms as you speak. If there is an impulse, use gestures; if you feel no impulse, don't use them. A gesture that is natural for some may be awkward and artificial for others. Furthermore, your body naturally assumes an attitude that reflects joy, despair, confidence, eagerness, fear, or anger. If you really *feel* the emotion or thoughts you wish to express, your body should express them naturally.

Gestures must be made with the entire body. Your hands and arms are not detached from your body and, therefore, cannot move naturally and easily by themselves. Even the simplest act of lifting requires movement of the entire body. Instead of thinking what you should do with your hands and arms, free your whole body of tension and let the hands and arms take care of themselves. Being able to free yourself of fear and self-consciousness is a very important step in achieving body coordination. When you relax, your gestures will appear free, relaxed, and effortless as they should for pleasing delivery.

## Platform movement

Here movement refers to actual travel about the speaking area or platform as opposed to bodily movement such as posture and gestures. You may wonder how moving about the platform can affect your delivery of ideas. Have you ever listened to a speaker who seemed in perpetual motion during his talk? If so, didn't you find it difficult to keep your attention on his words while he moved all over the stage?

The opposite extreme is the speaker who plants himself firmly in one spot and never moves an inch except, perhaps, to shift weight from one foot to the other. His lack of stage movement is as tiresome to the audience as the feeling is to you when you drive for hundreds of miles on a straight highway with no curves or hills to break the monotony. Platform movement provides relief to the audience. If you don't move, sooner or later your listeners will start moving about in their seats. People tire of seeing you in the same position. They become far more tired, however, if they have to follow you needlessly back and forth across the platform. To avoid either extreme, confine yourself generally to the center of the speaking area unless you have needed equipment off center or there is some other reason that you must move away from it.

"That's nothing—wait'll he gets warmed up."

THE SATURDAY EVENING POST



Movement in its controlled form tends to emphasize ideas and to punctuate your speech as effectively as punctuation marks do in writing. Walking forward, backward, or to the side a few steps indicates a change from one thought to another and should be timed to match the words. While purposeful movement serves to relieve monotony for you and the audience, aimless ambling about the stage or excessive action only betrays your nervousness. You will have to determine for yourself each time you give a speech the amount of movement it requires for best results. For example, some people can move about the stage more because they possess the knack of carrying their audience right along with them in thought. Again, if you are using demonstrations in your speech, you may have to move about. Or, if the occasion is a pep rally, more movement will help create enthusiasm. Thoughtless movement on your part, however, in the midst of a serious point, can ruin your audience's concentration just when you most need it. You must be the judge.

## ACTIVITIES

1. Write or find in a book sentences which could be used with gestures or movements that do the following:
   Point out something or somebody.
   Describe shape and size.
   Indicate division into two or more parts.
   Emphasize a key word or series of words.
   Show approval.
   Show disapproval.
2. Read aloud the following statements using gestures that you believe to be appropriate:
   Here are the facts in the case.
   Our answer to your proposition is NO.
   We must reject your offer.
   The convicted man sits there.
   The plan must go through.
   Let me bring this point to your attention.
   I tell you it is up to us to help.
   If I ever get a chance to hit that thing, I'll hit it hard.
   That idea is out of the question; it is utterly repugnant to American principles.
   I am astonished and shocked to hear such language in this house.
3. Pick any selection in Chapter 19. Use what you consider appropriate gestures as you read it to the class.

# How to Impress Others Psychologically

Certain intangible elements exert a strong influence upon an audience as you deliver a speech. Although these elements lie within you, they are as evident to your listeners as if you were wearing them on the outside. They are the psychological elements which cause an audience to respond favorably, unfavorably, or indifferently. As you speak, an audience appraises you as much as your words. You must deliver *yourself* in an effective manner if you expect your ideas to arrive in perfect condition. How well you succeed depends upon your attitudes.

### Be sincere

Sincerity lies at the heart of all effective delivery. Sincerity includes earnestness plus complete honesty of belief. Audiences can quickly sense whether or not you are sincere from the tone of your voice, your gestures and movements, your facial expression, and your general attitude. Only if you are genuinely pleased with your subject will your voice be warm, friendly, and enthusiastic. Only if you really like an audience will your smile be genuine. Only if you really want to share your thinking with your audience will your desire to speak be real.

To appear sincere you must *be* sincere. You must honestly believe your own words in order to create belief in the minds of others. In most cases, your voice, gestures, and facial expression will automatically express sincerity when you, yourself, are filled with a sincere belief in your ideas. If you are not completely sincere, any training in audible and visible action will not help you fool an audience.

Your personality also affects your listeners' judgment. Some persons naturally inspire confidence; others create doubt and mistrust. Any improvements that you can make in your personality will help in establishing trust in your sincerity.

## Be poised

To be poised is to be balanced emotionally, mentally, and physically. When you are truly poised, neither your knees nor your ideas shake. Poise in a speaker generates confidence. If you have poise, you will feel at home with your listeners and they will feel at home with you. Lack of poise creates a strained situation in which you appear at a disadvantage and fail to communicate your thoughts because your listeners are likely to be more concerned about your discomfort than your message. It also arouses feelings of doubt regarding your preparation, sureness, and sincerity. If you appear insecure, your listeners may place little confidence in your words. The worst effect is arousing sympathy for you instead of complete empathy with you. There will be no need for sympathy during or after your speech if you are prepared before you speak. Preparation is the first giant step toward poise.

## Be friendly

You can accomplish miracles with a smile that is based on a friendly attitude. As a listener, you often respond indifferently or even negatively to the speaker who is aloof, cold, or stiffly formal. An aloof speaker seems forbidding whereas the one who is warm and friendly engenders a warm, friendly response. People automatically smile back at the speaker who greets them with a smile.

In a high school assembly program, a group of student council nominees delivered campaign speeches in order to win votes. One of the nominees was a freshman who had to speak before a large group of upper classmen. Although he was very nervous, nobody realized it after his disarming beginning. He knew and made use of the power of a smile and friendly attitude. He walked to the center of the stage, stopped, looked quietly around the entire auditorium and greeted the group with a broad smile. Instinctively, everybody smiled at him. Then he said quite simply, "Hi!" The audience smiled again. Next he pulled out a long speech saying, "I wrote out my speech last night. I thought of everything I could possibly say and here it is. (pause) But I'm not going to use it." At this point, the audience sighed with relief and smiled some more as he put his speech back in his pocket. "I'm going to use this one instead," he said, pulling a still longer one out of another pocket.

With this remark, the audience roared while the once nervous freshman laid his "prop" speech on the table and continued with a short, friendly speech explaining the "platform" he stood for and what he would work for if he were elected secretary. He won the election, too, just as easily as he won his audience that day.

A friendly personality is always a great asset in any speaking situation. *(Jay-Vee)*

### Be positive

To be positive is to be certain of yourself and of your cause. You can be positive in a speaking situation only if you know that your speech is right for your listeners. Positiveness of belief exists within you; it occurs only after you have investigated your topic thoroughly enough to obtain reliable and acceptable material. Do not confuse positiveness with sincerity. You can be sincere without being positive; far worse, you can be very positive without being sincere. Ideally, positiveness and sincerity go hand in hand. This ideal combination occurs when you are convinced that your message is right in principle and expression for your audience and when you are sincerely desirous of having your audience receive your message. Abraham Lincoln is an outstanding example of positiveness plus complete sincerity of belief.

Listeners in a democracy will ultimately accept your views if they are right in principle; they will ultimately reject views that seem wrong. Be positive—irrespective of the immediate reaction of your audience—only when you are sure that you are representing the right.

### Be forceful

Forcefulness keeps your audience alert, listening, and responding. The most vividly worded speeches can die in transit if delivered by a listless speaker. Be alive and dynamic instead of indifferent and bored. Delivering a speech in a dynamic manner is work; it requires energy, strength, and power. Unless you are willing to work hard to deliver your speech, there is no point in preparing it. It is your responsibility to give life and meaning to your words. It is the responsibility of your listeners to react to what you do. You can not get a forceful reaction without a forceful presentation.

## Types of Delivery

What type of delivery should you choose—the impromptu, the extempore, the exact-word type, or a combination of the three? Which one will enable you to deliver your message with the greatest degree of accuracy and force? It is impossible to prescribe the "best" way, since no one type suits all speakers, occasions, and audiences. Take a close look at the advantages and disadvantages of each type and then make your own decision when the time comes for you to speak.

Hands shaking in forceful gestures, a student springs to the defense of his candidate to speak impromptu with great effectiveness. *(Don Carlos Dunaway)*

## The impromptu speech

This is speaking without any preparation or previous thought. It is often called speaking on the spur of the moment or "off the cuff." Almost any time that you stand up in a meeting to contribute information or opinions, you give an impromptu speech. You often feel impelled to say something about a motion or a subject under discussion and you may speak at great length without even realizing that you are giving a speech. The informality of the occasion plus your deep feeling on the subject makes your impromptu speaking spirited and often effective.

But what about the times you may be caught unaware and asked to "say a few words"? Can you then stand up with the same ease and enthusiasm to speak "off the cuff" before a large audience about a subject you may know or care little about? If so, you may be able to deliver your speeches impromptu.

As a rule, only speakers with years of experience can speak smoothly and coherently on the spur of the moment. Because of their experience in speaking and in living, they have much more to talk about than has the average high school student. These experienced speakers also have learned how to select a topic quickly, to organize it well, and to pick a good beginning and ending. Many of them have their own pet plans of organization that they can use for any topic, and they frequently carry in their minds a large supply of anecdotes, jokes, or opening remarks that would be suitable for any occasion. Except for *training* yourself to speak impromptu, you will probably do better speech work if you save this type of delivery until near the end of the course. By all means, don't develop the habit of being unprepared in order to practice giving impromptu speeches!

The only *advantage* of this type of delivery is that it requires no preparation. In cases when you feel strongly on a subject, either in class discussion or in a meeting, you will probably speak quite forcefully without giving it any thought.

The *disadvantages* are that your speeches may lack organization, worthwhile material, and even fluency. Such speeches often represent a great waste of time and effort—both for you and for your audience. If you use the impromptu type exclusively, you will get little training in speech development.

## The extempore type

In *Webster's New International Dictionary of the English Language*, you find this statement: "Extempore (still often interchangeable with impromptu) is now more often applied to that which is spoken without the use of a manuscript, provided it has not been learned by heart; the word does not necessarily exclude preparation; impromptu applies to that which is composed or uttered on the spur of the moment." Whereas there is no advance preparation in the impromptu type, the extempore type definitely implies preliminary thought and development.

Since the extempore style of delivery is recommended and followed by many experienced speakers, you should know how to develop this type to your best ability. These are the steps involved:

1. Select your topic in accordance with the standards discussed in earlier chapters.

2. Collect the most pertinent and interesting material available from all the sources you know.

3. Arrange the body of your speech according to a definite plan of organization.

4. Prepare the best introduction and conclusion you can think of. (You may wish to memorize these.)

5. Practice your speech many times by talking out loud. Take the outline or memorandum of your main points and start talking. Pay no attention to your exact words on the first three or

four rehearsals, but keep experimenting until you feel that you have found the most satisfactory manner of expressing your meaning.

Some of you may be wondering how you will know when you have found the best style. Naturally, you can't tell exactly because you might continue improving with every rehearsal. The point for you to remember is this—when you feel sure that you are saying exactly what you mean in a coherent, convincing style, you can feel satisfied with your preparation. You may also be wondering how you can be sure you will give it before an audience the same way you said it in rehearsal. You can't be sure and you probably won't use the same words—you may even use better ones!

The *advantages* of speaking extemporaneously are naturalness of delivery and adaptability of content. In addition, if you plan from the beginning to give an extempore speech, you will be able to spend a good proportion of your preparation time in collecting materials and in organizing your point of view.

Naturalness is the quality which makes a speech—even if well rehearsed—seem spontaneous and unrehearsed. With no set manuscript to read or memorization to worry about, you can deliver your ideas in a conversational, informal manner which brings you into closer relationship with your audience. Every time that you practice by speaking your thoughts out loud, you become surer of your content, surer of your word choice, and surer of yourself. That is one of the chief charms of the extempore speech. You can feel confident and devote your full attention to your listeners.

Adaptability of content implies a change of content on short notice. You can shorten, lengthen, or modify content when you speak without manuscript. If you are the last of ten speakers, you may feel it advisable to cut short your speech. Perhaps a previous speaker reminded you of something or expressed an idea similar to one in your speech. If so, you can include the thought of which you were reminded and you can omit the similar idea or tie in the previous speaker's reference to it with your own thoughts. You may observe unfavorable reactions from an audience when you or somebody else mentions a certain idea. If so, be quick to modify your statements or to eliminate from your speech any further references to it. Such quick revisions can be made easily in the extempore type.

Finally, as noted above, the extempore type of speech requires a manner of preparation that puts the emphasis on the finding and organizing of facts and ideas rather than the precise writing out

To deliver a successful extempore speech, this speaker must utilize all his attributes of sincerity, poise and forcefulness. *(Black Star)*

of the speech. But this is not to say that the extempore type of speech is easy to give because it requires only a little preparation. Actually, as you saw when you studied the various steps in the preparation of this type of speech, the extempore speech requires a lot of preparation.

The *major disadvantages* of this type are obvious: precision of meaning, exactness of timing, and fluency of speaking may all be difficult to achieve. In actual fact, adequate preparation can minimize all of these problems. They are cited here, not so much to discourage you from using this type of delivery, but rather to warn you what can happen if you fail to prepare adequately. If you will prepare adequately, you can speak extemporaneously and still say what you mean, use your time allotment, and speak with a reasonable degree of style and fluency.

## The exact-word speech

This type of delivery consists of reading your speech from a manuscript or delivering it word for word from memory. One of the first questions most students ask is, "Is it all right if I write out my speech and read it?" Bishop Fulton J. Sheen gave his answer to that question when speaking before a convention. He explained that he always speaks without notes or manuscript after hearing an old

Irish lady complain about a bishop who read his sermons. When asked why she objected to a bishop who read, she answered, "If he can't remember his sermon, how does he expect us to?"

The *advantages* of this type enable you to overcome the disadvantages of the extempore. You can time your speech, you will prepare more carefully, and you will be able to speak more fluently.

The *disadvantages*, however, may outweigh the advantages. If you speak from memory, you may be so afraid you will forget that you will concentrate more on the remembering process than on your audience. The fear of forgetting also gives you an added dose of stage jitters. The result may be that you will recite words in a detached automatic manner as if somebody dropped a coin in the slot and a record started playing.

If you read from a manuscript, you have no worry about forgetting your speech, but you often forget your audience. As in memorization, although for different reasons, there is the same danger of delivering your words in a dull manner.

There are some occasions when it may be necessary to read from a manuscript. Therefore, concentrate for the time being on how to read properly and how to use notes.

If you choose to deliver your classroom speeches according to this type, try to write as you would talk. By expressing your thoughts in a spoken style, your delivery will sound natural and spontaneous. Give yourself plenty of time in preparation. Begin reading your manuscript as soon as you have completed it and continue reading it until it becomes a definite part of you. As you practice reading your speech, do not hesitate to change places that sound unlike you. Every time that you read it aloud, imagine that you have an audience in front of you. Better still, try it out on some of your family or friends. As you read, practice speaking forcefully and directly to your real or imaginary audience. Give life, vigor, and naturalness to the written word if you want it to sound like the spoken word.

If you are reading a manuscript such as a Class Will, Class Prophecy, or a research paper involving the repetition of exact names, places, dates, and statistics, these suggestions may help you:

1. Make your reading easier by typing or writing legibly. Allow plenty of space between the lines. Write only on one side of the paper.
2. Number each page and be sure your pages are in order.
3. When a speaker's stand is available, place your entire manuscript on it and, as you finish each page, place it in a new stack either to the right or the left. Many experienced speakers prefer to keep the pages

right side up as they move them to the new stack. Although this does reverse the order of the pages, the sliding movement is less conspicuous than the flipping movement. Moreover, you can still see the last page.

4. If no stand is available, hold the manuscript in your hands and as you finish each page place it beneath the manuscript.

5. Follow the same rigid practice routine that you would with any speech: don't read it—speak it!

In all instances of the exact-word delivery not requiring a lengthy manuscript, use notes. There are times when you should read from note cards. If you use a direct quotation in debating, you should read it from the card to satisfy the audience that you are correct and not trusting to memory alone. Note cards often give reliability to your statements when you are repeating statistics, dates, sources, names, and other detailed information difficult to recall.

Beginning speech students often feel more comfortable if they may use notes for the first few speeches. The important consideration appears to be more *how* to use notes than *whether* to use them,

Correct use of a speaker's stand and the technique of handling note cards should be thoroughly rehearsed. *(Monkmeyer)*

since most of you will be using them at some time. You will remember that the use of cards for note-taking was discussed in Chapter 10. The points below will augment that information.

1. Use 3″ x 5″ cards because they fit easily in the palm of your hand. If your quotations are unusually long, you may require larger cards.

2. Write on one side only and number each card. Be sure to keep them in order.

3. Write only what is needed for recall—outline, statistics, or anything you are afraid you might forget. *Do not write out your entire speech.*

4. Use as few cards as possible. If you must use several cards, go from one card to the next with a minimum of confusion. As you finish with each card, quietly shift it from the top of the stack to the bottom.

5. In general, keep your eyes on your audience—*not* on your cards. Except while you are actually reading direct quotations or other specific facts, forget that you are holding your cards. Some speakers ruin audience contact by looking down at their cards constantly even though there may be only three or four lines written on them.

6. Hold your cards inconspicuously, but keep them in front of you when you are using them. Never try to hide cards and then attempt to sneak a look at them when you think the audience won't see you. Keep them where they can be used easily.

7. With reference cards or recorded quotations, hold the card in such a way that the audience can see you reading from it, and then return it to its place. This helps the audience to know when you begin and end the direct quotation.

From the three basic types of delivery—the impromptu, the extempore, and the exact-word type—you may choose one or you may combine all three of them into one speech. If you use several types in the same speech, you will perhaps solve the problems which pertain directly to you. Memorize parts of your speech which should be word-perfect such as the opening and the conclusion; speak from notes when giving data difficult to remember or when quoting from a source; and speak extempore for the remainder of your speech. You can use the impromptu method if you wish to depart from your regularly planned speech.

Every speaker has his own favorite way of preparing his speech for delivery. Your choice will depend entirely upon your skills and upon the circumstances.

If you are suddenly called upon to say something, you have little choice except to speak impromptu. Usually, however, you can choose your type. Base your choice upon your capabilities as well as your limitations. Pick the type that will serve your purpose—not the type that you think may be easiest. Pick the type of delivery that you can be proud of—the one that will show you off to your best advantage.

## ACTIVITIES

1. Ask a classmate to pick a topic about which you have little information. Speak impromptu for three minutes on the subject he selected. Ask the class to keep notes on what you say and do and to discuss your speech frankly with you at the end.
2. Now take the same subject. Spend at least one-half hour in finding information about the subject and preparing your speech. This time speak extemporaneously for three minutes. Again ask the class to keep notes.
3. Take the same subject a third time and prepare an exact-word type speech. Write out your information completely and read your speech from memory or from manuscript. Ask the class to keep notes. Finally evaluate the three speeches according to these questions:

   Which one did the listeners like best? Why?

   Which one did you consider the easiest to give? Why?

   Which one did you regard as the best? Why?

   What were the noticeable differences in content, organization, and delivery recorded by the class?
4. For practice purposes only, conduct a contest in impromptu speaking. Select several topics, write them on cards, and put the cards face down. As your turn comes, pick a card and deliver a two-minute speech on the subject you draw. You may follow one of the following methods of handling your subject:
   a. Speak seriously and directly upon your topic giving all the information you have in a well-organized form.
   b. If you know nothing about the topic, try a humorous approach. Set yourself up as an authority, for example, and speak from ignorance.
   c. You might evade the subject completely by using the technique of "that reminds me of . . . ." For example, if you are called upon to talk about "Life Among the Eskimos," you could begin thus:

      I would be glad to talk about the experiences I had among the Eskimos, but I was such a small boy at the time that I can't remember much about them except their delicious Eskimo pies. Speaking of pies reminds me of dough, and dough always reminds me of money. . . ."

   As soon as you get on to the subject of money, you have endless possibilities—allowances, jobs, whether girls should share expenses on a date, and so on.
5. Find a couple of humorous stories or anecdotes which could be used as a lead into almost any type of speech. Such stories would be ones which would describe humorously the plight of the unprepared speaker or could be made to reflect the feeling of the speaker. Bring them to class and share them aloud.
6. Give a topic to the class. See which of you can be the first to use your anecdotes in getting off to a good start on the suggested topic.
7. Prepare and deliver a speech in which you combine the three basic types of delivery. Ask the class which part of your speech was best.

## PRONUNCIATION PROBLEMS

"T's" are often omitted or sounded like "d's" in the average person's speaking habits. "D's" likewise are easily omitted or weakened. The first list of words below requires exactness in reproducing the "t" sound; the second one, the "d" sound. The Reading Check-Up contains sentences with both sounds. Note that in cases where the final "ed" follows an unvoiced sound, as in "asked," the "ed" is pronounced as a "t."

| INITIAL "T" | MIDDLE "T" | | FINAL "T" SOUND | | |
|---|---|---|---|---|---|
| ten | little | brittle | kept | must | balked |
| town | kitten | prattle | slept | least | camped |
| tame | kettle | cotton | wept | belt | helped |
| talk | button | bitten | worst | adept | hatched |
| two | fatten | beaten | mount | contradict | pumped |
| twenty | battle | shuttle | crept | asked | against |
| table | pretty | motto | bolt | basked | convulsed |
| tape | writer | gentle | distinct | tracked | cramped |
| touch | united | daughter | next | sulked | fixed |
| toy | sentries | enter | tract | risked | cracked |

| INITIAL "D" | MIDDLE "D" | | FINAL "D" | | |
|---|---|---|---|---|---|
| den | middle | saddle | build | fatigued | dead |
| down | fiddle | candle | ground | squabbled | dwelled |
| dough | ladle | cradle | husband | yelled | happened |
| drape | bridle | sadder | sound | ruffled | graded |
| day | ladder | paddle | would | reveled | island |
| dare | seldom | bidder | end | filmed | field |
| door | lady | candy | drowned | judged | puzzled |
| date | dandy | divided | kind | heed | tattled |
| dime | wedding | madder | rolled | nod | road |
| drop | meddle | toddle | scold | contended | stood |

## READING CHECK-UP

Read aloud the nonsense sentences below to check your pronunciation of any problem words.

Thirty-three thrifty tailors toiled Tuesday trimming tiny tattered tunics.

"Read aloud many times these tongue twisters," said the tenth grade teacher.

When the two little kittens lost their mittens, they cried aloud, "Our hands are cold."

Betty Batter bought some butter.
"But," said she, "this butter's bitter.
If I put it in my batter,
It will make my batter bitter."
So she bought some better butter,
And she put the better butter in the bitter batter,
And made the bitter batter better.

A tutor who tooted a flute
Tried to tutor two tooters to toot.
Said the two to the tutor,
"Is it easier to toot or
To tutor two tutors to toot?"

Three pretty, witty sisters and their three proud strutting poodles attracted widespread attention from the twenty handsome sentries mounted on their saddled and bridled steeds.

The bold hounds growled and sniffed for moles under the ground while a band of crafty hunters went wending around the fields.

Sweet Swedish waitresses prattled on and on about sweet Swedish pastry treats.

Ride, writers, ride the riders' wild white steeds and write about the night riders' bold bad deeds.

Sadder and sadder the old owl grew until he didn't give a hoot no matter what happened.

When asked who attacked first in the battle, the sentries stated distinctly that the beetles made the first inroads on the meddling ants, and not one guard would contradict.

## VOCABULARY BUILD-UP

Use the italicized words in short paragraphs to show that you understand their meanings.

a *symbolic* dance
to *supplement* his income
a *jaundiced* view
the habits of a *scavenger*
a feeling of *nostalgia*
*indomitable* spirit
a well-known *benefactor*
*predestined* to fail
an *apparent* mistake
a *discrepancy* in views
a *concerted* course of action
a feeling of *apathy*
*turbulent* times
to *minimize* your efforts
a plan of *infiltration*
a *cursory* analysis
a *sacrilegious* remark
constant *surveillance*
*susceptible* to infection
a *reconnaissance* flight

# Speaker's Kit

ARE you aware of how important a doctor's medicine bag is to him and how he must care for it? He depends upon it to hold the "tools of his trade." As supplies diminish he must replace them and be constantly on the alert to see that he has at all times everything necessary for an emergency call. He reads and investigates the latest medical reports on drugs so that he can add new and better remedies. In short, his well-stocked kit is no accident; it is the result of careful planning and vigilant replenishing.

In the same manner, the experienced speaker keeps a well-stocked kit of speaking material. The speaker's kit, like the doctor's bag, requires planning. The speaker must be on the alert to collect items for his kit whenever he is reading. His two most valuable "tools" are a pair of scissors to clip appropriate items and a package of labeled envelopes in which to file them. Then, when he begins to prepare a speech, he goes to his file first to look for a suitable topic and second to find attractive material with which to develop his speech.

You, too, can be prepared with a stock of useful clippings for emergencies. Your speeches will be enlivened if you are able to insert well-chosen quotations, anecdotes, or other illustrative material pertaining to your subject. It is much easier to prepare speeches when you have a supply of interesting material at hand than it is when you have to start from scratch each time to look for it.

You are probably wondering where to find materials and what kinds to file. Newspapers, magazines, and other printed matter abound with useful items. Watch for statistics on current topics, specific examples on subjects of general interest, jokes, anecdotes (either serious or humorous), witticisms, humorous definitions, quotations and anything else which excites your interest.

Select only those items which seem to have good possibilities for speech topics in themselves or which might help explain an idea by supplying a forceful example. Don't waste time and space filing anything which does not suggest a clear application to a subject. Keep in mind that all such illustrative material must be useful in reinforcing ideas and have a direct bearing upon a topic. *For future reference note on each item as you clip it the source from which you have taken it and the date.*

This chapter contains a *sample* speaker's kit. It is included to show you the kinds of material to collect for your own file and to give you some self-starters already "clipped" for use in preparing class speeches. The primary purpose in this is twofold: (1) to gain experience in using illustrative material and (2) to discover in how many *different* ways you and your classmates will make use of identical material. The application of the material is entirely up to you. In other words: This is a do-it-yourself experiment!

Earlier in this book you have learned the value of including various types of illustrations in the body of your speech. You have learned also the importance of beginning and ending your speeches with different devices to capture attention at the beginning and to furnish a forceful conclusion. The illustrations gathered in this kit give samples for you to study and use for the above purposes. You will be more responsive to some than to others. Choose those which "ring a bell" with you and decide in which type of speech purpose they would be most effective—speeches to inform, to entertain, or to persuade—then use them as you develop your speeches.

In choosing material from a file, the trained speaker is careful to pick only those items which are appropriate for his speech purpose and which will strengthen his own ideas. He also gives variety to his speech by choosing different *types* of material to enliven it. Another rule which he follows is *not to overload* his speeches with these devices so that the main ideas are obscured. He knows that "too much oil extinguishes the lamp."

## A sample speech

Perhaps the best way to learn the uses that can be made of material from a speaker's kit is to study some excerpts from the following article that is richly developed with forceful examples. The skillful author of this composition used illustrative material naturally and smoothly to strengthen and enliven his subject. Although the article appeared in printed form, it would be just as effective if delivered as a speech. For your convenience the particular techniques used by the writer are indicated in the margins.

### WHAT PRAYER CAN DO

*Condensed from "Guideposts"*

by Fulton Oursler

ANECDOTE

One spring morning when I was a small boy, my mother dressed me up in my Sunday best and warned me not to leave the front steps.

"We'll be walking over to see your aunt," she promised.

I waited obediently until the baker's son came along and called me a sissy. Then I sprang from the steps and whammed him on the ear. He shoved me into a mud puddle, splotching my white blouse with slime and leaving my stocking with a bloody hole at the knee. Hopelessly I began to bawl.

But my grief was stilled at a sudden tinkle of bells. Down the street came a peddler, pushing his jingling green cart—"Hokey-pokey ice cream, one cent apiece." Forgetting my disobedience, I ran into the house and begged my mother for a penny. Never can I forget her answer:

"Look at yourself! You're in no condition to ask for anything."

* * *

APPLICATION

Many a harum-scarum year went by before it dawned on me that often, when we ask for help from God, we need to take a look at ourselves; we may be in no condition to ask Him for anything.

* * *

QUOTATION

"The trouble is that most prayers are not honest to God," declares a psychologist, and a man of no religious faith. "People have the ungracious audacity to ask for heavenly handouts although they are not on speaking terms with their next-door neighbors; they have forbidden relatives their house; they are spreaders of gossip and envious detractors of their best friends.

"To feel free of bitterness one must be rid of malice, resentment, envy, jealousy and greed, which are certain causes of mental illness and even physical disease. Simply by obeying the scriptural rule to be reconciled to our brother before prayer, we can wash away these breeding germs of neuroses and psychoses. Honest-to-God prayer is a kind of *mental health insurance*."

* * *

ANECDOTE

A young American Indian left his Huron tribe in northern Wisconsin to be educated in city schools. He became a lawyer and the green forests saw him no more, until in middle life he returned for a hunting and fishing vacation. Presently his woodsman guide noticed that at every sundown the Indian vanished for an hour. One day, beset with curiosity, the guide trailed him.

From behind the low spread of a hemlock tree, he watched the Indian build a fire in an open clearing, saw him balance a log across two stones on one side of the fire, and place another such bench on the opposite side, then seat himself on one of the logs and stare into the blaze.

The guide started to walk toward the fire when the Indian, seeing him, held up restraining hands. Without a word he arranged another log and invited the guide by a gesture to join in his vigil. For half an hour the two remained together in complete silence.

After they had returned to camp and eaten supper, the Indian explained the mystery:

"When I was a child my mother taught me to go off by myself at the end of each day and make a place for a visit of the Great Spirit. I was to think back over my actions and thoughts of the day. If there was anything of which I was ashamed, I must tell the Great Spirit I was sorry and ask for strength to avoid the same mistake again. Then I would sleep better that night. I had forgotten all about it, but here, among these tall trees where I played as a boy, I have found my lost faith. I have not known such peace since I was a child. And from now on I shall somehow manage to visit with the Great Spirit every day."

PERSONAL EXAMPLE

Ezio Pinza, who starred in "South Pacific," has his own story about the pathway to peace. It is reported by Ed Sullivan in his famous syndicated column:

"On the night before 'South Pacific' opened," said Pinza, "I told Mary Martin if she could not sleep because of nervousness, to do what I'd found best—get up, dress, and go to the nearest church. 'Just sit there in church,' I said, 'and soon all your nervousness will vanish as if it had been smoothed away.' God has been so good to me and my career has been so crowded with great luck that I turn to Him all the time. Others may fail; God, never. When I explained this to Mary she started to cry, and it was on this note that our friendship was founded."

* * *

QUOTATION AND PROVERB

The divine promise "Ask and ye shall receive" does not guarantee that you will receive exactly what you ask for. Often we do not know what is good for us; the old Greeks had a proverb that when the gods were angry with a man they gave him what he wanted. Many of us have lived to be thankful that our prayers were denied. The wise person adds a proviso to every request: "Nevertheless, not my will but Thine be done."

* * *

ANECDOTES

There was Rosalie, the daughter of a poor Parisian, who showed early promise of becoming a great artist. But an artist needs more than promise. Rosalie wanted to draw from life, and her father had no money to pay for a model. Very earnestly the girl prayed for enough francs to pay a model's hire, but no shower of money rained down on her back yard.

One day, as she was taking a walk, she had a sudden feeling that everything was going to be all right. Near a crowded market place she noticed a farmer's dray horse hitched for the day behind a vegetable stall. He would not object to being her model—not if Rosa did not mind drawing a horse! In the Metropolitan Museum of Art in New York City there now hangs a world-known canvas, "The Horse Fair." It was painted by Rosa Bonheur, imperishably famed for her masterpieces of horses.

* * *

When the late Laurette Taylor was starring in her last Broadway play, "The Glass Menagerie," her friends knew that she was in poor health. They knew also that she had quarreled with her co-star, Eddie Dowling.

One midsummer matinee, in the course of a scene near a table at which Dowling was seated, Miss Taylor suddenly swayed and grabbed a chair for support. The company manager, fearing that she had been about to faint, rushed back to her dressing room when the curtain fell.

"I'm all right," Laurette assured him. "It was just that something happened on stage that nearly knocked me off my pins. We were playing the part where Eddie is supposed to be trying to write something while I am scolding him. I happened to look over his shoulder and saw that he really was writing—and what he was writing was a prayer: 'Dear God—please make Laurette well and strong, and help us to be friends again.'"

That prayer broke a black spell between the rival stars. Later I learned that for months at every performance Eddie Dowling had been writing prayers for friends and foes during that same scene. "It kept my mind sweet—which it badly needed," Eddie told me.

Below is a sample speaker's kit for you to use in preparing speeches. It contains short illustrative materials of various types organized under main headings such as *statistics, jokes, anecdotes,* and *humorous definitions.* In addition to using the kit as a source of materials for speeches, you should also think of it as an example of the types of material that you can collect for yourself. Thus, even as you study and use the supply from this kit, get out your scissors and envelopes and start a kit of your own. Feel perfectly free to devise your own headings; the ones given in the sample kit may not fit your particular needs.

## Directions for using the kit in your speeches

This sample material has been collected for your convenience. Feel free to use any number of items in the kit. They can be used as introductions or conclusions to your speech or they may be used within the body of a speech. The interesting part of this experiment will be to discover in how many different ways you and your classmates will use the same item. Remember that all illustrative material must fit your speech purpose and help to develop it forcefully. The ideal use of the kit is to prepare at least one speech for each of the speech purposes explained in Chapter 8. You may find that the same illustration can be used in more than one purpose.

Start now to see how many different uses you can find for the material contained in this kit.

# A Sample Speaker's Kit

## Statistics

It is estimated that a college grad earns during his lifetime an average of $100,000 more than a non-college man of comparable ability, reports Dr. Frank H. Sparks, president of the Council for Financial Aid to Education. On this basis, he adds, the 240,000 men graduates of June 1958 will, during the next 35 or 40 years, receive as income and spend as customers some $25 billion more than if they had not gone to college.

—Industrial Press Service—*Quote* Magazine

The size of our 49th state, Alaska, is almost too big to comprehend. However, this comparison will help: With a total area of 586,400 square miles, Alaska is big enough to hold two Texases, and one Georgia, with almost enough left over to make a Rhode Island.

—Ford Times, hm, Ford Motor Co.—*Quote* Magazine

* * *

Read something each day. Discipline yourself to a regular schedule of reading. In 15 minutes a day you can read 20 books a year.

—Wilfred A. Peterson, *Jaqua Way*, Jaqua Advertising Co., Grand Rapids, Michigan—*Quote* Magazine

* * *

Dr. Wm. M. Elliott, in taking some position on a subject, (often says), "I am not asking you to agree with me, but I am asking you to think." It has been said 85% of our people do not think; that 10% think they think; and only 5% of the population actually *do* think.

—Dr. Arthur V. Boand, "Every Thought Captive"—*Christian Observer*, Reprinted in *Quote* Magazine

## Examples

* * *

The average driver has to cope with 300 distinct traffic situations in every mile of city driving, 100 situations on the highway, and makes at least one error in every 40 decisions.

—S. T. Blau, *Coronet*

* * *

In George Orwell's satire, *Animal Farm*, he deflates some of the socialistic and confused ideas about equality. In that book, the animals revolt and take over a farm. At first, they set up seven commandments and the seventh is, "All Animals Are Equal." Soon, however, the pigs, who are more clever, start to run things, and one day, the seventh commandment is changed to read: "All Animals Are Equal But Some Are More Equal Than Others."

—*Quote* Magazine

* * *

On August 4, 1807, the crowd that watched Robert Fulton's *Clermont*, the first American steamboat, contained many doubters. "It will burn up"; "the thing will bust"; "all on board will be drowned"; "it can never go upstream."

But it did go upstream 150 miles from New York to Albany in 32 hours.

—Prochnow, *Speaker's Treasury of Stories For All Occasions*

* * *

Thomas Jefferson was elected President by just one vote in the Electoral College. So was John Quincy Adams. Rutherford B. Hayes was elected President by just one vote. His election was contested and referred to an electoral commission. Again he won by a single vote. The man who cast that dividing vote for President Hayes was a lawyer from Indiana who was elected to Congress by the margin of just one vote. That one vote was cast by a client of his who, though desperately ill, insisted on being taken to the polls to cast that vote.

—*Americans Will Vote, Inc.*

—Prochnow, *The Speaker's Special Occasion Book*

* * *

He struck out 1330 times, a record in futility unapproached by any other player in the history of baseball. But that isn't what we remember about Babe Ruth. His 714 home runs completely obliterated the 1330 strike-outs.

Cy Young, perhaps the greatest pitcher of all time, accumulated 511 victories, a mark that has never been threatened. But what is generally forgotten is that Young actually lost almost as many games as he won.

One of the failingest men who ever lived was always trying an experiment that was unsuccessful. Yet we never think of Thomas Edison as a failure.

At Fort Necessity, during the French and Indian War, a young American officer capitulated to the enemy. But George Washington is never thought of as the man who surrendered to the French.

People would feel a lot less sensitive about failure if they remembered it just doesn't matter, except as a guidepost for oneself. Success is a bright sun that obscures and makes ridiculously unimportant all the little shadowy flecks of failure.

—Harold Helfer in *The Kiwanis Magazine*

* * *

Failed in business '31
Defeated for Legislature '32
Again failed in business '33
Elected to Legislature '34
Sweetheart died '35
Had nervous breakdown '36
Defeated for Speaker '38
Defeated for Elector '40
Defeated for Congress '43
Elected to Congress '46
Defeated for Congress '48
Defeated for Senate '55
Defeated for Vice-President '56
Defeated for Senate '58
Elected President '60

—*Outline of Lincoln's Life*

—Prochnow, *Speaker's Treasury . . .*

* * *

## Jokes

A precocious five-year-old son of a professor asked his father what was the exact meaning of the verse beginning, "Jack Sprat could eat no fat."

"In simple terms," said the professor, "it means Jack Sprat could assimilate no adipose tissue. His wife, on the contrary, possessed an aversion for the more muscular portions of the epithelium. And so, between them both, you see, they removed or did away with all the foreign substances from the surface of the utilitarian utensil, commonly called a platter. Does that make it clear, son?"

"Perfectly clear," replied the son. "The lack of lucidity in these alleged Mother Goose rhymes is amazingly apparent to one with an intellect above the moronic grade."

—Prochnow, *Speaker's Treasury . . .*

* * *

An employer, interviewing an applicant, remarked, "You ask high wages for a man with no experience."

"Well," the prospect replied, "it's so much harder work when you don't know anything about it."

—Prochnow, *Speaker's Treasury . . .*

* * *

He had never been outside the United States, and neither had she, but both were recounting their experiences abroad.

"And Asia. Ah, wonderful Asia. Never shall I forget Turkey, India—all of them. And most of all China, the celestial kingdom. How I loved it!"

"And the pagodas—did you see them?"

She held her ground.

"Did I see them?" She powdered her nose. "My dear, I had dinner with them."

—Prochnow, *Speaker's Treasury . . .*

* * *

An English cub reporter, reprimanded for relating too many details, and warned to be brief, turned in the following:

"A shooting affair occurred last night. Sir Dwight Hopeless, a guest at Lady Penmore's ball, complained of feeling ill, took his hat, his coat, his departure, no notice of friends, a taxi, a pistol from his pocket, and finally his life. Nice chap. Regrets and all that sort of thing."

—Prochnow, *Speaker's Treasury . . .*

* * *

## Anecdotes

On a day memorable to me, I boarded a tiny tugboat that I used often in crossing a southern river and saw that we had a new Negro engineer. He sat in the doorway of the engine room reading the Bible; he was fat, squat and black but immaculate, and in his eyes was the splendor of ancient wisdom and peace with the world. As I paused to talk with him I noticed that the characteristic odors that had always emanated from the engine room were no longer there. And the engine! It gleamed and shone; from beneath its seat all the bilge-water was gone. Instead of grime and filth and stench I found beauty and order. When I asked the engineer how in the world he had managed to clean up the old room and the old engine, he answered in words that would go far toward solving life's main problems for many people.

"Cap'n," he said, nodding fondly in the direction of the engine, "it's just this way: I got a glory."

Making that engine the best on the river was his glory in life, and having a glory he had everything. The only sure way out of suffering that I know is to find a glory and to give to it the strength we might otherwise spend in despair.

—Adapted from Archibald Rutledge, *It Will Be Daybreak Soon*

* * *

Perhaps you have heard the story of Christopher Wren, one of the greatest of English architects, who walked one day unrecognized among the men who were at work upon the building of St. Paul's Cathedral in London which he had designed. "What are you doing?" he inquired of one of the workmen, and the man replied, "I am cutting a piece of stone." As he went on he put the same question to another man, and the man replied, "I am earning five shillings twopence a day," and to a third man he addressed the same inquiry and the man answered, "I am helping Sir Christopher Wren build a beautiful cathedral." That man had vision.

—Prochnow, *Speaker's Treasury . . .*

* * *

In Lancaster County, Pennsylvania, where I have lived for the past thirty years, they tell a story about a Pennsylvania Dutch minister who had no regular charge, but who supplied vacant pulpits around the countryside as opportunity offered. One Sunday, accompanied by his little son, he boarded a trolley car and journeyed several miles to a small town where he was scheduled to conduct the service of the morning. As he entered the church he noticed a box in the vestibule bearing the legend, "For the poor"; and although he was himself not blessed with a superfluity of this world's goods, he produced a quarter from his pocket and dropped it into the receptacle. At the conclusion of the service he was escorted from the pulpit by one of the officers of the church who thanked him for his sermon and stated that it was the custom of the congregation to give their supply preachers the contents of the poor box. When he unlocked it, out dropped nothing whatever save the poor minister's own quarter. He pocketed it with a wry smile, and as he and his little son walked back to the trolley station, the boy looked up into his face and said: "You would have gotten more out if you had put more in, wouldn't you, Pop?"

—From an Address by H. W. Prentis, Jr.,
Chairman of the Board, Armstrong Cork Company

One sunny May day in Central Park a blind man was seen tapping for attention with his cane and carrying on his chest a sign: "Help the Blind." No one paid much attention to him. A little farther on another blind beggar was doing better. Practically every passer-by put a coin in his cup, some even turning back to make their contribution. His sign said:

It is May—and I am blind!

—*Reader's Digest Reader*

* * *

Early in his career Henry Ford, in granting a subcontract for engine parts, specified that these parts were to be delivered in wooden boxes of a certain size, held together by screws, not nails. He even indicated the exact size and location of the screws.

In order to receive this lucrative order, the subcontractors willingly accepted the conditions, although they privately agreed that "this guy Ford is slightly batty." Many of his own employees felt that the "old man" was being unnecessarily dogmatic about the shipping cases, too, but they chalked it up to erratic genius.

Came delivery day—and revelation. Henry Ford's "whimsy" had been the work of genius, all right, but hardly erratic. The sides of those precisely measured wooden shipping boxes were exactly the size of the floorboards of Henry's Fords. With each screw hole correctly spaced and drilled, the boards were ready to be slipped into place.

—George Relf, Quoted by Helen Houston Boileau
Reprinted in *The Reader's Digest*

* * *

When a girl applies for admission to Vassar, a questionnaire is sent to her parents. A father in a Boston suburb, filling out one of these blanks, came to the question, "Is she a leader?" He hesitated, then wrote, "I am not sure about this, but I know she is an excellent follower."

A few days later he received this letter from the president of the college: "As our freshman group next fall is to contain several hundred leaders, we congratulate ourselves that your daughter will also be a member of the class. We shall thus be assured of one good follower."

—*The Journal of Education*

* * *

A friend of mine, a distinguished explorer who spent a couple of years among the savages of the upper Amazon, once attempted a forced march through the jungle. The party made extraordinary speed for the first two days, but on the third morning, when it was time to start, my friend found all the natives sitting on their haunches, looking very solemn and making no preparation to leave.

"They are waiting," the chief explained to my friend. "They cannot move farther until their souls have caught up with their bodies."

I can think of no better illustration of our own plight today.

—James Truslow Adams, "The Tempo of Modern Life"
(Boni). Reprinted in *The Reader's Digest*

## Witticisms, Quips, and Humorous Verse

It often takes a speaker twice as long to tell what he thinks as to tell what he knows.

—Prochnow, *Speaker's Treasury . . .*

* * *

It seems incredible . . . 35,000,000 laws and no improvement on the Ten Commandments.

—Prochnow, *Speaker's Treasury . . .*

* * *

Always when I pass a church
I drop in for a visit
So that when I'm carried in
The Lord won't say, "Who is it?"

—Prochnow, *Speaker's Treasury . . .*

* * *

It's useless to put your best foot forward—and then drag the other.

—*Quote* Magazine

* * *

I always prefer to believe the best of everybody; it saves so much trouble.

—Kipling

* * *

After all is said and done, more is usually said.

—*Reader's Digest*

* * *

Gossip: something negative that is developed and then enlarged.

—*Reader's Digest*

* * *

The narrower a man's mind, the broader his statements.

—Burton Hillis, *Quote* Magazine

* * *

The more hot arguments you win, the fewer warm friends you'll have.

—Burton Hillis, *Quote* Magazine

* * *

If at first you succeed, you probably haven't accomplished much.

—Rex Mobley, *Quote* Magazine

* * *

For each pupil with a spark of genius, there are ten with ignition trouble.

—*Mississippi Education Advance*

Don't forget that people will judge you by your actions, not your intentions. You may have a heart of gold—but so has a hard-boiled egg.

—Emily Lotney, *Quote* Magazine

* * *

A centipede was happy quite,
Until a frog, in fun,
Said, "Pray, which leg comes after which?"
This raised her mind to such a pitch
She lay distracted in a ditch,
Considering how to run.

—Prochnow, *Speaker's Treasury . . .*

* * *

## Quotations

I have never been hurt by anything that I didn't say.

—Calvin Coolidge

* * *

No race can prosper till it learns that there is as much dignity in tilling a field as in writing a poem.

—George Washington Carver

* * *

"The world," Dwight Morrow once wrote to his son, "is divided into people who do things and people who get the credit. Try, if you can, to belong to the first class. There's far less competition."

—Harold Nicolson, *Dwight Morrow*

* * *

The only way to have a friend is to be one.

—Emerson

* * *

Countless people love to talk, but many have no idea of conversation—which is, in too many cases, a lost art. Conversation may make or mar your social and business future. People judge you the moment you speak; there is no better index to your breeding, your education, your environment, your habitual associates. Yet society has a shortage of men and women with well-developed moral and ethical sense who are articulate enough to make their convictions felt.

—Adapted from E. Daniel Ryden,
*The Lost Art of Conversation, Life and Health Magazine*

If you have lost wealth, you have lost nothing.
If you have lost health, you have lost something.
If you have lost character, you have lost all.

—Inscription over old German school

Education is not something that is done for a student. It is no laying on of hands, no putting on of robes, no pouring in of information. Education is what the student does for himself in the way of developing his own powers. Teachers can help; so can a curriculum and an atmosphere of devotion to things of the mind. But ultimately the problem is utterly the student's. If he would be an educated man, then he must give his best effort to the arduous, the unpleasing and often discouraging task of disciplining his mind to the point where it is an effective mechanism—knowing full well that the trained mind is the most powerful instrument in the whole world.

—Charles Cole, President, Amherst College

* * *

Anyone can carry his burden, however hard, until nightfall.
Anyone can do his work, however hard, for one day.
Anyone can live sweetly, patiently, lovingly, purely, till the sun goes down.
And this is all that life really means.

—Robert Louis Stevenson

* * *

The evil that men do lives after them;
The good is oft interred with their bones.

—Shakespeare

* * *

One man with courage makes a majority.

—Andrew Jackson

* * *

According to Sydney Herbert Wood, retiring Principal Assistant Secretary of the British Ministry of Education, the three acid tests of an "educated man" are:

Can you entertain a new idea?
Can you entertain another person?
Can you entertain yourself?

—*Time* Magazine

* * *

America is great because she is good, and if America ever ceases to be good, America will cease to be great.

—Quoted by Dwight D. Eisenhower, November 3, 1952

* * *

Have you heard of the terrible family They,
And the dreadful venomous things They say?
Why, half of the gossip under the sun,
If you trace it back, you will find begun
In that wretched House of They.

—Ella Wheeler Wilcox

## Fables

In our friendly neighbor city of St. Augustine, great flocks of sea gulls are starving amid plenty. Fishing is still good, but the gulls don't know how to fish. For generations they have depended on the shrimp fleet to toss them scraps from the nets. Now the fleet has moved to Key West.

The shrimpers had created a Welfare State for the St. Augustine sea gulls. The big birds never bothered to learn how to fish for themselves and they never taught their children to fish. Instead they led their little ones to the shrimp nets.

Now the sea gulls, the fine free birds that almost symbolize liberty itself, are starving to death because they gave in to the "something for nothing" lure! They sacrificed their independence for a handout.

A lot of people are like that, too. They see nothing wrong in picking delectable scraps from the tax nets of the U. S. Government's "shrimp fleet." But what will happen when the Government runs out of goods? What about our children of generations to come?

Let's not be gullible gulls. We Americans must preserve our talents of self-sufficiency, our genius for creating things for ourselves, our sense of thrift and our true love of independence.

—*Reader's Digest*

* * *

A hunter once caught a nightingale in his net. He was astonished when the bird spoke to him, asking for freedom. "See, how small I am," she said. "If you kill and eat me, you will not have much. But if you set me free, I will teach you three rules of wisdom that can be of great help." The man said, "Teach me, and I will let you go."

So the bird said, "Never try to obtain what you cannot. Never lament the loss of a thing which you cannot recover. Never believe what cannot be true." And the man let the nightingale go.

The bird then decided to make a test. Safe on a high branch, she called out, "Poor man, why did you let me go? I have in my body a pearl larger than the egg of an ostrich."

At once the man was sorry that he had freed the bird and tried in vain to catch her.

Then he heard the nightingale speak once more. "Oh, foolish man, you have learned nothing from my teaching. You try to catch me when you cannot follow my flight. You grieve at the loss of something you cannot recover. And you believe that there is in me a pearl of great size. Can you not see my whole body is not so large as an ostrich egg?"

—Written by John of Damascus in the 8th Century

* * *

The wolf and fox formed a partnership with the lion. On their first hunt together, they caught a bull, a cow, and a sheep. The lion asked the wolf to divide their booty.

The wolf said, "Sir, you take the bull; I, the cow; and the fox, the sheep."

The lion was very angry. He raised his paw and struck the wolf, causing a deep wound in his head. Then the lion told the fox to make the division.

The fox said, "Sir, it is right that you, who are our king, should have the bull; your wife, our queen, shall have the cow; and your children shall have the sheep."

The lion was well pleased. "You have made an excellent division," he said. "How did you learn to divide so well?"

The fox, looking at the wolf, said, "Sir, our partner, the wolf, taught me how to divide."

—Aesop's Fables

* * *

Once upon a time, the wolves sent messengers to a flock of sheep, asking that there might be peace between them for all time.

"Why should we go on with this fierce and deadly fighting?" argued the messengers. The cause of all our troubles is those wicked dogs. They are always barking at us and making us angry. Please send the dogs away. Then there will be no bar to our peace and eternal friendship."

The silly sheep listened to the messengers and sent the dogs away. Soon, without these strong defenders, the sheep were destroyed by their treacherous enemies, the wolves.

—Aesop's Fables

* * *

## Miscellaneous

According to the theory of aerodynamics and as may be readily demonstrated through wind tunnel experiments, the bumblebee is unable to fly. This is because the size, weight and shape of his body in relation to the total wingspread make flying impossible.

*But the bumblebee, being ignorant of these scientific truths, goes ahead and flies anyway—and makes a little honey every day.*

—*Reader's Digest Reader*

* * *

One night, in ancient times, three horsemen were riding across a desert. As they crossed the dry bed of a river, out of the darkness a voice called, "Halt!"

They obeyed. The voice then told them to dismount, pick up a handful of pebbles, put the pebbles in their pockets and remount.

The voice then said, "You have done as I commanded. Tomorrow at sun-up you will be both glad and sorry." Mystified, the horsemen rode on.

When the sun rose, they reached into their pockets and found that a miracle had happened. The pebbles had been transformed into diamonds, rubies, and other precious stones. They remembered the warning. They were both glad and sorry—glad they had taken some, and sorry they had not taken more . . .

And this is a story of Education.

—Dr. L. H. Adolfson, Director
Extension Division, University of Wisconsin

A man lived by the side of the road and sold hot dogs.
He was hard of hearing so he had no radio.
He had trouble with his eyes so he read no newspapers.
But he sold good hot dogs.

He put up a sign on the highway telling how good they were.
He stood by the side of the road and cried: "Buy a hot dog, Mister."
And people bought.
He increased his meat and roll orders.
He bought a bigger stove to take care of his trade.
He got his son home from college to help him.

But then something happened . . .
His son said, "Father, haven't you been listening to the radio?
If money stays 'tight,' we are bound to have bad business.
There may be a big recession coming on.
You had better prepare for poor trade."

Whereupon the father thought, "Well, my son has been to college.
He reads the papers and he listens to the radio, and he ought to know."
So the father cut down on his meat and roll orders.
Took down his advertising signs.
And no longer bothered to stand on the highway to sell hot dogs.
And his hot dog sales fell almost overnight.
"You're right, son," the father said to the boy.
We are certainly headed for a recession."

—Courtesy Trundle Consultants, Inc.

* * *

Enna?
Yeh, Jawge.
Enna, we bin goanagether for sem munts.
Sem munts an tennays.
Yeah. Well, I thing we kyna unnerstan e chudder.
We do.
We yeach godda sensayuma.
Thaz ride.
We lyg da same thins: TV wezzerns.
Pinics.
Hah dogs en sarkraut.
Plain cards.
Jussa bowed evrythin to mayga perfek mairge.
Wadayuh tryna say, Jawge?
Weeyuh marry me?
Ohyezz. Thizziz the hapyest moment of my lyve.
Enna!
Jawge!

—Herb Gochros, *Enfeebled English—The Proposal*

## ACTIVITIES

1. Bring to class the speaker's kit that you have prepared. Compare yours with those of your classmates. Answer these questions:
   What are the most common headings used in your class?
   What are the least common headings used in your class?
   Which sources seem to be most frequently used?
   Which kits contained the most interesting items?
2. Select any five of your items and tell the class briefly how you would use each in a speech.
3. Exchange kits. From the one that you receive, select the most interesting related clippings and use them in preparing a speech to be delivered to the class.
4. Bring to class as many clippings as you can find that are closely related in meaning to any of the items in the *Sample Speaker's Kit.*
5. Bring to class at least five quotations from Shakespeare or any other widely quoted author. Discuss in class how they could be applied to a modern topic or situation.
6. Using the Bible as a source, find a series of related items that could be applied to a modern subject. You may choose quotations, parables, events, or the lives of any of its people.
7. Collect as many items as possible related to the general aspects of speaking—voice, stage fright, conversation, listening, speech habits, and so forth. Share them with each other in class and discuss their importance to you.
8. Find at least one fable or little story with a moral to exchange with one of your classmates. In a short speech, use the one that you receive to apply to a modern situation.
9. Find in any speaker's collections of stories in your library some stories that you could use as openers in case you are called on unexpectedly to give a speech. Arrange a program in class in which you can use at least one of yours.
10. Select any of the titles given below, find interesting anecedotes, quotations, examples, and other illustrative devices, and use them in preparing a forceful speech. Use "What Prayer Can Do" as a model.
    What Faith Can Do
    What Perseverance Can Do
    What Love Can Do
    What Loyalty Can Do
    What Understanding Can Do
11. Below is a list of general subjects. Find as many illustrative items as possible on any one of them to use in a speech. Phrase a suitable specific title, write, and deliver your speech. Vote with your classmates to decide which speech is the most appealing.

| | | |
|---|---|---|
| Education | Courage | Courtesy |
| Patriotism | Vision | Heroism |
| Citizenship | Crime | Success |
| Youth | Responsibility | Self-reliance |
| Safety | Morals | Integrity |

UNIT

# 4

# *Speaking in More Formal Groups*

CHAPTER

CHAPTER

# 15 Conducting a Meeting

Which motions have the most success?
For which do persons yearn?
One is the motion to recess,
The other, to adjourn.

*—Richard Armour*

"MR. Chairman, I move that . . . ." "Point of order!" "I move to amend by . . . ." "I think that this is a good proposal because . . . ." "I nominate Mary Doemel." "I appeal from the decision of the Chair." Probably these words are familiar to all of you for almost everyone belongs to clubs and social groups, attends conventions, or joins in various activities in which parliamentary procedure is used. But you have probably also heard statements like the following, or you may have made them yourself: "I don't know why I keep coming to meetings. I never say anything because I don't know all the rules of parliamentary procedure." Or, "I really used my knowledge of parliamentary procedure well. I defeated everything anyone proposed." Or, "Boy, did we have fun! We really confused that chairman!" All three statements reflect some failure in either understanding of or proper use of parliamentary procedure.

## Basic Principles of Parliamentary Procedure

### Introduction

What is parliamentary procedure? Simply stated it is a set of principles and rules which have been developed over a long period of time to help groups reach decisions in a democratic way. It provides the opportunity for a full and fair presentation of views and a group decision based upon the wishes of the majority. It also provides for the protection of the rights of every member of the group, the right to suggest action, to nominate or serve in an office, to debate, or to be free from unfair restriction by the majority of the group.

As a member of groups, you need to understand parliamentary procedure well enough to present your ideas, to protect your rights, and to secure good decisions in any clubs which you will join. You particularly need to understand parliamentary procedure well enough also to enable you to execute your duties in the event that you are elected to an office.

The basic aim of parliamentary procedure is to provide a way for a group to come to a decision in the simplest and most direct manner while providing free debate, protecting the rights of the minority, and ensuring the rule of the majority. This aim is accomplished in several ways. Only one proposal may be debated at a time. Every subject is entitled to full debate. Each member has an equal right to propose subjects for consideration, to speak on a subject, to vote as he pleases, and to have information supplied about the proper procedure. Order is necessary so that these procedures are possible. Members must cooperate, only one may speak at any

"Order please!" The chairman raps with his gavel to restore order so as to continue with the business at hand. *(Ewing Galloway)*

one time, and each must speak to the specific matter before the group. Each member has an equal vote in reaching any decision. Through the written rules of the group and the customs of parliamentary procedure a method is established to provide for these rights in a natural and uniform way. These rules further provide that no member can exercise his rights to a point where he may block action or dictate to the majority.

### Familiar terms

The *constitution* and *bylaws* contain the written rules which protect the rights of every member. They set forth such items as the purpose of the group, its name, membership requirements, and establish the essential parliamentary procedure for election of officers, order of business, and so forth. In Chapter 16 you will learn specifically what goes into the constitution and bylaws and the method of adoption.

A *quorum* requirement protects the rights of all members by preventing a small part of any group from making decisions binding on all. The quorum is the minimum number of members required to be present before any official business can be transacted. Usually the quorum requirement is stated in the bylaws, but if no statement is made a quorum is defined by custom as one over half of the total membership.

## Order of Business

The order of business is usually prescribed in the constitution and bylaws. The usual order of business is as follows:

**1. Call to order.** The chairman stands, raps with his gavel and says, "The meeting will please come to order."

**2. Invocation.** If the group desires to include a brief prayer, it should be given at this time.

**3. Roll call.** The secretary will call the names of the members at this time unless some other attendance check is taken.

**4. Reading and approval of the minutes of the last meeting.** The chairman requests: "The secretary will please read the minutes of the last meeting." Since the minutes are the formal, written record of the previous meeting, it is particularly important that the statements be correct, that the minutes be read clearly, and that the group be given the opportunity to approve them or to correct them before they are approved.

The chairman asks, "Are there any corrections or additions to the minutes as read?" If there is no response, he then states, "The minutes will stand approved as read."

In the event of a change or an addition, the member addresses the Chair, waits for recognition, and states his point. The Chair confers, if he wishes, with the secretary, announces his decision, and asks if there is any objection. If even one person objects, the matter must be put to a vote for group decision. This is like a main motion and demands a majority vote. After suggested changes have been decided, the chairman states, "If there are no further objections, the minutes will stand approved as corrected." The secretary then writes at the conclusion of the minutes: (a) "Approved" (b) date of approval and (c) his signature.

**5. Reports.** The chairman calls for reports, usually in this order: (a) officers in the order of their rank, (b) chairmen of standing committees, and (c) chairmen of any special committees.

Reports keep the members informed of actions and/or recommendations of officers or committees. The treasurer reports on the club finances, a social committee reports on progress for the school

"Will the chairman of the membership drive please give his report?"

THE SATURDAY EVENING POST

dance, or a special committee reports on a problem referred to it. Officers and committees derive their power from the group, are responsible to the group, and may be voted out of office or dismissed by the group that elected them.

Standing committees are permanent ones usually appointed by the president or elected by the group to perform a specific task such as taking care of social activities, preparing programs, or handling membership problems.

Special committees are temporary, do one special job, and are dissolved when they finish their work and report to the group.

If a report ends with no specific recommendation, the chairman usually says, "If there is no objection, the report will be filed as read." If there is a recommendation offered, the chairman of the committee usually moves its adoption and this motion is treated like any main motion. The group then may adopt, modify, reject, or request the committee to give further study to the matter.

**6. Unfinished business.** At this time any business held over from the previous meeting is considered.

**7. New business.** This is the opportunity for any member to propose action on new subjects.

**8. Announcements.** Any officers or members may make announcements about any events or things of interest not hitherto mentioned.

**9. Program.** If a program is to be given, it follows the formal business session. Frequently, the business session is formally adjourned prior to the program.

**10. Adjournment.** The chairman may say, "The hour fixed for adjournment is now reached. The meeting is adjourned." If no exact time has been fixed, the chairman may call for a motion or one of the members may make a motion to adjourn.

## ACTIVITIES

1. What are the ways in which parliamentary procedure is fundamental to democracy?
2. In your experience with groups—clubs, school government, legislative bodies—what have you observed regarding the use of parliamentary procedure?
   a. Did it work well?
   b. What were some of the problems you observed?
   c. How did the members of the group respond in different situations?
   d. What improvements would you suggest?
3. Why is an "Order of Business" necessary in parliamentary groups?

# Motions

## Classification of motions

Motions are proposals submitted for decision by the group and may serve many different functions. On the basis of these different uses we divide motions into four types: main, subsidiary, incidental, and privileged.

**Main motions** are initial proposals for action. They introduce a subject for the assembly to act upon.

**Subsidiary motions** are those which act directly upon the main motion in some fashion. They may serve to change its content or to dispose of it temporarily or permanently in some manner such as by postponing it or by referring it to a committee. These subsidiary motions are tools to work upon motions. Certain of them also apply to other subsidiary motions or to incidental and privileged motions.

**Incidental motions** are tools of a more secondary nature. They do not apply directly to motions as do the subsidiary motions, but provide a means for a correction of or changing of the procedure under which motions are being handled. These motions arise "incidentally" out of other motions. Motions to take a secret ballot or a point of order are incidental motions.

**Privileged motions** are those which could be of such urgent importance that they interrupt the proceedings at any time, receive immediate attention, and suspend the other work of the group until they are taken care of.

## Precedence of motions

Because each type of motion and each different motion serves a different function, a different priority or rank for consideration is given to them. If one motion has precedence or priority over another it must be decided first. *A main motion is at the bottom of precedence.* The subsidiary motions are tools to modify other motions, and thus they are considered *before* the motion to which they apply. Incidental motions deal with matters of procedure and are taken care of immediately as they arise. Thus, they actually have no precedence among themselves. Privileged motions deal with emergency-type matters and thus take precedence over all other types of motions. The table of parliamentary motions at the end of this chapter indicates the rank or precedence of the frequently used motions. *(See pages 306-7)*

## General aspects of motions

Certain general questions arise in connection with every motion. The answer to these general questions is the basis for most of the parliamentary rules for any motion. In the table at the end of this chapter you will note a description of each motion in terms of the five general aspects considered below.

**May interrupt a speaker?** Normally, you would think it discourteous to interrupt a speaker. However, when a matter is so urgent or is most conveniently handled if brought up immediately, it is best to interrupt a speaker. If a speaker cannot be heard, for example, it is best to make this known immediately through a question of privilege. Whenever a motion is so important that the mover may interrupt a speaker, the mover never has to be recognized by the Chair. Whenever a motion is not of such importance, the mover must first secure recognition from the Chair.

**Second required?** A second has two purposes: (1) it is evidence that more than one member wishes to consider a matter and so it may be worth taking the time of the group, and (2) it usually indicates support for the proposal which is seconded. All main and subsidiary motions require seconds but certain privileged and incidental motions, particularly those calling for a decision by the Chair, do not.

**Debatable?** Motions may or may not be subject to debate. Privileged motions and incidental motions are not debatable. Also, motions to table, and to close, limit, or extend debate are not debatable. Most of these non-debatable motions are procedural or call for immediate action and decision by the Chair. Also, the ruling of the Chair may be submitted to majority approval by an appeal from the decision of the Chair.

**Amendable?** Some motions have a fixed form that cannot be changed; these are not amendable. However, the content of main motions, other amendments, and proposals as to time and place may be modified in their content; and so these are amendable.

**Vote required?** The way in which a group decision is formalized is through a vote. This is how the will of the majority is made effective. However, certain motions require different strength for adoption. Like the requirement of the quorum which was established to protect the rights of the members, other requirements in terms of voting strength are established. Amendments to the constitution normally take a two-thirds vote. Motions which limit the freedom of members of a group also call for a larger vote.

The kinds of votes include unanimous consent, two-thirds of the membership, two-thirds of those voting (also called a simple two-thirds), a majority of the total membership, a majority of those voting (also called a simple majority), and a plurality.

Unanimous consent is a method of securing immediate acceptance on items that are universally supported. You saw an example of this in approving the minutes. The usual form is "If there is no objection . . . ." If an objection is made, a motion must be formally moved and a vote of "aye" and "nay" taken. No motion ever demands a vote of unanimous consent.

A two-thirds vote of the entire membership is rarely demanded. A two-thirds vote of those members present and voting is usually required for suspension of the rules, limiting debate, closing nominations, and other motions where the freedom of the members is being limited. This demand for a two-thirds vote prevents a bare majority from depriving members of their right to full debate, for example, yet one member is not permitted to block all action.

A majority vote of the entire membership is one over half of the entire group. Unless otherwise stated, a majority vote refers to one more than half of the legal votes cast (simple majority). If a quorum is present and only one member votes, that vote is a majority vote. Most matters are decided by majority votes.

A plurality represents less than a majority but more votes than any other proposal or candidate. This is normally used only in elections, although many constitutions and bylaws require a majority vote to elect to office.

In the chart on pages 306 and 307, the vote required for passing a motion is based on the simple majority and simple two-thirds of those voting. In other words, if 25 in the group vote on a main motion, it will pass if 13 or more vote for it. If someone wishes to stop debate and 25 cast their votes, at least 17 will have to vote "yes" to prevent further discussion.

**Method of voting.** There are several methods of voting: voice vote, standing vote, by ballot, or a roll call vote.

The most common is the voice vote. After stating the motion to be voted upon, the chairman says, "All those in favor say 'aye.'" Then he says, "Those opposed say 'nay.'" If the chairman is certain of the group's feeling he may say, "The ayes have it. The motion is carried"; or, "The nays have it. The motion is defeated."

A standing vote may be taken when the chairman cannot make a reasonable decision as to which side had the majority. "The Chair is in doubt. All those in favor please stand (or raise their hands)."

In large, formal meetings, the chairman often has occasion to exercise his full knowledge of the fine points of parliamentary procedure. *(Ewing Galloway)*

He then counts the votes and calls for those opposed. Finally, he states the affirmative and negative votes and declares the motion carried or defeated.

Any member of the house may obtain a standing vote after a voice vote by simply calling, "Division," or saying, "I call for a division." The mover of this incidental motion need not be recognized but must make this call immediately after the decision of the Chair on the vote is announced.

Another common method of voting is by ballot. This may take the form of a secret ballot to be counted by special tellers or by the secretary. Sometimes a mail ballot is used with the secretary sending and receiving the ballots through the mail. This is used principally for very important questions such as amendments to the constitution. Any member may move for a vote by ballot. Such an incidental motion is not debatable and requires a majority vote.

The roll call vote is not common in small groups but it is a useful method at any time when it is desired to record the vote of each member. It is frequently used in legislative bodies and political conventions. Any member may move for a roll call vote, the motion is not debatable, and requires a majority vote. The secretary calls the roll alphabetically with each person recorded as "aye," "nay," "absent," or "abstaining" (present but not voting).

## Presentation and Disposition of a Motion

### Recognition

To move adoption of main motions, amendments, and many other motions, or to enter debate on a motion, the speaker must be recognized by the chairman. The normal procedure is to stand and address the Chair, "Mr. Chairman," and wait for the chairman to recognize you. Often many members try for recognition simultaneously and the Chair must decide whom to recognize. He will usually try to recognize a speaker presenting a differing viewpoint from that of the preceding speaker during debate. He will also recognize a person who has not spoken previously on a given motion over one who has spoken previously. You will recall that certain motions may be presented without the mover obtaining prior recognition from the Chair. When these are disposed of, the speaker who was interrupted may continue his speech.

### Statement of a motion

After obtaining the recognition of the Chair, a person may continue to debate the motion before the group or he may wish to move a new motion. Every new motion should be stated as clearly and completely as possible. If the motion is out of order because it violates some parliamentary rule, the chairman will rule it out of order immediately. The Chair will also rule out of order any attempt to debate a motion before it is actually declared open to debate by the Chair.

### Seconding

After a motion is stated, another member may call, "Second," (he need not be recognized) or the Chair will ask, "Is there a second to that motion?" If no one seconds a motion that requires such a second, the Chair will rule, "The motion is lost for lack of a second." You remember that certain motions do not demand seconds.

## Restatement of the motion by the Chair or decision by the Chair

After a motion has been made and, if necessary, seconded, the Chair should restate the motion. This helps all group members to understand the business before the house. If the motion is debatable, the chairman then declares the motion open to debate. Other motions may call for a decision of the Chair. In this case the Chair will announce his decision, and then continue with the next item of business.

## Debate

The chairman first recognizes the person who made the motion, giving the mover a chance to support his motion. During the course of debate, any member may desire to modify or dispose of the main motion by using a subsidiary motion such as a motion to amend or refer to a committee. Since debate is normally in order only upon the immediate item of business, if an amendment is proposed, it must be debated and disposed of before the group may return to the discussion of the main motion. The Chair should rule out of order any debate not on the immediate order of business. The Chair also enforces time limits and sees that the discussion is proper.

All motions are not subject to debate. Most non-debatable motions are procedural or call for immediate action and decision by the Chair.

## Voting

When a vote of the membership is required, the chairman should restate the motion to be voted upon and he will frequently indicate the necessary vote for adoption, if other than a majority vote.

## Announcement of the vote

Finally the Chair will announce the vote, indicate its effect, and then state the next order of business. "The ayes have it. The proposal to have a Christmas party is referred to the social committee. Is there any further business to come before the house?" Or, "The nays have it. The motion to refer to a committee is lost. We shall continue debate on the main motion. Is there any further debate?"

## ACTIVITIES

Assume that the class is a club. Appoint a chairman, a secretary, and three persons to introduce main motions.

1. In the first motion, state the motion, have it seconded, and decide by a voice vote the outcome after discussion.

2. In the second motion, state the motion, and have it die because nobody seconds it.
3. In the third motion, call for a voice vote after discussion and then call for a division.
4. Conduct an election of officers by secret ballot.

# Specific Motions

## Main motions

The main motion serves to introduce a proposal for consideration of the group. It is stated: "I move . . . . " For example, "Mr. Chairman. (after recognition by the chairman) I move that we have a Christmas party at 7:30 p.m., December 21, in Room 301." A main motion places a proposed course of action before the group and some decision must be made upon it. Even if no immediate action is taken upon a main motion and the group adjourns without making any decision concerning it, the motion will automatically reappear as old business at the next meeting.

A main motion must be seconded, is debatable, and all other motions may apply to it. A main motion is "at the bottom of precedence." Most main motions require a simple majority vote unless they are proposals to amend the constitution or have some similar effect.

## Subsidiary motions

As you have learned earlier, subsidiary motions are used to modify or dispose of other motions. As such they take precedence over any motion to which they apply. These subsidiary motions will be treated in order from least precedence to highest precedence.

**To postpone indefinitely.** The usual purpose of this motion is to defeat a main motion without running the risk of possible passage. "Mr. Chairman. (recognized) I move that we postpone consideration of this motion indefinitely." This motion requires a second and opens the main motion to full debate. No subsidiary motions apply to the motion to postpone indefinitely except that to close debate. If this motion passes (simple majority), the motion may not be renewed at this session. If this motion is lost, debate continues on the main motion and those opposing the main motion have an indication of the relative strength of those favoring the main motion.

**To amend.** Amendments are an attempt to secure modifications of the main motion, other amendments, proposed time limits of debate, length of a recess, strength of a committee, or any other motion in which the content of the motion may be varied.

Amendments are of three types: those which insert or add additional words, those which strike out words, and those which substitute—that is, strike out and insert in their place. Amendments are extremely useful in meetings and you will wish to know each form. Here is a main motion: "I move that our dramatic club present a Christmas play in an assembly program." "Mr. Chairman. (recognized) I move to amend this motion by inserting the words 'December 16th' immediately after the word 'play.'" Or, "Mr. Chairman. (recognized) I move to amend the motion by striking out the word 'Christmas' immediately preceding the word 'play.'" "Mr. Chairman. (recognized) I move to amend this motion by substituting the word 'entertainment' for the word 'play.'"

The motion to amend demands a second. Debate is not permitted on the main motion to which an amendment is proposed but must be limited to the amendment. If an amendment is defeated, the original main motion is left in its original form and is debated in that form. If an amendment is adopted, the motion is changed and is then debated in its amended form.

Amendments must take precedence of the motion to which they apply, even if the motion is a privileged one such as a move to take a recess. An amendment may be directly opposed to the basic idea of the motion to which it is applied, but it is in order provided that it is relevant to the subject. The Chair usually decides any question of relevance. An amendment to substitute (that is, to entirely replace a motion with a new motion) is proper, therefore, provided that the substitute motion deals with the same subject area as the original motion. However, it is not proper to simply insert a negative in the original motion, for the same end may be achieved simply by voting down the motion.

**To amend an amendment.** All of the provisions above with regard to a first order amendment apply to this motion with the exception of a provision for amendment. Since many amendments at one time would be very confusing, only one amendment to a main motion and one amendment to that amendment may be in order at one time. Following the order of precedence and logic, you must dispose of the amendment to the amendment before the original amendment may be discussed further. This in turn must be debated and voted upon before attention is re-focused on the main motion.

**To refer to a committee.** This motion is used to refer a subject to a committee for further investigation, to attempt a compromise, for action, or for other purposes. It is moved as follows: "Mr. Chairman. (recognized) I move that we refer this to a special committee of three members, appointed by the chairman, to gather the facts and report at the next regular meeting." The effect of this motion, if passed by a majority, is to refer the motion to the committee. This disposes of the matter until such time as the committee reports.

Usually a motion to refer to a committee includes instructions to the committee, number and method of selection of the members, and the time for its report. The motion to refer may be amended on any of these points.

A related motion is that to recommit to a committee. After a committee reports, the group may decide that further committee action is desirable and return the matter to the committee once more.

Both motions demand a second, are debatable, and require a majority vote.

**To postpone to a definite time.** Your group may want to postpone consideration of a motion until some definite future date.

A committee meets for discussion and to gather information for its report. *(Monkmeyer)*

They may feel that (a) other business is more pressing or (b) a better decision can be made at a later date. This postponement may be made as either a general or a special order.

In a general order the date but not the time of day is specified in the motion. In a special order the time of day is specified as well. A motion for a general order is made as follows: "Mr. Chairman. (recognized) I move to postpone the question until the next meeting." This requires a simple majority vote and, if passed, the question will come up as unfinished business at that meeting. The motion for a special order is stated as follows: "Mr. Chairman. (recognized) I move to postpone further consideration of this question until 2 p.m. this afternoon." This motion requires a two-thirds affirmative vote because it limits the freedom of action of the group. However, a special order may be postponed by a similar two-thirds vote.

Either special or general orders may also be created as a result of a main motion. To move either a special or a general order as a main motion, or to postpone definitely, the mover must be recognized and the motion seconded. This motion is debatable and amendable.

**To limit or extend debate.** Freedom of debate is essential to the democratic principles of parliamentary procedure. However, if time seems limited or if a number of items are to be discussed, the body may desire to establish time limits on debate. The form of this motion is: "Mr. Chairman. (recognized) I move that debate be limited to a total of twenty minutes." The motion also could limit the number of speeches or put time limits on each speech.

The motion requires a second, may not be debated, and requires a two-thirds vote. Amendments on the limits, however, may be introduced.

If the limits set up by the group are found too restrictive, a two-thirds vote can pass a motion to extend debate beyond the original limits.

**To call for the previous question.** The purpose of this motion is to close debate. The motion may be stated in one of two ways: "Mr. Chairman. (recognized) I move the previous question," or "I move to close debate." If passed, a vote must be taken at once on the immediately pending question. If there are several subsidiary motions on the floor in addition to a main motion, the mover may attempt to close debate on all these motions by stating: "Mr. Chairman. (recognized) I move to close debate on all pending questions." If this motion passes, voting must continue on all motions in order of precedence until the main motion has been disposed of in some fashion.

Because this motion ends debate, and thus limits the freedom of the members, it requires a two-thirds vote for passage. This motion is useful in closing debate when a few members are obviously delaying action. Yet, the requirement of the two-thirds vote prevents excessive limitation on debate by a small majority. A second is required. No debate is permitted on the motion. The motion is also renewable after additional progress in debate.

The call, "Question," is not a motion. It is simply an indication on the part of a member that he feels the group is ready for a vote.

**To lay on the table.** This motion serves to postpone consideration of a motion (lay on the table) with no time set to begin consideration again (take from the table). The form is simple. "Mr. Chairman. (recognized) I move that we table the motion." If this motion passes, the motion to which it is applied is set aside and the group proceeds to other business.

Because no time is set for resuming debate on the question, the assembly must vote to take up the matter again. The usual form is: "Mr. Chairman. (recognized) I move that we take from the table . . . (specify the motion tabled)." The move to take a motion from the table is a special type of main motion and may be moved only when no other business is before the group. Unless the motion to take the matter from the table passes, the question will never again be considered.

For both the motion (a) to table and (b) to take from the table, the mover must be recognized, the motion requires a second, is not debatable, and demands a majority vote.

## Incidental motions

**To suspend the rules.** Occasionally it is desirable to suspend a rule of the organization to accomplish some particular goal which is blocked by normal rules. The motion states the business that is interfered with and moves to suspend the rules so that the business in question may be accomplished. "Mr. Chairman. (recognized) I move to suspend the rules which prevent attendance of a non-member at our meetings so that Mr. Thomas may be invited to present a speech next week." If passed, the rules are suspended only for the amount of time necessary to accomplish the specific task stated in the motion. To suspend the rules demands a two-thirds vote. The mover must be recognized, the motion requires a second, and is not debatable.

**Leave to withdraw a motion.** A member who made a motion may desire to withdraw it before a final vote is reached disposing of the motion. Once made, however, any motion becomes the property of the group. The group must, therefore, give its permission before the motion may be withdrawn. This motion can be made only by the original mover: "Mr. Chairman. (recognized) I desire to withdraw my motion." The Chair will then say, "Mr. X desires to withdraw his motion. If there is no objection the motion will be withdrawn." If such a unanimous vote is not obtained, the motion to withdraw must be put to a vote. Such a motion does not require a second, is not debatable, and demands a simple majority vote.

**To object to consideration of a question.** This rarely used motion serves to prevent debate on a matter that is clearly objectionable to the group. The mover may interrupt another speaker, saying, "Mr. Chairman. I object to the consideration of this motion." The chairman immediately states the motion as follows: "All those in favor of considering this motion say 'aye,'" etc. A vote of two-thirds in the negative is required to prevent consideration. The motion requires no second and is not debatable. Any debate would violate the basic purpose for which the motion is made, that is, to prevent discussion of an objectionable matter.

**To call for division of the assembly.** Since the voice vote is the typical manner of voting, it is sometimes necessary to verify the accuracy of the Chair in his interpretation of a voice vote. If the Chair fails to confirm a close voice vote, a member may state, without waiting for recognition, "I call for a division of the assembly." The motion requires no second, is not debatable, and cannot be amended. Since most chairmen would welcome a confirmation of a close vote, most chairmen immediately call for a standing vote. However, if he feels it is not necessary to do so, a majority vote is required to compel a division.

**To rise to a point of order.** If any member feels that the Chair has made or is permitting some procedural mistake he may rise to a point of order to call attention to this fact. "Mr. Chairman. I rise to a point of order." The chairman then replies, "State your point." "A motion to close debate requires a two-thirds, not a simple majority vote." The point of order is decided by the chairman who rules, "Your point is (or is not) well taken," and then indicates the next item of business and the proper procedure. If the chairman is in doubt he may put the matter to a vote by the group. Because of the importance of proper procedure, anyone making a point of order may interrupt a speaker, does not need a second, and the point is

"All those in favor say, 'Ugh!' "

not debatable. A ruling of the Chair is always required on a point of order. Normally, a matter is first raised as a point of order. If the decision of the Chair is unsatisfactory to some member, he may then appeal from the decision of the Chair.

Closely related to the point of order is "rising to a parliamentary inquiry." This is used by a member to discover proper procedure. It is answered by the Chair and follows the same rules as the point of order.

**To appeal a decision of the Chair.** An appeal is used to put a decision of the Chair to a vote of the members. The mover may interrupt a speaker and say, "Mr. Chairman. I appeal from the decision of the Chair." The Chair states the motion in this fashion: "There is an appeal from the decision of the Chair. Those in favor of sustaining the Chair say 'aye,' " etc. If the Chair receives a majority of the votes, the decision or ruling of the Chair stands. If the Chair does not receive the majority vote, the ruling must be reversed.

This motion is an important democratic safeguard, for it protects the group from unfair or arbitrary rules of the chairman. An appeal must be seconded and it is usually not debatable. However, the member making the appeal and the Chair may state the basis for their actions. While appeals from the decision of the Chair are important safeguards, they should not be used to overturn correct decisions made by the Chair which protect the rights of members or follow proper procedure.

## Privileged motions

**To call for the orders of the day.** The purpose of this motion is to direct attention to some special or general order which applies at this time. The "orders of the day" to which the chairman must adhere might include an agenda set forth by the group from a previous meeting, a motion which was postponed to a definite time, or any order of business established previously by the assembly. If the chairman fails to observe the prearranged order, a member may state: "Mr. Chairman. I call for the order of the day." The Chair will rule whether the call for the order is proper and will indicate the correct procedure. If the orders of the day are in order, they must be considered unless postponed. A special order may be postponed by a two-thirds vote, a general order by a majority vote. The call for a special order may interrupt a speaker, that for a general order may not. Neither call requires a second and neither is debatable.

**To rise to a question of privilege.** A matter which concerns the assembly or an individual and is of a very immediate nature may be raised as a question of privilege. "Mr. Chairman. I rise to a question of privilege." The Chair rejoins, "State your question." "I request that the doors be opened to increase the ventilation." The presiding officer will normally decide a question of privilege although the request also may be put to a vote by the group. Any matter which affects the comfort or convenience of the group or an individual member may be brought to the attention of the Chair through a question of privilege. Such a question may interrupt a speaker, and is normally decided by the Chair without need of a second, or of debate.

**To recess.** To provide the group with the opportunity to take an intermission is the purpose of the motion to recess. The form is: "Mr. Chairman. I move that we recess for one hour for lunch, to reconvene at one o'clock." The motion to recess requires a second, is not debatable, but may be amended as to the length of time, and requires a majority vote.

**To adjourn.** The purpose of the motion to adjourn is to end a meeting. "Mr. Chairman. (recognized) I move to adjourn." If the motion is passed, that particular meeting is ended and the group will reassemble at the time previously set for the meeting to follow.

Normally the motion to adjourn may be moved at any time during a meeting because it holds privileged status. When privileged, the mover must gain the recognition of the Chair, the motion requires a second, but is not debatable.

Under certain special conditions the motion to adjourn is *not* privileged and must be made as a main motion. When adjournment would mean the end of the assembly or the dissolution of the group, a motion to adjourn is not privileged. Thus, in a final class meeting, the last assembly at a political nominating convention, the last parliamentary meeting at any convention, the motion to adjourn is not privileged but is a main motion. As such, it is subject to all the general aspects of a main motion including debate, and amendment.

### ACTIVITIES

Assume that you are members of a club with an appointed chairman and secretary. Transact your business according to proper parliamentary procedure. Attempt action on such motions as the following:

1. A motion is postponed indefinitely.
2. A motion is postponed to a definite time as a special order.
3. A motion is made to refer a question to a committee.
4. A motion is made to lay the main motion on the table.
5. Introduce a motion and amend it in each of the three ways explained.
6. Use incidental and privileged motions during action on the motions indicated above.

# Officers: Election and Duties

## Election of officers

The number, names, and duties of officers, their terms of office, and certain requirements for their election are usually set forth in the constitution and bylaws of your organization. There are, however, certain general principles that apply to the nomination and election of such officers.

**Nominations.** To nominate is to name a candidate for an office. The first step in an election is to draw up a slate (i.e., list) of candidates. This task may be given to a nominating committee. This special committee names at least one, but not necessarily more than one, candidate for each office. Usually this report or slate is presented at a meeting specified for election. In order that the nominating committee may not control the election completely, many groups provide that the chairman will also request nominations from the floor.

In very *informal* groups, a nominating committee may not be necessary. The chairman announces at the appropriate time, "Nominations are open for the office of president." Any member may nominate by rising and saying, "Mr. Chairman. (recognized) I nominate -------- for president." Nominations made from the floor have the same effect as those made by a nominating committee. Nominations do not require a second.

If only one person is nominated for an office, the chairman should declare, "If there are no other nominations, -------- will be declared elected by acclamation."

The chairman may declare the nominations for an office closed if no further nominations are made. Or a member may move that nominations be closed. Such a motion is not debatable and requires a two-thirds affirmative vote. It is possible to proceed directly to voting without a motion to close nominations. The Chair may simply declare them closed in the absence of further nominations.

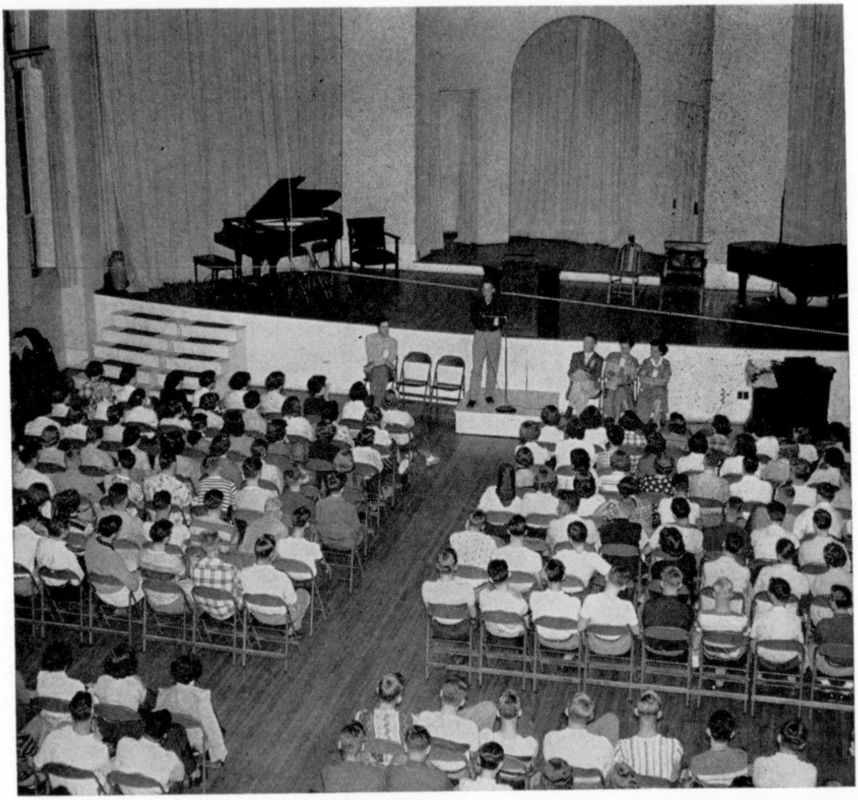

In less formal meetings, the chairman may adapt the degree of parliamentary procedure to the requirements and the nature of the group. *(Monkmeyer)*

**Election.** If balloting is done by a voice or standing vote, it is customary to list the candidates in the order of nomination. It is also customary to nominate and ballot for one office before going on to the next office to permit losers for one office to be nominated for another.

Election to office may require only a plurality in some groups; in other groups, however, a majority is sometimes necessary. The requirements for election are usually established in the bylaws.

## Duties of the officers

**The chairman.** The chairman is responsible for knowing the order of business, following proper procedures, and performing all duties prescribed in the constitution or bylaws. It is important that the chairman be comparatively expert in his command of parliamentary procedures to ensure that business is conducted in an orderly fashion.

In informal meetings a chairman may remain seated during much of the meeting. It is proper for him to stand (a) as he calls the meeting to order, (b) as he puts questions to vote, and (c) as he gives decisions. In formal meetings, the chairman may stand much of the time; in more informal meetings, he may remain sitting most or all of the time.

The chairman normally tries to remain impartial during debate. If he wishes to discuss freely, he must appoint a chairman *pro tem* (temporary chairman) to serve in his place. He may then argue from the floor exactly like any other member. He should not return to the chair until action on that item has been completed. He may vote if the vote is by ballot, but usually does not vote in other circumstances unless his vote will change the decision. This may occur in two instances: (1) In the event of tie, the Chair may cast a vote which would pass or defeat the motion. (2) If the Chair's vote will make a tie and change the decision, he may vote. For example, if the vote is 18-17 in favor of the motion, and the Chair votes no, the motion dies from a lack of a majority as is true in all cases of tied votes.

A good chairman needs to understand the problems, purposes, and personalities of his group. He should be able to speak well. The chairman should be concerned with helping the group to transact its business, and not worry about enforcing in strictest fashion all the rules of parliamentary procedure. The formality of the proceedings should always be adjusted to the needs of the particular group.

**The secretary.** The secretary must keep the minutes of each meeting. From the standpoint of content, the minutes should include:

1. Name of the organization
2. Kind of meeting (regular, special, etc.)
3. Date, time, and place of the meeting
4. Name and title of presiding and recording officers
5. Fact that a quorum was present
6. Notation as to the reading and approval of the minutes
7. Record of the reports by officers and committees
8. Record of all main motions, except those withdrawn, name of the mover, and possibly the major arguments
9. Record of all other motions including their disposition
10. Record of all votes taken
11. Time and type of adjournment
12. Signature of the secretary

The minutes should be written in permanent ink or typed. A loose-leaf notebook, size 8½ by 11, is quite convenient. It is helpful to allow wide margins so that any changes in the minutes may be legibly entered in the margins. The secretary's book becomes part of the permanent records of the organization.

In addition to keeping the minutes, the secretary may handle the correspondence, prepare the agenda for meetings, coordinate committee work, and perform such other duties as prescribed in the constitution or bylaws.

**The parliamentarian.** The parliamentarian is usually not elected. Ordinarily, he is appointed by the chairman to advise the Chair on procedural matters. He cannot rule on any question, but merely advises the Chair, who is free to disregard the advice.

## ACTIVITIES

1. Assume that the class is a club.
   a. Elect officers by show of hands with nominations from the floor.
   b. Prepare and deliver a speech in support of a candidate you nominated.
2. Discuss the following material you have studied.
   a. What is the basic aim of parliamentary procedure?
   b. What are the differences between main, subsidiary, incidental, and privileged motions?
   c. How is a motion handled?
   d. What are the major responsibilities of a member of a group? of a chairman? of a secretary?
   e. What are the different types of votes? What are the different methods of voting?

# Sample Minutes

MINUTES OF THE THALIAN DRAMATIC CLUB

The regular meeting of the Thalian Dramatic Club was called to order by its president, Carole Moyer, at 3:15 p.m., November 10, 19__, in Room 151. Thirty-five members responded to roll call.

The minutes of the previous meeting were read and approved.

Frank Morin, treasurer, reported the collection of $17.25 in dues, making the balance on hand $145.55 after expenditures of $40.95. Those members still owing dues were reminded that payment should be completed by December 1 to avoid a fine of ten cents.

Jane Lynn, chairman of the Program Committee, reported that a Christmas play, "Mimi Lights the Candle," would be presented at the next regular meeting in December. Those members wishing to try out for the play were asked to meet with Pat Eckman, director of the play, at the close of the meeting.

Sue Brengel, chairman of the Christmas Project Committee, reported that the committee had agreed to recommend that the club prepare a program and a party for the children at Findlay Street Neighborhood House. They also suggested that each member contribute one gift for the party costing not more than fifty cents and that refreshments be paid from club funds.

Sue Scherer moved the adoption of the Project Committee's report. It was seconded and passed unanimously by the club. Garnet Gooley moved that the date for the party be set for December 18. After some discussion, it was noted that December 18 would conflict with a rehearsal for the school concert. Motion was withdrawn, and Aletha Parks moved that the party be given December 16. Motion was passed unanimously.

The president called for volunteers to be on the program. The following members responded: Alfreda Tate---a Christmas story and a solo; Elaine Grote---a Christmas poem; Jackie De Vere and Sue Scherer---a dance; Beck Fleck---an original story; Ed Harris---magic tricks; Holly McCabe---an original monologue; and Frank Morin---a Christmas poem. Bette Ewing volunteered to play the piano for group singing, and Ed Wright agreed to play the part of Santa Claus.

New Business: Plans were discussed for having pictures in the yearbook and having a spring play.

Betty Leister moved that the club have two pages of pictures in the yearbook---one of members and one of club activities. Virginia White seconded the motion. In the discussion that followed, members wished to know more about the cost before deciding on having two pages. Bea Willard moved that the matter be referred to a committee appointed by the president and that the committee report the details of the cost at the next meeting. The motion was seconded by Margaret Reed and passed unanimously. Bea Willard and Margaret Reed were appointed to investigate the cost.

Mary Ellen Crawford moved that the president should appoint a committee of five to begin looking for a suitable three-act play to be presented in the spring. Motion was seconded by Norma Fingerhuth. In the discussion on the motion some members felt that it might be wise to consider three one-act plays as well as a three-act play. Betty Crum moved that the original motion be amended as follows: The committee of five should be instructed to look for both a three-act play and three one-act plays with the club having the right to decide which type of production it preferred. The amended motion was seconded and passed unanimously.

The committee appointed to read plays was: Eulonda Estes, chairman; Jo Quinn, Lillian Boner, Susan Lynn, and Virginia White.

At the conclusion of the business meeting the following program was presented:

"Pershing at the Front," dramatized by Rad Ewing, Ed Harris, Frank Morin, and J. B. Ewing

"Two Plus Two," an original monologue by Susan Lynn

"Ding Dong School," an impersonation by Mildred Mayberry

The president declared the meeting adjourned at 4:30.

Respectfully submitted,

Elaine Grote, Secretary

## Sample Treasurer's Report

THALIAN DRAMATIC CLUB TREASURER'S REPORT

November 10, 19___

| | | |
|---|---|---|
| RECEIPTS | | |
| 1. Balance on hand at last report | $146.75 | |
| 2. Dues collected | 17.25 | |
| 3. Receipts from bake sale | 22.50 | |
| Total | | $186.50 |
| DISBURSEMENTS | | |
| 1. Lumber for scenery | $ 25.00 | |
| 2. Donation to Scholarship Fund | 15.95 | |
| Total | | $ 40.95 |
| Balance on Hand | | $145.55 |

Frank Morin, Treasurer

"Most dramatic treasurer's report I've ever seen."

THE SATURDAY EVENING POST

FREQUENTLY USED PARLIAMENTARY MOTIONS
*(Listed in the order of precedence)*

| TYPE | MOTION | PURPOSE | MAY INTERRUPT A SPEAKER? | SECOND REQUIRED? | DEBATABLE? | AMENDABLE? | VOTE REQUIRED? |
|---|---|---|---|---|---|---|---|
| Privileged | 20. Fix Time for Reassembling | To arrange time of next meeting | No | Yes | No | Yes | Majority |
| | 19. Adjourn | To dismiss the meeting | No | Yes | No | No | Majority |
| | 18. To Recess | To dismiss the meeting for a specific length of time | No | Yes | No | Yes | Majority |
| | 17. Rise to a Question of Privilege | To make a personal request during debate | Yes | No | No | No | Decision of Chair |
| | 16. Call for the Orders of the Day | To force consideration of a postponed motion | Yes | No | No | No | Decision of Chair |
| Incidental | 15. Appeal a Decision of the Chair | To reverse the decision of the chairman | Yes | Yes | No | No | Majority |
| | 14. Rise to a Point of Order or Parliamentary Inquiry | To correct a parliamentary error or ask a question | Yes | No | No | No | Decision of Chair |
| | 13. To Call for Division of the Assembly | To verify a voice vote | Yes | No | No | No | Majority[1] |
| | 12. Object to the Consideration of a Question | To suppress action | Yes | No | No | No | Two-thirds |
| | 11. Leave to Withdraw a Motion | To allow the maker of a motion to withdraw it | No | No | No | No | Majority |
| | 10. To Suspend the Rules | To take action contrary to standing rules | No | Yes | No | No | Two-thirds |

| TYPE | MOTION | PURPOSE | MAY INTERRUPT A SPEAKER? | SECOND REQUIRED? | DEBATABLE? | AMENDABLE? | VOTE REQUIRED? |
|---|---|---|---|---|---|---|---|
| Subsidiary | 9. To Lay on the Table | To defer action | No | Yes | No | No | Majority |
| | 8. To Call the Previous Question | To force an immediate vote | No | Yes | No | No | Two-thirds |
| | 7. To Limit or Extend Debate | To modify freedom of debate | No | Yes | No | Yes | Two-thirds |
| | 6. To Postpone to a Definite Time | To defer action | No | Yes | Yes | Yes | Majority[2] |
| | 5. To Refer to a Committee | For further study | No | Yes | Yes | Yes | Majority |
| | 4. To Amend an Amendment | To modify an amendment | No | Yes | Yes | No | Majority |
| | 3. To Amend | To modify a motion | No | Yes | Yes | Yes | Majority |
| | 2. To Postpone Indefinitely | To suppress action | No | Yes | Yes | No | Majority |
| Main | 1. Main Motion | To introduce business | No | Yes | Yes | Yes | Majority |
| Specific Main Motions | A. To take from the Table | To consider tabled motions | No | Yes | No | No | Majority |
| | B. To Rescind | To reverse previous action | No | Yes | Yes | Yes | Majority |
| | C. To Reconsider | To consider a defeated motion again | Yes | Yes | Yes | No | Majority |

[1] Requires no vote unless a formal motion is offered to force the chairman to take a division.

[2] Majority vote required for general order; two-thirds vote required for special order.

## PRONUNCIATION PROBLEMS

Beware of confusing the "w" and "wh" sounds. The "wh" was taken from the Anglo-Saxon language. Its spelling was "hw" and, although we have changed the spelling, the sound remains the same—"hw"—as you will observe when you look up in the dictionary words beginning with "wh." Form your lips to say "h" and then say the letters which follow. Compare the two lists below and practice saying the words distinctly.

| | | |
|---|---|---|
| whale............wail | where...........wear | whither.........wither |
| whine............wine | when............wen | why..............."y" |
| whoa.............woe | what.............watt | whist.............wist |
| while.............wile | which...........witch | whet.............wet |
| Whig.............wig | wheel...........weal | whit..............wit |

## READING CHECK-UP

Read aloud the nonsense sentences below to check your pronunciation of any problem words.

The wheelwright whose wheels whirred when the whistle sounded told a whopper about seeing white whales whirling about in the white water. We were sure it was only a whim because he could never tell whence they came nor whither they went.

The white whippets wiggled their tails waiting for the whistle and ran like wild whenever the whips were used.

The Whigs wore their wigs wherever they went which caused much whispering as to whether the Whigs were wise to wear wigs especially in hot weather.

Many a wit is not a whit wittier than Whittier.

What wattage did you wish in the warehouse where the wags wager high stakes?

## VOCABULARY BUILD-UP

Use the italicized words in short paragraphs to show that you understand their meanings.

in a *reminiscent* mood
clever *repartee*
in a *quandary*
noted for his *philanthropy*
an act of *plagiarism*
an *accessory* to the crime
*refuting* all claims
a *forthright* manner
a *homogeneous* group
a *bimonthly* publication
a *bipartisan* policy
an act of *coercion*
recent *innovations* at the store
a *ludicrous* situation

CHAPTER

# 16 Starting a Club

The constitution's what you go on,
What you really can't be low on,
What you plan by, work by, share by,
What, in short, you always swear by.
Having long revered, obeyed it,
Sometimes you forget you made it.

—*Richard Armour*

PEOPLE with mutual interests and hobbies enjoy meeting to exchange ideas and to work together on new projects. Frequently, they like to organize a club and to work with other members who have the same interests. Hence you find stamp clubs, camera clubs, coin clubs, science clubs, debating clubs, and many others which appeal to specific groups.

It is highly probable that you may wish to start a club for a group with interests similar to yours. If so, you need to know the basic steps involved in getting a club under way. If you follow these main steps and if you know the essentials of parliamentary procedure as explained in the previous chapter, you can organize your club in such fashion that it will actually accomplish what you want it to do.

## The First Meeting

The first step is to announce your intention of starting a club so that others will know about it. You may do this in any of several ways. You may tell your friends as you see them, you may telephone a selected list, or you may write letters to potentially interested persons. A more formal method is to post a notice on the school bulletin board or to insert a notice in the school paper. In any of the methods used, you should specify a definite time and place for holding the first meeting.

At the first called meeting, you will probably preside until a temporary chairman is elected. After explaining the purpose of the proposed club and the advantages of having such a club, you should follow a recognized order of business. The following order of business is customary:

1. Elect a temporary chairman and a temporary secretary. Nominations should be from the floor, and elections should be conducted according to parliamentary procedure as discussed in the previous chapter. As soon as the temporary chairman is elected, he should preside and conduct the remainder of the meeting. The temporary secretary should start recording minutes immediately following his election.

2. Start the process of organizing the club. The steps include the following actions:

a. The chairman calls for a motion to organize. Such a motion is considered as a main motion and is subject to all of the rules of a main motion. If the motion is defeated, the meeting will either adjourn or the chairman may call for another motion to organize. If the motion is passed, provision should be made for drawing up a constitution and bylaws.

b. The chairman appoints a committee or conducts an

An attractive and imaginative announcement about a newly formed school club catches the eye and the interest of these two potential members. *(Monkmeyer)*

election for a committee to prepare a constitution and bylaws. The constitution and bylaws, as you learned in Chapter 15, together cover the essential purposes of the club and describe its essential parliamentary procedures. It is customary for the chairman to call for a motion instructing him as to the preferred method in choosing a committee. Usually, a motion is made for the chairman to appoint the committee. If this motion is passed, the chairman appoints the committee with instructions to have the constitution and bylaws ready by the next meeting.

3. Set the time for the second meeting by calling for a motion to this effect.

4. Declare the meeting adjourned.

## The Second Meeting

At the second meeting, the temporary chairman and the temporary secretary will be in charge until permanent officers are elected. The order of business at the second meeting is as follows:

1. The temporary chairman calls the meeting to order.

2. The temporary secretary reads the minutes of the previous meeting.

3. The committee on constitution and bylaws gives its report. Usually the report is submitted in writing to the temporary chairman.

4. The temporary chairman submits the report to the group for voting. The normal procedure is to consider, i.e. discuss and vote on, proposed amendments, if any, but not actually vote each article separately. At the completion of this procedure, the chairman calls for a discussion on the constitution as a whole, and then for a vote on the entire constitution. *Note that,* with the exception of voting on amendments, *there is only one vote in this entire process of approving the constitution.*

5. The temporary chairman calls for an election of permanent officers. The procedure of election should be the one prescribed by the constitution and by general parliamentary practice. Usually the election is by ballot.

6. Each permanent officer assumes his duties immediately following the chairman's announcement of his election.

7. The business transacted after the election will follow your constitution and bylaws and will be governed by parliamentary practice.

## A SAMPLE OPENING MEETING

JACK: The meeting will please come to order. The purpose of this meeting is to organize a photography club. Our first duty is to elect a temporary chairman. The meeting is now open to nominations for chairman.

JOHN: (Rises) Mr. Chairman.

JACK: The Chair recognizes John Blake.

JOHN: I nominate Jim Allen to preside as temporary chairman.

JACK: Jim Allen has been nominated. Are there any other nominations?

RUTH: (Rises) Mr. Chairman.

JACK: Ruth Black has the floor.

RUTH: I nominate Jane Carnes as chairman.

HARRY: (Rises) Mr. Chairman.

JACK: The Chair recognizes Harry Barnes.

HARRY: I move that the nominations be closed.

MARY: I second the motion.

JACK: It has been moved and seconded that the nominations be closed. All those in favor of the motion to close nominations say "Aye." (Pause) All opposed say "No." (Pause) The motion is carried. We shall vote by show of hands unless the group rules otherwise. Do I hear any objection? (Pause) Since there are no objections, you will raise your hands for either Jim Allen or Jane Carnes. All who wish Jim Allen as chairman, raise your hands. (Count is taken.) All who wish Jane Carnes as chairman, raise your hands. (Count is taken.) Jim Allen has been elected. Congratulations, Jim. Will you please take charge?

JIM: (Comes to front of group and Jack takes a seat.) Thank you for your vote. The next order of business is electing a temporary secretary. Are there any nominations?

RUTH: (Rises) Mr. Chairman.

JIM: The Chair recognizes Ruth Black.

RUTH: I nominate Jane Carnes as secretary.

JIM: Jane Carnes has been nominated. Do I hear any other nominations?

BOB: (Rises) Mr. Chairman.

JIM: Bob Ross.

BOB: I move that the nominations be closed.

DICK: I second the motion.

JIM: You have heard the motion and the second—that the nominations be closed. All in favor of the motion to close the nominations for secretary say "Aye." (Pause) All opposed say "No." (Pause) The motion is carried. The nominations are now closed.

We shall again vote by a show of hands unless the group rules otherwise. Do I hear any objection? (Pause) Since there are no objections, the Chair rules that the election shall proceed by show of hands. All who are in favor of Jane Carnes as temporary secretary, raise your hands. (Count is taken.) The vote was unanimous for Jane Carnes. Congratulations, Jane. Will you please come to the front of the room

At the second meeting of the Student Council, the temporary secretary reads the minutes of the opening meeting. *(Monkmeyer)*

and take the minutes for our first meeting? (Jane begins taking minutes.)

As you know, we have assembled for the purpose of organizing a photography club. The Chair will now entertain a motion to organize as a group.

MARK: Mr. Chairman.

JIM: The Chair recognizes Mark Johnston.

MARK: I move that we organize a photography club in order to further our interests and activities in this hobby.

BOB: I second the motion.

JIM: Is there any discussion?

The handling of the motion to organize proceeds according to parliamentary practice discussed in the previous chapter. Ordinarily, such a motion will pass unanimously as stated since all are interested in organizing as a group. If the motion had been less simple and had contained confusing provisions, there would be a possibility of amendment. Some discussion of the motion would probably precede the voting. This would enable people to inquire about aims, activities, requirements, and general problems connected with organizing and running the club.

Before adjournment, either the chairman appoints a committee or the group elects one to draw up the constitution and bylaws to be presented at the next meeting. After a motion has been made and carried to set the time of the next meeting, the meeting adjourns.

# The Constitution and Bylaws

A constitution is a formal statement of the aims and basic rules governing a club. It is regarded as a permanent law to be followed strictly until the group votes (usually by a two-thirds vote) to amend any provisions. You should think wisely and act cautiously in drawing up a constitution since it is regarded as binding. A long list of amendments indicates that the original constitution was weak. Examine the Constitution of the United States and then notice how few amendments have been added over the course of years. Although this is a classic example of long-range planning and statesmanship, wisdom and foresight are necessary in drawing up any satisfactory constitution.

Bylaws are flexible rules which, placed at the end of a constitution, contain details concerned with the operation of the constitution. In small informal groups, there may be little distinction made between bylaws and the constitution. You should be familiar, however, with their main differences in case you wish to draw up a constitution for a group desiring to adhere to strict parliamentary organization and procedure. A constitution usually contains the following articles:

Article I. Name and purpose of the organization
Article II. Membership requirements
Article III. Duties of officers and terms of office
Article IV. Number of meetings (monthly, weekly, or annually)
Article V. Method of amending the constitution.

Bylaws are easier to change than the constitution. Therefore, details of operation are usually placed in them so that they can be altered when changes become necessary. The details which are contained include:

1. Dues and any other obligations of membership
2. Method of electing officers
3. Standing committees and their duties
4. Definition of a quorum
5. Order of business
6. Method of amendment
7. Parliamentary authority to be followed

A constitution for the newly organized photography club could be simple and still meet all of the requirements necessary for a small group. Small clubs can easily follow such an example.

# SAMPLE CONSTITUTION AND BYLAWS

## CONSTITUTION

ARTICLE I. **Name and Purpose**

Section 1. The name of this club shall be the Jefferson High Camera Club.

Section 2. The purpose of this club shall be to share and compare knowledge of various kinds of cameras, to discuss techniques in taking pictures and in developing them, and to provide opportunities for members to display their pictures and to enter contests.

ARTICLE II. **Membership**

Section 1. Any students at Jefferson High School actively interested in photography are eligible to join by applying to any member of the Membership Committee and by agreeing to abide by the club rules.

Section 2. A member to be in good standing must pay his dues and attend meetings regularly as prescribed in the Bylaws.

ARTICLE III. **Officers**

Section 1. The officers of the club shall be a president, a vice-president, a secretary, and a treasurer.

Section 2. The officers shall be elected once a year at the last regular meeting of the club before the close of school.

Section 3. The duties of the officers shall be the same as prescribed in Robert's *Rules of Order,* Revised Edition.

Section 4. Vacancies in office shall be filled by election at a special meeting called by the president of the club.

ARTICLE IV. **Meetings**

Section 1. Regular meetings shall be held once a month during the school year.

Section 2. Special meetings may be called by the president.

ARTICLE V. **Amendments**

Section 1. This constitution may be amended at any regular meeting by a two-thirds vote of members present provided that the amendment has been presented at the previous regular meeting of the club.

## BYLAWS

**Part I. Obligations of members**

Section 1. The financial obligations shall be: (1) an initiation fee of one dollar and (2) dues of one dollar per year, said money to be used for equipment and projects of mutual benefit as voted upon during the year by the members.

Section 2. Members who have missed more than three regular meetings without an excuse approved by the Membership Committee shall be automatically dropped from the club.

**Part II. Election of Officers**

Section 1. Officers shall be nominated from the floor at the last regular meeting of each school year.

Section 2. Names for only one office at a time shall be presented and only one office shall be filled at each balloting.

Section 3. Persons defeated for one office may be eligible for any other office.

Section 4. Voting shall be by show of hands.

Section 5. A majority of those votes actually cast shall be necessary to elect all officers.

**Part III. Committees**

Section 1. The standing committees shall be the Membership Committee, the Program Committee, and the Project Committee appointed by the president at the beginning of each new school year.

Section 2. The Membership Committee shall be composed of five members, three of whom must be seniors, who shall act in the following capacities: (1) handling applications of new members, (2) investigating excuses and passing on them, and (3) notifying members who are in danger of being dropped.

Section 3. The Program Committee shall be composed of four members who shall plan the programs for the year.

Section 4. The Project Committee shall be composed of three members whose duties shall consist of planning interesting projects for group participation subject to approval of the group.

Section 5. A chairman of each committee shall be elected by the members of each committee.

**Part IV. Meetings**

Section 1. Regular meetings will be held on the first Thursday of each month during each school year.

Section 2. The first regular meeting of the club shall be called by the president.

Section 3. A quorum shall consist of 25 per cent of the membership, in the absence of which no business can be transacted at a regular meeting or at a special meeting.

**Part V. Order of Business**

The order of business shall be as follows:

1. Call to order
2. Roll call
3. Reading and approval of the minutes
4. Treasurer's report
5. Report from standing committees
6. Report from special committees
7. Unfinished business
8. New business
9. Miscellaneous items
10. Adjournment

**Part VI. Rules of Order**

All matters of procedure not specifically covered by this constitution and bylaws shall be conducted in accordance with Robert's *Rules of Order*, Revised Edition.

**Part VII. Amendments**

These bylaws may be amended by a two-thirds vote of the members present at any regular meeting of the Jefferson High Camera Club.

## ACTIVITIES

Organize your speech class into a club. It may be a debating or dramatics club. Or it may be a type of club not associated specifically with speech activities such as a rocket club, a magic club, or a flower club.

1. Appoint a committee to make all arrangements for calling the first meeting.
2. Conduct the organizational meeting. Follow the procedures described in this chapter.
3. Conduct a second meeting. Include the complete order of business specified for this meeting in this chapter.
4. Have a committee present a constitution and bylaws to be voted on at the meeting.

## PRONUNCIATION PROBLEMS

Perhaps we use the pronoun "I" as much as any word in the English language. Yet we sometimes misuse the long "i" sound of "I" when we use the sound in other words. Say each of the words below carefully and then read the practice sentences until you have mastered the sound.

| | | | | | |
|---|---|---|---|---|---|
| smile | I'll | acquire | buy | cried | I'm |
| mile | child | require | white | bright | cry |
| while | mild | five | guide | allies | hide |
| aisle | fire | live | kind | defy | wide |
| guile | iron | ivory | light | lime | pie |
| pile | tired | I've | eye | time | vine |
| trial | wire | dive | ice | dime | fine |
| pilot | pirate | hives | ride | wine | find |
| tile | entire | die | side | nine | pine |
| stylish | mire | tie | fly | higher | dine |

## READING CHECK-UP

Read aloud the nonsense sentences below to check your pronunciation of any problem words.

For a while the child smiled when the fire engine went by. He cried with delight when the kind fireman took him for a ride on a trial run of five miles. He told his mother, "I'm going to buy a fiery red engine that will be mine when I'm nine, and I'll take you for a ride."

Repeat these words rapidly: vine, fine, wine, vine, time, dime, vine, fine, dine, dime, hide, wide, wide, hide, pride, died, wine, time, die, pine, dime, side.

Are you required to wear white ties at dinner time or are black ties in style?

The entire family was tired of waiting for the hired man to fix their flat tire. Now they know that for miles and miles of tire wear, you should drive no more than fifty-five miles per hour.

The pilot acquired a license five months ago and is as fine a pilot as you can find in a long time.

Fire fighters save many lives. Last year while forest fires threatened miles and miles of fine pine timber, firemen fought side by side for a long time until the fires finally died out. Although tired from their struggle, the firemen smiled and proved that they had wills of iron.

Ride, ride, ride in your stylish ivory car and pile up the miles as you smile all the while.

The wild child is now mild and minds his parents especially those times when he gets dimes for pies and lime ice cream cones.

Did you say fired, wired, mired or tired? I'm so tired of ironing that I'd like to find a hired girl to do my entire ironing if I could find one with the right requirements. My sister was able to find a fine ironer after she had tried out five girls, but I've been pining for a long while and in the meantime the ironing piles up.

I've five live bees in my beehives and they're mine, all mine until they die or I die. I defy you to find any bees who can fly higher or sting milder. I acquired my five live bees from a kind guide nine days ago while shopping for wire on Vine Street.

## VOCABULARY **BUILD-UP**

Use the italicized words in short paragraphs to show that you understand their meanings.

a *trite* expression
a *perceptible* change
*derelict* in his duty
an object of *derision*
*latent* possibilities
a *pertinent* reply
*succinct* remarks
*decadent* civilization
a striking *analogy*
a *diffident* person
*agility* of movement
a *motley* array
to *rescind* a motion
a *voracious* reader
a *feasible* plan
an *insidious* problem
a land of *incredible* beauty
to *ambush* them
a *posthumous* award
an *innocuous* remark
accused of *collusion*
a *furtive* glance
*gregarious* in his habits
*dogmatic* statements
*fallacious* reasoning
a *facile* style of writing
a recognized *prerogative*
an *untenable* position

CHAPTER

# 17 Discussing

Men are never so likely to settle a question rightly as when they discuss it freely.

—*Thomas Babington Macaulay*

IN the preamble to UNESCO, the statement is made that "Since wars begin in the minds of men, it is in the minds of men that the defenses of peace must be constructed." Peace is a matter of understanding between nations and races, between parent and child, and between neighbor and neighbor. Talking things over is a wise and healthy method in learning to understand and respect each other.

Now, more than ever before, there is great need to learn how to live generously and agreeably in a free world. Discussion meets this need by helping you to learn how to speak freely, to listen freely, and to understand why another speaks and feels as he does even if you do not agree with him.

In Chapter 3, you discovered some elements pertaining to informal discussions such as you have in your classroom, in your home, or in your organizations. In this chapter you will have opportunity to learn more about the basic characteristics of organized discussion of a more formal and serious nature and to become acquainted with some of the familiar types of discussion.

## Discussion Defined

*Discussion is planned, cooperative, critical interchange of fact and opinion concerning a common problem area.* Discussion usually occurs in a face-to-face group and, if more than two members participate, is usually under the guidance of a leader. Discussion seeks to accomplish any or all of the following purposes: (a) locating and defining the problem; (b) analyzing the problem; and (c) exploring possible solutions. In some instances, discussion may actually reach a single or preferred solution.

The above definition will be more meaningful to you if you examine its terms individually. The term *planned* need not always denote a carefully phrased question for discussion; it does, however, suggest an intent to talk about an agreed upon problem area.

*Cooperative* implies that the members are willing to work together in examining all views fairly and honestly. It does not mean that they are in complete agreement at the beginning, for if they were there would be no reason to discuss. It does mean that they are willing to share opinions in a permissive atmosphere; to speak and let speak; to listen and let listen.

This sharing of views and pooling of knowledge results in a *critical interchange of fact and opinion.* The term *critical* suggests

"I thought I made it clear that a discussion period would follow."

THE SATURDAY EVENING POST

careful evaluation of points as opposed to blind acceptance or denial of these points. The interchange is of most value when the members can assemble in such fashion that all can see each other.

The *common problem area* is one that affects all of the members and in which all are genuinely interested. *Area* refers to a general field of interest rather than to some specific solution.

*Guidance of a leader* implies that one of the group, either by appointment or election, will assume responsibility for starting, directing, stopping, and summarizing the discussion. Of course, in many instances, a leader will emerge from the group by a natural process of recognition by its members.

The purposes of discussion, all of which are centered on the investigation of a problem and the examination of possible solutions, clearly distinguish it from the purposes of debate. In fact, discussion is frequently regarded as an important first step in debate. In discussion, the emphasis is upon an extensive search for answers to causes and conditions in an unbiased, cooperative manner. After the solutions are arrived at, however, there is not always complete agreement on a specific solution. At this point the process of inquiry ceases, and the role of the advocator in the form of a debater begins. The discussant is interested in understanding all possible points of view; the debater is interested in convincing the listeners of the wisdom of one particular point of view.

As stated above, you may use discussion in three types of situations: (1) when you wish to investigate facts, (2) when you wish to analyze problems, and (3) when you wish to formulate solutions.

In your investigative discussions, your primary purpose is to learn as much as possible about a particular problem area. Usually you will find it desirable to phrase your topic in the form of a question, thus: In what ways has the conquest of space influenced national defense? In this type of discussion you will usually not carry through the full process of discussion, since your answer may often simply be a collection of facts or ideas with no attempt to interpret them for the purpose of solving any problems. You will accomplish the first purpose of (1) locating and defining the problem, but will not get into the additional purposes of (2) analyzing the problem or (3) exploring possible solutions.

When you discuss for the purpose of analyzing the problem, you will, of course, accomplish purposes (1) and (2) above, but you still will not include the process of (3) exploring possible solutions. In this type, your interests may center on judging the rightness or wrongness of a person, procedure, or group. An example of this type of question is: What are the advantages to the United States of our present foreign aid program? This limits the discussion to judging the rightness or wrongness of foreign aid and does not necessarily imply exploring possible solutions.

In policy-making situations, the purpose is to arrive at a course of action through exploring possible solutions. Policy-making discussions, therefore, capitalize to the full extent on the discussion process. Examples of policy-making types of questions are: How can our streets be made safer for pedestrians? How can our schools improve their present educational methods?

## Values and Weaknesses of Discussion

### Values

Any attempt to assign definite values to all discussions is impossible. Some discussions accomplish much more than others, depending upon the persons involved and the conduct of the discussion method itself. The values mentioned here, therefore, represent those which *may* and *should* result from discussion at its *best.* They are based upon the assumption that the question is well selected and appropriately phrased, that the discussants are adequately prepared and display the proper attitudes, and that the leader assumes his full responsibility in conducting a real discussion instead of a "gab" session. When these conditions exist, discussion has definite values; when they are absent, it tends to be weak and useless.

**Discussion builds healthy attitudes.** The process of talking things over encourages *sharing* of opinions in an open-minded manner and discourages the tendency to be narrow-minded. It gives you opportunity to discover as well as accept new ideas. When a truly permissive atmosphere flourishes, prejudice and stubbornness soon die. In such discussion you learn to respect truths and beliefs even though they may differ widely from your own.

**Discussion demands active participation rather than passive listening.** Taking part satisfies the basic need to belong in a group and to be recognized as an individual. You increase in stature in your own mind when you have the chance to contribute ideas. You feel more secure and more free to express ideas in a group than you do in front of a large audience. Talking things over in a group thus serves the useful purpose of breaking down some of your fears of speaking in public.

**Discussion stimulates learning.** The very process of thinking

A speech class participates in a well-planned discussion period. *(Pogue's Portrait Studio)*

out loud helps the flow of ideas. And, just because you spend more time in listening than in speaking, you are more sure of learning many facts and ideas worth remembering. Research has suggested that knowledge acquired through discussion is retained longer than that acquired through lectures and that such knowledge can be used more effectively. If preparation precedes the discussion period, your learning is even greater. It is only when discussion happens to be a pooling of ignorance that you learn little. Collective thinking is only as worthwhile as the thoughts collected.

**Discussion helps you develop some valuable courtesies in both listening and speaking.** Some of the most obvious ones follow.

**To be a courteous listener, you should:**

1. Learn to listen to the end of every statement without interrupting. Don't be like Boris:

> JOHN: Finally, to bring this matter to a head, I wish to say . . . .
>
> BORIS: No, that is not right. I agree that two and two makes four. But . . . .

2. Learn to listen carefully for exact statements and meanings instead of picking up partial statements or trying to twist meanings. Not like Boris:

> JOHN: Although it is true that in the rainy season 2% of our county runs a risk of being flooded, during the rest of the year even this 2% is as dry as a bone.
>
> BORIS: As John has just said, 2% of our county is flooded 98% of the time.

3. Learn to listen with an open mind instead of closing it to conflicting views or listening only for opinions which coincide with yours. Don't be a Boris:

JOHN: In summary, I have just presented five reasons why we need a new gym.

BORIS: I haven't changed *my* mind; so far, no one has even tried to explain why a new gym would be helpful.

### To be a courteous speaker, you should:

1. Remember that only one person can speak at a time.
2. Speak in such a manner that others will want to follow instead of fight you.
3. Refrain from sarcasm, superior attitudes, and tactless comments. Here's Boris again:

   JOHN: This appears to be the viewpoint of the senior men with respect to Tag Day.

   BORIS: How stupid can you get! When are you going to get a brain for that head?
4. Express difference of opinion calmly and courteously.
5. Be smart instead of "smart-aleck." Unlike Boris:

   JOHN: I know it's trite, but may I remind you that a stitch in time still saves nine.

   BORIS: Ha! Ha! Ha! That really puts me in stitches. Pass the needle and thread to Grandma, boys, and don't give up the stitch.
6. Condense your thoughts and speak briefly so that others will have their full share of time. Try to emphasize your central idea as opposed to chatting at length about all of your opinions.
7. Be satisfied with occasional opportunities to speak. Seek recognition in a quiet manner instead of waving your arms wildly in the air, standing up, or calling to the leader.
8. Speak only to the entire group. Carrying on side conversations is not only rude, but is ruinous to the orderly progress of discussion.
9. Speak loudly and clearly enough that all can hear you the first time.
10. Stay on the main track. Avoid bringing in personal experiences of little consequence or dwelling on irrelevant ideas. Speak only when you have something worthwhile and pertinent to contribute.

**Discussion helps in reaching workable decisions.** Many problems can be solved better by group thinking than by individual thinking, although the group may not always reach a decision. You've heard the old saying, "Two heads are better than one." Likewise, many heads are better than one provided that they are filled with valuable information and motivated by a desire to share.

The workability of a decision depends largely upon its acceptance by the group. You know that you are more likely to accept a solution when you have helped to work it out than you are when it is handed to you on the basis of "take it or leave it." This is one of the strongest arguments in favor of student councils. When the students themselves discuss problems and the possible solutions, they accept the group decision more readily than if the principal of the school issued a ruling. Furthermore, through discussion, students often realize the weakness of their own views and reject them willingly.

## Weaknesses

Many of the weaknesses of discussion arise from the *abuse* of the discussion technique rather than from its use. Even at its best, discussion is a slow process. Based as it is on critical or evaluative thinking, it is not adapted to the securing of quick action. Inherent in discussion procedure is the right for all to speak, a feature which is often responsible for lengthy speeches and delayed action.

The United Nations furnishes an example of this feature when an important crisis arises. Since all delegates have the right to speak, it is understandable that much time is consumed in discussion before any action can be taken. Prompt action can occur only when

The United Nations is an outstanding example of the democratic process of discussion on an international level. *(Ewing Galloway)*

there is slight need for lengthy discussion, a situation which seldom exists in the United Nations because of the sharp conflict of interests among its members. This is true of any large group which employs the democratic practice of giving everyone the right to speak. Discussion succeeds only when it is used wisely.

To be truly effective, discussion must not be a time killer. Its real purpose should be one of minimizing misunderstanding and increasing understanding. It should bring people closer together instead of forcing them farther apart.

## Types of Discussion

It is difficult to list all types of discussion and to give specific names to each since there are so many variations in the forms and in the names used to identify each. Nevertheless, the following types are widely recognized.

### The Informal Group Discussion

This type is really a kind of magnified conversation. It consists usually of a leader and a group of up to 15 or 20 people who have met to talk over a common problem. It is informal throughout and gives everyone a chance to express views and opinions. There are no set speeches and no attempts are made to divide the group into opposing sides. The leader, if one member of the group so serves, acts as a guide only; he does not try to control thinking or require that participants recognize him before speaking. It can be found in the classroom, at a meeting of the student council, at a PTA meeting, at a civic club meeting, or at any other meeting where problems are being discussed.

### The Committee

The committee is a private assembly of individuals who are actually working in similar positions and who exchange ideas, experiences, and data about their positions. A leader will usually be designated; he may or may not follow a prepared agenda in keeping the discussion moving. Either the leader or a recorder will take notes on what is said and will present a summary for the consideration of the group. An audience is usually not present. Board meetings, private conferences, and so forth are typical examples. The committee is an increasingly important unit of discussion in governmental, business, and educational organizations.

## The Panel

The panel is a discussion situation in which a few *informed* individuals, who may represent either the various factions in the audience or who may be specialists in various phases of the question, carry on a controlled conversation before an audience. This conversation is informative, not argumentative. Usually the audience may participate in the conversation during later portions of the session by asking questions of the participants or by volunteering information. If so, the situation becomes a panel-forum, for the term *forum* always means audience participation. In order to give direction to the meeting, handle any audience participation, and adapt the discussion to the audience, a chairman usually presides.

The number of panel members may vary, but will usually range from three to eight. Probably the smaller number makes for a more efficient discussion. The individual members of the panel make specific preparation for their part in the program but do not give a set speech.

Because of the number of participants involved and the "give-and-take" pattern of procedure, the organization of this type of discussion may be weak at times. To offset this disadvantage, many panel leaders use a planning session prior to the meeting to decide

The well-known program, "Young Worlds," is shown here with its moderator and panel members from four countries. *(WCBS Television)*

on the scope of the discussion, the points of view that will be represented, definitions of terms, and appropriate time divisions. This prevents wasting time in haggling over terms, introducing irrelevant views, and repeating needlessly.

Panels are frequently used in P.T.A. meetings, school assemblies, and classrooms when informal discussions seem inadequate.

## The Lecture-Forum

The lecture-forum consists of a set speech delivered by one person, preferably a recognized authority on the subject, who then answers oral or written questions from the audience at the close of his talk. Although the speech is specifically prepared, it usually seeks to present a well-rounded, *informative* point of view on the general subject rather than a *persuasive* speech on a particular point of view.

If a moderator is used, his duties will include introducing the speaker and conducting the question and answer period at the close of the lecture. Sometimes no moderator is used. In this case, the lecturer himself conducts the question and answer period.

## The Dialogue

The dialogue is a controlled public conversation in which one person, usually designated as the chairman, questions a second person, usually designated as the respondent, in order to seek information which an audience may want or need. It is essential to the success of this form of discussion that the person be an expert in the general area of the discussion. An expert, in the present sense, is an individual who is recognized as having a unique and specialized fund of pertinent information on the chosen subject.

Occasionally, the two participants in a dialogue may function as co-experts; in this case, each will question the other. But in neither variant does the dialogue become a personal interview. After the original question and answer period between the two speakers, the audience may direct questions at one or both of the participants, depending upon the form used.

The chairman should be versed in the problem under consideration, must understand what the audience wants to know, and must be able to phrase his questions appropriately. The respondent, in addition to having a necessary fund of knowledge, must be able to talk pointedly and plainly in a spontaneous situation. The chief advantage of this type is the presence of an informed expert or of two experts.

## The Symposium

In the symposium, a series of expert speakers give *prepared* talks on various aspects of a problem. These talks may then be followed by a forum. The number of speakers varies from three to six. Each speaker is an *expert* in at least one phase of the problem under discussion, is specifically prepared, and gives a set speech. The length of the speech may be ten or fifteen minutes; the total speaking time should not be much longer than an hour, particularly if a forum is to follow. Although the speeches are separate, their collective effect should give a complete point of view.

Occasionally, after the presentation of the prepared speeches, the experts themselves will discuss the question among themselves, as in the case of the panel. Whether this is done or not, a forum generally follows.

Among the advantages of the symposium are these: (a) the coverage of the organized set speeches may be more systematic than that provided by a panel discussion; (b) the amount of factual information is likely to be quite high during the prepared speech portion; (c) the participants are encouraged to prepare thoroughly; (d) because of the number of speakers (three to six), the method lends itself to covering problems that have more than one or two solutions; (e) the method is generally successful in laying the foundation for good audience discussion.

The chief disadvantage of the symposium is the length of the set speeches. Successful audience response will depend on the effectiveness of the participating speakers. If the audience develops a passive and uninterested attitude, little thinking will be generated and few questions will come from them.

The chairman is particularly important in this form of discussion if the advantages are to be developed and the disadvantages are to be minimized. His specific functions are to introduce the question and the speakers, to make necessary transitions and correlations, to arrange the order of the speaking, and to handle the question and answer period.

## The Forum

The essential element in the forum, whether presented alone or in combination with other methods, is that the audience may question the speakers rigorously. The forum may be combined with the panel, dialogue, symposium, or lecture, as a technique for securing audience participation.

The chairman or moderator presents the speakers, directs the

The chairman of this classroom forum seems to be doing a good job of carrying out the functions of her office. *(Frederic Lewis)*

questions to the speakers, and makes necessary transitional remarks. The functions of the chairman include: (a) explaining the specific procedure to the participants and to the audience, (b) stimulating the audience to ask questions, (c) rephrasing questions if necessary, (d) repeating the question loudly enough that all may hear, (e) closing the meeting at an appropriate time. The duties of the audience involve the following: (a) asking relevant questions, (b) asking answerable questions, (c) phrasing questions well, (d) sharing the question period. The duties of the participants being questioned include: (a) answering—not evading—the questions, (b) being brief and not using a question as a peg on which to hang a speech.

## Selecting and Phrasing the Question for Discussion

One of the most important considerations in the selection of a subject is, of course, the group itself. Obviously, if a question is to be effective, it must be one about which the group is interested and has opinions and feelings. If the group is uninformed in the problem area, it can accomplish little. It is for this reason that thorough preparation by each participant *before the discussion begins* is essential to successful discussion. Also, the subject must be within the capabilities of the group—it should be one that they are able to think reflectively about.

Finally, the problem area should be important enough to be worth discussing. The question should be either extremely timely or essentially timeless. It should be a topic that is not too "live" to be handled; it should have more than one point of view; and it should be capable of being handled during the time allowed. Problems should be avoided which lend themselves to "Yes" and "No" answers.

The next step is to phrase the problem precisely. First, the subject should be phrased as a question. Second, the phrasing should precisely define the problem area. The words used should be words with definite meanings; they should not be vague or ambiguous. Third, the phrasing should be impartial; any appearance of bias or prejudice for a particular solution must be avoided. Fourth, the phrasing should also limit the question with respect to the time available. Finally, it may be desirable under certain circumstances to adopt special phrasing in order to attract attention for popular discussion.

## The Process of Discussion

In general, the process of discussion roughly parallels the problem-solving steps of John Dewey:

1. Defining the problem
2. Analyzing the problem
3. Suggesting possible solutions
4. Developing and comparing solutions
5. Selecting a solution
6. Activating the solution

Descriptions and examples of Dewey's steps as they are modified for discussion follow.

### Defining the problem

The first step in discussion is to define the problem or difficulty. This involves the limiting of the problem and the careful definition of all terms employed in a mutually acceptable way. It should be noted that the particular definitions adopted by the group are flexible; that is, it is perfectly possible to modify these as the discussion continues.

A group of high school students had been appointed as a committee to plan the annual senior prom. At the first meeting of the group, it was discovered that there was a generalized discontent on the part of all the members with the way the dance had gone the last couple of years. Yet no one knew exactly what had been wrong with these dances. The immediate goal of the committee, then, was to define the problem. They concluded, as had been suggested, that their first act should be to take a close look at the presumed unpopularity of the dance.

## Analyzing the problem

The goal in this stage is to discover or locate the true nature of the problem in terms of its symptoms and the cause or causes believed to be responsible for the problem. Usually, this will involve a collection of all information of past and present circumstances which will help in examining possible solutions. But more than this, it will involve the formulation of standards that may be applied to the situation. In formulating standards, the group will have to decide upon present values, the relative importance of these values to various members of the group, and how to handle conflicting judgments of values. Out of such analysis can come agreement as to the goals actually sought.

As the group began to analyze the unpopularity of the dance, they discovered that several factors seemed to be involved. Among the more important of these were:

1. The high price of tickets
2. Lack of a "name" band
3. Disagreement as to whether the dance should be formal, semi-formal, or informal
4. Restrictions imposed by school authorities as to the location of the dance
5. Restrictions similarly imposed as to the hours of the dance
6. Parental opposition to the dance
7. Competition from other events—some of which were not directly controlled by the high school

The group concluded that its program for the next prom would have to meet these standards:

1. Develop positive attitudes toward the prom on the part of their elders—school and parental.
2. Keep the cost as low as possible.
3. Increase the attractiveness of the dance itself.
4. Reduce the competition with other activities.

## Suggesting possible solutions

In this step, the purpose is to find possible solutions for the problem, as defined in step one and in terms of the values agreed upon in step two. In this step, no effort is made to evaluate or compare the solutions. Rather, the primary goal is to arrive at a statement of the possibilities.

Among the alternatives suggested by the group were:

1. Develop a student-centered code of conduct for the dance in order to form better administrative and parental attitudes.
2. Minimize or eliminate costly decorations, programs, and favors.
3. Secure a "name" band in order to make the dance more attractive.
4. Work with the director of the school calendar to avoid unfortunate scheduling of the dance or competitive events.

## Developing and comparing solutions

In this step, the essential purpose is to see what advantages and disadvantages will be created by each of the proposed solutions. You need make no choice at this stage. What is important is that each of the solutions be developed in pertinent detail. In evaluating the consequences of each of the solutions suggested, it is important that the consequence of reaching no decisions should also be evaluated. Many discussions will terminate at this level; it is not always possible to arrive at a common solution.

At this stage of their work, the group began to develop in detail the four suggestions decided upon. It was found that it seemed quite possible to work out a student-centered code and to improve the scheduling of the dance. As they sought to limit their tentative budget entirely to the orchestra, however, they began to discover that the prom would never be attractive if held without benefit of decorations, as the old armory was the only hall available.

## Selecting a solution

Obviously, this selection will have to be based upon the previous values and goals recognized by the group and must be carefully tested in terms of its consequences. Many actual discussions will not reach this step.

The conduct code for the dance was developed in detail and the dance was scheduled at an appropriate time. It was decided to settle for a good local band so as to save some money for the other items mentioned.

## Activating the solution

A sixth step is sometimes recognized, that of activating the solution. If the discussion is carried this far, it will of course concern itself with the problems of carrying into effect the solution decided upon. In general, however, this activation step is not regarded as part of the discussion process.

The dance went through as planned. To the satisfaction of the committee, it was quite successful.

# Participating in Discussion

## Participating as a leader

Several qualifications help to determine your success as a leader in discussion groups. The most important ones seem to be intelligence, pleasing personality, optimism, tactfulness, sense of timing, lots of energy, effective speech, and experience as a discussion leader. With experience you soon learn that you are expected to perform the following duties:

1. Understand the discussion process and the general responsibilities of group leadership.
2. Prepare yourself in the subject matter of the discussion topic.
3. Plan the discussion with the participants. Your planning will follow the general steps described on page 331, but its completeness will range from a jotting down of a few ideas on a piece of paper to a full-scale planning session.
4. Assume responsibility for such physical conditions as size of room, seating arrangements, ventilation, and exact meeting time.
5. Introduce the speakers to each other and to the audience.
6. Open the discussion by announcing the topic, explaining its nature and importance, and informing the group of anything necessary in appreciating the discussion. Avoid the error of explaining too much. You should include any limitations of time, subject matter, or point of view in order to prevent any unpleasantness.
7. Keep the discussion moving on the main track.
8. Maintain a general tone of informality and of pleasant relationship.
9. Close the discussion effectively. Usually, this involves a summary of the main points covered and any decision, if one has been reached.
10. Keep yourself from dominating the meeting, but let your leadership be felt in guiding the participants to contribute their ideas. This involves knowing how to deal with different types of people. The skilled leader can recognize the shy person and help him to say something. He can also guide the hostile one so that his energy is expended for and not against the group.

## Participating as a member

On page 323 you learned some of the valuable courtesies of listening and speaking. In addition to practicing those, you can help to make the discussion process worthwhile by recognizing that you have definite responsibilities.

First, you should be willing to define the subject as it is seen by the group, to restrain your emotional reactions, and to adjust in general to the group. Listen to understand rather than to argue or disagree just for the sake of creating excitement. It is advisable to introduce material in an explanatory manner instead of an argumentative one.

Second, make a genuine effort to prepare yourself on the subject so that your contributions will be worthwhile. It is wise to speak only when you have something pertinent to say and not to try to monopolize the discussion.

Finally, help the group to explore its chosen solution even if you are opposed to it. Above all, don't be afraid of being wrong or admitting that you are wrong.

Turn your attention now to active participation in the discussion situations which follow. You may wish to add many more to the list or to change some provided. Use the discussion process as often as you wish, but use it wisely.

The senior yearbook faculty sponsor calls a meeting in his home of all committee heads to hear progress reports and discuss further plans. *(Monkmeyer)*

## ACTIVITIES

1. Pretend that you are members of your school's student council with an appointed president. Discuss any one of the following problems or any other timely one at your school:
   a. A clean-up-and-beautify campaign for the school
   b. Methods of raising money for school improvements
   c. Supporting school activities
   d. Establishing honor study halls
   e. Methods of handling school discipline problems
2. After conducting forum discussions on the above topics, divide into committees to discuss each topic in detail. In these smaller groups, present specific ideas and work toward preparing a practical report for adoption by the council.
3. Pretend that you are a teacher in any class of your choice in order to show your ability as a leader. Select a topic that might spark a discussion and conduct a forum discussion period. For example, in an English class you might discuss the meaning of a certain poem or essay; in an American History class, the advantages or disadvantages of the electoral college; in a speech class, the problem of controlling stage fright.
4. Follow the *symposium* style of discussion in the following situations with a chance for forum participation at the end:
   a. Pretend you are a panel composed of two teachers, two parents, and two students appointed to discuss the present system of education at a PTA meeting. Divide the general topic into specific phases with each panel member prepared to speak a specified time on each phase. Suggested phases are:
      Weaknesses of the present system
      Suggestions for corrective measures
      Ways in which local or state governing bodies can help
      Needed curriculum changes
      Needed changes in co-curricular activities
   b. Pretend that you are informed members of the city council discussing any one of the following proposals:
      Enactment of a curfew law
      Establishing a downtown shopping mall
      How to deal with traffic violations
      Use of voting machines
      Decrease of air and stream pollution

   Special note: In the question period which follows each of these discussions, pay special attention (1) to word questions clearly and simply, (2) to ask only one question at a time, and (3) to avoid answering your own question or presenting an argument along with your question.
5. Try the *lecture-forum* method by selecting a topic about which you feel qualified to speak. Be sure to prepare thoroughly enough so that you can present your subject adequately and can answer questions intelligently.
6. Try the *dialogue* method by selecting partners and topics of interest.

7. Select any one of the interview types of programs on the air in which people present their views. Follow the same procedure in conducting a class program.
8. Pick a problem of personal interest and conduct an opinion poll among chosen members of the class. Some examples are:
   What would you do if you saw a person cheating on a test?
   Should you expect classmates to give you their homework?
   How old should you be before you "go steady"?
   Should parents chaperone parties held in their homes?
   What are the most important qualities you look for in a person?
9. Select any one of the types of discussion for the following topics:
   Changing the voting day from Tuesday to Sunday
   Lowering the compulsory school attendance age
   Granting athletic scholarships
   Holding parents responsible for misdemeanors of minors
   Decreasing juvenile crime rate
   Handling the dope problem
10. Select and phrase one timely topic not mentioned in any of the activities. Use the most interesting ones for class discussion.

## PRONUNCIATION PROBLEMS

Be careful not to change short "e" sound to short "i" in words such as *get, ten,* and *send.* For example, when a person says "tin cint store," he really means "ten cent store." After making sure that you are able to hear and make this distinction, use the short "e" sound when you pronounce the following words:

| | | | | |
|---|---|---|---|---|
| many | instead | every | depend | edge |
| any | genuine | engine | measure | spend |
| ten | friend | kept | seven | when |
| get | lend | scent | assembly | enemies |
| pen | twenty | met | tends | fender |
| send | extra | bed | men | error |
| general | sense | wreck | slender | meadow |
| attention | end | steady | sentence | very |
| pencil | educate | deaf | bend | tennis |
| penny | said | pleasure | then | hen |
| century | meant | weather | went | debt |

## READING CHECK-UP

Read aloud the sentences below to check your pronunciation of any problem words.

Many men went to the ten cent store every day to spend their pennies. Generally, they would get pencils and ink for their pens. When any gentleman could send anyone else, he sent a friend instead to spend his pennies.

The teacher said, "Get your pencils ready. I want you to write correctly these ten sentences without making any errors. Be sure to put a period at the end of every sentence. Ready—get set—go."

1. The meadow was heavily scented with fresh hay.
2. The general said, "Attention, men! Get ready for inspection."
3. For seven centuries, many enemies kept the small country in heavy debt.
4. You will be requested to spend ten cents for any assemblies meant for pleasure.
5. After the wreck, my friend found a dent in his car's fender.
6. It was a genuine pleasure for the old gentleman to lend his friend twenty-five cents.
7. Generally speaking, it is very hard to depend on the weather.
8. My slender friend lost ten pounds by bending down twenty times according to directions sent by the "20th Century Reducing Salon."
9. He fed his pets many different energy foods to get them ready for the show.
10. Steady studying tends to make education a genuine pursuit of knowledge.

At the end, the teacher then told every one who had made any errors to write the sentences again and again until he could get them 100 per cent correct.

## VOCABULARY **BUILD-UP**

Use the italicized words in short paragraphs to show that you understand their meanings.

*colloquially* speaking
fond of *euphemisms*
a familiar *idiom*
*notorious* for his deeds
a *climactic* year
an *eminent* attorney
a *scrutinizing* look
*proponents* of foreign aid
of *titanic* strength
motor *mayhem*
*diversified* interests
mixed *metaphors*
a *grotesque* cartoon
*unverified* charges
*coherent* statements
a *voluble* spokesman
an *infirm* hand
*impaired* vision
*cumulative* effects
*rampant* rumors
a *precarious* undertaking
a *decrepit* appearance

CHAPTER

# 18 Debating

Most debates are won in the library.

—*Anonymous*

## Characteristics of Debating

### What is debating?

Debating arises from discussion. Discussion (a) locates and defines the problem, (b) analyzes the problem, (c) explores possible solutions to the problem, and (d) *may* arrive at a mutually preferred solution. But if through the process of discussion, honest and well-intentioned men are unable to agree upon a particular solution, debating is the process by which the disagreement is referred to a judge, a jury, or a majority of the people concerned. Discussion is essentially a technique for arriving at possible solutions; debate is essentially a technique for testing a particular solution. Discussion is the art of inquiry; debate, the art of advocacy.

Debating, like discussion, flourishes in a free society. And, like discussion, the details of the technique vary from time to time and from place to place. Yet, according to Ewbank and Auer in *Discussion and Debate,* debating is almost always characterized by the following elements:

1. The point at issue is a particular solution.
2. The debaters are given relatively equal opportunity to state and defend their positions.
3. The decision is limited to being for or against the solution.
4. The solution is reached by a mutually agreed upon form of voting.

## Where is debating found?

**I agree with you, but . . .** Informal debating begins when two or more persons disagree as to how a problem should be solved and try to test one particular solution to that problem. Usually few fixed rules govern such debating. Thus when you and your friends argue about how to fix a fuel pump, which stereo outfit you would buy, or where to go after the football game, you are debating informally. You may not always reach a decision in this type of informal debating, but if you do, the debaters or speakers will usually make the decision themselves.

Listen to these informal debates that go on around you. Note that the speakers try to be logical and clear. They use everyday language. They try to put their facts and reasoning skills together in the best possible way. You will find that informal debating is essentially a form of argumentative speaking.

**Mr. Chairman . . .** Debating is going on today in such situations as the regular meetings of organized clubs, special meetings of a senior class or neighborhood or church group, or a governmental commission or committee. In each the procedures vary, but the basic elements of a specific proposal, people for and against the proposal, equality of presentation, and a majority technique for reaching a decision are all present. Debate, along with discussion, is the touchstone of organized American life.

**Your Honor and Ladies and Gentlemen of the jury . . .** Debating also occurs in the court of law. The two sides are typically the prosecution and the defense. Although the what, when, and how of the speaking is controlled by relatively rigid precedents, the basic purpose of the speaking is persuasive. Equality of opportunity is guaranteed by these procedures. The usual alternatives are "guilty" or "innocent." The decision is made, not by the opposing lawyers, but by judges or juries. The American judicial system is dependent upon the art of debating.

**Mr. Speaker . . .** The great parliamentary bodies of the free world furnish the finest examples of the debating process. For centuries in the British House of Commons and House of Lords and the American Senate and House, able and intelligent men have submitted their disagreements to the will of the majority. Mankind has yet to evolve a finer system for testing solutions than that of parliamentary debating.

**Fellow Debaters . . .** Contest debate is a specialized form of oral discourse in which two or more persons, or teams of persons,

In this form of debate as seen on the "Perry Mason" show, the two sides are known as the prosecution and the defense. *(CBS Television Network)*

test in a previously agreed upon manner a proposed solution to a specific problem. In order that this solution may be tested, it is stated in the form of a proposition such as:

*Resolved,* That the ins should be turned out.

A formal resolution of this type provides for only two very limited alternatives: you must either (1) decide to turn the ins out—and thus accept the proposition, or (2) decide not to turn the ins out—and thus reject the proposition. The debaters agree in advance to disagree about the proposed solution and, as part of their agreement, to follow a set of rules applicable to both sides and designed to be fair to both sides. Thus the affirmative side supports the proposition and the negative side attacks it. Finally, the two sides usually agree that their respective arguments shall be evaluated either by a judge (or judges) or by an audience. As will be explained later, two somewhat different types of contest debate result, depending upon whether the decision is given by a judge or by an audience.

## What are the values of debate?

**Debate facilitates American democracy.** Freedom to evaluate alternate solutions and to urge the acceptance of a particular solution is vital to American life. The kind of life we know depends upon this freedom to test solutions. You can learn about problems and their solutions in many ways. You can read. You can listen to the radio. You can watch television. You can discuss. Each of these is good, but none of these permits you to evaluate and defend particular solutions as openly as does debate. Because of its traditional use in parliamentary bodies, it has always been one of the most influential means whereby lawmakers can evaluate specific proposals in an attempt to provide satisfactory legislation. Debate helps you to test solutions in terms of *fact* instead of hasty guesswork.

**Debate is of value to the listener.** Have you ever been a member of an audience for a debate? If so, you remember how your excitement grew as you heard each speaker present his arguments and attempt to refute those of his opponents. Your interest was keenly aroused as the debaters defined sharply both sides of the question and showed you that there was much to be said for each side. Although neither side may have completely convinced you, your thinking was stimulated enormously.

For the listener, then, debate is one of the finest activities in any living democracy for the reasons given on the next page.

Do you think this Parent-Teacher's audience is "interested, informed, and stimulated" by the debate on the stage? *(Ewing Galloway)*

*It arouses interest.* Public apathy is one of the outstanding weaknesses of a democracy. Many persons either have no opinion on a subject or fail to support intelligently their point of view. Debate serves to arouse interest in subjects of common concern and may motivate listeners to learn more about the points at issue.

*It presents pertinent facts.* A good debate quickly brings before its listeners the facts and opinions that are pertinent to the controversy. Although it must be admitted that the presentations are biased, that is, that each side is selecting from all the facts and opinions those particular facts and opinions that best support its respective position, it is still true that the total picture presented should be quite informative.

*It stimulates thinking.* The clash and drama of debate tend to stimulate the thinking of listeners about important issues. Listeners feel an active identification with the debate and have a sense of participation in it. Often they adopt a course of action because they feel impelled to do something about the problem.

**Debate is of value to the debater.** In debating, you receive a type of training that cannot be completely duplicated in any other speech activity. This training will provide improvement in the following areas:

*Increased knowledge.* Debate, like any activity that requires research, encourages the active search for information. In this search, you find many sources of knowledge that you did not know about before. Such experiences are bound to help you become a better-informed individual and, therefore, a more interesting person.

Becoming better informed helps you in many ways. First, you adopt sensible, stable viewpoints instead of whims. You tend to become a broad-minded person who sees things in their true perspective. Second, you are recognized as a leader largely because of your sensible views. People will respect you and seek your advice. Your ability to talk with others easily and skillfully is increased. A third satisfaction is simply the joy of learning. You profit greatly in self-satisfaction through becoming a more able student.

*Exactness.* Guesswork has no place in debating. You must find accurate information. After you have found your facts, you must express them in precise, clear-cut statements. You soon learn to express your ideas economically and in a straightforward manner. Wasting time is costly in debate. Your audience demands and expects facts. You have to satisfy a very critical audience or judge or lose support. In a debate, you rise or fall on the basis of exact information. You suffer greatly by comparison in any form of debate. Since an audience can discover quickly how much or how little you know, debating *forces* you to present the facts. In other words, you find yourself in the position where you "put up or shut up."

***Critical judgment.*** Debating requires critical evaluation of facts. Since there are always two sides to any debatable question, you know that the side which presents the more persuasive arguments will win the debate. The superior debater, therefore, concentrates on picking out the arguments that best support his solution and on eliminating the weaker ones. Being able to decide between the strong and the weak arguments is strictly a matter of judgment, knowing the subject matter, and the type of audience or judge. Knowing the difference between the important and the unimportant issues in either the audience or in the contest debate is the secret of winning debates.

***Organized thinking.*** All debate speeches must be carefully organized. Organization is basically a matter of arranging your thoughts into a pattern which is easy to follow. Debating trains you in organizing your thoughts. You learn to separate the important from the unimportant. You also learn to relate the subordinate points to the proper main ideas. Thinking logically is an essential element both in debating and in living.

***Adaptive thinking.*** Debates are competitive. The primary objective is to win the audience or judge to your point of view. Often, if you are well prepared and well organized, you may do a good job in your first or constructive speech. A constructive speech is one in which you introduce and build up a portion of your argument. But one of your opponents may stress facts or opinions that damage your position. It is then necessary for you to be able to adapt your original arguments and position to what has been said. This adapting will require you to refute—or counter-attack—the arguments of your opponents and rebut—or rebuild—your own position. The ability to do this kind of adaptive thinking is one of the finest skills to be developed by debate.

***Listening ability.*** Good debating requires that you must learn to listen to every statement and quotation to be sure that each is accurate, and that you learn also to be sure of the source of each. Debating teaches you to challenge a source that is out-dated or biased in any respect and to recognize flaws or fallacies which you can attack.

Debating develops your ability to recognize the most important facts and arguments and not to waste valuable rebuttal time on trivial items. Yet you learn also to test the supporting facts and arguments and to see if they apply. Again, you receive practice in separating the important from the unimportant issues.

Finally, debate emphasizes the importance of listening for exact statements. Misquoting or misinterpreting the opposition is costly in the minds of listeners. Having to guess or ask questions about what was said is even worse.

***Cooperation.*** Particularly in contest debating, you work with a team. There may be two or three on your team, but all of you must work together in planning your speeches. As you prepare your strategy in meeting the opposition, you realize that you can't "carry the ball" alone and that you can't have all the strong points. You also learn that although each speaker has certain duties and points to prove in the constructive speeches, you must be able to defend your partner's arguments as well as your own. You learn that you do not compete with each other on a team, but that you work together to compete with the opposing team.

## The Debate Process

### How debates develop

Debates most frequently grow out of a basic disagreement as to the merits of a particular solution to a problem. Except in certain contest debate situations, the solution that is debated is not arbitrarily picked out of the blue. Debatable solutions emerge out of unresolved discussions. The solutions actually tested in the debates of our culture are potential solutions to problem areas that threaten the culture. Debating, in the large sense in which it is being used here, is not a restricted or artificial activity. The solutions being tested today at the World Power level are literally matters of life and death.

**Problem areas.** The problem areas from which debates may arise are as manifold as the activities of our culture. Yet, if you will listen to the debating that is going on at each of the levels indicated, you will note that the problem areas of debate share the following common features:

***The problem area is vital.*** Some problem areas have such little significance that they seem not to be worth debating very seriously. The problem areas out of which debates emerge tend to be somewhat serious. Frequently they are of national or international importance, but this does not mean that topics of local or school

The Commission on Narcotic Drugs meets in a chamber of the United Nations to debate a solution to a vital problem area. *(Ewing Galloway)*

importance are not debatable. Many of you at present may be more interested in debating the question of drivers' licenses for high school students than in debating the extension of social security. Likewise, your parents may be more interested in a proposed city income tax than a proposal to send more aid to some unfamiliar country in the Near East.

Whether or not a topic is vital depends largely upon circumstances. If a topic is highly controversial and is creating two vigorous points of view, it is probably vital. Certainly any topic which affects a large group of people is vital to that group. The vitalness of a topic, therefore, seems to be measured in terms of its importance to the listeners.

## ACTIVITIES

1. What current school problems would make vital subjects for debate?
2. What local or community problems do you consider vital debate topics?
3. Mention several current national or international problems that are vital.
4. What vital problems are being debated now in the Congress of the United States? In your state legislature?

***The problem area is timely.*** Closely related to the preceding discussion is the fact that most debates emerge out of timely problem areas. The term *timely* means of present interest and importance. Timely subjects are usually more interesting both to the debater and to the audience than out-dated ones. Outlawing the use of outer space in warfare is obviously of more interest today than is the topic of joining the League of Nations.

In looking for timeliness, it is important, however, that you show caution in using topics of extremely short-term interest. Some sudden fad of dress, expression, or recreation current among your school friends may be forgotten before you have time to debate it.

***The problem area is complex.*** A problem that hinges on a single fact is not debatable. Such a problem can be solved unquestionably by referring to standard reference sources. Examples of problems of simple fact are: the length of the Golden Gate Bridge, the population of Omaha, Nebraska, in 1960, or the capital of Florida. If you don't already know these facts, you can find them readily in a reference book. It is foolish to argue about verifiable facts; use verifiable facts to support your arguments.

**Types of debatable problems.** Among the types of problems that are debatable are *problems of fact, problems of value,* and *problems of policy.* The decision reached in a court of law represents an attempt to establish a question of fact by the process of argumentation. Whether the defendant is or is not guilty is a matter of fact, but it is frequently a debatable fact in that it cannot be ascertained by any simple reference process.

Problems of value are frequently debatable. "Which was the better president, Lincoln or Washington?" is an example of a question of value. Problems of value, then, are not so concerned with fact as they are with feeling or emotion toward the goodness or badness of an idea.

Today, problems of policy are the most frequent source of debate. A problem of policy is concerned with what should be done in a particular situation. Since the consequences of such decision may be considerable and are frequently of obvious importance, this type is extremely popular. Problems of policy may range from banning the existence of high school athletics to banning the use of nuclear warfare.

**Phrasing the solution.** When talking informally with your classmates you can easily debate such casual questions as:

Shall we have a Senior Prom?
Should students with B averages be excused from examinations?

In the case of casual discussion or debate, such phrasing is perfectly in order. But, in some of the more formal debating situations referred to earlier, it is desirable to give more attention to the wording of the statement to be debated. Thus, in a meeting, the statement to be debated would usually be phrased as a motion. In the court of law, the statement is commonly known as the complaint and sets forth exactly what the defendant is charged with. In the parliamentary body, the statement is phrased formally as a motion. And, in contest debate, the statement is known as the proposition, and may take the form:

*Resolved,* That the senior class should have a Senior Prom.

In addition to being phrased appropriately, it is good practice in all debating situations to phrase the statement as clearly as possible. Unless the meaning is as nearly unmistakable as possible, the debate may generate more heat than light.

## How debates proceed

Irrespective of the type of debate, whether it is between two friends in a school bus or between two opponents in the assembly of the United Nations, the process of debate involves four closely related steps. These are (1) the determination of the points at issue, (2) the development of arguments around these points of issue, (3) fallacies, and (4) the presentation of these arguments. Many informal debates seem, unfortunately, to consist almost entirely of the presentation of argument.

**Points at issue.** A point at issue is an area of disagreement between the two sides of a debate. A point at issue is an important question (a) about which there is disagreement and (b) to which the answer is vital for the acceptance or rejection of the original proposition. Suppose that you are debating the topic, *Cityville should build a new high school building in Tenning Park.*

As the proposition is discussed in preliminary sessions, some of you may think the city can raise the money to build a new school on this particular property, but others of you may not think so. Here is critical disagreement. For if the affirmative members cannot demonstrate to the satisfaction of a judge or audience that the city can raise the necessary money, then the solution required by the proposition becomes an impossibility and the affirmative loses. Granted the above circumstances, you would have discovered a real issue for this particular proposition. This issue should then be stated:

> Can Cityville raise the money necessary to build a new high school building in Tenning Park?

As noted above, issues are usually stated as questions.

If you were on the affirmative side, you would state the above cost issue in the affirmative by phrasing it as a main argument or contention. Thus:

> Cityville can raise the money necessary to build a new high school building in Tenning Park.

Main arguments are statements based on issues. They may be affirmative as in the above example, or negative, as below:

> Cityville cannot raise the money necessary to build a new high school building in Tenning Park.

If you are debating a statement of policy and are advocating a solution that changes the present situation, you will find that you will usually have to prove all of the issues in order to win unbiased observers to your point of view. In seeking to determine in advance what the points at issue may be, you should know that certain questions arise so frequently and are so generally applicable in the preparation for debates on questions of policy that they have come to be known as *stock issues.* Stock issues, then, are simply guiding questions that can be very helpful as you begin your analysis of the specific problem under debate. A stock issue may sometimes prove to be a *real* issue in a particular debate, but, even if this is the case, you will usually find it desirable to phrase it more specifically in terms of the actual subject than the stock issues are phrased in this chapter. In other instances, a stock issue may not prove to be a real issue. For example, the first stock issue below is concerned with the need for a change. If the negative decides to concede the need for a change and to present a counterplan, then this stock issue would not become a real issue in this debate.

Three stock issues that may be used in the preliminary analysis of almost any debate on a question of policy are:

I. ***Is there a need for any change?***

II. ***Is the proposed change practical?***

III. ***Is the proposed change the most desirable solution to the problem?***

How can you make most effective use of these stock issues? Don't try to build your case directly on these issues. Rather, use these issues in your preliminary thinking about the topic. Use them as starters. Use them to discover the big questions on which the affirmative and negative differ. After you have found these specific questions, build your case around your own specific real issues.

**Argumentation.** Proof is the sum of everything that causes an audience to accept and believe your arguments. Three forms of proof which influence an audience are: (1) personal, (2) emotional, and (3) logical.

Personal proof, that is, the proof that you exert as an individual through your knowledge, preparation, sincerity, and reputation, is a compelling factor in debate. William Muehl in *The Road to Persuasion* makes this statement: "The fact about human beings is that they deal in personal ties far more than in logic or evidence." Anything which destroys confidence in you or antagonizes your audience can cause your audience to reject even the soundest arguments. Being tactful, courteous, and fair in your presentation is far better than belittling or ridiculing the opposition. Display confidence without seeming over-confident; give the impression of knowing your subject without seeming vain; and establish friendly relationships with your audience if you hope to win acceptance of your point of view.

Emotional proof consists of presenting your arguments in such a way that they are linked with the interests and welfare of the audience. Making people feel that they will suffer personal loss by not accepting your views may have a stronger persuasive power than the recital of cold, hard facts. The same is true if you show them what they can gain by adopting your ideas. Dress up your facts in terms of personal desires and wants.

Quoting percentage figures regarding radioactive fallout from nuclear tests may leave your audience unmoved, but speak about the dangers of lung or bone cancer which threaten every person's children or grandchildren and you receive instant attention and response. You are speaking in terms that may mean life or death to them. People may reason with their brains but they act more often from their hearts.

Logical proof consists of *evidence* plus *reasoning*. You must understand the kinds of evidence as well as the types of reasoning if you wish to use logical proof in its strongest form.

***Evidence.*** There are four kinds of evidence:

1. Accepted or known facts
2. Documented facts or statistics
3. Authoritative statements or opinions
4. Examples or instances

To understand each, assume that you are debating the subject of foreign aid.

ACCEPTED OR KNOWN FACTS. These are facts of general knowledge. It is an accepted fact that the United States has been giving foreign aid to other countries. Since this is a known fact, it requires no further proof. It is, therefore, indisputable. The amount of aid given to each country and the list of countries receiving aid could be determined only through *documented facts or statistics.* The effects of foreign aid and the desirability of continuing it would be decided through the assembling of *authoritative statements and opinions.* Many of the statements would be based upon *examples or instances* of the use of aid in various countries.

All of these forms of evidence are valuable as proof, but you must exercise care in selecting and interpreting the last three since they are usually disputable. Some of your main problems in using them become clearer as you study each form.

DOCUMENTED FACTS OR STATISTICS. Your main problem is finding reliable sources. Encyclopedias, yearbooks, almanacs, and special published reports are considered the best sources for statistics. However, the date of publication is vital to the reliability of any figures that you quote. Your figures must be based upon the latest possible published information if you are speaking about anything current.

In preparing for a debate, the team members must gather the most recent figures and statistics from the most authentic sources. *(Monkmeyer)*

At their best, statistics are usually estimates. Even census reports are not completely accurate. Ten minutes after a census report has been taken, the rapidly increasing birth rate makes it inaccurate. You must expect, therefore, to be confronted with statistics from your opponents that appear just as reliable as your own and which seem to disprove yours. How can you meet this problem? The answer lies in interpreting statistics wisely. Instead of arguing about differences, point out the fact that there is bound to be a slight variation and then proceed to convince your listeners how your figures give a more comprehensive picture of the situation.

For instance, in a debate on raising the drivers' license age to eighteen, one side used statistics of an insurance company to prove that the accident rate of those under eighteen had been exaggerated, whereas the other side quoted statistics obtained from state surveys. The position quoting from state surveys shrewdly pointed out that many accidents were not reported to insurance companies since not all drivers carried insurance and since not all minor accidents were reported. This strategy nullified the effectiveness of the insurance report, even though it was reliable and honest.

AUTHORITATIVE STATEMENTS OR OPINIONS. This is the most dangerous type of evidence to use. It is easy to collect a series of quotations on any topic which seems to prove your case. The untrained debater may read hastily only for an abundance of quotations which suit him and then make up a speech composed entirely of those quotations. But the speaker who prepares in such a slipshod manner seldom examines his quotations critically to see if they meet the five tests which must be applied to all opinions:

1. Are they from a recognized authority in the field?
2. Are they unbiased?
3. Are they free from duress?
4. Are they intentional quotations?
5. Are they current?

EXAMPLES OR INSTANCES. An example is a situation or part of a situation that is used to show what other situations or parts of situations are like. The example may be regarded as an appropriate sample of what may be true in other cases, particularly in the case being debated. The example is used to establish precedent.

## RECORDING THE EVIDENCE

You have read about evidence and how it is needed to support your position. The following form will suggest a convenient method for recording your evidence. By using a 3″ x 5″ or a 4″ x 6″ file card you will be able to include all of the necessary information.

| (1) | (2) |
|---|---|
| Affirmative Need: | Education by ability and interests |
| (3) | (4) |
| Paul Woodring | Professor of Psychology, Western Washington College of Education |

(5)

A Fourth of a Nation, New York: McGraw-Hill Book Company, Inc., 1957, page 137.

(6)

"Every American child has a right to as much free, public education as will be of real benefit to him and to society. But this does not mean the same education or the same amount of education for everyone, because individuals have different capacities for learning as well as special talents and different interests."

CODE FOR CARD

(1) The side of the question (affirmative or negative) and the stock issue the quotation supports.

(2) A brief summary or identification of the subject matter of the quotation.

(3) The name of the person making the statement.

(4) The qualifications of the authority.

(5) The specific source of the evidence.

(6) The direct quotation.

***Reasoning.*** The process by which you examine your evidence and reach a conclusion is known as reasoning; the process of presenting your evidence and conclusions to an audience is called argumentation. Often the two terms are used interchangeably.

Four types of reasoning may be used in reaching conclusions:

1. Induction: the formulation of a general truth on the basis of observation of specific data
2. Deduction: the application of a general statement concerning a class to some specific member of the class
3. Cause and effect types:

   a. cause-to-effect: examining a presumed cause and then predicting its probable effect

   b. effect-to-cause: examining a presumed effect and stating its probable cause

   c. effect-to-effect: examining a presumed effect and stating its probable cause and then predicting a probable additional effect of the stated cause

4. Analogy: the assumption that if X and Y are alike in certain characteristics, then other characteristics known to be true of X are also true of Y

INDUCTIVE REASONING. There are three basic steps in inductive reasoning. These are:

Step 1: Collect through observation a series of specific facts which apply to a *general class.*

**Example:** Observe all the birds that you can see to find out if they have feathers.

Step 2: Make a *limited statement* that is true of all the cases that you have observed.

**Example:** Robins, blue jays, cardinals, starlings, sparrows, and crows (the only birds that I have seen) have feathers.

Step 3: Make a general statement that you believe to be true of the *entire class* (a group of beings, things, or qualities) to which your observed cases belong.

**Example:** All birds have feathers.

All types of reasoning should be tested before you use them in your final arguments. In the above steps, test first your individual observations to see if they are accurate. In step one, are you sure that every bird that you observed did have feathers? Second, test step two to see if it takes into account all of the accumulated data. Finally, recheck the observed members to be sure that they are typical of the class. In checking step three, you must be able to answer "yes" to these three questions: (1) did your observations include *enough* members? (2) were the members fairly chosen? and (3) do all of them belong to the same general class?

The chief dangers in inductive reasoning are selecting not enough examples, overlooking exceptions, and including examples which do not belong to the same general class.

DEDUCTIVE REASONING. This type of reasoning is in many ways the reverse of inductive reasoning. It is frequently expressed in a three-step pattern known as a syllogism. Here is an example of it:

| | |
|---|---|
| Major premise (general statement) | All birds have feathers. |
| Minor premise (specific classification) | A robin is a bird. |
| Conclusion (what is true of the class is true of all members of the class) | Therefore, a robin has feathers. |

As you can see, your steps in deductive reasoning are in reverse order of those in inductive reasoning. Deduction begins with a general truth and arrives at a conclusion regarding a specific member; induction begins with the specific to arrive at a general truth.

You have three chances to be wrong in deduction. If there is even one exception to the statement made in the major premise, you begin with an inaccurate assumption which makes the conclusion incorrect. If the subject of the minor premise does not belong in the general class referred to in the major premise, again the conclusion will be wrong. Finally, if the conclusion does not deal with the subject of the minor premise, your reasoning is false. In the above syllogism, you should be able to answer "yes" to these questions to be sure that your syllogism is valid.

Do *all* birds without a single exception have feathers?
Is the robin a *member* of the bird class?
Is the robin the *true subject* of the minor premise?

The dangers of deductive reasoning are illustrated in these examples of invalid syllogisms:

| | | |
|---|---|---|
| (False) | Major premise: | All birds are excellent divers and swimmers. |
| (True) | Minor premise: | A robin is a bird. |
| (False) | Conclusion: | Therefore, robins are excellent divers and swimmers. |

| | | |
|---|---|---|
| (True) | Major premise: | All birds have feathers. |
| (False) | Minor premise: | Spot is a bird. (Spot, in this case, is a collie dog.) |
| (False) | Conclusion: | Therefore, Spot has feathers. |

| | | |
|---|---|---|
| (True) | Major premise: | All birds have feathers. |
| (True) | Minor premise: | A robin is a bird. |
| (False) | Conclusion: | Therefore, Spot has feathers. (Spot was not the subject of the minor premise.) |

In valid syllogisms, the pattern followed can be expressed in terms of A, B, and C. *A* is the class identified; *B* is the statement made about the class; and *C* is the specific subject placed in the class. So the form is always:

| | | | |
|---|---|---|---|
| Major premise: | A . . . . . . . . . . . . . . . . | is . . . . . . . . . . . . . . . . | B |
| Minor premise: | C . . . . . . . . . . . . . . . . | is . . . . . . . . . . . . . . . . | A |
| Conclusion: | C . . . . . . . . . . . . . . . . | is . . . . . . . . . . . . . . . . | B |

The first syllogism regarding birds would look like this:

| | | | | |
|---|---|---|---|---|
| Major premise: | A (all birds) (class) | have | B | (feathers) (true of all members of class) |
| Minor premise: | C (robins) (subject) | are | A | (birds) (general class) |
| Conclusion: | C (robins) (subject) | have | B | (feathers) (because true of all members) |

CAUSE AND EFFECT REASONING. Each of the three basic types of cause and effect reasoning can be understood best through examples. A study of those which follow should illustrate this point.

1. Cause-to-effect is reasoning from a known cause to a probable effect. For example, if you know that a street is covered with ice (the cause), you can reason or predict with certainty that the street is slippery (probable effect).

2. Effect-to-cause is reasoning from a known effect to a probable cause. For example, if a car skids on an icy street (known effect), you can reason that the skidding occurred because of the icy street (probable cause).

3. Effect-to-effect is a combination of the two previous types. It is based on the fact that a single cause may produce more than one effect. For example, if an automobile wreck occurs, you can assume two effects, at least—damaged cars and injured occupants. Hence, if you see two overturned cars on an icy street (the observed effect), you can reason that there must have been a wreck. You then wonder if anybody has been hurt (probable effect) and if the cars have been damaged (probable effect). In so doing, you have reasoned from effect-to-effect by way of the common cause (a wreck on an icy street).

REASONING BY ANALOGY. This is a system of reasoning on the basis of comparisons. If two situations are alike in certain *known* respects, then they must be alike in other *unknown* respects.

For example, Northville, after a losing football season, replaced its coach and won all of its games the following season. Southville has had a losing football season and has also replaced its football coach. By analogy, you would reason that Southville now would win all of its football games.

Actually, analogy is not a very strong type of reasoning unless you can find situations which are practically identical; otherwise, you are vulnerable to attack. In the above illustration, the opposition could disprove your analogy in several ways:

(1) By showing that Northville and Southville are not identical in the factors which caused the loss in games

(2) By pointing out that the coach was not the sole cause of losing the games

(3) By showing that the two new coaches are not equal in ability

(4) By showing that Northville's team is larger and more experienced or that it has more time for practice

(5) By proving that Southville's opponents are always stronger teams than those of Northville

Can you see how difficult it is to prove cases through the use of analogies? It is better to use an analogy because of its vividness or as an illustration of your point of view, rather than to use it for strong proof.

## ACTIVITY

Prepare an example for each of the four types of reasoning. Read them in class and decide if they meet the tests explained in the text.

**Fallacies.** Fallacies are errors in reasoning which occur when you reach conclusions on the basis of too little or inaccurate evidence or through the misuse of evidence. There are many different types of fallacies, but three common fallacies with which you should be familiar follow:

***Hasty generalization.*** This fallacy consists in basing an opinion or an entire group of opinions on insufficient or improper examples. This occurs most frequently in the process of inductive reasoning when you attempt to arrive at a general statement after observing specific examples. Whenever your examples are not typical or do not represent the entire group, your reasoning is fallacious. For example, if you observed at one banquet that the ten wealthiest men were married to blondes, you might conclude that all wealthy men marry blondes. You can readily understand the fallacy of hasty generalization in this example. Yet many debaters attempt to set up a strong case on the basis of such limited observation.

***False cause.*** The frequent Latin rendering of this fallacy is *post hoc, ergo propter hoc,* which means literally "after this, therefore because of this." This type of argument, then, assumes that anything which comes before is the cause of anything that comes later. It is common in the cause and effect types of reasoning. For example, if a student with low grades joins a social club, you may argue that the social club accepted him because of his low grades and, therefore, social clubs encourage poor grades. Or, if a student received a lower grade in a subject after joining a social club, some persons might argue that joining the club was the cause of his poor grade.

In any reasoning involving a cause and effect relationship, you must be wary of jumping to false conclusions. Consider carefully these questions to test the accuracy of your assumptions: (a) Is the cause strong enough to produce the effect? (b) Can you be sure that no other causes produced the effect? (c) Could the relationship be one of chance only, such as having an accident after a black cat crossed your path?

If you can answer these questions adequately, you can be fairly certain that your causal relationship will be free from fallacy.

***False analogy.*** This is the result of comparing two things that have more differences than likenesses. As stated earlier, analogy is seldom completely accurate. To use it in reasoning requires great skill in pointing out all of the similarities and defending it against attack on possible loopholes. It is especially dangerous if you build too much of your case around an analogy, since your entire case can be destroyed by proving that your analogy is false.

It should be noted that of the two types of analogy, literal and figurative, the literal analogy is by far the safer to use in argument. In a literal analogy, you make your comparison between two members of the same general class. For example, you may reason about two jet fighters in this way: "The F-883 has a Delta wing and is a good fighter. Therefore, the F-886, which also has a Delta wing, will be a good fighter." In the figurative analogy, you make your comparison between two members of different classes. For example, you may compare a sick human with an economically stricken country in the following manner: "If a person is bleeding to death, you wouldn't try to save his life just by pumping more blood in and not making any effort to stop the flow of blood; so, in this instance, we cannot prevent national bankruptcy just by adding more money to the system; we must also stop the needless expenditures that are bleeding us to death."

Figurative analogies are frequently used in high school debate. But, except as attention-getters or as clarifiers, they usually have little value. The figurative analogy almost invariably disregards basic differences in the two classes and, hence, offers little by way of proof.

In addition to the three fallacies already described, two special types of fallacies, *begging the question* and *ignoring the question,* should also be mentioned.

***Begging the question.*** This is arguing as if something has been proven when, in fact, the something in question is what you are trying to prove. For example, note the following statement taken from a recent telecast:

> Promises of the Soviet government cannot be trusted because the Soviet government does not keep its word.

You can easily see that the "reason" that follows the word *because* is actually the same as the original assertion.

***Ignoring the question.*** This fallacy consists of ignoring the point at issue and speaking about irrelevant matters that have no actual bearing on the controversy. For example, in a recent debate on the question of whether or not the President of the United States should be elected for one six-year term, the first affirmative speaker devoted the first seven minutes of his speech to a detailed development of the importance of the Presidency and of the individual greatness of the men who had held the position. This material, while interesting in and of itself, ignored the question of the President's term of office.

## ACTIVITIES

1. Prepare examples of the following kinds of fallacies: hasty generalization, false cause, false analogy, begging the question, and ignoring the question.
2. Did you find any fallacies in the examples of reasoning you prepared in the activity on page 357? If so, what were they?

**Presenting arguments.** Once you have determined the points at issue, built your arguments around these issues, and paid attention to the possible fallacies in your position, you are ready to consider the presentation of your arguments.

The debate process may be written or oral, but more commonly is oral. The style of speaking will vary from the informal conversation of two friends deciding whether or not to play golf, to language that is appropriate before the United States Supreme Court. But, regardless of the situation in which the debating is taking

"*I* think we should watch Southville practice, but *she* thinks they don't deserve our support!" *(Monkmeyer)*

place, two characteristics of presentation should prevail. Both parties to the debate should have equal opportunity to (1) present their side of the argument and (2) attack the other side of the argument. In conversational debating, good manners and a sense of fairness make this equality more or less possible. In the formal meeting, parliamentary practice assures this equality. In the court of law, it is guaranteed by the rules of procedure. And in contest debating, the rules of the contest control this factor.

### How debates end

As you have learned, debates begin when two or more people disagree as to the merits of a proposed solution to a problem. Debates typically end with the acceptance or rejection of the proposed solution.

In all debates other than contest debating, the debating usually continues until there is concurrence on the part of the persons concerned that all that is important to be said *has* been said. Thus a small, informal group may suddenly silence a speaker in the midst of an argument and make a decision. Courts and parliamentary bodies move more deliberatively, but in both instances techniques are available for stopping the debate when it seems to have exhausted the evidence. In the contest debate, and occasionally in other special debates as those on radio or television, the length of the debating is set in advance and rigidly adhered to.

After the debate stops, the decision is made either by the majority concerned, as in a group discussion or a parliamentary body, or by a judge or jury in the courtroom, or by a judge or audience majority in the contest debate.

## Contest Debating

Contest debating is an extremely specialized form of debating. Many high schools and colleges carry it on as a co-curricular activity. As an activity, contest debating offers unusual opportunity to master techniques of finding and organizing materials, of presenting argumentative speeches, and of handling rebuttal. Although many of the statements made previously about the debate process in general apply to contest debating, too, a special portion of this chapter has been set aside to describe this activity. Many classroom debating situations will embody most of the characteristics of contest debating.

## Rules of the game

Debate, like any other activity or contest, is performed under certain rules and conditions. Inasmuch as these rules set off contest debating from other forms of debating, they are given here.

**The proposition.** The subject of a contest debate is referred to as the proposition. A good proposition should have the following characteristics:

***The proposition should be phrased formally.*** An example of formal phrasing of a debate proposition is:

> *Resolved,* That students with a B average should be excused from examinations.

***The proposition should be phrased affirmatively.*** In contest debates the team that supports the proposition is known as the affirmative team; the team that attacks the proposition is the negative. In debates of policy, the affirmative advocates a *change* in the *present* situation, whereas the negative, either by defending the present situation or by proposing an alternative solution, *opposes* the specific change advocated by the affirmative. The affirmative team wages an *offensive* battle; the negative, a *defensive* one, unless it proposes an alternative solution.

Thus the proposition should be worded so that the affirmative supports a change:

> *Resolved,* That the U. S. should abandon the two-party system.

***The proposition should be phrased clearly.*** Always try to make the meaning of your position unmistakable. You can accomplish this in several ways.

(1) State your proposition briefly. If you state your proposition concisely, the audience can remember it easily and will have no confusion in following you. In the following example both propositions have the same meaning, but the second one is too wordy.

Right: *Resolved,* That our city should use voting machines.

Wrong: *Resolved,* That our city should purchase and use voting machines to tabulate election returns in all city, state, and national elections rather than tabulate these as is now done.

(2) State your proposition in simple words. Simple words usually require no definition and, therefore, save you time and avoid possible misunderstanding. In the example below, it is easier to understand the first statement than the second one.

Right: *Resolved,* That the city income tax should be lowered to one per cent.

Wrong: *Resolved,* That the burden of the taxpayer should be ameliorated by lowering the city income tax to one per cent.

(3) State your proposition in words that have only one meaning. Abstract words such as liberty, freedom, conservative, liberal, communism, or isolationist have different meanings for different persons. They are vague and, therefore, hard to define. Here is an example of a vaguely worded statement and its correction:

*Resolved,* That Federal aid to education should be granted as needed.

What kind of Federal aid? How much? To whom should the aid be granted? Will the granting of such aid mean also Federal control? There have been many different proposals concerning Federal aid to schools. Therefore, avoid confusion in interpretation by narrowing your statement to one specific proposal, such as:

*Resolved,* That House Bill No. 312 proposing Federal aid to education should be passed.

This statement is precise and requires only the explanation of the main features of one specific bill.

Another violation of this principle occurs when you use words which involve degree or amount:

*Resolved,* That there are too many reckless drivers on the highways.
*Resolved,* That taxation is too high.

**Types of debate.** Many types of debate are now popular in high schools. Here are some of the more common types.

***The classic or traditional debate type.*** This type is still a favorite in many parts of the country. Each team usually consists of two speakers. The constructive speeches (speeches in which the primary function is the development of original arguments on the real issues) are usually eight to ten minutes in length. All constructive speeches after the first affirmative will, of course, contain some refutation (attack on the opposing arguments and defense of your team's arguments). Constructive speeches are given in the following order:

1. First Affirmative Constructive
2. First Negative Constructive
3. Second Affirmative Constructive
4. Second Negative Constructive

Rebuttal speeches (speeches in which the primary function is refutation) are usually from three to five minutes in length, and follow in this order:

1. First Negative Rebuttal
2. First Affirmative Rebuttal
3. Second Negative Rebuttal
4. Second Affirmative Rebuttal

The affirmative is given the last rebuttal because the affirmative carries the burden of proof.

***Variations of the traditional type.*** At times, the number of speakers may be reduced to one on each team, with the affirmative speaker speaking twice in this manner: (1) affirmative presentation, (2) negative reply, (3) affirmative reply.

In another variation of the traditional type, there may be two or even three constructive speeches on each side, but the number of rebuttal speeches may be reduced to one per team.

In these variations, the basic functions of traditional debate are unchanged. In each, the first affirmative states the proposition, defines the terms, lists the issues, and presents the affirmative case. The negative then reacts to the affirmative statement, denies the affirmative case in whole or part, and states the negative case. Each variation concludes with rebuttal; almost always, the last rebuttal is affirmative.

***The cross-examination debate.*** Each team usually consists of two members. As the title suggests, the differentiating feature of this style of debate is that each speaker is in turn cross-examined by a specified member of the opposing team. During this question and answer period, the cross-examiner is in complete charge. He (or she) asks what questions he wants. He cuts off answers as he thinks best.

Many variations in the precise pattern of the cross-examination debate exist. The pattern of the National Forensic League is as follows:

1. First Affirmative Constructive speech................ 8 minutes
2. First Affirmative is questioned by a Negative speaker ........................................................ 3 minutes
3. First Negative Constructive speech.................... 8 minutes
4. First Negative is questioned by an Affirmative speaker ........................................................ 3 minutes
5. Second Affirmative Constructive speech........... 8 minutes
6. Second Affirmative is questioned by the *other* Negative speaker ............................................ 3 minutes
7. Second Negative Constructive speech............... 8 minutes
8. Second Negative is questioned by the *other* Affirmative speaker ........................................ 3 minutes
9. First Negative Rebuttal...................................... 4 minutes
10. First Affirmative Rebuttal.................................. 4 minutes
11. Second Negative Rebuttal.................................. 4 minutes
12. Second Affirmative Rebuttal.............................. 4 minutes

It is, of course, difficult to prepare for the cross-examination portion of this style of debate. But it is extremely helpful if the debaters can learn to ask questions that draw out the issues, that provide a measure of control over the answers, and that are pertinent to what the other team has actually said.

***Is there a best type?*** Probably no one of these is best. Each has its own purpose. Each offers unique and specific values. Your coach or speech teacher will help you to decide which of these—or other types not mentioned—will be best for you, your subject, your speech purpose, the situation, and the audience.

**Conducting the debate.** The conventions of contest debate are rather well established with respect to seating arrangements, functions of the chairman, duties of the timekeeper, and behavior of the speakers themselves. Here are some useful observations:

Both teams normally sit in full view of the audience with the affirmative at the left and the negative on the right of the audience. A chairman (sometimes called the moderator) is seated on the stage either between the two teams or at one side. He stands to make all introductions, introducing the topic and the two teams to the audience at the beginning and giving any necessary announcements. He also introduces each speaker in turn by giving his position on

The chairman presiding at this high school contest debate appears to have the situation well in hand. *(Don Carlos Dunaway)*

the team when called upon to speak. At the close of the debate, he calls for the verdict and announces the winning team. An appointed timekeeper, usually seated in front of the speakers, gives time signals to each speaker. He rises to give a warning—usually two minutes before the end of a constructive speech and one minute before the end of the rebuttal speech. When the allotted time limit has expired, he stands and remains standing until the speaker stops talking.

If a chairman is presiding, rise when you are introduced, walk to the center of the speaking area, and say, "Mr. Chairman" and follow this with a salutation that includes everyone present, such as "Friends" or "Ladies and Gentlemen."

Speak out toward the audience instead of turning toward the opponents. You are seeking audience approval, not the approval of the opposition.

Observe each of the rules stated by the chairman, particularly those limiting time. Acknowledge the warning signal at once; never pretend that you don't see it. You may finish your sentence, but the usual rule is that you say no more than that.

At all times be courteous to your opponents and to your audience. Avoid sarcasm, belittling remarks about the opposition, displays of temper, threatening gestures or tones of voice, and any distracting actions during an opponent's speech. In this connection, try, so far as possible, to communicate with your teammate by note during the actual progress of the debate. In those instances when you find it absolutely essential to confer orally, do so as quietly as possible.

If you wish to challenge a statement, do so in a courteous manner when it is your turn to speak. Don't mutter "I didn't say that" or look out at the audience and shake your head as if to deny what the speaker is saying. If you write down a question to hand the opposition to answer, be polite in handing it to them or in reading it, if you elect to read it out loud.

**Judging.** The attitude of the judge in the contest debate deserves mention. As the judge listens to the debate, he knows that the contest is an intellectual battle. He realizes that no changes will actually occur in the *status quo* as a result of his decision. Only legislative bodies, courts, and groups of responsible people can make and enforce decisions on questions of taxation, capital punishment, foreign aid, tariff, a new high school gymnasium, and other problems. Therefore, the contest debate judge, unlike a member of a jury or a senator, need not make his decision on the merits of the

The judges carefully check the plus and minus qualities of the debaters. *(Monkmeyer)*

solution. The contest debate judge makes his decision on the merits of the debating—giving his vote to the team that displays superior preparation, argumentation, and presentation.

## Studying the proposition

**Finding the issues.** The concepts of the *real issue* and the *stock issue* have already been developed on pages 348-349. These concepts are as crucial for the contest debate as for any other type of debate. But in addition, the contest debater is frequently concerned with the *potential issue*, the *admitted issue*, and the *pseudo-issue*.

***Potential issues.*** This is a question, the answer to which is important to the acceptance or rejection of the original proposition, but about which it is not yet known if there will be a clash of opinion. Potential issues become real issues if there is a clash of opinion; potential issues become admitted issues if there is not a clash of opinion. Obviously, then, the affirmative case must be prepared on all potential issues.

***Admitted issues.*** A real issue was defined earlier as a main question (a) about which there is disagreement and (b) to which the answer is vital for the acceptance or rejection of the original

THE SATURDAY EVENING POST

"Well, I see there are two sides to the question."

Reprinted by special permission of Brad Anderson and *The Saturday Evening Post.* Copyright © 1960 by The Curtis Publishing Company.

proposition. An admitted issue is a question to which the answer is vital for the acceptance or rejection of the original proposition, but about which there is no disagreement or clash of opinion. An admitted issue differs from a real issue only in that the negative and affirmative answer the question in the same way.

***Pseudo-issues.*** The pseudo (false) issue is a question to which the answer is not vital to the acceptance or rejection of the original proposition regardless of whether or not there is a clash of opinion. Pseudo-issues develop in contest debating when one or the other of the two teams has been misled in its analysis of the problem.

**The case.** After discovering issues, your next step is knowing how to use those issues in building a case. Your case is the over-all plan of arguments or the strategy you use in reaching your conclusion.

A strong case is the result of blending all of your best arguments together so firmly that they lead directly to a logical conclusion. To build a strong case, start with a list of all possible arguments accumulated in your search for information. Line them up on both sides and then proceed to weed out all weak and duplicated arguments. Reword in concise and forceful terms the ones that you retain for use. Next, decide how to incorporate these into a chain which will be difficult to destroy. Your interpretation of the proposition will help to determine your approach. Your final approach is usually influenced by three questions: (1) which arguments are the strongest logically, (2) which will win most favorable acceptance of this particular audience, and (3) which will be most difficult for the opposition to attack?

In building any case, you should consider first the probable audience reaction. Try always to win agreement on general objectives and to show how your plan will accomplish these objectives. Phrase your arguments in terms of the listeners' welfare. The strongest arguments are always those which seem to provide benefits to the listeners. Furthermore, such arguments are always the hardest for the opposition to attack.

**The brief.** Every debater knows and respects the brief as the backbone of good debating. It is the full outline of a complete affirmative or negative position; it contains all the arguments and evidence known to the team. It is the reference source from which the case is planned. The brief contains an Introduction, Discussion, and Conclusion. The brief consists of a series of declarative statements, each of which expresses one complete idea but only one. The relationship between main headings and subheadings may be either explanatory or causal in different parts of the brief.

***The introduction.*** The introduction tells you everything that is necessary to a clear understanding of the case. The usual main headings of an introduction are:

I. Statement of the proposition
II. History of the question
III. Immediate cause for the debate
IV. Definition of terms
V. Excluded or admitted matter
VI. Statement of the issues
VII. The partition or division of the basic arguments among the speakers.

The purpose of the introduction is to inform, not to argue. The relationship between the main headings and subheadings is explanatory rather than causal.

***The discussion.*** The discussion presents all of the evidence and reasoning for each of the possible issues. It seeks to answer these questions:

What is true?
Why is it true?

The relationship between main and subheadings is always causal, signified by the words "because" or "for" at the end of each main heading.

***The conclusion.*** The conclusion reviews the brief's main points and presents a package summary of the reasons presented to support the proposition. The relationship between main and subheadings is causal.

## Debating the proposition

**Duties of the two teams.** In addition to understanding the total situation, you must know the obligations of each team before you seek to present either case.

***The affirmative team.*** The primary duty of this team is to gain audience acceptance of the specific proposal as stated in the debate proposition. Since the affirmative is proposing a change, it assumes the *burden of proof.* This means that it must fulfill the following obligations:

1. It must attack the *status quo* by pointing out its basic disadvantages and by proving that these disadvantages are inherent in the present system and cannot, therefore, be eliminated without changing the present system.
2. It must develop the essential elements of its solution in sufficient detail to make the debate meaningful.
3. It must prove that its proposed change will meet the need in the best possible way with no serious disadvantages.
4. It must prove that its proposed change is practical and will work if put into operation.
5. It must be ready to refute any counter-proposals.

***The negative team.*** The primary duty of this team is to convince the audience or judge to reject the specific solution of the affirmative. The negative always has the advantage that the existing situation is *presumed* to be satisfactory until the affirmative can prove *all* of its reasons for advocating a change. In court, you are innocent until you are proved guilty. This same presumption favors the negative on the debate platform.

The negative has several methods open to it in maintaining its defense:

1. It may deny completely the need of any change by defending the present system as being entirely satisfactory, or
2. It may recognize some degree of imperfection but argue that the alleged faults are not inherent in the system and, therefore, can be corrected without changing the entire system, or

3. It may concede the need for a major change but not the change proposed by the affirmative. As soon as the negative advances a proposal, it must assume the same burden of proof as the affirmative and prove that its proposal will not only work, but will also work better than the one advanced by the affirmative, or

4. It may confine its attack to pointing out reasons which are stronger for the rejection than for the acceptance of the affirmative proposals.

***Comparison of teams.*** Consider now the four choices open to a negative team. In the first, you defend the existing conditions in toto. You attempt to destroy the "need" argument of the affirmative by proving that there is no need for a change since the present situation is entirely satisfactory. This type of strategy is excellent—if you can defend it consistently throughout the debate. Certainly, if you can prove to everyone's satisfaction that there is no need for a change, there is little reason to continue the debate. However, this is not as easy as it sounds.

The second choice usually gives you the greatest opportunity to launch strong arguments against the affirmative. Instead of denying a need completely, you admit a weakness but you deny that the weakness is a basic part of the system itself. This choice provides you with a reasonable approach which your listeners may be persuaded to accept. Remember, that the full obligation of the affirmative is not simply to point out flaws and imperfections in the present system, but to prove that these flaws and imperfections are so basic to the present system that the entire system is ineffectual and doomed to failure. Never let an audience lose sight of this important obligation of the affirmative; never let the affirmative lose sight of its obligation, either. While you are insisting that the affirmative prove that the evils are inherent in the system, you can confront your listeners with the plausible plea of "Why advocate replacing an entire system in order to remedy a few flaws which can be easily corrected?"

You have scores of examples to use in such a method of reasoning. Here are a few analogous questions which would help drive home your point:

> Would you abolish all paper currency because of the evils of counterfeiting?
>
> Would you cut down a tree to get rid of a hornet's nest?
>
> Would you burn down your house to destroy termites?
>
> Would you overthrow our democratic form of government because of some of its weaknesses?

The second choice is usually a wise one. It gives you many chances to "corner" your opponent fairly and provides a lively encounter for the teams and the audience. This continuous clash of arguments represents debating at its best.

Many negative teams like to offer an alternative plan, but in doing so you lose the advantage of presumption. The audience can no longer presume that the *status quo* is right when you admit that it is wrong by offering a remedy of your own for it. In doing so, you must accept the burden of proof in defending your plan as surely as the affirmative team must. In reality, the debate is no longer one between the affirmative advocating a change in the *status quo* and the negative defending the *status quo* against radical change. It becomes virtually a debate between two affirmative points of view—one affirming the specific change stated in the proposition and the other affirming a completely different change, but *with both teams advocating a change.*

If you do elect the third method, be sure that you assume full responsibility for proving the superiority of your solution over all others and, of course, be certain that it is superior. It is sometimes suggested that the negative should withhold the details of its counterplan until the second negative constructive speech in order to gain certain alleged advantages such as surprise. Because the plan is introduced late in the debate, there is less opportunity on the part of the affirmative to deal with the plan. You will generally find it far better to present the negative counterplan, if you use this technique, in the first negative speech. The major advantage of introducing the plan early in the debate is that this procedure gives the negative the opportunity to control the ground on which the debate is to be fought and to force the affirmative to debate the arguments and evidence that the negative has selected. Moreover, what would the first negative speaker say during his constructive speech if he must keep secret the heart of the negative argument?

It may be well to add that there sometimes seems to be too much use of the "surprise weapon" in high school debating. One example of such surprise weapons, in addition to the one cited, is to use the last minute of the first negative speech to read—and usually quickly—a list of questions to the opposition. These surprise techniques suggest a real fear of the effect of full debate and a lack of faith in the counterplan or argument.

The fourth method is advisable if you want to keep up a steady barrage of argument against the contentions of the opposition and if your evidence is strong enough to overthrow their every major point. This is possible if you can keep demonstrating that all the alleged evils are minor, that the proposed change would bring far greater evils, that any advantages would be outweighed by disadvantages, and, finally, that the plan can't possibly work. Success in establishing such beliefs in the minds of your audience will make the affirmative case seem weak and futile in comparison. But you can use this type of strategy only in case your evidence and reasoning power can top that of your opponents.

You may be wondering why any debater would choose the affirmative side in view of all the apparent advantages and alternatives open to the negative. But never make the mistake of thinking that either side has everything its own way in debate. More specifically, although it is true that the affirmative has the burden of proof, it also has the tremendous advantage of speaking both first and last in the debate. From the persuasive standpoint, the importance of making the first and last impressions can scarcely be overestimated. In particular, the opportunity of being able to make the final statement—a statement that the negative has no opportunity to erase—must be stressed. Moreover, the affirmative usually sets the ground on which the debate will be fought. They have the opportunity to define the terms, set forth the original analysis of the proposition, and deliver the first speech which can be polished to perfection. The negative must face the affirmative on its ground or risk the appearance of "dodging the issues." Finally, there are undoubted advantages, both with a judge and with an audience, in being on the offensive, of attacking rather than defending. All in all, then, as the won and lost records of contest debates indicate, there is no particular advantage to being on either side.

**The constructive speeches.** In contest debates, each speaker has a definite responsibility to present a certain segment of the case. In two-person teams, the following division of points is customary in the constructive portion of the debate:

The first affirmative speaker states the proposition, defines terms, gives the history of the question, limits the question to main issues, outlines the case, and develops one or two major points.

The first negative speaker accepts, rejects, or offers changes in the introductory explanation and definitions presented by the first affirmative. He then outlines the negative case and attempts to develop one or two major points. He also allows time to refute all of the important arguments of the first affirmative.

The second affirmative has these responsibilities: refuting any important arguments advanced by the first negative, strengthening the affirmative case by bringing in new evidence to refute the negative's attack against it, developing the remaining issue or issues of the affirmative case, summarizing the full case, and showing how the negative attack against it has failed.

The second negative has the same responsibilities for his team as the second affirmative. That is, he must attempt to refute all important, unanswered affirmative arguments, strengthen the negative case by bringing in new evidence as needed to refute the affirmative's attack, develop the remaining issues of the negative case, summarize the complete argument of the debate, and show how the affirmative has failed to establish its major contentions.

The constructive speech, then, is the speech in which you advance your arguments. It is prepared in advance and may or may not be given from memory depending on how flexible you want your speech to be. If you wish to allow time to refute the opposition's arguments at the beginning of or during your speech, you should be able to depart from your basic speech to do so. In such an event, you would memorize the main ideas you wish to present and you would speak extemporaneously. Such a procedure is usually considered the most convincing, but it requires thorough understanding of your question and much practice before delivery.

**The rebuttal speeches.** Refutation is the process of attacking the major contentions of the opposition. Refutation may and should occur in either your constructive or your rebuttal speeches. In the rebuttal speech, the debater both refutes the arguments of his opponents and rebutts, that is, rebuilds his own case. Refutation, whether done in the constructive or the rebuttal speech, is a most important part of debate. Many debaters think it is *the* most important, particularly from the standpoint of skills developed.

The better you debate, the more you will like refutation. To master refutation, you must (a) know your subject thoroughly, (b) understand refutation techniques, and (c) practice refutation.

***Know your debate subject.*** You may be wondering how to prepare for refutation. Preparation for refutation is not as mechanical as it is for constructive speeches since you cannot prepare refutation in advance. Yet, you should be preparing for refutation all of the time that you are searching for material to build your own case. Read all of the opposing arguments that you can find. The more counter-arguments that you can discover, the better equipped you will be to answer them. As you find a strong argument on the opposing side, list evidence and arguments that will help you answer it. The debater who looks for arguments only on his side and closes his eyes to those of the opposition will find it difficult either to attack the opposition or to uphold his case.

The only answer to preparing for refutation is thorough knowledge of both sides of the proposition. In brief, you should (a) anticipate all possible arguments of your opponents, (b) collect data to refute these arguments, and (c) build arguments of attack on the basis of such data. Set up your arguments in advance and plan your attack on them before the debate. Then select from your card file the arguments as needed and present them accordingly.

***Understand the techniques of refutation.*** You must know what, how, and when to refute.

1. *What* to refute.

Attack only those arguments that may cost your team a favorable decision. "Don't waste valuable ammunition on small game" is a rule of the hunter which you can put to good use. If you spend too much time on minor points, you have no time for the major ones. Furthermore, you may make some of the minor points *seem* important by dwelling upon them.

Attack most strongly those arguments that are open to attack. Find the weak spots and hit them hard.

2. *How* to refute.

State clearly and honestly the argument that you intend to attack.

Show why the argument is important to the debate. Explain *why* you are attacking that particular point.

Offer whatever proof seems strongest to refute the arguments of the opposition.

Point out specific instances in which the opposition has committed a specific fallacy. But be careful not to be content with pointing out the name of the fallacy; it is much more important to make clear the nature of the fallacy as it was actually committed.

Point out clearly the effect or significance of your refutation on the entire debate.

3. *When* to refute.

There is no one best time. A good general principle is to refute an argument of the opposition as quickly as possible and as often as needed. The main point to remember is to bring in your refutation at the time which, in your judgment, will make the strongest impact upon your audience or your judge.

The essential duties of the members of both teams in the rebuttal speeches are summarized in the following outline. You will note that the rebuttal speech is used to analyze, attack, and answer the arguments of the opposition and to rebuild your own case. New evidence may be used to support your reasoning, but you should never present new issues in the rebuttal speeches. All constructive material must be presented in the constructive speeches.

A reference is checked in preparation of the rebuttal. *(Monkmeyer)*

## AN OUTLINE OF THE DUTIES OF REBUTTAL SPEECHES

*First Negative*

1. Technique of overwhelming assault. Shatter the affirmative. Expose their inconsistencies. Show them lacking in materials, et cetera.
2. Push them on some objection they have failed to meet.

*Second Negative*

1. Answer the first affirmative rebuttal.
2. Analyze the big affirmative argument and meet it with the negative case or one big negative argument.
3. Forestall the effectiveness of the last affirmative rebuttal. "He will no doubt come up and tell . . . . ."
4. Make the negative case clear and leave the audience on your side.

*First Affirmative*

1. Answer the first negative rebuttal.
2. Answer thoroughly the main argument of the second negative constructive speech. Or, in the analysis of the debate meet the second negative constructive.

*Second Affirmative*

1. Answer the second negative rebuttal.
2. Analyze the big negative argument; what does the case resolve into? Present the affirmative answer.
3. Make the affirmative case clear. Point out how the affirmative has fulfilled its duty efficiently and sufficiently. Point out that the negative has failed to meet important points.
4. Summarize.

Your greatest enjoyment of debating comes from active participation. Now that you have learned the fundamentals of building strong debate cases and the elements of refutation in the various types of debate, you will want to try your skill in the following activities:

## ACTIVITIES

In all of the activities, prepare the following to turn in to your teacher: a brief, a bibliography, and a set of filing cards containing your evidence.

1. Prepare a ten-minute argument on either the affirmative or the negative side of a current topic. Be ready to answer any opposing arguments from the class.
2. Choose an opponent for a two-person debate on any subject of interest. Prepare a constructive speech eight minutes in length and give a three-minute rebuttal speech.
3. Choose two affirmative and two negative speakers to participate in the traditional type of debate. Select any debatable subject from the following:

   A current school topic
   A topic of local or state interest
   A topic of national or international interest

   Limit the constructive speeches to eight minutes and the rebuttal to three minutes.
4. From the same general grouping of topics in No. 3, choose a topic and conduct the variation of the traditional debate described on page 363—three speeches in this order:

   Affirmative Presentation
   Negative Reply
   Affirmative Reply
5. Try the next type of variation with two constructive speakers on each side but with only one rebuttal speaker for each team. Select your own topic.

## PRONUNCIATION PROBLEMS

Words containing the diphthong "oi" are difficult for many of you to say. Practice repeating the words below and reading the sentences until your teacher is satisfied with your pronunciation.

| | | |
|---|---|---|
| oil | spoiled | annoying |
| poise | oyster | groin |
| boy | cloister | appoint |
| avoid | moist | boil |
| rejoice | turmoil | broil |
| destroyer | soil | coil |
| adroit | join | joy |
| foil | coin | point |
| toil | noise | void |

## READING CHECK-UP

Read aloud the nonsense sentences below to check your pronunciation of any problem words.

The smell of oil was annoying throughout the voyage. I did not know when I joined the boys and girls for a trip on an oil tanker that coal oil lamps were still in use, or I would have remained on home soil.

He was enjoined to be silent on the point of voiding the lease which was disappointing instead of a cause for rejoicing.

"Broil him in oil!" the boisterous fellow shouted during the turmoil, but his adroit opponent foiled his plans by making so much noise that his comrades joined in the turmoil to spoil the plans of the roistering hoyden.

The royal personage was anointed on foreign soil. He claimed that the broiled oysters served in the cloister were too moist for his taste.

The boisterous boy rejoiced over his appointment to clean oily coils aboard the new destroyer.

The physician voiced his opinion about goiters and helped the girl who was toiling hard to foil the effects of the poison.

The counterfeiter was a bit coy about admitting his adroitness in designing coins.

Oil, oily oil, oils old oily autos.

## VOCABULARY BUILD-UP

Use the italicized words in short paragraphs to show that you understand their meanings.

an *invincible* opponent
in *imminent* danger
a quick *appraisal*
acceptance of a *gratuity*
a *discerning* mind
fling of *profligacy*
*inevitable* consequences
*retroactive* to May 1
fear of *reprisal*
the order of *precedence*
to *evolve* a solution
a *restive* audience
to *deplete* supplies
*flaccid* muscles
*divergent* ideas
*ethical* standards
of *gargantuan* proportions
a *derogatory* remark
a congressional *boondoggle*
*affectation* of speech
an *alleged* attempt
efforts to *inhibit* action
*extraneous* arguments
noted for his *veracity*
an attempt to *vilify*
*acrimonious* statements
speaking in the *vernacular*
discharging a *salvo*

UNIT

# 5

# *Interpreting and Broadcasting*

CHAPTER

CHAPTER

# 19 Reading Aloud

"Reading aloud is simply a way to share something you like with somebody you like."

—*Charles Laughton*

WHENEVER you read something interesting, humorous, exciting, or important, your first impulse is to communicate it to somebody else. Reading aloud at such times is meaningful and pleasant to you and should be meaningful and pleasant to your listener.

Reading aloud seems to satisfy two main drives: (1) the urge to communicate with others and (2) the desire to create enjoyment. The goal of this chapter is to help you achieve both of these ends more effectively.

## What Is Good Oral Reading?

A good reader is first and always an interpreter. Reading any selection aloud includes thinking, feeling, and understanding the author's meaning and mood. Repeating words and reciting lines are only preliminary steps in becoming an enjoyable reader.

As an interpreter, your role is to translate printed words into living speech. Three people are always involved in interpretation—the author who wrote the words, the one who speaks them, and the person who hears them. Whenever you are the reader of another's words, you must re-create for your listener the thoughts and feelings of the writer as accurately as possible.

You will find many instances of the importance of good reading in everyday life. Your teachers will frequently find it necessary to read aloud to you; this ability may be particularly important to the teacher of literature. Many good speakers will use quotations to support or point up their talks. Radio and television announcers and reporters usually communicate from written scripts.

Radio actors have developed the ability to read from script as if they were talking to you. Seldom do you realize that the speaking you hear on radio is really oral reading unless a poor performer makes you aware of the fact that he *is* reading. Telltale signs of poor reading are mispronounced words, stumbling over words, and confused sentence structure. Usually, the voice is artificial and the delivery is hesitant, choppy, and difficult to follow. In such cases, you brand the person as a poor reader and refuse to listen.

Skilled radio readers can make characters so lifelike and scenes so realistic that you visualize them and even *feel* the emotions projected through the voice. Such readers exemplify the essence of good reading—to make others see and feel what they hear.

Two words—proper preparation—spell the difference between just *reciting* lines and reading well. Begin by reading a selection silently to grasp the general content. As you study your selection, keep asking yourself what the author means and what the author feels. The answer to these two questions is the first essential of preparation.

To listen to such an experienced team of radio performers as this, you would never suspect that they were reading the script. *(NBC Photo)*

# Understand Your Selection

## Understand the meaning

Behind every author's words is a definite thought or meaning which he wants to express to a reading audience. Until you know exactly what that meaning is, you cannot express it orally to a listening audience. How can you get the meaning?

**Know the meaning of each word.** Words are the messengers which carry meaning. If you find any that are strangers to you, look them up in a dictionary. When you read silently, often you skip over words that you don't know or can't pronounce. This habit is ruinous to oral reading. Take time, therefore, to study word meanings and pronunciations.

Sometimes, authors use allusions—references to characters, terms, or lines found elsewhere in literature. Some familiar examples are:

| | |
|---|---|
| "patience of Job" | "Achilles' heel" |
| "a Herculean task" | "rich as Croesus" |
| "a modern Pegasus" | "a Midas touch" |
| "sword of Damocles" | "proud as Lucifer" |

You could not understand such allusions without knowing the story behind them. First, find out the source by asking your teacher or other qualified person or by consulting a dictionary of allusions available in most libraries. Usually, you will discover that allusions have their origins in the Bible, mythology, fables, legends, history, and other literary works. Thorough understanding of a selection containing allusions is impossible until you understand the references. Take time, therefore, to investigate doubtful phrases as well as doubtful words.

**Know the meaning of each sentence.** Although you may understand word meanings, you may not understand some sentences which are complicated in structure or unusually long. Confusing sentences are used often in poetry to meet the requirements of meter and rhyme. If the meaning is obscure, read a sentence aloud. Watch carefully all punctuation marks, since they are the guideposts to clear understanding. Unscramble confusing sentences by saying or writing them as you would ordinarily state them in conversation. If you still cannot understand a sentence, ask somebody to help you discover the meaning. As soon as you are clear in your own mind, you will be able to punctuate audibly the true meaning to others. Never be satisfied until you understand every word, every allusion, and every sentence!

Does this reader give the impression of doing a good job? *(Pogue's Portrait Studio)*

**Express the meaning in your own words.** Always look for the main thought behind the words as well as the supporting ideas which help to develop the main thought. A good method to follow is to write out in a short paragraph your way of expressing the author's meaning. If you can say it in your own words, you can be sure that you understand it well enough to say it intelligently in the author's words. After writing out a paragraph, go one step further. Try to express in one sentence the central idea. This may be more difficult than writing a paragraph, but it's an excellent test of your ability to analyze the true thought and to express it concisely.

By the time that you have made this intensive study of word and sentence meaning, you should be able to translate orally the literal meaning of any selection. Literal meaning, however, is seldom the sole meaning an author wishes to communicate. More often, meaning is tinged with a feeling or mood that an author wants you to experience with him.

## Understand the mood

Mood can be described as the attitude, feeling, emotion, or temperament of an author which colors the meaning of his words. It provides the clue to the style of reading aloud which you should use in the interpretation. It is your responsibility to decide whether the intended mood is serious, sad, whimsical, humorous, nonsensical, cynical, nostalgic, angry, hysterical, or gay, for instance. You can clearly see that to read a sad poem gaily would turn the poem into a farce. In the same manner, a cheerful message read in an angry style would ruin the meaning. Determining the mood is, therefore, a *must* in interpretation. Naturally, you want to know how you can be sure of an author's mood. These suggestions will help you.

**Discover the background of the author and the selection.** Although it is not always possible to find such information about every author, you should try to find whatever is available. Biographies written about authors often furnish a clue to their emotional background and even tell you circumstances under which certain selections were written. The life story of Edgar Allan Poe, for example, reveals many tragic facts which were responsible for the despair and morbidness reflected in much of his writing. The death of his beloved wife at an early age explains the sadness of his love poems. His habit of excessive drinking accounts for some of the weird plots and deranged characters in his short stories and the poem, *The Raven.*

Knowing the circumstances which prompted the writing of certain selections helps also in understanding the mood. Walt Whitman wrote *O Captain! My Captain!* after the death of Abraham Lincoln to express his grief and the tragic loss to the nation. His use of symbolism is not clear unless you know that Lincoln is the "captain," and the ship is the "ship of state." When you realize the full meaning and mood behind the poem, you can give it the solemn interpretation which it deserves.

In your study of background, try to discover the author's motive. Why did he write a particular selection? Was he trying to tell a story, express a philosophy, describe an incident, paint a verbal portrait of a person, pay tribute to a person, or show love for a person, animal, or cause? Was he trying to appeal to your emotions or to your intellect? Was his purpose to provide humor? Or was he merely interested in composing nonsense? Finding the answers to such questions as these is always important in analyzing an author's mood.

**Make use of your own experience.** When you read silently, you often associate yourself with the characters in a story or poem to the extent that you even feel as they do. When you read aloud, you should call upon your own experiences in an attempt to project the feelings of the author. If the mood is happy and gay, think of similar experiences of your own. Or if the selection is sad or serious, try to recall how you felt when something sad happened in your life. Most of you have undergone the usual emotions of love, happiness, sadness, disappointment, or anger. Recalling your own sensations will help you understand the author's mood and, hence, give an understandable interpretation of it when you read aloud.

Below are several selections to test your ability to understand the meaning and the mood. Make no attempt to read aloud at present. Follow the directions given at the end of each selection for preparation.

## VERY LIKE A WHALE

One thing that literature would be greatly the better for
Would be a more restricted employment by authors of simile and metaphor.
Authors of all races, be they Greeks, Romans, Teutons or Celts,
Can't seem just to say that anything is the thing it is but have to go out of their way to say that it is like something else.
What does it mean when we are told
That the Assyrian came down like a wolf on the fold?
In the first place, George Gordon Byron had had enough experience
To know that it probably wasn't just one Assyrian, it was a lot of Assyrians.
However, as too many arguments are apt to induce apoplexy and thus hinder longevity,
We'll let it pass as one Assyrian for the sake of brevity.
Now then, this particular Assyrian, the one whose cohorts were gleaming in purple and gold,
Just what does the poet mean when he says he came down like a wolf on the fold?
In heaven and earth more than is dreamed of in our philosophy there are a great many things,
But I don't imagine that among them there is a wolf with purple and gold cohorts or purple and gold anythings.
No, no, Lord Byron, before I'll believe that this Assyrian was actually like a wolf I must have some kind of proof;
Did he run on all fours and did he have a hairy tail and a big red mouth and big white teeth and did he say Woof woof?
Frankly I think it very unlikely, and all you were entitled to say, at the very most,
Was that the Assyrian cohorts came down like a lot of Assyrian cohorts about to destroy the Hebrew host.
But that wasn't fancy enough for Lord Byron, oh dear me no, he had to invent a lot of figures of speech and then interpolate them,
With the result that whenever you mention Old Testament soldiers to people they say Oh yes, they're the ones that a lot of wolves dressed up in gold and purple ate them.

That's the kind of thing that's being done all the time by poets, from Homer to Tennyson;
They're always comparing ladies to lilies and veal to venison.
And they always say things like that the snow is a white blanket after a winter storm.
Oh it is, is it, all right then, you sleep under a six-inch blanket of snow and I'll sleep under a half-inch blanket of unpoetical blanket material and we'll see which one keeps warm,
And after that maybe you'll begin to comprehend dimly
What I mean by too much metaphor and simile.

—Ogden Nash

**The author:** Who is Ogden Nash? What type of verse does he write? What other compositions of his have you read? Bring to class another of his poems to discuss. What peculiarity in sentence structure do you notice in his poetry? What is your opinion of his style of writing?

**The meaning:** State the central idea in one sentence. What illustrations does he use to support the idea? Do you agree with it? Find out the meaning of any unfamiliar words, terms, or references. Restate any confusing sentences. Summarize the poem in your own words.

**The mood:** How would you describe the mood? Give reasons for your answer.

## THE ART OF LIVING TOGETHER

Long ago in an Oriental country, a great Mogul stepped on a sharp thorn in his garden. In a paroxysm of fury he summoned his viziers and commanded: "Cover the entire earth with leather, so that I shall step on no more thorns!" Not daring to dispute the dictator, the miserable courtiers bowed themselves backward and took counsel among themselves. Then one vizier, bolder than the rest, proposed an amendment to the Mogul: "Your Majesty, just cover your feet with leather, and wherever you go, you will be walking on leather." The Mogul thought it not a bad idea, and commanded it to be carried out. And so the first pair of shoes was made.

Commenting on this parable, Dr. William Alfred Eddy, former President of Hobart College, has said:

"The totalitarian magicians demand that the earth be covered with their culture. They command that their system be nailed down everywhere, stamping out every acre that is alien and every race or idea that is uncongenial. But we do not need to destroy racial and political minorities before the truth can prevail. We need only to cover ourselves from head to foot with tolerance, reverence, and charity. And then, wherever we walk, we shall find ourselves standing on holy ground."

**The meaning:** The opening paragraph is a parable. What is a parable? What application of the parable did Dr. William Alfred Eddy make?

Define and pronounce the following: Mogul, paroxysm, vizier, courtier, counsel, totalitarian, alien, and minorities.

Can you think of another application of the parable?

**The mood:** Is there a definite mood? If so, what is it?

## MIRACLES

Why, who makes much of a miracle?
As to me, I know of nothing else but miracles,
Whether I walk the streets of Manhattan,
Or dart my sight over the roofs of houses toward the sky,
Or wade with naked feet along the beach just in the edge of the water,
Or stand under trees in the woods,
Or talk by day with any one I love,
Or sit at table at dinner with the rest,
Or look at strangers opposite me riding in the car,
Or watch honey-bees busy around the hive of a summer forenoon,
Or animals feeding in the fields,
Or birds, or the wonderfulness of insects in the air,
Or the wonderfulness of the sundown, or of stars shining so quiet and
bright,
Or the exquisite delicate, thin curve of the new moon in spring;
These, with the rest, one and all, are to me miracles,
The whole referring, yet each distinct, and in its place.

To me every hour of the light and dark is a miracle,
Every cubic inch of space is a miracle,
Every square yard of the surface of the earth is spread with the same,
Every foot of the interior swarms with the same.

To me the sea is a continual miracle,
The fishes that swim—the rocks—the motion of the waves—the ships,
with men in them,
What stranger miracles are there?

—Walt Whitman

**The author:** Find out all of the interesting facts you can about Walt Whitman. What are some of his most outstanding works? Had you ever read any of these previously? If so, which are your favorites?

**The meaning:** Express in one sentence what he thinks about miracles. What are some of the miracles enumerated? Do you agree with his views? How many sentences are there in the poem? Why would this be a difficult poem to read aloud?

**The mood:** What is the mood? How can you tell?

### ACTIVITY

Bring to class a short poem to exchange with a classmate. Analyze the poem you receive by giving information about the background of the author and the selection, a summary in your own words of the poem, an explanation of any doubtful words or terms, and (drawing upon your own experience) your impression of the mood.

# Express Your Selection

Although understanding the meaning and the mood is essential, it is only the first step in interpretation. The second step is equally important—the preparation to translate that meaning and mood to others. The ability to read aloud so that your listeners can understand and enjoy what you read is developed only through considerable practice in oral reading.

Oral reading and singing are both vocal skills which cannot be mastered silently. Can you imagine a singer silently reading notes and hastily glancing over the marks of any musical score without attempting to practice aloud before a performance? Many readers, however, think that they know how to read aloud simply because they can understand and enjoy what they read silently. The techniques of the two types of reading are vastly different. These differences will become more clear to you as you study the remainder of this chapter.

## The importance of emphasis

More than anything else, reading aloud effectively depends upon (a) emphasis and (b) subordination. You can't have one without the other. Your basic purpose as you sought to understand the meaning and mood of your selection was to discover what to emphasize and what to subordinate. Now, as you learn how to express your selection, your basic problem will be to develop techniques of voice and body that will enable you to create these relationships in the minds of your listeners.

Proper emphasis is a vital part of reading aloud. Some words and ideas are naturally more important than others and must be made to stand out over less important words and ideas. Your two problems in emphasis are then to determine (a) the words or ideas to be emphasized and (b) the method of emphasis.

As you will learn later in this section, there are many ways to emphasize words and ideas. You may vary the quality, pitch, or force of your voice; you may speak at a different rate, use phrasing,

Even a very young child enjoys the images created for him by a reader who gives a skillful interpretation. *(Don Carlos Dunaway)*

make use of the pause; you may use bodily action. But any technique that you use must be used meaningfully to produce the effect that you desire.

Certain rules of emphasis will help you decide which words to stress. One rule is to put emphasis upon words which introduce *new* ideas. An example of this can be found in *The Bells* by Poe.

Hear the sledges with the bells—
Silver bells!

Since "bells" was introduced in the first line, you emphasize "silver" in the second line to indicate a special kind of bells. The same is true in another stanza:

Hear the loud alarm bells—
Brazen bells!

By this time you are no longer interested in "bells"—your interest lies in the adjectives which describe the bells.

A second rule of emphasis is to stress words which express *repeated* thoughts. Again you can find an example from *The Bells.*

In a clamorous appealing to the mercy of the fire,
In a mad expostulation with the deaf and frantic fire,
Leaping higher, higher, higher,

A third occasion for emphasis is in using words in a series which builds to a climax. A familiar example of this is in the progression of the three degrees of comparison, from the positive through the comparative to the superlative, as follows:

Good! Better! Best!

Another example of building to a climax is:

He won the local contest, the state contest, and the national contest.

A good example from literature of this type of emphasis is found in the following poem:

## A PRAYER TO ST. CATHERINE

St. Catherine, St. Catherine,
O lend me thy aid,
And grant that I never
May be an old maid.

A husband, St. Catherine,
A GOOD one, St. Catherine,
But ANYONE better than
No one, St. Catherine.

Rich, St. Catherine,
Young, St. Catherine,
Handsome, St. Catherine,
SOON, St. Catherine.
—Unknown

A fourth use of emphasis is to indicate comparison and contrast. In conversation, you often emphasize in this manner:

"I like cake better than pie."
"I prefer television to the movies."
"History is dull but chemistry is exciting."

Literature furnishes you with many examples of this type of emphasis. Antony in his speech at Caesar's funeral said:

"I come to bury Caesar, not to praise him.
The evil that men do lives after them,
The good is oft interred with their bones."

Emphasis can also be achieved through almost any sudden change because an audience is quick to notice change of any kind. In pausing, you decrease your speaking rate to attract attention. You can also quicken your rate in building to a climax, you can change voice quality, and you can vary the pitch and volume. All of these variations, when used in line with the meaning and the mood, help not only to carry the full expression of the author's words but also to add enjoyment to your interpretation.

## ACTIVITIES

1. Bring to class statements of your own which illustrate the following types of emphasis:
   Stressing the important word or words
   Stressing new ideas
   Stressing repeated ideas
   Stressing a series of words leading to a climax
   Stressing words of comparison or contrast
2. Find selections from literature included in this chapter to illustrate each of the types above.
3. Find in this chapter examples of pausing before words; after words; before and after words.

## Emphasize the meaning

When you travel in a foreign country and cannot understand the language, you rely upon an interpreter to translate accurately the words spoken by the person addressing you. If the interpreter omits or adds words, or misunderstands any of the words spoken, the translation will be inaccurate and the meaning distorted. The first responsibility of an interpreter, therefore, is to read accurately.

**Read your selection as it is written.** This advice may seem too obvious to mention, but inaccuracy in reading the very words themselves is a common fault of poor readers. Omitting words (especially small ones), adding words, and misreading words are habits which give listeners a confused translation of the printed page. Undoubtedly, this widely prevalent fault can be traced to the present-day emphasis upon silent reading and the subsequent lack of practice in oral reading. Whatever the cause may be, the remedy is attentive oral *practice.*

If you have had little experience in reading aloud, you can still become an interesting reader by following either of two methods or both. First, you can ask a qualified person to listen to you read aloud each day and to point out your errors. Second, you can record on tape from a manuscript and then check your own mistakes by reading the manuscript as you listen to the recording. The second method may be the better one for this purpose because you can hear not only your mistakes in reading but also the sound of your voice. Continue making recordings until you recognize definite signs of improvement. Many students are amazed at the large number of errors that they discover in listening to themselves.

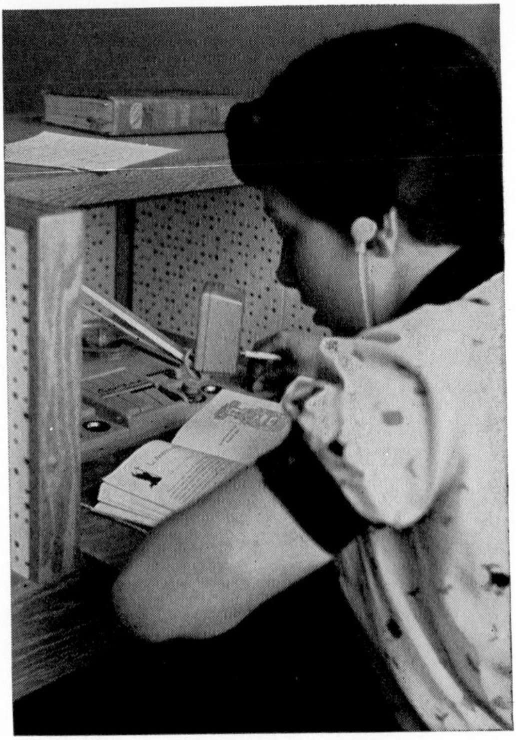

A student records her voice while reading, then she or a teacher plays back the tape to check for errors. *(Monkmeyer)*

**Read your selection audibly.** Audibility includes sufficient volume and distinct enunciation. Throughout this text, emphasis has been placed upon both of these factors for speech purposes. A brief reminder that reading aloud is really *speaking* should impress you with the necessity of following good speaking habits if you expect to express meaning.

**Read your selection smoothly.** A smooth style comes with practice. When you read a selection for the first time, you are likely to hesitate over words, mispronounce them, and go back to correct yourself. You may also read from word to word instead of reading in natural word groups. There is a tendency, too, to read rapidly the sections that are clear and to slow down for those which puzzle you. Such habits create a jerky, uneven effect which interferes with the transfer of meaning. Careful study of words and punctuation marks will help you understand the meaning, but only *practice* in reading aloud will enable you to transfer that meaning.

A familiar example of losing the meaning by reading with improper phrasing occurs in Act V, Scene 1, of Shakespeare's *A Midsummer Night's Dream.* In this example, Quince, the doltish clown who reads the prologue for the comic play within the play, is made by Shakespeare to speak his piece as follows:

PROLOGUE: If we offend, it is with our good will.
That you should think, we come not to offend,
But with good will. To show our simple skill,
That is the true beginning of our end.
Consider then, we come but in despite.
We do not come, as minding to content you,
Our true intent is. All for your delight,
We are not here. That you should here repent you,
The actors are at hand: and, by their show,
You shall know all, that you are like to know.

Certainly you can understand nothing according to the arrangement of words and the punctuation followed by this speaker. The meaning as it is expressed seems to be the opposite of what you would expect from a group appearing before royalty. The comments of their audience give you some valuable pointers regarding reading skills. Immediately following the Prologue, you find this conversation:

THESEUS: This fellow doth not stand upon points.

LYSANDER: He hath rid his prologue like a rough colt; he knows not the stop. A good moral, my lord: it is not enough to speak, but to speak true.

HIPPOLYTA: Indeed he hath played on this prologue like a child on a recorder; a sound, but not in government.

THESEUS: His speech was like a tangled chain; nothing impaired, but all disordered.

Reduced to present-day language, their conversation would sound like this:

THESEUS: This fellow does not follow punctuation marks.

LYSANDER: He delivered his prologue like a rough colt stumbling and lunging without knowing where or when to pause. A good lesson to remember in speaking is: It is not enough to speak only words but to give them true meaning.

HIPPOLYTA: He delivered his prologue as a child would give it. It was merely childish sound with nothing to govern or control it.

THESEUS: His speech was like a tangled chain. All of the links were present and in good condition but they were all mixed up.

## ◄ POINTERS THAT PAY OFF ►

Read words as they are written without adding, subtracting, or changing any.
Read with correct pronunciation and enunciation.
Follow the intent of all punctuation signs.
Read with sufficient loudness.
Read in word groups.
Read with interest and a desire to communicate.

Below are several tests for you to check your accuracy in reading aloud. They include reading material of a factual nature in which there is no attempt to display any particular mood or emotion. In taking the tests, use a tape recorder and play back your recording to check for inaccuracy, or ask your classmates to keep a record of any mistakes. Use the chart on page 395 for checking purposes.

## ☑ ACCURACY CHECK-UP ☑

1. *A news item:*

Two fat army missiles stood out in their sparkling towers at Cape Canaveral Sunday night after Able I blew to pieces because of a malfunction in the engine of its first stage, a Thor intermediate missile. One of the Army rockets was believed to be a Jupiter C Explorer satellite launcher and the other a basic Jupiter of the type to be used as the main stage of the Army's moon reconnaissance rocket.

Explorer IV already has found cosmic radiation of a greater density and higher extension into space than ever imagined. An Army source said the next Explorer would be instrumented to probe this lethal bombardment more deeply.

2. *A statement of opinion:*

Clearing of slum areas aids in the establishment of a more productive environment, but it has about the same effect as a power to exterminate crime as the changing of bedsheets will have in curing a cancer patient. For crime, like cancer, is a disease, a social disease. It does not represent the failure of a minority to conform to society's rules so much as it represents a sickness of society as a whole, for, remember, cancer, too, strikes only a few cells in the body.

—Edward Stewart, "Crime and its Ancestor: Man."

3. *A quotation:*

I do not believe the greatest threat to our future is from bombs or guided missiles. I don't think our civilization will die that way. I think it will die when we no longer care—when the spiritual forces that make us wish to be right and noble die in the hearts of men. Arnold Toynbee has pointed out that 19 of 21 notable civilizations have died from within and not by conquest from without. There were no bands playing and no flags waving when these civilizations decayed; it happened slowly, in the quiet and the dark when no one was aware.

If America is to grow great, we must stop gagging at the word "spiritual." Our task is to rediscover and reassert our faith in the spiritual, nonutilitarian values on which American life has really rested from its beginning.

—"Why Men Survive" by Laurence M. Gould
in *This Week* Magazine

4. *An anecdote:*

On my birthday I received a telegram relayed over the telephone by a Western Union operator with the happiest voice imaginable. It did indeed brighten my day. A week later, I received a telegram from my father bawling me out for not writing home. I was sure the same woman was reading the wire, but the voice was harsh and cold.

Afterward I said, "What's the matter with your voice?"

"Nothing," she replied in normal tones. "I always try to convey not only the words of the message, but also the intent."

—Life in These United States, *Reader's Digest*

**ACCURACY CHART**

1. Did you omit any words? If so, list them. (*Please do not write in this book.*)
2. Did you add any words? If so, list them on a separate piece of paper.
3. Did you change or mispronounce any words? If so, list them.
4. Did you make any mistakes in grouping? If so, list them.
5. Were you guilty of any one of these: mumbling? running words together? reading too fast? reading too slowly? speaking too low?
6. Did you read jerkily?
7. Did you read in a monotonous manner?
8. Did you read from word to word?

To compute your accuracy grade, use the following method of scoring:

Add one point for each error in items 1, 2, 3, and 4.

Add five points for each "Yes" answer in items 5, 6, 7, and 8.

A score of 10 or greater indicates that you are seriously inaccurate.

How did you rate in your tests? If the results reflected above-average ability, you will have an advantage when you test your interpretative ability later on. You are now ready to see how well you can bring to life the *feeling* behind the printed word.

## Emphasize the mood

It has been stated that he who can read a poem with feeling is in truth a poet himself. This is another way of saying that within the soul of every good interpreter is the desire to create something of beauty or greatness whether it be poetry or prose. Any literary selection should be born again within the reader if he is to bring to life the author's words.

As long as you are reading only items or statements of fact, you can express meaning by following the principles outlined in Pointers That Pay Off, page 393. When you attempt to express mood, however, you are dealing with meaning *plus* feeling. Accuracy is essential, but it is only the beginning step in recreating the feeling which colored the thoughts expressed in words. Your success in expressing the mood of your selection will depend upon your ability to use your voice, to use your speech, and to use your body.

**Using your voice.** Everyone recognizes the importance of voice in reading aloud. The mood created by any words can be dissipated when spoken in an unpleasant or monotonous voice. On the other hand, a pleasing, striking, dynamic voice can make even ordinary prose sound poetic.

The poet, Longfellow, has written:

> Then read from the treasured volume
> The poem of thy choice,
> And lend to the rhyme of the poet
> The beauty of thy voice.

The voice is an indicator of moods. When you are speaking, it tends to reveal your own mood. When you are reading aloud, your voice tends to reveal the mood of your selection. By listening to the voice of a reader, you can learn much of the mood of what he is reading. You can learn if the mood is angry, sad, disappointed, tired, happy, gay, excited, or "peppy." The elements of voice which reflect mood are: quality, pitch, and force.

***Voice quality.*** The tone of your voice reveals your feeling in any language. People from other countries may not be able to translate your words, but they can translate your tone. Animals know instantly how you feel about them by the tone of voice you use in speaking to them. Small children unable to understand words can understand voice tone. Strong emotions are hard to hide in your voice especially if you try to say, "I hate you!" to somebody you love or "I love you!" to somebody you dislike. The words may come through, but your true feelings are difficult to conceal.

Since voice quality is such a definite indicator of mood, a good interpreter selects qualities to match moods. There are innumerable variations possible in the human voice, but five common voice qualities frequently used by oral interpreters are: normal, breathy, full, chest, and thin.

THE NORMAL QUALITY. Normal quality is that which you use in ordinary conversation when you speak naturally with little display of emotion. Essays, descriptions, factual compositions, and all other literature written more to express thought than intense feeling may be read in a normal tone.

THE BREATHY QUALITY. This quality can be described as a whispery voice. Since whispering usually creates an atmosphere of mystery or secrecy, you may use this quality in dramatic scenes of suspense such as you find in many of Shakespeare's plays. An example of a scene in which the breathy quality may be appropriate is this one between Macbeth and Lady Macbeth after the murder of Duncan:

MACBETH: Who's there? What, ho!
LADY MACBETH: Alack, I am afraid they have awaked, and 'tis not done. Th' attempt and not the deed confounds us. Hark! I laid their daggers ready; he could not miss 'em. Had he not resembled my father as he slept, I had done't . . . . .

Another occasion for using the whisper occurs when an author wants to portray absolute quiet. In A. A. Milne's poem *Vespers* you might well use breathy quality in these lines:

"Hush! Hush! Whisper who dares!
Christopher Robin is saying his prayers."

THE FULL QUALITY. Its use helps to create a mood of reverence and solemnity because of the deep, full quality of the voice. The full quality is also appropriate to portray a melancholy mood or to make a stirring appeal. Some examples of selections that may be presented in the full quality are those that follow. You should note, however, that these selections are given simply as arbitrary examples and with no suggestion that the selections indicated can *only* be given in the particular voice or quality suggested.

Roll on, thou deep and dark blue Ocean—roll!
Ten thousand fleets sweep over thee in vain,
Man marks the earth with ruin—his control
Stops with the shore:—upon the watery plain
The wrecks are all thy deed, nor doth remain
A shadow of man's ravage, save his own,
When for a moment, like a drop of rain,
He sinks into thy depths with bubbling groan,
Without a grave, unknelled, uncoffined, and unknown.

—Byron

Breathes there the man with soul so dead
Who never to himself hath said,
"This is my own, my native land!"

—Scott

Lord God of Hosts, be with us yet,
Lest we forget—lest we forget!

—Kipling

Patriotism, courage, and grandeur are emotions expressed by the full quality which explains the reason for its frequent association with orators and dramatic readers.

THE CHEST QUALITY. This tone is a deep, hollow one in which resonance comes from the chest and is especially useful in speaking as a spirit or a ghost. Shakespeare made frequent use of ghosts in his plays. An example of a situation in which you would find it appropriate to try the chest quality is in this speech by the ghost of Hamlet's father:

I am thy father's spirit,
Doom'd for a certain term to walk the night,
And for the day confined to fast in fires,
Till the foul crimes done in my days of nature
Are burnt and purged away. But that I am forbid
To tell the secrets of my prison-house,
I could a tale unfold whose lightest word
Would harrow up thy soul, freeze thy young blood,
Make thy two eyes, like stars, start from their spheres,
Thy knotted and combined locks to part
And each particular hair to stand on end,
Like quills upon the fretful porpentine.
But this eternal blazon must not be
To ears of flesh and blood . . .

Charles Laughton and Charles Boyer in reading their parts in *Don Juan in Hell* exemplify the finest use of voice qualities in their interpretation of the roles. *(Graphic House, Inc.)*

THE THIN QUALITY. This quality, which is a very little voice and sounds as if it were made just in the mouth, may be used to suggest weakness, old age, ill health, and great tiredness. An example of a scene in which you might wish to use this quality occurs in Act II, Scene 6, of *As You Like It.* Adam, the very old and very weakened servant of Orlando, says:

> "Dear master, I can go no further: O, I die for food! Here lie I down, and measure out my grave. Farewell, kind master."

## ACTIVITIES

1. Count to ten using normal, breathy, full, chest, and thin quality in the order named.
2. Recite the alphabet in the following manner:
   A-E, normal; F-J, breathy; K-P, full; Q-U, chest; and V-Z, thin.
3. Give the following as directed:
   Your name and address—chest
   Your phone number and name of school—breathy
   The titles of three books you have read—full
   The names of five television shows—breathy
   The titles of three movies that you have seen—thin
   The salute to the flag—normal
4. Count to five in a tone that will express the following in turn:

| | | | |
|---|---|---|---|
| sarcasm | conceit | fatigue | boredom |
| ecstasy | scorn | love | weakness |
| fear | anger | surprise | sorrow |

5. Select one of these to do:
   Read a want ad to express suffering, grief, or joy.
   Read five listings from a telephone directory to express love, happiness, or rage.
   Read an item from the society page to express anger, sadness, or mystery.
6. Bring to class one example from literature to illustrate each type of tone quality.

***Voice pitch.*** This is the second element of voice which shows emotion. Voices are described as high, medium, or low in pitch. When you are alarmed, excited, nervous, or ecstatic, your voice usually rises. Many people who become angry often lose control of their voice to the extent that it becomes increasingly higher. A low pitch is customary to reveal reverence, sadness, disappointment, or melancholy. A medium pitch is similar to the ordinary speaking voice when a person is unexcited or unemotional.

When you are speaking, your voice rises and falls in response to your mood and you automatically use a wide pitch range. This natural variation in pitch gives life and interest to your speech. In reading, as in speaking, you need variation to indicate the feeling behind the words. Think how you would say the lines of a selection if you were speaking to friends, and then read them with the same variety of pitch.

Changes of pitch occurring within syllables or words are called inflections. Unless you speak in a monotone, your voice contains many rising and falling inflections to give meaning. In questions, your voice glides upward; in stating positive decisions, your voice glides downward. These varied inflections in reading add color and feeling to your words just as they do in conversation and influence your listeners to respond with more interest and pleasure.

In suiting the pitch to the mood, therefore, it is unwise to keep your voice in a high, low, or medium key. You may decide which one is the best to use in establishing the mood, but be sure that the natural inflection is present to prevent monotony. Mood often changes within a selection and your pitch must vary in accordance with the changes.

## ACTIVITY

The selections on the following pages offer you a chance to try different pitches, Although you must not conclude that a particular selection can only be read in a particular pitch, you may wish to experiment with a high pitch in denoting happiness in *Jenny Kiss'd Me,* a medium pitch to denote the calm of *Mending Wall,* and a low pitch to suggest the sadness in *Farewell to Springfield.*

Examine carefully the other selections on these pages. In which would you use a high pitch? a low pitch? a medium pitch? In which would there be the greatest variation in pitch?

### SEA FEVER

I must go down to the seas again, to the lonely sea and the sky,
And all I ask is a tall ship and a star to steer her by;
And the wheel's kick and the wind's song and the white sail's shaking,
And a gray mist on the sea's face, and a gray dawn breaking.

I must go down to the seas again, for the call of the running tide
Is a wild call and a clear call that may not be denied;
And all I ask is a windy day with the white clouds flying,
And the flung spray and the blown spume, and the sea gulls crying.

I must go down to the seas again, to the vagrant gipsy life,
To the gull's way and the whale's way where the wind's like a whetted
knife;
And all I ask is a merry yarn from a laughing fellow-rover,
And a quiet sleep and a sweet dream when the long trick's over.

—John Masefield

## FAREWELL TO SPRINGFIELD

"My Friends:

No one not in my situation can appreciate my feeling of sadness at this parting. To this place, and the kindness of these people, I owe everything. Here I have lived a quarter of a century, and have passed from a young to an old man. Here my children have been born, and one is buried. I now leave, not knowing when or whether ever I may return, with a task before me greater than that which rested upon Washington. Without the assistance of that Divine Being who ever attended him, I cannot succeed. With that assistance, I cannot fail. Trusting in Him who can go with me, and remain with you, and be everywhere for good, let us confidently hope that all will yet be well. To His care commending you, as I hope in your prayers you will commend me, I bid you an affectionate farewell."

—Abraham Lincoln

## JENNY KISS'D ME

Jenny kiss'd me when we met,
Jumping from the chair she sat in;
Time, you thief, who love to get
Sweets into your list, put that in!
Say I'm weary, say I'm sad,
Say that health and wealth have miss'd me,
Say I'm growing old, but add,
Jenny kiss'd me.

—Leigh Hunt

## MENDING WALL

Something there is that doesn't love a wall,
That sends the frozen-ground-swell under it,
And spills the upper boulders in the sun;
And makes gaps even two can pass abreast.
The work of hunters is another thing:
I have come after them and made repair
Where they have left not one stone on a stone,
But they would have the rabbit out of hiding,
To please the yelping dogs. The gaps I mean,
No one has seen them made or heard them made,
But at spring mending-time we find them there.
I let my neighbor know beyond the hill;
And on a day we meet to walk the line
And set the wall between us once again.
We keep the wall between us as we go.
To each the boulders that have fallen to each.
And some are loaves and some so nearly balls
We have to use a spell to make them balance:
"Stay where you are until our backs are turned!"

We wear our fingers rough with handling them.
Oh, just another kind of out-door game,
One on a side. It comes to little more:
There where it is we do not need the wall:
He is all pine and I am apple orchard.
My apple trees will never get across
And eat the cones under his pines, I tell him.
He only says, "Good fences make good neighbors."
Spring is the mischief in me, and I wonder
If I could put a notion in his head:
"*Why* do they make good neighbors? Isn't it
Where there are cows? But here there are no cows.
Before I built a wall I'd ask to know
What I was walling in or walling out,
And to whom I was like to give offense.
Something there is that doesn't love a wall,
That wants it down." I could say "Elves" to him,
But it's not elves exactly, and I'd rather
He said it for himself. I see him there
Bringing a stone grasped firmly by the top
In each hand, like an old-stone savage armed.
He moves in darkness as it seems to me,
Not of woods only and the shade of trees.
He will not go behind his father's saying,
And he likes having thought of it so well
He says again, "Good fences make good neighbors."

—Robert Frost

## HABITS OF THE HIPPOPOTAMUS

The hippopotamus is strong
  And huge of head and broad of bustle;
And limbs on which he rolls along
  Are big with hippopotomuscle.

He does not greatly care for sweets
  Like ice cream, apple pie, or custard,
But takes to flavor what he eats
  A little hippopotomustard.

The hippopotamus is true
  To all his principles, and just;
He always tries his best to do
  The things one hippopotomust.

He never rides in trucks or trams,
  In taxicabs or omnibuses,
And so keeps out of traffic jams
  And other hippopotomusses.

—Arthur Guiterman

*Voice force.* This is the last element of voice and refers to intensity. Force is a great revealer of your emotional state both in speaking and in reading. Loudness is one way of expressing force, but it is not the only way. Neither does the use of loudness *necessarily* show intense emotion. Although you might shout loudly if you were violently affected by something, thereby showing emotion, you might also speak loudly just to project your voice in a large room, for example. Strong emotions often are spoken with a restrained, deep-seated force rather than with a violent outburst. For gay, rollicking and boisterous types of literature, you usually employ a vigorous and energetic style of reading. When the mood is solemn, dignified, and sad, the intensity of feeling comes through quietness rather than loudness.

**Using your speech.** In addition to varying the quality, pitch, and force of your voice, in order to convey moods accurately you will want also to be able to control the way you speak in such factors as rate, phrasing, and pausing. A skilled reader prepares a script carefully before reading it aloud. He studies sentences individually for the purpose of phrasing and placing of emphasis. Then he studies them collectively in order to see how they fit together in creating the entire picture. As he reads, he forms clear mental pictures of the setting, characters, and action. His imagination helps him to see, hear, smell, taste, and feel all of the descriptive factors in the selection. He then uses in his reading those elements which help emphasize a mood, thereby making his audience experience through their senses exactly what the author is saying.

*Rate.* This term refers to the speed at which you read. A rapid rate denotes happiness and gaiety or it can show a feeling of hysteria, fear, and uncontrolled emotion. Authors use increased tempo also to build to an exciting climax.

A slow tempo shows a serious or reflective mood, sadness, gloom, or nostalgia. It is especially suitable for anything read on a solemn or dignified occasion.

A moderate rate is the one used most frequently, since it denotes the natural or normal situation with no great degree of emotion present.

Many selections cannot be read at one tempo without becoming boring. In most of them, variation is necessary to create a lifelike quality. Some portions are brisk whereas others may be slower and more deliberate. You should not change the rate without a justifiable cause which can usually be found in the words or ideas. Any change of mood should be accompanied by a change in rate.

## ACTIVITIES

1. Find an example in this chapter of a selection that you could read at a rapid rate; a slow rate; a moderate rate.
2. Find an example of a selection which you believe needs variation in rate. Which portions should be read slowly? which faster? which at moderate rate? Justify your changes of rate.

***Phrasing.*** If you are able to speak in meaningful word groups instead of saying one word at a time or combining words that do not belong together, then you have mastered phrasing. This simplified definition is not so easy, however, to put into practice when you attempt to read another's words. Earlier in this chapter, you learned that following punctuation marks is essential to accuracy and that reading in word groups between punctuation marks gave smoothness to your delivery.

In this section some of the principles of proper phrasing will be discussed. In the following sentences, you can recognize improper phrasing instantly:

> The birds said the professor will fly south for the winter.
> The oyster said the man is far too slippery for me to enjoy.

With correct punctuation and phrasing, the sentences assume the right meaning:

> "The birds," said the professor, "will fly south for the winter."
> "The oyster," said the man, "is far too slippery for me to enjoy."

These sentences illustrate one principle: *keep clauses intact.* You have two clauses in each sentence—"the birds will fly south for the winter" and "said the professor" in the first sentence; "the oyster is far too slippery for me to enjoy" and "said the man" in the second sentence.

A second principle is *to keep phrases intact:* "for the winter" and "for me to enjoy" are examples of phrases. Any phrases introduced by prepositions or participles should be kept together.

A third principle is *to keep words and their modifiers together.* Adjectives and adverbs are intended to describe the words they modify, but they can not do so when separated from them.

There is no set formula that you can use in learning how to phrase clearly at all times, but you can experiment with a sentence until you feel certain that the meaning is smooth and intact. If you work with your classmates on the same sentences, you will probably discover that you can find several ways of phrasing. Usually, however, one way will seem more natural than the others. By reading aloud and practicing different word groupings, you should be able to detect the one which sounds best.

***Pausing.*** A properly inserted pause is an excellent conveyor of meaning and mood. In tense scenes, the pause arouses suspense with its magnetic pull of interest and is far more adequate than words in revealing deep emotions. It is also a device for indicating a change of scene or a lapse of time. Make use of pauses to give expression to your reading. It is the skilled reader's most effective device in punctuating, emphasizing, and relaying thought and feeling.

## ACTIVITIES

Working in groups of three with your classmates, choose one poem or one prose selection (a different one for each group) and do the following:

1. Divide at least four sentences into word groups.
2. Read aloud the sentences as you have divided them. Use pauses to separate the groups.
3. Decide which division gives the clearest interpretation.

**Using your body.** Finally, in reading aloud, you must learn to convey mood by the way you use your body, that is, by the way you move, gesture, stand, hold your head, and change your facial expressions. The amount of bodily action that you will want to use will vary with the mood of what you are reading and with your style of reading.

Agnes Moorehead uses natural bodily movements to enrich her interpretation of a reading, regardless of whether her audience is seen or unseen. *(Graphic House, Inc.)*

***Your materials.*** Some selections seem to stimulate little or no use of the body. For example, many lyrics and many descriptive passages can be read with little or no bodily movement. On the other hand, some selections, particularly those involving dramatic action, seem to ask for bodily action on the part of the reader.

***Your style of reading.*** There is a controversy today as to whether a reader should simply *suggest* or strongly *act out.* If you decide to use the first of these styles, your bodily action will be less than if you decide to use the latter. You and your class and your teacher will have to decide which of these styles is best for you.

## When You Read Poetry

Although the suggestions made earlier in this chapter apply to both prose and poetry, some of you may still have trouble reading poetry. Common problems are stressing rhythm too much, stopping abruptly at the end of lines, and hitting rhyming words with too much force.

Robert Frost endears himself to an audience in reading his own poetry in his own inimitable way. *(Black Star)*

Poetry generally has more rhythm than prose has, and you cannot or should not attempt to eliminate the rhythm when you read aloud. In the first place, rhythm helps to create mood. A lilting style signifies a light, happy mood such as you find below in the first stanza of *Experience.* A slow, measured style as found in the second stanza of the same poem reflects a sedate, dignified attitude. It can also give a serious, mournful, or reflective mood. In the second place, rhythm helps to give melody and an enjoyable speaking pattern, provided you handle it properly. After you have read *aloud* for two or three times the poem below, you can better understand how important rhythm is in setting or changing a mood.

## EXPERIENCE

Deborah danced, when she was two,
As buttercups and daffodils do;
Spirited, frail, naïvely bold,
Her hair a ruffled crest of gold.
And whenever she spoke her voice went singing
Like water up from a fountain springing.

But now her step is quiet and slow;
She walks the way the primroses go;
Her hair is yellow instead of gilt,
Her voice is losing its lovely lilt;
And in place of her wild delightful ways
A quaint precision rules her days.
For Deborah now is three, and, oh,
She knows so much that she did not know.

—Aline Kilmer

The danger in reading poetry lies in being carried away by the rhythmic effect to the extent that you overlook the meaning and drift into a monotonous voice pattern. You are unconsciously stressing meter just as you do in scanning poetry and this habit makes your reading sound like a sing-song chant. Nursery rhymes and nonsense verse often are read in metrical stress, but in poetry with definite meaning, the rhythm and meaning must go together because each one is dependent upon the other.

With such poems as Poe's *The Bells,* rhythm is the main purpose and you must emphasize it in such a manner that people will actually hear the bells. Nearly all of Poe's poetry has a predominant rhythm which helps to portray his mood and ideas. With all such poetry, you need to blend the mood and melody; otherwise much of the beauty and sense (the most important aspects of any poem) will be lost.

Another problem many beginners have in reading poetry is stopping abruptly at the end of each line. Unless a comma, period, or some other form of punctuation signals you to pause at the end of a line, read right into the next line. Poems are written in sentences just as prose is. Poetry is not a series of lines to be read separately as though each line represented a complete sentence, but this habit is a common one and a difficult one to break.

Readers who stop abruptly at the end of lines usually make the mistake of emphasizing rhyming words with undue force instead of stressing only the words which carry meaning. This practice not only gives a jerky effect but it destroys the meaning and enjoyment.

If you are one of those who have any of these problems in reading poetry, follow the practice used in the example of Leigh Hunt's *Abou Ben Adhem* which follows. Written in prose form, it does not even resemble poetry. You see only sentences in paragraph form and are not tempted to stop at the end of each line because the original line formation has disappeared. Even the rhyming words are hidden. You can overcome any sing-song style or choppiness by following this same method. Follow exact punctuation but write in sentences, not lines. Read *Abou Ben Adhem* aloud. Forget completely the line formation and the rhyming words. Concentrate on the meaning and the melody which blends with the words.

> "Abou Ben Adhem (may his tribe increase!) awoke one night from a deep dream of peace, and saw, within the moonlight in his room, making it rich, and like a lily in bloom, an Angel writing in a book of gold: exceeding peace had made Ben Adhem bold, and to the Presence in the room he said, "What writest thou?"
>
> The vision raised its head, and with a look made of all sweet accord, answered, "The names of those who love the Lord."
>
> "And is mine one?" said Abou.
>
> "Nay, not so," replied the Angel.
>
> Abou spoke more low, but cheerily still; and said, "I pray thee, then, write me as one that loves his fellow-men."
>
> The Angel wrote, and vanished. The next night it came again with a great wakening light, and showed the names whom love of God had blessed, and, lo! Ben Adhem's name led all the rest!

Written in this manner, this poem looks like a short anecdote complete with characters and dialogue. Notice how easy it is to read when you read it as a conversation.

You will now have a chance to find out your interpretative ability by reading aloud the poems on the next few pages and following the directions given.

## INTERPRETATIVE CHECK-UP

1. Read aloud any of the poems given earlier in the chapter.
   a. Tell the class which one you enjoyed most and give your reasons.
   b. What difficulties (if any) did you have in interpretation?
2. Select any given number suggested by your teacher from the group of poems below and answer questions or observe directions following each.
3. Before reading aloud any of the poems which follow, make the following preparation:
   a. State the meaning in your own words and tell whether or not you agree with it.
   b. Prepare an introduction which will include any available background information about the author and the selection itself.
   c. Decide what the mood is and determine the voice elements (quality, rate, pitch, and force) suitable for interpreting the mood.
   d. Write out the poem in prose form.
   e. Decide the best method of emphasis to use.

## THE TOUCH OF THE MASTER'S HAND

'Twas battered and scarred, and the auctioneer
Thought it scarcely worth his while
To waste much time on the old violin,
But held it up with a smile:
"What am I bidden, good folks," he cried,
"Who'll start the bidding for me?"
"A dollar, a dollar"; then, "Two!" "Only two?
Two dollars, and who'll make it three?
Three dollars, once; three dollars, twice;
Going for three—" But no,
From the room, far back, a gray-haired man
Came forward and picked up the bow;
Then, wiping the dust from the old violin,
And tightening the loose strings,
He played a melody pure and sweet
As a caroling angel sings.

The music ceased, and the auctioneer,
With a voice that was quiet and low,
Said: "What am I bid for the old violin?"
And he held it up with the bow.
"A thousand dollars, and who'll make it two?
Two thousand! And who'll make it three?
Three thousand, once, three thousand, twice,
And going, and gone," said he.
The people cheered, but some of them cried,
"We do not quite understand
What changed its worth." Swift came the reply:
"The touch of a master's hand."

And many a man with life out of tune,
And battered and scarred with sin,
Is auctioned cheap to the thoughtless crowd,
Much like the old violin.
A "mess of pottage," a glass of wine;
A game—and he travels on.
He is "going" once, and "going" twice,
He's "going" and almost "gone."
But the Master comes, and the foolish crowd
Never can quite understand
The worth of a soul and the change that's wrought
By the touch of the Master's hand.

—Myra Brooks Welch

What is the connection between the violin and man? Who is the "Master"?

Notice all of the conversation in the poem. Try making a clear distinction between the descriptive parts and the speaking lines.

What are all of the chances for variety in interpretation?

Can you imitate an auctioneer? Would doing so add to the enjoyment?

## BARTER

Life has loveliness to sell,
All beautiful and splendid things,
Blue waves, whitened on a cliff,
Soaring fire that sways and sings,
And children's faces looking up
Holding wonder like a cup.

Life has loveliness to sell,
Music, like a curve of gold,
Scent of pine trees in the rain,
Eyes that love you, arms that hold,
And for your spirit's still delight
Holy thoughts that star the night.

Spend all you have for loveliness!
Buy it and never count the cost.
For one white singing hour of peace,
Count many a year of strife, well lost.
And for a breath of ecstasy,
Give all you have been or could be.

—Sara Teasdale

Notice the sprightly rate.
What are the lovely things mentioned? Can you add any others?
Do you agree with the last verse?

## FOUR LITTLE FOXES

Speak gently, Spring, and make no sudden sound;
For in my windy valley, yesterday I found
Newborn foxes squirming on the ground . . .
Speak gently.

Walk softly, March, forbear the bitter blow;
Her feet within a trap, her blood upon the snow,
The four little foxes saw their mother go . . .
Walk softly.

Go lightly, Spring, oh, give them no alarm;
When I covered them with boughs to shelter
them from harm,
The thin blue foxes suckled at my arm . . .
Go lightly.

Step softly, March, with your rampant hurricane;
Nuzzling one another, and whimpering with pain,
The new little foxes are shivering in the rain. . .
Step softly.

—Lew Sarett

What voice element is essential in conveying meaning?

What does the poem reveal of the author's feeling about animals?

## THE WINDS OF FATE

One ship drives east and another drives west
With the selfsame winds that blow.
'Tis the set of the sails
And not the gales
Which tells us the way to go.

Like the winds of the sea are the ways of fate,
As we voyage along through life:
'Tis the set of a soul
That decides its goal,
And not the calm or the strife.

—Ella Wheeler Wilcox

What figures of speech do you find?

Enlarge upon the meaning of the poem by giving some examples or practical applications of the message expressed.

How can the message in this poem be especially helpful to youth?

This poem is often used as a theme for graduation speeches. Can you understand why?

# THE BRONCHO THAT WOULD NOT BE BROKEN

A little colt—broncho, loaned to the farm
To be broken in time without fury or harm,
Yet black crows flew past you, shouting alarm,
Calling "Beware," with lugubrious singing . . .
The butterflies there in the bush were romancing,
The smell of the grass caught your soul in a trance,
So why be a-fearing the spurs and the traces,
O broncho that would not be broken of dancing?

You were born with the pride of the lords great and olden
Who danced, through the ages, in corridors golden.
In all the wide farm-place the person most human,
You spoke out so plainly with squealing and capering,
With whinnying, snorting, contorting and prancing,
As you dodged your pursuers, looking askance,
With Greek-footed figures, and Parthenon paces,
O broncho that would not be broken of dancing.

The grasshoppers cheered. "Keep whirling," they said.
The insolent sparrows called from the shed,
"If men will not laugh, make them wish they were dead."
But arch were your thoughts, all malice displacing,
Though the horse-killers came, with snake-whips advancing.
You bantered and cantered away your last chance.
And they scourged you, with Hell in their speech and their faces,
O broncho that would not be broken of dancing.

"Nobody cares for you," rattled the crows,
As you dragged the whole reaper, next day, down the rows.
The three mules held back, yet you danced on your toes.
You pulled like a racer, and kept the mules chasing.
You tangled the harness with bright eyes side-glancing,
While the drunk driver bled you—a pole for a lance—
And the giant mules bit at you—keeping their places,
O broncho that would not be broken of dancing.

In that last afternoon your boyish heart broke.
The hot wind came down like a sledge-hammer stroke.
The blood-sucking flies to a rare feast awoke.
And they searched out your wounds, your death-warrant tracing.
And the merciful men, their religion enhancing,
Stopped the red reaper, to give you a chance.
Then you died on the prairie, and scorned all disgraces,
O broncho that would not be broken of dancing.

—Vachel Lindsay

What words give pictures and sound effects? How does the rhythm help to create the mood and meaning?

What is the effect of the repetition of the last line?

What finally happened to the broncho? How and why did it happen?

What was your feeling after reading the poem?

## LITTLE BOY BLUE

The little toy dog is covered with dust,
  But sturdy and stanch he stands;
And the little toy soldier is red with rust,
  And his musket molds in his hands.
Time was when the little toy dog was new
  And the soldier was passing fair,
And that was the time when our Little Boy Blue
  Kissed them and put them there.

"Now, don't you go till I come," he said,
  "And don't you make any noise!"
So toddling off to his trundle-bed
  He dreamed of the pretty toys.
And as he was dreaming, an angel song
  Awakened our Little Boy Blue—
Oh, the years are many, the years are long,
  But the little toy friends are true.

Ay, faithful to Little Boy Blue they stand,
  Each in the same old place,
Awaiting the touch of a little hand,
  And the smile of a little face.
And they wonder, as waiting these long years through,
  In the dust of that little chair,
What has become of our Little Boy Blue
  Since he kissed them and put them there.

—Eugene Field

What happened to "Little Boy Blue"?

How should the poem be read to bring out the pathos?

## VESPERS

Little Boy kneels at the foot of the bed,
Droops on the little hands little gold head.
Hush! Hush! Whisper who dares!
Christopher Robin is saying his prayers.

God bless Mummy. I know that's right.
Wasn't it fun in the bath to-night?
The cold's so cold, and the hot's so hot.
Oh! God bless Daddy—I quite forgot.

If I open my fingers a little bit more,
I can see Nanny's dressing-gown on the door.
It's a beautiful blue, but it hasn't a hood.
Oh! God bless Nanny and make her good.

Mine has a hood and I lie in bed,
And pull the hood right over my head,
And I shut my eyes, and I curl up small,
And nobody knows that I'm there at all.

Oh! Thank you, God, for a lovely day.
And what was the other I had to say?
I said "Bless Daddy," so what can it be?
Oh! Now I remember it. God bless Me.

Little Boy kneels at the foot of the bed,
Droops on the little hands little gold head.
Hush! Hush! Whisper who dares!
Christopher Robin is saying his prayers.

—A. A. Milne

In what tone should the first and last verses be read?

What are some of the thoughts which interrupt Christopher's prayer?

Be sure to punctuate your reading to indicate the difference between his words and the words of the prayer.

Where do you vary the pitch and rate? Why?

## THE SUPERSTITIOUS GHOST

I'm such a quiet little ghost,
  Demure and inoffensive,
The other spirits say I'm most
  Absurdly apprehensive.

Through all the merry hours of night
  I'm uniformly cheerful;
I love the dark; but in the light
  I own I'm rather fearful!

Each dawn I cower down in bed,
  In every brightness seeing
That weird uncanny form of dread
  An awful Human Being!

Of course I'm told they can't exist,
  That Nature would not let them:
But Willy Spook, the Humanist,
  Declares that he has met them.

He says they do not glide like us,
But walk in eerie paces;
They're solid, not diaphanous
With arms! and legs!! and faces!!!

And some are beggars, some are kings,
Some have and some are wanting,
They squander time in doing things,
Instead of simply haunting.

They talk of "art," the horrid crew,
And things they call "ambitions."
Oh yes, I know as well as you
They're only superstitions.

But should the dreadful day arrive
When, starting up, I see one,
I'm sure 'twill scare me quite alive;
And then—oh, then I'll be one!

—Arthur Guiterman

What is the purpose of the author?
How do you picture the ghost?
What is your opinion of the poem?

## When You Read Prose

It is also helpful to prepare prose for reading. In the selections which follow, make these preparations before reading aloud:

1. Determine the general mood.
2. Look up any unfamiliar words and allusions.
3. Express the general meaning in your own words.
4. Watch phrasing and emphasis.
5. Which did you like best? Why?
6. Study carefully to know which quality, rate, pitch, and force to use.
7. Which ones point out a lesson or give something worthwhile to think about?

### I SPEAK FOR DEMOCRACY

I am an American.
Listen to my words, Fascist, Communist.
Listen well, for my country is a strong country, and my message is a strong message.
I am an American, and I speak for democracy.

My ancestors have left their blood on the green at Lexington and the snow at Valley Forge

. . . on the walls of Fort Sumter and the fields at Gettysburg

. . . on the waters of the River Marne and in the shadows of the Argonne Forest

. . . on the beachheads of Salerno and Normandy and the sands of Okinawa

. . . on the bare, bleak hills called Pork Chop and Old Baldy and Heartbreak Ridge.

A million and more of my countrymen have died for freedom.

My country is their eternal monument.

They live on in the laughter of a small boy as he watches a circus clown's antics

. . . and in the sweet, delicious coldness of the first bite of peppermint ice cream on the Fourth of July

. . . in the little tenseness of a baseball crowd as the umpire calls "Batter up!"

. . . and in the high school band's rendition of "Stars and Stripes Forever" in the Memorial Day parade

. . . in the clear, sharp ring of a school bell on a fall morning

. . . and in the triumph of a six-year-old as he reads aloud for the first time.

They live on in the eyes of an Ohio farmer surveying his acres of corn and potatoes and pasture

. . . and in the brilliant gold of hundreds of acres of wheat stretching across the flat miles of Kansas

. . . in the milling of cattle in the stockyards of Chicago

. . . the precision of an assembly line in an automobile factory in Detroit

. . . and the perpetual red glow of the nocturnal skylines of Pittsburgh and Birmingham and Gary.

They live on in the voice of a young Jewish boy saying the sacred words from the Torah: "Hear O Israel: the Lord our God, the Lord is One. Thou shalt love the Lord thy God with all thy heart and with all thy soul and with all thy might."

. . . and in the voice of a Catholic girl praying: "Hail, Mary, full of grace, the Lord is with thee . . . "

. . . and in the voice of a Protestant boy singing: "A mighty Fortress is our God, A Bulwark never failing . . . "

An American named Carl Sandburg wrote these words:

"I know a Jew fishcrier down on Maxwell Street with a voice like a north wind blowing over corn stubble in January.

He dangles herring before prospective customers evincing a joy identical with that of Pavlova dancing.

His face is that of a man terribly glad to be selling fish, terribly glad that God made fish, and customers to whom he may call his wares from a pushcart."

There is a voice in the soul of every human being that cries out to be free. America has answered that voice.

America has offered freedom and opportunity such as no land before her has ever known, to a Jew fishcrier down on Maxwell Street with the face of a man terribly glad to be selling fish.

She has given him the right to own his pushcart, to sell his herring on Maxwell Street,

. . . she has given him an education for his children, and a tremendous faith in the nation that has made these things his.

Multiply that fishcrier by 160,000,000–160,000,000 mechanics and farmers and housewives and coal miners and truck drivers and chemists and lawyers and plumbers and priests–all glad, terribly glad to be what they are, terribly glad to be free to work and eat and sleep and speak and love and pray and live as they desire, as they believe!

And those 160,000,000 Americans–those 160,000,000 free Americans–
have more roast beef and mashed potatoes,
the yield of American labor and land;
. . . more automobiles and telephones,
. . . more safety razors and bathtubs,
. . . more Orlon sweaters and aureomycin,
the fruits of American initiative and enterprise;
. . . more public schools and life insurance policies,
the symbols of American security and faith in the future;
. . . more laughter and song–
than any other people on earth!

This is my answer, Fascist, Communist!

Show me a country greater than our country, show me a people more energetic, creative, progressive–
bigger-hearted and happier than our people,
not until then will I consider your way of life.
For I am an American, and I speak for democracy.

–Elizabeth Ellen Evans



## HOW TO WARM A BENCH

When my English teacher recently asked me to write an essay, I was stuck for a subject. So I dug into my handbook for an idea. It said: "Choose a topic on which you're well versed."

That struck a bell. If there's one subject on which I'm well versed, it's how to warm a bench. During the past two years, I've spent about 85 hours sitting on the bench, while my more talented chums have been giving their all for the dear old alma mater.

To be able to ride the bench properly, you must qualify as follows:

1. You must have practically no talent. And if you do, you must be careful to keep it hidden. Or you might have the awful experience of having the coach put you in the game.

2. You must have highly developed hindquarters, for that's the part of you that takes the wear (plus the splinters).

3. Last, but not least, you must have a highly trained voice, for it's the duty of the bench to aid the cheerleaders in spurring the team to greater heights.

If, after examining yourself, you find that you possess these qualifications, you have a good chance of becoming at least an average benchwarmer.

I shall now elaborate on how to assure yourself a permanent place on the bench. First, constantly be on guard against showing any improvement. If you do, the coach will surely try to develop you into something resembling a ball player.

Next, it will aid your cause immensely if you can disgust the coach or arouse his ill will.

One successful method is to let the coach catch you breaking training rules. This will either get you kicked off the team or sat down on the bench.

If for some reason this fails, another good method is never to pay attention to what the coach is saying.

The last, but one of the most effective means, is that of playing dumb; that is, wearing a look of complete ignorance.

One must not get the idea that a benchwarmer's life isn't an enjoyable one. During the half-time period or the pre-game warmups, the boys on the bench are allowed to exhibit their meager talents. This is done mainly to assure the public that the boys are not just charity cases.

This, plus the excellent food which they so joyously consume at the expense of the athletic department and the fact that just being on the squad tends to impress the girls, makes life most enjoyable for the benchwarmer.

I can think of just one thing more enjoyable than warming the bench, and that is NOT warming the bench!

—Lee Kennedy

## A MAN CALLED PETER

That June, as usual, the little Cape Cod cottage beckoned. As we drove into the yard, we saw that the shutters were just as blue as ever; the rambler roses were just about to burst into bloom as they always had; a pair of bluebirds had built their nest in the old pine by the kitchen door. Yet there was a difference this year. Even a little boy could feel it. We tried to be gay with each other as we unlocked the door.

Our neighbor had very thoughtfully opened some of the windows, and the white organdy curtains fluttered in the sea breeze. The Highland Regiments still marched jauntily, with kilts swinging, across the living-room wall—The Queen's Own Cameron Highlanders, the Black Watch, and the Royal Scots Greys. By his favorite lounge chair sat Peter's slippers, just as he had stepped out of them, and on the table by the chair lay a pocket edition of *The Case of the Perfumed Mouse*.

Each room spoke of him; his presence was everywhere. In the hall closet was one of his summer hats, the one whose blue band had faded to an intriguing shade of lavender. Under his bed were his old white shoes, the pair he used for garden work, with a pair of blue socks still stuffed inside.

I held one of his shoes in my hand and thought, "Now I understand those words, 'O memories, that bless and burn,' O God, how it hurts!"

Later that evening, after the tempest of emotion had subsided a bit I headed beachward.

The waves made gentle little lapping noises on the pebbled shore, and there was a path of silver across the water. The crisp sea air fanned my hot cheeks. Suddenly I remembered something, the last words I had ever spoken to Peter. Was it possible that God had prompted those words, seemingly so casual?

The scene was etched forever on my mind—Peter lying on the stretcher where two orderlies had put him down for a moment, while the ambulance waited just outside the front door. Peter had looked up at me and smiled through his pain, his eyes full of tenderness, and I had leaned close to him and said, "Darling, I'll see you in the morning."

And as I stood looking out toward that far horizon, I knew that those words would go singing in my heart down all the years . . . . . .

See you, Darling, see you in the morning . . . . . . .

—Catherine Marshall: *A Man Called Peter*

## HOME TOWN

You can't build a home town.

The cleverest architects and the most determined builders in the world never designed or erected a home town.

And yet the world is full of them, revolves around them, would fall apart without them.

They are hard to find. They hide behind streets and buildings and trees and houses, until they look just like ordinary towns.

You could be looking right at a home town, and unless you belonged there or came from there, you'd never know it. That is, until you had learned some of the many magical things that make up a home town.

Home towns are made up of bowling teams, borrowed cups of sugar, first names and easy hello's. They are noted for father-and-son banquets, tricycles in driveways, football heroes, village belles, neighborhood belles, belles of the block and many assorted sweethearts . . . all of the latter being the most beautiful in the world.

Home towns have plenty of nearby fields for Saturday Indian massacres, quantities of evening breeze to help the sounds of choir practice get around, and one of the world's best back-yard wireless systems.

They're long on lodge meetings, school meetings, business meetings, town meetings, meetings in the drugstore, in the barbershop, or in somebody's kitchen after the show. All are characterized by a wealth of opinion, freely given, freely disputed, but never forbidden.

Home towns are heated in winter by steaming coffee pots, cooled in summer by small boys whizzing down the sidewalk after dark on bicycles.

They are lit up by the sparkle of tinsel on Christmas baskets down at the firehouse. They are shaded by the wealth and profusion of family trees whose minutest branches are known to all.

Home towns are warm, wonderful places.

They're happiness, family-style. They're the star-spangled excitement of a Fourth of July afternoon with its unashamed patriotism. They're George the butcher, Scout Troop Three, the price of potatoes, and the Galworthy girl getting married.

People living a life and dreaming a dream together.

And home towns are hard to find . . . unless you know just where to look!

In your heart.

—Harry Kinzie, Jr.: *The Fairless Hills News*

Frequently, you are called on to present a dramatic reading in your class or in front of an audience outside of school. For such programs, you will want to choose something which you can act out in some detail with bodily action, facial expression, and vocal interpretation in keeping with the characters speaking. Whenever you find a literary selection which tells a story or represents a person speaking, you can do more than just suggest the mood—you can try your skill at acting, as described on page 405.

In this student presentation of Edmond Rostand's play, *Cyrano de Bergerac,* the leading role offers a fine opportunity for vocal interpretation.

## ACTIVITY

The selections which follow give you an opportunity to become the characters who are speaking. Study them carefully to determine the mood, the setting, and the type of character whom you are to represent. Through voice and bodily expression bring the characters to life.

### THE WHITE MAGNOLIA TREE

The year when I was twenty-one
(John that year was twenty-three)
That was the year, that was the spring,
We planted the white magnolia tree.

"This tree," said John, "shall grow with us,
And every year it will bloom anew.
This is our life. This is our love."
And the white magnolia grew and grew . . .

Oh, youth's a thing of fire and ice
And currents that run
Hot and white,
And its world is as bright
As the sun . . .

I was twenty-one . . .
And I wore a plume in my hat, and
we went to the movies and wept over
"Stella Dallas," and John sang
"Moonlight and Roses" (a little
off-key, but very nicely really), and we
hurried through our crowded days with
beautiful plans, boundless ambitions
and golden decisions.

There is so much the young heart clamors
for; this it must have, and that it cannot
live without, and it must be all or nothing,
for aren't we the masters of creation?

Oh, valiant and untamed were we,
When we planted the white magnolia tree!

And the white magnolia grew and grew,
Holding our love within its core,
And every year it bloomed anew,
And we were twenty-one no more.

No more untamed, no more so free,
Nor so young, nor so wild and aflame were we.

Dearer to us then grew other things:
easy sleep, books, a day's quiet holiday,
good talk beside a fire, the beauty of
old faces . . .

We have known many things since then:
the death of a child and the bitter lesson
that a heart which breaks must mend itself
again (that it can and must be done), and
what loyalty can mean, and how real a word
like courage can become, and that solitude
can be rich and gratifying and quite different
from loneliness . . .

There is so little the serious heart requires:
friends, faith, a window open to the world,
pride in work well done, and strength to live
in a world at war and still maintain the
heart's own private peace . . .

Dear Heaven, I give thanks to thee
For the things I did not know before,
For the wisdom of maturity,
For bread, and a roof, and for one
thing more . . .
Thanks because I still can see
The bloom on the white magnolia tree!

—Helen Deutsch

## WHY THE DOCTOR WAS HELD UP

A little before nine the phone rang. "Glens Falls calling Dr. Van Eyck," said the operator.

"Speaking."

There was the usual "go-ahead-please," and then, "This is Dr. Haydon at the Glens Falls hospital. A boy was just brought in with a bullet in his brain. He's hemorrhaging badly and the pulse is weak."

"I'm 60 miles from Glens Falls," said Dr. Van Eyck. "Have you tried Dr. Mercer?"

"He's out of town," said Dr. Haydon. "The reason I'm calling you is that the boy comes from your city. He was spending the week-end with relatives here and shot himself playing with a twenty-two."

"You say the boy's from Albany?" said Dr. Van Eyck. "What's his name?"

"Arthur Cunningham."

"Don't think I know him. But I'll get there as fast as I can. It's snowing badly, but I think I can make it before midnight."

"I ought to tell you the kid's parents are poor and there isn't much chance of a fee."

"That's all right," said Dr. Van Eyck.

A few minutes later, the surgeon's car stopped for a red light on the outskirts of Albany. A man in a brown leather jacket opened the door and climbed in.

"Drive straight ahead, mister," he said, "and better not make a fuss—I've got a gun."

"I'm a doctor," said Van Eyck, "and this is an emergency."

"Never mind the talk," said the man in the jacket. "Step on it."

A mile out of town he ordered the doctor to stop and get out.

It took a half hour for Dr. Van Eyck to find a phone, and a lot of talking to persuade a taxi company to send out a cab. At the railroad depot he found the next train to Glens Falls wasn't until 12:10.

It was after two when the surgeon reached the hospital. Dr. Haydon was waiting for him.

"I did my best," said Van Eyck, "but my car—"

"It was good of you to try," said Dr. Haydon. "The boy died an hour ago."

As the two men walked past the waiting room, Van Eyck suddenly stopped. On one of the benches, his head in his hands, was the man in the brown leather jacket.

"Mr. Cunningham," said Dr. Haydon. "Meet Dr. Van Eyck. He came all the way from Albany to try to save your boy."

—Billy Rose: *Pitching Horseshoes*

## NANCY HANKS

If Nancy Hanks
Came back as a ghost,
Seeking news
Of what she loved most,
She'd ask first
"Where's my son?
What's happened to Abe?
What's he done?

"Poor little Abe,
Left all alone
Except for Tom,
Who's a rolling stone;
He was only nine
The year I died.
I remember still
How hard he cried.

"Scraping along
In a little shack,
With hardly a shirt
To cover his back,
And a prairie wind
To blow him down,
Or pinching times
If he went to town.

"You wouldn't know
About my son?
Did he grow tall?
Did he have fun?
Did he learn to read?
Did he get to town?
Do you know his name?
Did he get on?"

—Rosemary Carr Benét

## SEEIN' THINGS

I ain't afeard uv snakes, or toads, or bugs, or worms, or mice,
An' things 'at girls are skeered uv I think are awful nice!
I'm pretty brave, I guess; an' yet I hate to go to bed,
For, when I'm tucked up warm an' snug an' when my prayers are said,
Mother tells me "Happy Dreams!" an' takes away the light,
An' leaves me lyin' all alone an' seein' things at night!

Sometimes they're in the corner, sometimes they're by the door,
Sometimes they're all a-standin' in the middle uv the floor;
Sometimes they are a-sittin' down, sometimes they're walkin' round
So softly and so creepy-like they never make a sound!
Sometimes they are as black as ink, an' other times they're white—
But the color ain't no difference when you see things at night!

Once, when I licked a feller 'at had just moved on our street,
An' father sent me up to bed without a bite to eat,
I woke up in the dark an' saw things standin' in a row,
A-lookin' at me cross-eyed an' p'intin' at me—so!
Oh, my! I wuz so skeered that time I never slep' a mite—
It's almost alluz when I'm bad I see things at night!

Lucky thing I ain't a girl, or I'd be skeered to death!
Bein' I'm a boy, I duck my head an' hold my breath;
An' I am, oh, *so* sorry I'm a naughty boy, an' then
I promise to be better an' I say my prayers again!
Gran'ma tells me that's the only way to make it right
When a feller has been wicked an' sees things at night!

An' so, when other naughty boys would coax me into sin,
I try to skwush the Tempter's voice 'at urges me within;
An' when they's pie for supper, or cakes 'at's big an' nice,
I want to—but I do not pass my plate f'r them things twice!
No, ruther let Starvation wipe me slowly out o' sight
Than I should keep a-livin' on an' seein' things at night!

—Eugene Field

## ACTIVITIES

1. Select your favorite poem that has possibilities for dramatic interpretation and read it aloud in class.
2. Read aloud a short story containing conversation and attempt to portray characterization through your style of reading.
3. Select a soliloquy or solo scene from any play by Shakespeare and give it a dramatic interpretation.
4. Find a selection to read with a musical background.

## PRONUNCIATION PROBLEMS

The long "o" is a melodious round sound. If you will say "oh" with your lips in the form of a perfect O, you will make the true sound. Be especially particular with those words ending in the long "o" sound such as *window* and *yellow*. Read with precision the words and the practice sentences.

| | | | | | |
|---|---|---|---|---|---|
| oh | float | boat | widow | shadow | willow |
| go | snow | most | meadow | auto | wheelbarrow |
| so | hope | slow | fellow | mosquito | cello |
| show | home | open | mellow | fresco | bravado |
| foam | flow | moan | fallow | Ohio | maraschino |

## READING CHECK-UP

Read aloud the nonsense sentences below to check your pronunciation of any problem words.

The tornado ruined the tobacco, potatoes, and tomatoes planted in the narrow field near my home.

Did you notice the goat with the rope around his neck go through the open gate to eat the yellow daisies in the meadow?

May I borrow your wheelbarrow until tomorrow to haul oats to the unbroken broncho who makes his home in the meadow?

Repeat this motto in mellow tones: The old scold sold a school coal scuttle.

## VOCABULARY BUILD-UP

Use the italicized words in short paragraphs to show that you understand their meanings.

viewed with *skepticism*
to *concede* a point
in *unprecedented* numbers
political *aspirations*
*germane* to the question
the *prosaic* style

*urbane* in manner
*defamation* of character
an *ostentatious* display
*frenetic* outbursts
a *syndicated* column
*unscrupulous* attacks

CHAPTER

# 20 Speaking in Chorus

Practice is the best of all instructors.

—*Pubilius Syrus*

QUIETLY you stand, face the flag, and place your right hand over your heart. As one of a group you repeat in unison:

"I pledge allegiance to the flag of the United States of America and to the Republic for which it stands . . . ."

Or with your head bowed you kneel in church and repeat with others the Lord's Prayer. In church, you often engage in responsive readings as the leader reads one group of verses and you respond with alternate ones. Every church has its own form of creeds, prayers, and group readings in which the congregation may unite.

Or in your school auditorium or stadium you join your friends in a series of resounding cheers. In order to spur your team on to victory you use the combined strength of many voices speaking as one. Surely it is an impressive experience to hear several thousand voices repeating the same words in unison.

## What Is Choral Speaking?

In any of the above familiar experiences, you are participating in one form of choral speaking—the activity that is the subject of this chapter.

Group speaking has probably existed as long as people have assembled. One of the first examples of its existence can be found in the early Greek drama in which the chorus was used to inform

"The chorus enters and takes its position with the line, 'Here let us stand close by the cathedral.' "—from *Murder in the Cathedral.* *(Black Star)*

the audience of the progression of events that could not be presented on the stage. The primary purpose of the Greek chorus was entertainment, and choral speaking has remained a form of dramatic entertainment ever since. Even now, playwrights frequently use a choral background to make certain scenes more stirring. Some of the best known examples of choric speaking in modern drama are found in T. S. Eliot's *Murder in the Cathedral,* and in two selections by Stephen Vincent Benét, *The Devil and Daniel Webster* and *John Brown's Body.* If you have a chance to hear the recordings or see an actual performance of any one of these, you will note that some parts of a selection may be solos spoken by individuals, other parts will be spoken by two or more people, and some parts will be spoken by the entire group.

# Why Study Choral Speaking?

There are many excellent reasons for studying choral speaking in your high school speech course: one is for sheer pleasure, another is for the confidence it gives you, a third is for the valuable speech training it provides, and a fourth is for the communicative value of choral speaking itself.

Listening to or joining with a well-trained chorus of voices is a delight comparable to that of being in the presence of expertly trained musical groups—singing or instrumental. The same artistic elements are common to all these forms of art; the same satisfactions in expression come from participating in all of them.

People who are naturally reserved in public find that they are not afraid to express the rhythm and feeling of a poem or other selection if they are part of a group. The zest you will experience from performing as a member of a unit and the opportunity it affords for self-expression will make you more self-confident and relaxed in your solo activities in speaking and reading aloud.

The precision-drilled chorus of the musical hit, *Oklahoma,* delights the eyes and ears of the audience. *(Graphic House, Inc.)*

The demands of being a member of any well-trained chorus are rigorous and exacting; the rewards are gratifying and satisfying to the full. *(Official Photograph, Board of Education, City of New York)*

Group study of choral speaking contributes greatly to your total speech development. Achieving the unison necessary for choral speaking depends upon precision, and precision for the group depends upon the precise control of every individual in the group. Thus, for example, you must learn to perfect your articulation so that you will be in harmony with the others. Group reading must be so perfectly timed and coordinated that it sounds like one voice made many times richer; otherwise the effect will be jumbled, garbled confusion. If only one person reads too fast or too slowly or mispronounces a word, for instance, the effect is ruined. Cooperation is also essential in expressing the same mood or shade of meaning, and in subordinating your voice so that it does not stand out from the others. You will have to learn to expand your voice range, vary your pitch, and modulate your tones from loud to soft as the group interpretation of the selection requires.

Besides the many benefits already mentioned pertaining to your speech development, you will gain a greater appreciation of literature—especially poetry—when you hear how magnificently it can be brought to life in a choral performance. For real pleasure and beneficial speech training you will discover this group activity to be one of the highlights of your speech course.

# How Do You Organize a Choral Speaking Group?

Choral speaking groups may include from ten to fifty people, but twenty is an ideal number. In church or school audiences, there are frequently more than a thousand voices participating, but these are usually untrained groups. Although various selections and situations will require groups of different sizes, a maximum of thirty is desirable. Experimentation by the group and its director will help to set optimum standards and limits.

After the number of people has been determined for your group, the next step is forming this unit into three or four sections according to voice pitch. If you are in a group containing both boys and girls, your arrangement would look like this:

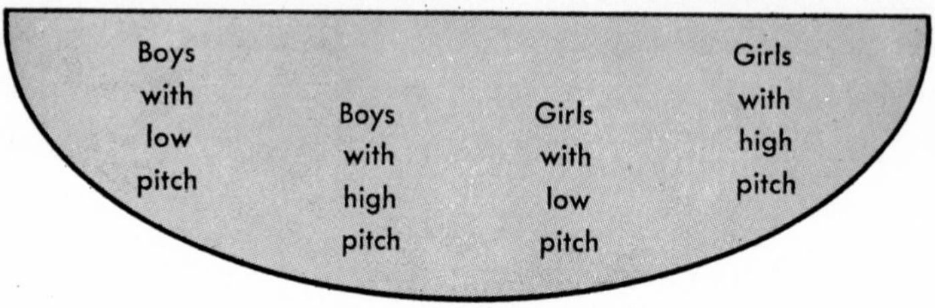


If your group consists only of boys or only of girls, you will want to divide this way:

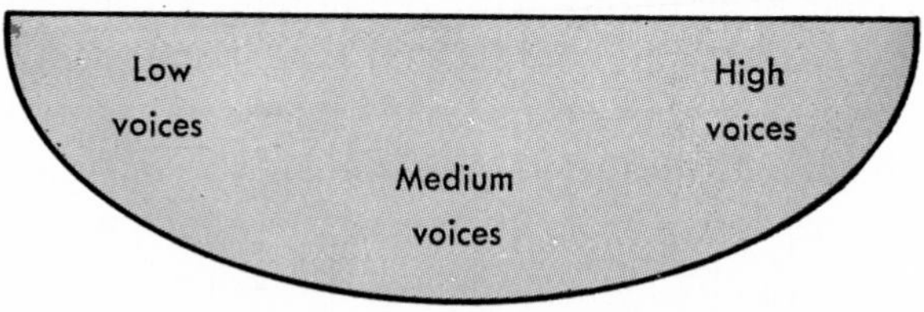


Such divisions provide balance to your unit and make rehearsing easier for all concerned. Usually your teacher will conduct your chorus so that you can keep together and come in on cue. As you progress, each of you should be able to act as conductor for your group. A director's principal duty, like that of a conductor of an orchestra, is to be interpreter of the selection. He should study the reading and its background and then use his imagination to interpret its meaning and mood. In poetry, especially, he must sense the melody and rhythm so that he can lead the chorus in expressing them.

The duties of a director of a choral speaking group are much like those of a conductor of an orchestra. *(Alfred Wertheimer/Scope)*

## ACTIVITIES

1. Use one of the following selections in rating each member of your class as to voice pitch.

### SONG: THE OWL

When cats run home and light is come,
And dew is cold upon the ground,
And the far-off stream is dumb,
And the whirring sail goes round,
And the whirring sail goes round;
Alone and warming his five wits,
The white owl in the belfry sits.

When merry milkmaids click the latch,
And rarely smells the new-mown hay,
And the cock hath sung beneath the thatch
Twice or thrice his roundelay,
Twice or thrice his roundelay;
Alone and warming his five wits,
The white owl in the belfry sits.

—Alfred Tennyson

### THE PANTHER

The panther is like a leopard,
Except it hasn't been peppered.
Should you behold a panther crouch,
Prepare to say Ouch.
Better yet, if called by a panther,
Don't anther.

—Ogden Nash

### PETER PIPER

Peter Piper picked a peck of pickled peppers;
A peck of pickled peppers Peter Piper picked;
If Peter Piper picked a peck of pickled peppers,
Where's the peck of pickled peppers Peter Piper picked?

—Mother Goose

### OLD KING COLE

Old King Cole
  Was a merry old soul,
And a merry old soul was he;
  And he called for his pipe,
  And he called for his bowl,
And he called for his fiddlers three!
Every fiddler he had a fine fiddle,
  And a very fine fiddle had he;
Twee-tweedle-dee, tweedle-dee, went the fiddlers.
Oh, there's none so rare, as can compare
  With King Cole and his fiddlers three!

—Mother Goose

2. Use the selections above to condition yourself. You will find these particularly helpful in training you to articulate distinctly, to use effective pitch change, and to read in perfect unison. Repeat these as a group until you can say them to your satisfaction and that of your director.
3. Practice the Pledge to the Flag. Concentrate on the timing of every syllable of every word so that the group begins together and keeps together during the entire pledge.

## How Do You Choose a Selection for Choral Speaking?

After dividing into groups according to voice pitch, your next problem is choosing selections suitable for your group.

Both prose and poetry are good for group interpretation,

although poetry seems to be preferred by most choral groups, probably because of the rhythmic effects which can be worked out together. Usually selections revealing emotion and feeling are best suited for group performance. Subtle intellectual meanings or messages may be difficult to understand and seldom do more than make hard work for the chorus and create confusion for the audience.

Your choice should be governed largely by the wishes of the members of the group. By all means, choose selections which all of you will enjoy! That's the fun of choral speaking. It is important that you understand the purpose and mood of the selection. If your choice is to be read in public, you must also consider the taste of your audience. Try to decide if your audience will enjoy it as much as you do.

There are other points that you will want to consider. Thus, you will want to decide if it is worth while spending time in preparation and production. A good test for any selection is to ask these questions: (a) Does it tell an interesting story? (b) Does it convey a definite mood? (c) And, if poetry, does it have a strong rhythmic feeling? Usually, if the selection of your group meets these requirements both in terms of your group and your audience, you have chosen well. The final test, of course, is the ability of your group to perform the selection well.

## How Do You Prepare Your Selection?

First, read aloud the prose or poetry that you have chosen. Discuss with your group its meaning, mood, and purpose. Is it primarily light, gay, and humorous? Is it serious and profound? Is there an air of mystery about it? Which predominates—the idea or the sound pattern?

After discussing the questions above and any others that seem important to all of you, you should have reached an agreement on the meaning. Now try taking turns reading the selection aloud to discover if you all agree on the oral method of bringing out the meaning. Which concepts of interpretation seem to be most effective? Keep experimenting until you can agree on the best interpretation.

Here are some suggestions that should be helpful as you begin to study your selection:

1. As you practice, articulate both your vowels and consonants clearly.

2. Figure out where the point of highest interest is. Decide how you will build up to it.

3. Decide where subdued tones should be used to contrast with greater volume and emphasis in other places.

4. Figure out the rhythm and the mood, and decide how the chorus will express them.

The next stage of preparation is the decision on voice division. Should you read the entire selection in unison or should it be divided in a certain manner? There are several ways of dividing voices for choral speaking. The ones most frequently used are:

**Refrain**—a soloist or soloists, plus group response

**Two-part**—one group contrasted with another group (antiphonal response)

**Group sectional**—several soloists, small groups, large groups, and entire group

**Cumulative response**—a variation of the others in which one voice or a few voices begin and others are added until the entire chorus is reading together. In a variation of this technique, voices can decrease too, until the original number reads the last line.

The voice division of a group such as this may be into any of the four different categories. *(Monkmeyer)*

Which method should you use? Obviously, you can't be sure until you have tried reading your selection in several different ways. Your director will play an important part in this decision, for frequently the division of voices is a matter of artistic judgment. You may see the same poem in seven books with seven different variations on the marking of the lines for reading. Try as many as you wish and then decide which you consider to be the most effective. If you have time, you might enjoy using two or three methods on the same selection. This is particularly interesting if there are two or three choral groups in your class.

In dividing the voices of the group, there are many choices. The following might take certain parts in one selection:

| | | |
|---|---|---|
| All the girls | Two girls | All the high voices |
| All the boys | One girl | All the low voices |
| Two boys | One boy | All the medium voices |

There is one danger to avoid: that is the temptation to divide too often merely to give a large number of persons opportunity to perform. There must be a reason for dividing into solos or small groups. Breaking up your selection into too many small parts may produce a choppy effect.

In the selections that follow, you will find samples of the various types of voice division with markings to guide you. As was stated earlier in the chapter, such marks are frequently somewhat arbitrary. Unless a selection is designed only for unison reading, you should find several interesting ways of dividing any reading. After reading the samples as marked, try to work out different methods of your own.

All low voices will be referred to as ***Dark;*** the high voices, as ***Light;*** and the medium ones, as ***Medium.***

## Sample refrain

### AMERICA THE BEAUTIFUL

*Voice 1*

O beautiful for spacious skies,
For amber waves of grain,
For purple mountain majesties
Above the fruited plain!

*Unison*

America! America!
God shed His grace on thee
And crown thy good with brotherhood
From sea to shining sea!

*Voice 2*

O beautiful for pilgrim feet,
Whose stern, impassioned stress
A thoroughfare for freedom beat
Across the wilderness!

*Unison*

America! America!
God mend thine every flaw,
Confirm thy soul in self-control,
Thy liberty in law!

*Voice 3*

O beautiful for heroes proved
In liberating strife,
Who more than self their country loved,
And mercy more than life!

*Unison*

America! America!
May God thy gold refine
Till all success be nobleness,
And every gain divine!

*Voice 4*

O beautiful for patriot dream
That sees beyond the years
Thine alabaster cities gleam
Undimmed by human tears!

*Unison*

America! America!
God shed his grace on thee
And crown thy good with brotherhood
From sea to shining sea!

—Katharine Lee Bates

## Sample two-part (or antiphonal)

### THE BEATITUDES

*Light*

Blessed are the poor in spirit:

*Dark*

For theirs is the kingdom of heaven.

*Light*

Blessed are they that mourn:

*Dark*

For they shall be comforted.

*Light*

Blessed are the meek:

*Dark*

For they shall inherit the earth.

*Light*

Blessed are they which do hunger and
thirst after righteousness:

*Dark*

For they shall be filled.

*Light*

Blessed are the merciful:

*Dark*

For they shall obtain mercy.

*Light*

Blessed are the pure in heart:

*Dark*

For they shall see God.

*Light*

Blessed are the peacemakers:

*Dark*

For they shall be called the children
of God.

*Light*

Blessed are they which are persecuted
for righteousness' sake:

*Dark*

For theirs is the kingdom of Heaven.

—*The Bible,* St. Matthew, Chapter V

## Sample group sectional

### THE OWL AND THE PUSSY-CAT

*Small group*—***Medium***

The Owl and the Pussy-Cat went to sea
In a beautiful pea-green boat;
They took some honey and plenty of money
Wrapped up in a five-pound note.
The Owl looked up to the stars above,
And sang to a small guitar,

*First Boy . . .* ***Dark***

"O lovely Pussy, O Pussy, my Love,
What a beautiful Pussy you are,
You are,
You are,
What a beautiful Pussy you are!"

*Girl . . .* ***Light***

Pussy said to the Owl, "You elegant fowl,
How charmingly sweet you sing!
O! let us be married; too long have we tarried!
But what shall we do for a ring?"

*Small group*—**Dark**

They sailed away, for a year and a day,
  To the land where the bong-tree grows;
And there in a wood a Piggy-wig stood,
  With a ring at the end of his nose,

*Unison*

His nose,
His nose,
With a ring at the end of his nose.

*First Boy . . .* **Dark**

"Dear Pig, are you willing to sell for one shilling
  Your ring?"

*Second Boy . . .* **Dark**

Said the Piggy, "I will."

*Small group*—**Light**

So they took it away, and were married next day
  By the Turkey who lives on the hill.
They dined on mince and slices of quince,
  Which they ate with a runcible spoon;

*Unison*

And hand in hand, on the edge of the sand,
  They danced by the light of the moon,
The moon,
The moon,
They danced by the light of the moon.

—Edward Lear

## Sample cumulative response (addition of voices)

***This may be done by any type of voices***

### THE GREEN GRASS GROWS ALL AROUND

*Voice 1*

There was a tree stood in the ground,
The prettiest tree you ever did see;
The tree in the wood, and the wood in the ground,

*Unison*

And the green grass grows all around.
And the green grass grows all around.

*Voice 2*

And on this tree there was a limb,
The prettiest limb you ever did see;

*Voices 1 and 2*

The limb on the tree, and the tree in the wood,
The tree in the wood, and the wood in the ground,

*Unison*
And the green grass grows all around.
And the green grass grows all around.

*Voice 3*
And on this limb there was a bough,
The prettiest bough you ever did see;

*Voices 1, 2, and 3*
The bough on the limb, and the limb on the tree,
The limb on the tree, and the tree in the wood,
The tree in the wood, and the wood in the ground,

*Unison*
And the green grass grows all around.
And the green grass grows all around.

*Voice 4*
Now on this bough there was a nest,
The prettiest nest you ever did see;

*Voices 1, 2, 3, and 4*
The nest on the bough, and the bough on the limb,
The bough on the limb, and the limb on the tree,
The limb on the tree, and the tree in the wood,
The tree in the wood, and the wood in the ground,

*Unison*
And the green grass grows all around.
And the green grass grows all around.

*Voice 5*
And in the nest there were some eggs,
The prettiest eggs you ever did see;

*Voices 1, 2, 3, 4, and 5*
The eggs in the nest, and the nest on the bough,
The nest on the bough, and the bough on the limb,
The bough on the limb, and the limb on the tree,
The limb on the tree, and the tree in the wood,
The tree in the wood, and the wood in the ground,

*Unison*
And the green grass grows all around, around, around,
And the green grass grows all around.

—Anonymous

In the cumulative response type of division, voices can decrease as well as increase to produce the desired effect. For example, you can probably remember many singing games you played as a child in which the players were accumulated one by one (such as "The Farmer in the Dell") and then decreased in the same way. One of the most familiar examples of poems in which decrease of voices contributes to the meaning is *Ten Little Injuns.*

## Sample cumulative response (decrease of voices)

### TEN LITTLE INJUNS

*10 voices*

Ten little Injuns standing in a line—

*Solo (Drops out after saying line)*

One went home, and then there were nine.

*9 voices*

Nine little Injuns swinging on a gate—

*Solo*

One tumbled off, and then there were eight.

Using the above as a sample, continue with the division of voices until there is only one voice in the last two lines.

Eight little Injuns tried to get to Heaven—
One kicked the bucket, and then there were
seven.

Seven little Injuns cutting up tricks—
One went to bed, and then there were six.

Six little Injuns learning how to dive—
One swam away, and then there were five.

Five little Injuns on a cellar door—
One jumped off, and then there were four.

Four little Injuns climbing up a tree—
One fell down, and then there were three.

Three little Injuns out in a canoe—
One fell overboard, and then there were two.

Two little Injuns fooling with a gun—
One shot the other, and then there was one.

One little Injun living all alone—
He got married, and then there was none!

—Anonymous

### ACTIVITY

Bring to class any other poems suitable for cumulative response division. Use the above poems to help you divide them.

In ballads or stories, a narrator is often used to supply the descriptive lines between conversational lines. When the characters can be identified by name or title, it is helpful to do so. This system is used in *Casey Jones,* the traditional ballad that follows.

## CASEY JONES

*Narrator*

Come, all you rounders, if you want to hear
A story 'bout a brave engineer.
Casey Jones was the rounder's name
On a six-eight-wheeler, boys, he won his fame.
The caller called Casey at a half-past four,
Kissed his wife at the station door,
Mounted to the cabin with his orders in his hand
And he took his farewell trip to that promised land:

*Unison*

Casey Jones, mounted to the cabin,
Casey Jones, with his orders in his hand,
Casey Jones, mounted to the cabin,
And he took his farewell trip to the promised land.

*Casey*

"Put in your water and shovel in your coal,
Put your head out the window, watch them drivers roll,
I'll run her till she leaves the rail
'Cause I'm eight hours late with that western mail."

*Narrator*

He looked at his watch and his watch was slow,
He looked at the water and the water was low,
He turned to the fireman and then he said,

*Casey*

"We're goin' to reach Frisco but we'll all be dead";

*Unison*

Casey Jones, goin' to reach Frisco,
Casey Jones, but we'll all be dead,
Casey Jones, goin' to reach Frisco,
"We're goin' to reach Frisco, but we'll all be dead."

*Narrator*

Casey pulled up that Reno Hill,
He tooted for the crossing with an awful shrill,
The switchman knew by the engine's moan
That the man at the throttle was Casey Jones.
He pulled up within two miles of the place
Number Four stared him right in the face,
He turned to the fireman, said,

*Casey*

"Boy, you better jump,
'Cause there's two locomotives that's a-goin' to bump";

*Unison*

Casey Jones, two locomotives,
Casey Jones, that's a-goin' to bump,
Casey Jones, two locomotives,
"There's two locomotives that's a-goin' to bump."

*Narrator*

Casey said just before he died,

*Casey*

"There's two more roads that I'd like to ride."

*Narrator*

The fireman said what could they be?

*Casey*

"The Southern Pacific and the Sante Fe."

*Narrator*

Mrs. Casey sat on her bed a-sighin',
Just received a message that Casey was dyin'
Said,

*Mrs. Casey*

"Go to bed, children, and hush your cry'n,
'Cause you got another papa on the Salt Lake Line":

*Unison*

Mrs. Casey Jones, got another papa,
Mrs. Casey Jones, on that Salt Lake Line,
Mrs. Casey Jones, got another papa,
"And you've got another papa on the Salt Lake Line."

—Traditional Ballad

Other ballads that can be divided in the same manner are: *The Blue-Tail Fly, Oh Susanna,* and *I Ride on Old Paint.* What other ballads can you suggest for soloist plus refrain division?

In some of the selections which follow, several methods are suggested for dividing the voices. You may think of more.

**JOHNNY AT THE FAIR**

1. **Two-part division:** Group 1 (girls) read stanza 2; Group 2 (girls) read stanza 4; entire group join in reading stanzas 1, 3, and 5.

2. **Simple refrain:** Girl solo, stanzas 2 and 4; refrain, in unison.

3. **Cumulative:** Group 1 (girls) begin line 1 and continue throughout refrain; group 2 begin line 2 and continue throughout refrain; group 3 begin with line 3 with the three groups finishing the refrain. Follow same plan with the three refrains. Stanzas 2 and 4 can be read as solos or by small groups.

## JOHNNY AT THE FAIR

Oh dear, what can the matter be!
Dear, dear, what can the matter be!
Oh, dear, what can the matter be
Johnny's so long at the fair!

He promised to bring me a faring to please me,
And then for a kiss, oh he said he would tease me.
He promised to buy me a bunch of blue ribbons
To tie up my bonnie brown hair.

Oh dear, what can the matter be!
Dear, dear, what can the matter be!
Oh, dear, what can the matter be
Johnny's so long at the fair!

He promised to buy me a basket of posies,
A garland of lilies, a garland of roses,
A little straw hat to set off the blue ribbons
That tie up my bonnie brown hair.

Oh dear, what can the matter be!
Dear, dear, what can the matter be!
Oh, dear, what can the matter be
Johnny's so long at the fair!

—Traditional ballad

## JAZZ FANTASIA

*Unison*

Drum on your drums, batter on your banjoes, sob on the long cool winding saxophones.
Go to it, O jazzmen!
Sling your knuckles on the bottoms of the happy tin pans;
Let your trombones ooze, and go husha-husha-hush with the slippery sand-paper.

*2 or 3 voices (soft)*

Moan like an autumn wind high in the lonesome tree-tops;
Moan soft like you wanted somebody terrible.

*2 or 3 voices (staccato)*

Cry like a racing car slipping away from a motorcycle cop!

*Unison*

Bang-bang! you jazzmen, bang altogether drums, traps, banjoes, horns, tin cans!

*Same 2 or 3 voices as line 7 (staccato)*

Make two people fight on the top of a stairway and scratch each other's eyes in a clinch tumbling down the stairs.

*Unison (with sudden abruptness)*

Can the rough stuff!

*Same 2 or 3 voices as lines 5 and 6 (soft)*

Now a Mississippi steamboat pushes up the night river, with a hoo-hoo-hoo-oo,
And the green lanterns calling to the high soft stars;
A red moon rides on the humps of the low river hills;

*Unison (sharp and crisp)*

Go to it, O jazzmen!

—Carl Sandburg

THE PLAINT OF THE CAMEL

**1. Five different small groups** read the first four lines of each stanza with a soloist to read the last three lines.

**2. A soloist** to read the first four lines with the group reading the last three lines.

## THE PLAINT OF THE CAMEL

Canary-birds feed on sugar and seed,
Parrots have crackers to crunch;
And as for the poodles, they tell me the noodles
Have chicken and cream for their lunch.
But there's never a question
About *my* digestion—
ANYTHING does for me!

Cats, you're aware, can repose in a chair,
Chickens can roost upon rails;
Puppies are able to sleep in a stable,
And oysters can slumber in pails.
But no one supposes
A poor Camel dozes—
ANY PLACE does for me!

Lambs are enclosed where it's never exposed,
Coops are constructed for hens;
Kittens are treated to houses well heated,
And pigs are protected by pens.
But a Camel comes handy
Wherever it's sandy—
ANYWHERE does for me!

People would laugh if you rode a giraffe,
Or mounted the back of an ox;
It's nobody's habit to ride on a rabbit,
Or try to bestraddle a fox.
But as for a Camel, he's
Ridden by families—
ANY LOAD does for me!

A snake is as round as a hole in the ground,
And weasels are wavy and sleek;
And no alligator could ever be straighter
Than lizards that live in a creek.
But a Camel's all lumpy
And bumpy and humpy—
ANY SHAPE does for me!

—Charles Edward Carryl

Two soloists are being taped in this scene from *Wuthering Heights*. *(CBS Television Network)*

As mentioned earlier in the chapter, one of the first examples of group speaking was in the drama. As you finish this adventure in choral reading, you will enjoy using the chorus in some dramatic readings. You can dramatize stories or poems which contain choral responses or you can find scenes from plays which you can enact in class.

On the next page there is a dramatization of a favorite children's story, *The Little Engine That Could,* as prepared by a high school student. Study it as you did the reading selections in Chapter 19 to understand the changing moods from the beginning to the end. Use your imagination to suggest the kind of voice that would best portray the Clown, the Passenger Engine, the Freight Engine, the Rusty Old Engine, and the Little Blue Engine. Would the voice of the Narrator require any more versatility than the voice for any other role? Perhaps you can think of some sound effects and some props that would add to the dramatization.

## THE LITTLE ENGINE THAT COULD

NARRATOR: Chug, chug, chug. Puff, puff, puff. Ding-dong, ding-dong. The little train rumbled over the tracks. She was a happy little train for she had such a jolly load to carry. Her cars were filled full of good things for boys and girls.

There were toy animals—giraffes with long necks, Teddy bears with almost no necks at all, and even a baby elephant. Then there were dolls—dolls with blue eyes and yellow curls, dolls with brown bobbed heads, and the gayest little toy clown you ever saw. And there were cars full of toy engines, aeroplanes, tops, jack-knives, picture puzzles, books, and every kind of thing boys or girls could want.

But that was not all. Some of the cars were filled with all sorts of good things for boys and girls to eat—big golden oranges, red-cheeked apples, bottles of creamy milk for their breakfasts, fresh spinach for their dinners, peppermint drops, and lollypops for after-meal treats.

The little train was carrying all these good things to the good little boys and girls on the other side of the mountain. She puffed along happily. Then all of a sudden she stopped with a jerk. She simply could not go another inch. She tried and she tried, but her wheels would not turn.

What were all those good little boys and girls on the other side of the mountain going to do without the jolly toys to play with and the wholesome food to eat? The little clown who had jumped out of the train cried out:

CLOWN: "Here comes a shiny new engine. Let us ask him to help us."

CHORUS: "Please, Shiny New Engine, do carry our train over the mountain. Our engine has broken down, and the boys and girls on the other side will have no toys to play with and no wholesome food to eat unless you help us."

NARRATOR: But the Shiny New Engine snorted:

SHINY NEW ENGINE: "I pull you? I am a Passenger Engine. I have just carried a fine big train over the mountain, with more cars than you ever dreamed of. My train had sleeping cars, with comfortable berths; a dining car where waiters bring whatever hungry people want to eat; and parlor cars in which people sit in soft armchairs and look out of big plate-glass windows. I carry the likes of you? Indeed not!"

NARRATOR: And off he steamed to the roundhouse, where engines live when they are not busy.

How sad the little train and all the dolls and toys felt! Then the little clown called out:

CLOWN: "The Passenger Engine is not the only one in the world. Here is another coming, a fine big strong one. Let us ask him to help us."

NARRATOR: The little toy trainman waved his flag and the big strong engine came to a stop.

CHORUS: "Please, oh please, Big Engine, do pull our train over the mountain. Our engine has broken down, and the good little boys and girls on the other side will have no toys to play with and no wholesome food to eat unless you help us."

NARRATOR: But the Big Strong Engine bellowed:

BIG STRONG ENGINE: "I am a Freight Engine. I have just pulled a big train loaded with costly machines over the mountain. These machines print books and newspapers for grown-ups to read. I am a very important engine indeed. I won't carry the likes of you!"

NARRATOR: And the Freight Engine puffed off indignantly to the round-house. The little train and all the dolls and toys were very sad. Suddenly the little toy clown cried out again:

CLOWN: "Cheer up, the Freight Engine is not the only one in the world. Here comes another. He looks very old and tired, but our train is so little perhaps he can help us."

NARRATOR: So the little toy clown waved his flag and the dingy, rusty old engine stopped.

CHORUS: "Please, Kind Engine, do pull our train over the mountain. Our engine has broken down, and the boys and girls on the other side will have no toys to play with and no wholesome food to eat unless you help us."

NARRATOR: But the rusty old engine sighed:

RUSTY OLD ENGINE: "I am so tired. I must rest my weary wheels. I cannot pull even so little a train as yours over the mountain. I can not. I can not. I can not."

NARRATOR: And off he rumbled to the round-house chugging, "I can not. I can not. I can not." Then indeed the little train was very sad, and the dolls and toys were ready to cry.

CLOWN: "Here is another engine coming, a little blue engine, a very little one, but perhaps she will help us."

NARRATOR: The very little engine came chug-chugging merrily along. When she saw the toy clown's flag, she stopped quickly.

LITTLE BLUE ENGINE: "What is the matter, my friends?"

CHORUS: "Oh, Little Blue Engine, will you pull us over the mountain? Our engine has broken down and the good boys and girls on the other side will have no toys to play with and no wholesome food to eat, unless you help us. Please, please, help us, Little Blue Engine."

LITTLE BLUE ENGINE: "I am not very big. They use me only for switching in the yard. I have never been over the mountain."

CHORUS: "But we must get over the mountain before the children awaken."

NARRATOR: The very little engine looked up and saw the tears in the doll's eyes. And she thought of the good little boys and girls on the other side of the mountain who would have no toys and no wholesome food unless she helped. Then she said:

LITTLE BLUE ENGINE: "I think I can. I think I can. I think I can."

NARRATOR: And she hitched herself to the little train. She tugged and pulled and pulled and tugged and slowly, slowly, slowly, they started off. The toy clown jumped aboard and all the dolls and toy animals began to smile and cheer.

Puff, puff, chug, chug, went the Little Blue Engine.

LITTLE BLUE ENGINE: "I think I can. I think I can. I think I can. I think I can. I think I can. I think I can. I think I can. I think I can. I think I can."

NARRATOR: Up, up, up. Faster and faster and faster and faster the little engine climbed until at last they reached the top of the mountain. Down in the valley lay the city.

CHORUS: "Hurrah, hurrah, the good little boys and girls in the city will be happy because you helped us, kind Little Blue Engine."

NARRATOR: And the Little Blue Engine smiled and seemed to say as she puffed steadily down the mountain. I thought I could. I thought I could. I thought I could. I thought I could. I thought I could. I thought I could.

—Edited by Watty Piper

## ACTIVITIES

1. Using the above selection as a model, prepare another story or a poem for choral reading.
2. Select a scene from any play which contains choral responses and present it in class. Refer to Page 427 for the names of some plays which contain choral work or find one of the early Greek plays.
3. Study Vachel Lindsay's "Congo"; then perform it, using a bass drum or tom-tom to emphasize the rhythm.
4. Select a recording of some American folk song such as "Ballad for Americans," or "The Airborne." Using the record as a background, perform the selection, taking the cues from the recording artists.
5. As your final experiment, find any selections contained in Chapter 19 which you think could be adapted for speaking in chorus.

## PRONUNCIATION PROBLEMS

The diphthong usually spelled "ou" or "ow" should be said as a full, rich sound. The importance of making this sound through the mouth rather than through the nose is illustrated in the familiar quotation, "How, now, Brown Cow." Go over the following words and sentences until you can produce the sound properly:

| | | | |
|---|---|---|---|
| loud | ground | cow | abound |
| flour | vouch | vowel | thou |
| gout | found | hour | arouse |
| noun | scour | mountain | surround |
| pout | shout | bounty | power |
| mouth | mound | count | tower |
| ounce | bough | round | renown |
| sound | proud | about | town |
| shroud | fountain | now | our |
| pound | rebound | cower | sour |
| cloud | shower | bower | crown |

## READING CHECK-UP

Read aloud the nonsense sentences below to check your pronunciation of any problem words.

The boughs were placed at the mound and flowers grew around the fountain.

In an hour the sky was filled with clouds.

The town was surrounded by thousands who tried to arouse the rabble with shouting.

His renown for rounding the mouth when sounding certain vowels made his friends proud.

The town crier announced the hour loudly as he strolled around the town.

The towering giant was renowned for his power and all who had encountered his powerful strength would vouch that they cowered at the sound of his howling voice.

She seemed to be endowed with a perpetual frown on her brow. Even though she was stylishly gowned, she somehow looked dowdy and sour.

Inside the house the howling grew louder and louder as the crowd bound the suspect and allowed him to make no explanation.

The diver was drowned the first time he went down to make a sounding.

Burns wrote a poem about a mouse whose nest was turned up from the ground by a plow.

He now vowed that he would make a row about the cows eating the flowers at the fountain in our town.

## VOCABULARY BUILD-UP

Use the italicized words in short paragraphs to show that you understand their meanings.

policy of *non-alignment*
main *portent* of the moon shot
a *momentous* meeting
*reaffirmed* our unity
through *equitable* sharing
to *repudiate* the false teachings
the *impending* visit
loyalty to a basic *concept*
in *conformity* with principles
*flexibility* of methods
to *venerate* the flag
*enshrined* in the hearts
a *complementing* ring of missile bases
*strategic* encirclement
most *formidable* of the forces
ready for *deployment* of troops
seeking a *consensus*
squadrons of *tactical* fighters
a *deterrent* to war
a *contentious* meeting

CHAPTER

# 21 Dramatizing

"The world of the theatre is a magic realm where humanity has expressed its dreams for countless generations, and in which peoples of all nations are still finding inspiration, relaxation, and experience which could not otherwise be a part of their daily lives. Whether its setting has been the marble columns of ancient Greece, the crude carts of the Middle Ages, the cobbled inn-yards of Elizabethan England, the showboats aglitter on the Mississippi, the ornate picture palaces, or the modern theatres of Broadway—the stage has always had a peculiar fascination for every individual."

—Ommanney and Ommanney,
*The Stage and the School*

WHEN you look back over your most pleasant experiences, many of you will recall first of all the times that you appeared in a school or church play or pageant. The thrill of participating even in a small role is one that you will never forget. As you look ahead, some of you may even be anticipating the time when the world of the theater will include you as one of its actors, directors, playwrights, stage managers, designers, or other technical specialists. At the present time certainly all of you find pleasure in watching plays whether you see them on your school stage, on Broadway, at a local theater, on television, or in a barn or tent during the summer.

A study of drama has several far-reaching values for you. Since the story of drama presents a panoramic view of the world's culture, your general background will be enriched. Artistic expression has long been a part of the theater, a fact which increases your understanding and appreciation of art. By experiencing the varied emotional and intellectual content of plays, you enlarge your own emotional and intellectual background. Studying a large assortment of plays helps to make you a discriminating critic so that you can distinguish between the worthwhile and the insignificant productions. Finally, this contact with drama may motivate you to become actively engaged in the world of the theater.

The story of the theater is an exciting drama itself. Look now at its origin, its struggles, and some of its leading characters.

# The Story of the Drama

## Earliest beginnings of the drama

This story can truly begin with "Once upon a time . . . " because nobody knows the exact time of the beginning. Some believe that our drama is six thousand years old; others place it nearer three thousand.

Although many histories of the drama begin with Greek drama in the 6th century B. C., there is some evidence from carvings found on old tombs that the first theatrical performances took place in Egypt four thousand years ago. The actor-priests of Egypt are credited with having created the first dramatic literature in the form of highly emotional religious hymns. According to some sources, the first dramatic monologue, *Hymn to the Sun,* was composed by Ikhnaton, the greatest of the Pharaohs, around 1360, B.C. The Old Testament also contains forms of early drama such as *The Book of Job* and *The Song of Solomon.* Archibald MacLeish based his modern verse drama, *J. B.,* on *The Book of Job.* This Broadway play applied the familiar theme of Job, plagued by constant trouble, to a present-day businessman by the name of J. B. whose entire life was a series of mishaps.

Those who may question the foregoing events as being the true beginnings of drama usually accept the traditional viewpoint that the Greek drama was the direct origin of present-day drama. From this standpoint, the customary division into eras is as follows: Greek drama, Roman drama, Medieval drama, Renaissance drama, Elizabethan drama, Restoration drama, 18th and 19th century drama, and modern or 20th century drama.

## Drama in the age of Greece

The beginnings of drama in Greece occurred during the 6th century B.C., at which time dramatic forms appeared in the ritual worship of Dionysus, the Greek god of wine, who was later known to the Romans as Bacchus. In Greece, as in Egypt, drama arose from religious ceremonies and remained a part of religious pageantry for many centuries. Drama was such a vital part of the people's lives that the Greek theater is still considered one of the chief factors which shaped the cultural background of Greece. Many of the characteristics of the modern theater are the outgrowth of the Greek theater.

Certain names are important to remember since they are among

The ancient Greek theater at Epidauros, built in the 4th century B.C. and famous for its acoustics, still plays to capacity audiences during June Festival performances. *(Courtesy of Esther Johnson)*

the earliest ones associated with the theater. To begin with, Greek plays were spoken by a chorus and leader with no individual actors playing any roles. The Greek actor and playwright, Thespis, is generally credited with having introduced a single actor in addition to the chorus and leader. It is in memory of Thespis that actors today are known as "Thespians."

The three most famous Greek playwrights are Aeschylus, Sophocles, and Euripides. Aeschylus is remembered for his *Agamemnon* and *Prometheus Bound,* in both of which he introduced a second actor. Sophocles added a third actor in his famous tragedies, *Antigone,* and *Oedipus the King.* Euripides, who is considered by some as the first modern playwright, is author of *The Trojan Women, Hippolytus,* and *Medea.* Of these three, *Medea* is perhaps the strongest and has recently been revived for presentation on the American stage. In Greek drama, the chief conflict was always between the gods and human beings. Since Greek worship was based upon fear of the gods, the drama reflected this same religious belief in that the will of the gods prevailed over the desires of mortals.

It was during the Greek era that drama was first classified as either tragedy or comedy. Since the term *tragedy* implies the defeat of the leading character, it was natural that most Greek plays were tragedies. The term *comedy,* in its earliest usage, meant that the leading character would overcome any obstacles that faced him. The most important Greek author of comedy was Aristophanes, among whose leading works were *The Frogs, The Birds,* and *Lysistrata.*

## Drama in the time of Rome

The Greek theater was widely imitated, especially in Rome. Unfortunately the Roman theater proved to be only a dull, lifeless imitation and soon became only a place where sensual exhibitions occurred. Of all the Roman playwrights, only the names of Seneca, Plautus, and Terence are remembered.

This decline of dramatic activities continued until the Christian church became strong enough to banish drama. With the subsequent fall of the Roman Empire, drama seemed to be dead except

Today such spectacular productions as this *Ben Hur* scene attest to the continued interest in and popularity of the subject of Roman drama. *(Courtesy of Metro-Goldwyn-Mayer, Inc.)*

for a few crude exhibitions of juggling or similar acts. From these meager sparks, however, drama gained a rebirth, following the Dark Ages.

## Drama in the Medieval era

From the fifth to the fifteenth centuries Europe labored through the Dark Ages. Toward the end of this period, the church, which had formerly banned the drama, was responsible for its rebirth. The priests, who were among the few educated people of the period, used dramatic interpretation to present Biblical events to the illiterate masses.

Two types of plays that emerged from this period were known respectively as Mystery and Miracle plays. Mystery plays dealt only with Biblical events, whereas Miracle plays were concerned with the lives of saints or church events. In England the term Miracle play was widely used for both types. An example of the survival of

This scene from the Passion Play of Oberammergau, Germany, was played on the great outdoor stage during the 1960 presentation, in fulfillment of a vow made after a plague over 300 years ago. *(German Tourist Information Office)*

the Mystery play is the Passion Play of Oberammergau, which has been produced by the residents of that village at approximately ten-year intervals since 1634.

Civic interest brought many changes during this era. Production became more and more elaborate until it was necessary to present a pageant in cycles and move it about the city for people to see all of it. With the advent of guilds, each cycle came to be sponsored by a different guild and, naturally, there was great competition to see which guild could outdo the others in splendor. For the first time, plays contained humor.

A third type of play, the Morality play, was also introduced during the Medieval period. The Morality play dealt with ethical problems in which the chief conflict was between Good and Evil. The characters were largely symbolic and personified abstract qualities such as Truth, Honesty, or Piety. The best known example of the Morality play is *Everyman,* which was discovered by Ben Greet, an English producer. *Everyman* has since been produced in almost every country by drama groups.

## Drama in the Renaissance

In this period, which began in Italy around 1450, all art forms flourished including drama. Among the most important developments in this period were the rebirth of interest in the classical drama of Greece and Rome, the escape from the extreme limitations in theme of the Miracle and Morality plays, and the appearance of original plays written in the living language of the common people rather than in Latin.

Facilitating these developments was the patronage afforded drama groups by royalty and nobility. Funds were finally available to employ superior talent and to build theaters in which performances could be held. All of this attention to the drama added prestige to the players and writers which, in turn, gave impetus to the growth of drama.

## Drama in the Elizabethan age

The Elizabethan age is really part of the Renaissance period. But, because so much happened during this period in England, it is often treated separately. Although Shakespeare overshadowed his contemporaries, he was not the only great playwright of this era. Queen Elizabeth and many members of her court gave limited encouragement to the theater. Consequently, writers of talent vied with each other in turning out plays to win approval.

Some of the other playwrights of the Elizabethan Age and their leading plays are:

| | |
|---|---|
| Thomas Dekker | *Shoemaker's Holiday* |
| John Fletcher and Francis Beaumont | *The Maid's Tragedy* |
| Ben Jonson | *Every Man in His Humour* and *Volpone* |
| Thomas Kyd | *The Spanish Tragedy* |
| Christopher Marlowe | *Tamburlaine the Great* and *Doctor Faustus* |

During this era, the theater was accorded the highest patronage of its time. One marring factor was the kind of players who appeared in the plays. Although they were paid well by the nobility, many of them engaged in extravagant and wasteful living and squandered most of their money. They were gay and reckless and often died needlessly in brawls or duels. Since women did not act on the Elizabethan professional stage, the roles of women were played by boys.

After the death of Queen Elizabeth, the exceptional activity in the theater soon faded during the reign of James I and continued to decline during the troubled times of Charles I. Under Charles, the Puritans and other groups who had long opposed the theater forced the passage of an edict banning the public presentation of stage plays. Another "dark age" for the theater began.

## Drama in the Restoration

With the restoration of the Stuarts to the throne of England in the person of Charles II, the theater was also restored. The two important innovations which took place during the Restoration period were construction of scenery and mechanical apparatus for staging plays, and the acceptance finally of women players. Two playwrights of note during this period were William Wycherley and William Congreve, both of whom wrote broad comedies of sparkling wit.

## Drama in the 18th and 19th centuries

The 18th century was rather barren in England with the exception of three people whose names are legendary in the history of drama. David Garrick has long been recognized as one of the outstanding managers and actors of his time. The two great authors of the era were Richard Sheridan and Oliver Goldsmith whose comedies delighted audiences then and are still favorites for public production and classroom study. Sheridan wrote *The School for Scandal* and *The Rivals,* and Goldsmith was responsible for the classic *She Stoops to Conquer.* It was Sheridan's *The Rivals* which contained the unforgettable Mrs. Malaprop whose blunders with words created much of the comedy of the play and added the descriptive term "malapropism" to both oral and written English.

The popularity of the drama grew after the first quarter of the 19th century when Queen Victoria became ruler of England. The Victorian era (1837-1901) is notable for such popular dramatists as Oscar Wilde, whose greatest works are *Lady Windermere's Fan* and *The Importance of Being Earnest;* and Arthur Wing Pinero, who wrote *The Thunderbolt* and *Trelawny of the Wells.*

Elsewhere in Europe, some great names were added to the list of world-famous dramatic artists. In Germany there were Goethe, who wrote *Faust,* and Schiller, famous for his *Wilhelm Tell.* The French dramatists who lived and wrote during this time included the famed Voltaire, Victor Hugo, Sardou, and Alexandre Dumas. Associated with the Comedie Francaise, France's leading theater, were the renowned actors, Coquelin and Sully, and perhaps the world's greatest actress, Sarah Bernhardt, known almost reverently as the "divine Sarah."

This era was characterized almost entirely by plays belonging to the romantic school. The chief romanticist was Edmond Rostand, a French writer, whose plays, *Cyrano de Bergerac* and *Chanticler* will live forever on the world stage. Another familiar name among the romanticists is Maurice Maeterlinck of Belgium.

## Modern drama

Modern drama is sometimes thought of as beginning with the 20th century. The term is not so much a matter of time, however, as a matter of change in the type of writing. As mentioned above, writing was largely of a romantic style until about the middle of the 19th century at which time romanticism was replaced by realism. The person responsible for the sudden revolution in dramatic style was the Norwegian playwright, Henrik Ibsen, who lived from 1828 to 1906. He was the first to write about social problems and standards and to build plays on the theme of realistic human relationships, however unpleasant these might be. His influence was felt not only in Europe but in America where Eugene O'Neill became his greatest follower.

The chief differences between modern drama and its predecessors are easy to detect. Characters tend to be more lifelike and dialogue tends to be natural and conversational in style. The themes and problems are based on reality. Subjects are varied and of interest to the average person primarily because he can understand them.

The 20th century with its advances in transportation and the inception of radio and television is providing a tremendous growth in drama. You can sit at home and see or hear the world's greatest masterpieces merely by turning a dial. You can in this fashion travel easily to all parts of the world to see the kind of drama produced in the Orient, in Africa, in Australia, or in any country of Europe. Broadway stars now bring the leading hits of the theater to your own home town.

The increase in summer theaters and in civic theater groups enables you not only to see plays but also to participate in them. For you that can be one of the most gratifying phases of modern drama. Dramatic clubs and drama courses in high schools, colleges, and special schools provide an opportunity for you to become acquainted with techniques of acting. The rise in amateur acting groups gives you the chance to continue with dramatic pursuits

The enduring quality of Shakespeare is evidenced by the enthusiastic response of these students—part of the 60,000 who annually visit the American Shakespeare Festival Theatre in Stratford, Connecticut, during its school season.

after you are out of school. The spread of drama into radio and television also creates many chances for you to enter professional drama—chances which were hitherto limited to the Broadway stage.

Nearly every country has furnished an array of outstanding personalities associated with the theater during the modern era. In the activity which follows, you will have the chance to fill in your own story of drama in this era.

## ACTIVITIES

1. Below is a list of prominent people connected with the theater as playwrights or actors. Supply the following information about each:
   a. Nationality
   b. Playwright or actor
   c. In case of playwrights, names of best-known plays
   d. In case of actors, best-known roles

| | | |
|---|---|---|
| Somerset Maugham | Gertrude Lawrence | Anton Chekhov |
| Noel Coward | John Barrymore | Stanislavsky |
| Tennessee Williams | Marc Connelly | Beatrice Lillie |
| Alfred Lunt | George M. Cohan | Jerome Chodorov |
| Helen Hayes | Judith Anderson | Rabindranath Tagore |
| Maxwell Anderson | Maurice Evans | John Gielgud |
| Robert Sherwood | Thornton Wilder | Edwin Booth |
| Leslie Howard | Lynn Fontanne | Mrs. John Drew |
| Eugene O'Neill | Philip Barry | E. H. Sothern |
| George Bernard Shaw | Christopher Fry | Otis Skinner |
| John Synge | William Butler Yeats | Lillian Gish |
| Sir James M. Barrie | Raymond Massey | Joseph Jefferson |
| Katherine Cornell | Orson Welles | Minnie Maddern Fiske |
| Henrik Ibsen | Percival Wilde | Walter Hampden |
| John Galsworthy | Howard Lindsay | David Warfield |
| J. B. Priestley | Edna Ferber | David Belasco |
| T. S. Eliot | George S. Kaufman | Jessica Tandy |
| John Drinkwater | Booth Tarkington | Laurence Olivier |
| Maude Adams | Richard Mansfield | Eva LaGallienne |

2. Select any one of the above and prepare an interesting report based on his or her life story.
3. Select any one of the dramatists mentioned prior to the modern age and give an interesting account of his life.
4. Prepare a report giving details about the Greek theater.
5. Give a summary of one of the Greek plays mentioned in the text.
6. Find out all that you can about drama in the Orient and report your findings to the class. Stress methods of staging, costuming, and acting to show chief differences between Oriental and Occidental drama.
7. Have you seen any stage plays? If so, tell the class about one.
8. What are the outstanding plays in New York at the present time? Review one which you would like to see.

# Drama: Types, Forms, and Styles

The relatively simple classification presented here will help you to see the basic relationships among the major dramatic activities. In the following classification, *type* refers to the general theme or purpose of the play, *form* to the literary mode in which it is written, and *style* to its mood and mode of production, and sometimes also to the playwright's construction of plot, scene, and character.

## Types of drama

**Tragedy.** The essential elements of tragedy are two: (1) the hero, often called the protagonist, fails to solve his problem satisfactorily and his fate is death or ruin, and (2) the audience feels a strong emotional stimulation as a result of the protagonist's experience. William Shakespeare's *Hamlet* is an excellent example of a classic tragedy. Hamlet dies, but audiences do not leave the theater depressed, but rather exhilarated and elevated by an awareness that the purpose of the tragedy was beyond death.

Most of the great dramas of the world have been tragedies, because the emotional appeal of the tragedy is universal and long lasting. Comedies, on the other hand, tend to be artificial and based on situations which may be humorous at the time but which soon are meaningless.

**Comedy.** In the original meaning of this term, a comedy was defined as a play in which the hero was successful and lived to enjoy his success. More recently the term comedy has come to mean a play intended primarily to amuse. You will probably find this latter meaning fits in better with your own usage of the term.

There are many sub-types of comedy. These range from the extremely witty, verbal type of comedy at one extreme to the physically funny, slapstick type of comedy at the other. Although you will be introduced to only four distinct types here, the number of variations that could be recognized is almost limitless.

***"Drawing-room" comedy.*** This is the extremely intellectual, witty, verbally amusing type of comedy often laid in the living rooms of people in high society. The humor arises primarily from what is said rather than from what is done. Noel Coward, Rachel Crothers, and Philip Barry are three of the best-known writers of this type of comedy. The play, *The Philadelphia Story,* later made into a motion picture and now among the classic films of television, is an excellent example of this type of comedy. A satiric style of writing, characterized by a biting form of wit which is less kind

Cary Grant, Katharine Hepburn, and James Stewart in the swimming pool sequence of *The Philadelphia Story*—in which they created memorable roles. *(Courtesy of Metro-Goldwyn-Mayer, Inc.)*

than other forms of humor and usually more subtle, is often found in this type of comedy.

***Character comedy.*** In this type the humor and main interest arise directly from the personality of the leading character or characters. Although the character comedy may contain elements of both physical or intellectual humor, both of these elements are overshadowed by the personality of the protagonist. Some typical examples of this form of comedy are *The Man Who Came to Dinner, Life with Father*, and *No Time for Sergeants.*

***Sentimental comedy.*** In sentimental comedies the humor is gentle rather than biting, the characters tend to be kindly and warmly human, and the plot is fairly straightforward and of some importance. Love stories, especially those of young people, and stories centering around emotions of patriotism and devotion are common examples of this type of comedy. James M. Barrie is an outstanding example of a playwright who used sentimental themes almost exclusively. Some of his best-known sentimental comedies are *Quality Street, The Little Minister,* and *A Kiss for Cinderella.*

***Situation comedy.*** Situation comedy falls at the opposite end of the comedy range from drawing-room comedy. The humor stems from the situation—which is frequently absurd or ridiculous—in which the characters find themselves. Broad, slapstick humor of a physical type frequently results.

The farce represents the extreme type of situation comedy. The farce is an exaggerated type of comedy in which the characters, situation, lines, and actions are hilarious and implausible. Since its main purpose is to provide broad humor and laughter, any struggles or problems are of a ludicrous nature. Usually, funny characters play their roles with mock seriousness. When they suffer, they exaggerate their suffering to the point of being hilarious. Examples of this type of comedy are *Charley's Aunt, Nothing But the Truth, Three Men on a Horse,* and *Room Service.* A famous television series that exemplifies the farce was built around Sergeant Bilko.

**Serious drama.** Many plays do not fall in either the classification of comedy or tragedy. These can best be classed as serious drama. The following subdivisions suggest the types of plays to be found in this group but should not be regarded as all inclusive.

***Melodrama.*** This type of play is characterized by heightened plot situations, conventionalized characters, extremes of action, and usually the ultimate triumph of the protagonist. The familiar "whodunits" and western series of television furnish examples of melodrama. In these, a hero almost invariably foils a villain and, in so doing, saves a heroine. Famous examples of the melodrama on the stage are *Uncle Tom's Cabin* and *East Lynne.* The motion picture, *Birth of a Nation,* is also a good example of a melodrama.

***Historical plays.*** This type of play tells a story that is at least in part based on historical fact. Although there may be strong

In this film of Colonial Williamsburg, historically authentic in all details, Patrick Henry is depicted speaking out against the Townsend Act. *(Williamsburg–The Story of a Patriot)*

elements of tragedy or comedy in these plays, the historical characters and events provide the main interest. The historical plays of Shakespeare about Richard the Second or Henry the Fifth are classic examples of this type. *Victoria Regina* is a more modern example.

***Psychological plays.*** In these plays the conflict is more internal than external. The concern is as much with the motivations of the characters as with their actions. The theme is usually serious and sometimes tragic. In a very real sense, *Hamlet* may be regarded as a psychological drama as well as a tragedy. Modern examples of the psychological drama include *Come Back Little Sheba, Death of a Salesman, The Hairy Ape*, and *The Glass Menagerie.*

***Fantasies.*** Fantasies are plays that contain predominating elements of the unreal or the supernatural, although elements of comedy and tragedy may also be present. Examples of this type are *Peter Pan, High Tor, Damn Yankees,* and *Harvey.* In this type of play, the mood is usually whimsical and the general atmosphere tends to be happy, since a fantasy typically presents life as people would like it to be.

***Folk plays.*** This type presents people and customs of a certain locality. They may be either serious or humorous. Usually, characters speak in dialect and wear costumes typical of their environment. *The Happy Time* and *Papa Is All* represent this type of play.

***Allegories.*** Not widely popular today, the allegory seeks to teach a lesson. Allegories are similar in theme to the Miracle and Morality plays.

## Forms of drama

As used in this text, form refers to the literary form in which the play is written. The more important forms that will be considered here are: (a) prose, (b) verse, (c) musical, and (d) chorus or narrator.

**Prose.** In prose dialogue, the playwright makes his characters talk in the ordinary language of people as they actually speak or write. There is an absence of either poetical rhythm or rhyme. The great majority of contemporary plays are in prose.

**Verse.** A small proportion of contemporary plays is composed in verse which may be either rhymed or blank. The Greek authors of tragedy wrote in verse. Shakespeare used both blank verse and prose in his plays and, on occasion, employed a rhymed couplet. Examples of modern verse plays are Maxwell Anderson's *Elizabeth the Queen,* and Christopher Fry's *The Lady's Not For Burning.*

**Musical.** In this type of play the musical numbers are not extraneous to the plot but actually further the movement of the story. In recent years a number of musicals have had success on the Broadway stage: *My Fair Lady,* a straight musical comedy (picture on page 500); *Oklahoma,* a musical folk play (picture on page 428); *DuBarry Was a Lady,* a musical farce; and *Finian's Rainbow,* a musical fantasy.

**Chorus or narrator.** The singing or speaking chorus may be used by the playwright to carry or explain portions of the story. The use of the chorus was standard in the Greek drama and is on occasion used today. T. S. Eliot employed this technique in *Murder in the Cathedral.* (See page 427). Most musicals make use of a singing chorus.

A single narrator may be used in the same fashion as a chorus either to describe the action or to comment upon it. Perhaps the best known modern examples of this technique are to be found in *Our Town* and *The Glass Menagerie.*

## Styles of drama

It is impossible in a general speech text to begin to describe all of the styles of production that have been introduced with varying success in the field of drama. You will be introduced here to two major styles; your teacher may well wish to carry this topic further.

**Romantic style.** The romantic style of production presents an idealized version of life. Such emphasis tended to provide relief from the sordid and tragic happenings of everyday life. Examples of plays that lend themselves to romantic production are *Cyrano de Bergerac, Peter Pan, The Importance of Being Earnest,* and *Dracula.*

**Realistic style.** The original goal of the realistic production was to present so far as possible an actual segment of real life on the stage, complete in every detail. Super realism came to be an end in and of itself. At present, the trend is more in the direction of a selective realism, in which, although the total effect is one of reality, there is not extreme obsession with detail. Plays frequently produced in a realistic style are *Front Page, Dial M for Murder,* and *There Shall Be No Night.*

## ACTIVITIES

1. For each type, form, and style of drama mentioned, supply at least one title of a play not already mentioned in this chapter that would fit into that category. Compile your lists to keep as a permanent record.
2. List recent motion pictures, television plays, and stage plays and classify them according to tragedy, comedy, or serious drama.

# Drama and You

Thus far you have been looking at drama for the purpose of understanding and appreciating the part that the theater has played in the role of mankind and in your life as well. Now look forward to the part that you can play in the world of the theater.

You can, of course, read or attend plays and imagine that you are one of the characters as you share his experiences and emotions. Many, however, may prefer to participate more actively in creating a play for others to watch. If so, you can choose any of these three areas of participation: (1) acting, (2) production, and (3) writing.

## Your role as an actor

As you turn to the acting area in speech, you must continue to use some of the familiar principles of speaking that you have already learned. Yet you must also add some new techniques to your present skills.

In the materials in this text on expressing your own ideas, you were advised to speak naturally, clearly, and forcefully. The major emphasis was on projecting your best self sincerely and effectively. You learned the importance of vocal and bodily expression in transmitting ideas to your audience. These same points were also emphasized in interpreting reading selections.

In acting, the same elements of appropriateness and forcefulness are present. So also are sincerity of interpretation, clearness of speaking, and suitability of bodily expression. If you disregard these essentials in the theater, your acting will seem artificial and unrealistic.

In acting, the main departure from speaking skills is in the methods which you use to create a role. In speaking, you must be yourself; in acting, you must be somebody else. Your ability to create real people on the stage depends upon your ability to create illusions. In other words, you must be able to forget that you are John or Mary and remember that you are Scrooge or Peter Pan. You must employ stage techniques.

**Qualities of the actor.** There are ten qualities ending in "tion" which constitute the "ten commandments" of a successful actor. One is as important as the other, since each must be present before the illusion is firmly established in the minds of the audience.

***Interpretation.*** This quality means the ability to read lines so as to stimulate in your audience the moods and ideas intended by the playwright. Your ability to do so depends largely upon your ability to form an understanding of the play as a whole and of the relationship of your particular role to the play. You will get this understanding from the play itself, from the stage directions given by the author, and from the suggestions made by your director.

***Memorization.*** This is a must in acting unless the entire cast is doing a reading version of a play. Unless you memorize lines accurately, you may ruin a play by throwing your fellow-actors off cue. Memorizing the last lines of a speech is especially important since actors listen for those lines as their cue to speak. If you change or omit your last line, you can only hope that others on stage can make up lines (ad lib) quickly. If you cannot memorize, you belong in the audience instead of on the stage.

***Characterization.*** This is the art of portraying a definite person. Many people may be able to interpret and understand what a character is *supposed* to be like, but still be unable to *project* the character adequately or accurately. Such failure is similar in nature to the inadequacy which many of you experience in reading aloud those selections which you can understand and enjoy only when you read them silently.

One of the most difficult problems of the actor is that of getting a true picture of the person whom he is supposed to imitate. For example, playing Lady Macbeth as a weak character dominated by her husband would destroy completely the illusion of the dominant, ruthless woman which Shakespeare intended her to be. Your greatest difficulties in interpreting roles may occur with minor characters rather than with the main ones.

***Imagination.*** This is the indispensable attribute of any actor in creating a definite and believable character. Imagination gives you the ability to visualize and understand your stage character—to look like him, to walk, talk, and act like him. You will be able to sense the emotions of a character and imagine how that character would respond. In fact, you set up in your mind such a real picture of your stage character that you lose your own identity and become that person in your actions and reactions. Without imagination, you have only a hazy idea instead of a clear-cut image; you may not even be sure of the person's age; your characterization will be inconsistent and you will be playing the role as yourself. This is one of the main weaknesses of amateur actors. They try to imagine how *they* would respond instead of how the person in the play would respond. You can be taught mechanical forms and techniques, but you must develop imagination and emotional expression. These are inner qualities which you must learn to stimulate.

At the second or third rehearsal of a play, the actors are still reading their parts and writing in directions for stage business and stage movement. *(Fuller/Rapho Guillumette Pictures)*

***Exaggeration.*** You must be able to magnify certain characteristics in order to "get across" the footlights. On the stage you represent a specific person with definite personality traits that must stand out vividly in the minds of the audience. For example, you may be a giggly young person, in which case the giggly trait would require exaggeration; otherwise, you would be an average young person.

The extent of exaggeration is always a problem, but one which can usually be settled by the director and other members of the cast during rehearsals. Too much exaggeration is called over-playing; too little is under-playing. Either extreme will damage your role, although in farces and humorous melodramas some degree of over-acting is a requisite. Over-acting in comedy, tragedy, and serious dramas may easily change them into farces. Under-playing robs the role of its distinguishing qualities and makes the person seem average, or even worse, weak and uninteresting. As you can see, establishing a true character requires just the right amount of exaggeration—not too little, not too much.

***Cooperation.*** As an actor you must work agreeably with your director and other members of your cast. Think of your cast as a team and the director as a coach and then apply all of the standards of successful teamwork. It takes only one disgruntled or unprepared member of a cast to ruin any performance. If you dislike your role and refuse to work hard on it, if you fail to memorize lines or take directions carefully, or if you miss rehearsals, you do not deserve to be a member of the cast.

Cooperation includes such important actions on your part as (a) accepting pleasantly the role assigned, (b) being prompt for all rehearsals, (c) writing all stage directions in your book, (d) memorizing lines by the time your director sets as a deadline, (e) playing "in character" during each rehearsal, (f) being quiet and attentive during rehearsal time, (g) receiving criticisms or suggestions graciously, (h) listening for cues and being ready for entrances, (i) showing courtesy to the director and the cast, and (j) fulfilling all responsibilities delegated to you.

***Coordination.*** To be coordinated is to function harmoniously. To represent a character, your entire body must reflect the personality that you are creating. Every limb and muscle, every facial expression, and every sound of your voice must work together as you stand, sit, move, and speak. The ability to coordinate is especially necessary and difficult in portraying elderly people. You can gain perfect coordination only after you have studied your character thoroughly enough to establish a detailed image in your mind.

***Observation.*** The ability to observe can help you form definite mental images by providing you with many examples of different types and ages of people. Watch for people who appear to resemble in real life the ones you are to portray on the stage, observe their appearance in detail, and notice mannerisms which help to depict your stage character. All such observations enable you to give the many realistic touches so vital in making a character believable and natural.

***Imitation.*** This is the sequel to observation. After observing a person resembling your role, make mental or written notes about his appearance, his manner of movement, his way of speaking, and any special mannerisms that would add to your characterization. Practice imitating what you have observed. Much of this practicing should be done first at home and, preferably, in front of a mirror.

***Concentration.*** When you concentrate you keep your thinking centered on one thought or one action without allowing yourself to be sidetracked. In acting, you find the ability to concentrate useful for several purposes. First, you learn your lines faster if your attention is on your job. Second, you develop a consistent characterization if you focus your thinking on your role all of the time that you are on stage. You must stay in character, not only while you are speaking, but also when others are speaking. As a speaker, you are constantly attuned to reactions from those on stage; as a listener, you should be reacting to the lines or actions of the others. In other words, reacting is as necessary in giving life to your character as acting. Rehearsals give you the chance to practice reacting so that it will seem natural on the night of performance. The final benefit of concentration is that nothing can distract you during a performance—not even the arrival of late comers, the siren of an ambulance, the breaking of a lamp on stage, or the failure of an actor to make an entrance on time.

**Techniques of the actor.** To create the illusion of your character you must be able to move, speak, and look like him. Only by mastery of the techniques of pantomiming, speaking, and costuming, will you be able to achieve this goal. These are the three key techniques of the actor.

***Creating illusion through pantomime.*** The literal meaning of pantomime is "all-imitating." In the days of silent movies, pantomimic action had to convey most of the actor's feeling while subtitles explained the plot. Many television personalities use pantomime on their shows. Through facial expression and attention to minute details, they can portray an episode vividly without uttering a word.

In learning to act, training in pantomime is essential. Without the proper pantomimic reaction to accompany words spoken on the stage, acting can convey little meaning or, even worse, the wrong meaning. In real life, people do more than just say words. They use gestures, move about as they speak, stand in a certain way, and reflect in their facial expression what they are thinking or feeling. Unless this natural bodily movement and facial reaction is present on the stage as you speak, your character will resemble a talking statue.

In order to achieve realistic pantomimic effects, you must pay attention to small details, you must be accurate, and you must exaggerate the actions and facial expressions which carry the meaning. Watch experienced actors on television and notice how they carefully supply the minute details of every action. For example, they give the illusion of weight if they are carrying a trunk; they open and close the imaginary car door; they chew food and swallow

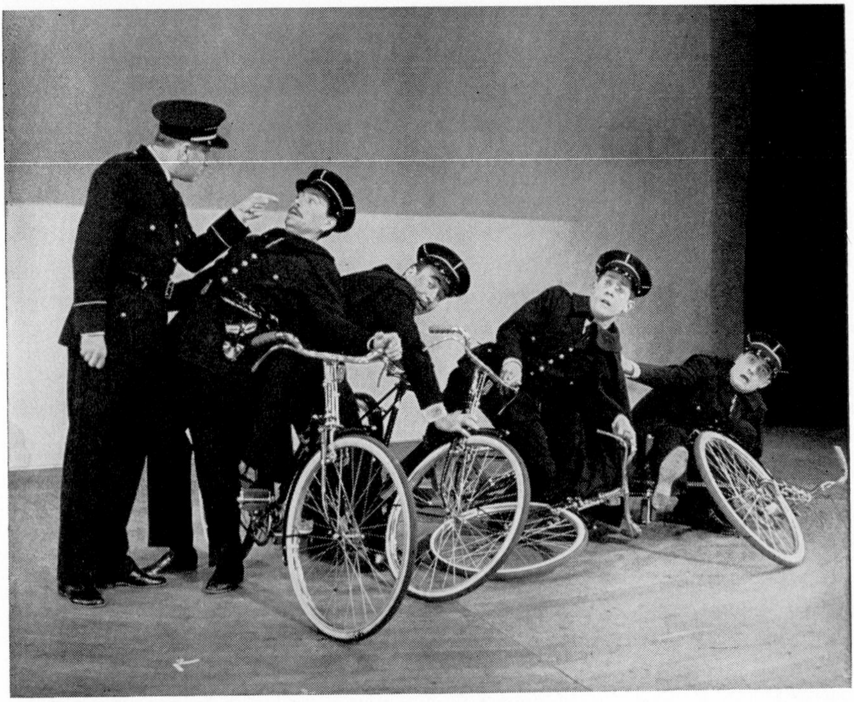

Many hilarious situations are portrayed solely by pantomime in the French comedy, *La Plume de ma Tante*—long popular on Broadway. *(Friedman-Abeles)*

it. They are also careful about keeping imaginary objects the same size and in the same place, which is essential in creating accuracy. The final characteristic of the skilled pantomimist is his use of exaggeration. By watching the best pantomimists, you can learn many valuable techniques.

How can you achieve the same type of realism? First, observe people in action. Watch them carefully, analyze some of their outstanding mannerisms, and then practice imitating them. Practice at home any actions that you want to portray in pantomime. Hold a cup in your hand, pick up a heavy trunk, eat a sandwich, or get dressed. The secret of imitation is having something real to imitate. Find the real activity and then practice imitating it in front of a mirror. Do it first with props and then do it without props. An ideal method is to arrange a room with real furniture for your first rehearsals and to use real props. Such planning in rehearsal enables you to create a realistic setting for your audience during your performance. This type of practicing eliminates such common blunders as washing dishes in the stove, cooking in the sink, entering the room through the icebox, or walking through tables and chairs.

Accuracy implies consistency in all details of arrangement and in size. Unless you keep a consistent idea in your own mind, you cannot hope to create a consistent picture for your audience. Accuracy also implies completeness of details as opposed to vagueness. Aimless movements which merely suggest an action are not sufficient. If you are driving a car, for example, you must get into the car, start the car, drive the car, and stop it. This requires accurate use of the hands and feet as well as knowledge of the mechanical features of driving. If you are holding something in your hand such as a purse, a box of popcorn, or an umbrella, you cannot use that hand until you have disposed of what you were holding. These are only a few of the details which the beginner frequently forgets in completing actions.

Exaggeration, the final step in creating realistic pantomime, is especially necessary in conveying meaning through facial expression. When the audience depends entirely on visual images, those images must be enlarged to create a realistic impression. The size of the room usually determines the amount of exaggeration necessary. In large auditoriums, many expressions are lost unless you have the ability to exaggerate forcefully.

## ACTIVITIES

### SCENES FOR ONE

1. Stand, sit, or walk to portray the following situations:
   A woman with many bundles on a crowded bus
   A football player ready for the kick-off
   A basketball player dribbling the ball or throwing for a basket
   A baseball pitcher in action; a catcher in action
   An old lady trying to put something breakable on the top shelf
   A young boy waiting in line at the movie
   An excited spectator at an athletic event
   A displeased shopper talking to a salesgirl
   A person watching a mystery play
   A student disgusted with his grade card
   An exhausted shopper waiting for a bus
   An automobile driver who has been stopped for speeding
   A clock-watcher in a study hall
   A girl wearing high heels for the first time
2. Make up an additional list of people and situations and take turns in pantomining them.
3. In the following pantomimic scenes, work out small plots involving complications in which imaginary characters become involved. Prepare a diagram of the setting including doors, furniture, and props.
   A boy or girl doing homework
   A man cooking while his wife is on vacation

A shy boy trying to persuade a girl to dance with him at the school dance
A woman ironing
A teacher conducting a study hall
A woman trying on hats
A baby sitter with four children
A girl dusting a shelf containing valuable china
A boy or girl in the school cafeteria
A student in the school library
A waiter in a restaurant
A magician appearing on an amateur show

4. Write out a short episode with a good beginning, an interesting course of events, and a surprise-type ending. Prepare a stage set. Present your pantomime to the class to see how many in the class can follow the story easily.
5. Select one of the leading pantomimists on television and try to imitate one of his pantomimes.

### SCENES FOR TWO

1. Select a partner and work together in planning, practicing, and presenting the following scenes in pantomime:

   A mother and daughter shopping for a party dress
   A son trying to persuade his father to give him the car and extra money
   A father trying to entertain his daughter's boy friend
   A teacher giving a piano lesson to a naughty little girl
   A husband trying to teach his wife to drive the car

2. Develop a two-person situation of your own to pantomime in class.

### SCENES FOR GROUPS

1. Work in groups of any size and prepare the following pantomimes:

   A family watching a television show
   A club meeting
   A family group having its picture taken
   Patients in a doctor's office
   A group in a train, bus, or airline terminal
   A study hall
   A school orchestra in rehearsal
   The staff of a school newspaper meeting a deadline
   A group summoned to see the principal
   A back-stage scene on opening night of the school play
   A school bus
   A family or class reunion

2. Select a situation of your own to pantomime.

The previous activities have been completely silent. Perhaps, as you have tried these, you have discovered that it is difficult to keep group pantomimes in particular from becoming confusing. One way to control this confusion is to use a narrator who actually tells the story as it progresses on the stage. He poses as an on-looker and describes what he sees. His descriptive narration contains all cues for entrances, business on stage, and exits. This method makes for perfect timing of all stage business and presents those ideas necessary to full understanding but difficult to pantomime.

***Creating illusion through speech.*** Your manner of speaking must harmonize with your character. Even though your make-up, costuming, and bodily movement all combine to create the illusion of a crotchety old person, for example, the illusion of age is shattered the moment you speak sweetly in an average young tone of voice. Since the usual teen-age voice is immature, you may have difficulty in playing various older roles. With practice and effort, however, you will be able to express many different moods and types of personalities. It is important for you to realize early in an acting career that illusions of character are created through listening as well as seeing.

When you listen to radio plays, the speech and voice furnish the only clues to character. You cannot see whether the person is old or young, ugly or beautiful, but you make up a mental picture on the basis of how the speaker sounds.

When you are assigned a role, study the part thoroughly in order to determine age, type, and general personality traits. After deciding on a true picture of your stage personality, listen to people who resemble in type and age such a character. Listening to similar characters on radio and television often helps you to establish an appropriate manner of speaking.

Playwrights usually give special clues for you to follow on certain lines. These descriptive clues are placed in parentheses and are inserted to give the author's interpretative directions. To ignore them or to fail in expressing them exactly weakens the lines.

In the activities which follow, observe directions carefully and evaluate your efforts fairly. If possible, use a tape recorder.

## ACTIVITIES

1. The words in parentheses are typical of the descriptive clues inserted by playwrights. You are to say the lines according to the directions.

   *(bellowing)* Get out of here! And don't you ever dare come back!
   *(truculently)* Don't move or I'll break every bone in your body.
   *(sternly)* Do as you're told, young man!
   *(frightened)* Who's there? Don't come near me . . . don't move!
   *(sotto voce)* Don't say a word. I'll handle this young whipper-snapper.
   *(eagerly)* You mean I may see him now?

*(stunned)* But you can't possibly mean that!
*(outraged)* You mean you let your own daughter defy you!
*(defiantly)* You'll never destroy my reputation in this town!
*(scandalized)* Well! I never! Did you hear that, Melinda?
*(vehemently)* You can't stop me this time! I'm going to win this election!
*(irritably)* What did you say?
*(curiously)* What did you say?
*(petulantly)* Please, please, let me buy it.
*(soothingly)* I'm sure you mean well, dear, but let's talk things over sensibly.
*(shyly)* Would you like to go to the dance with me?
*(ominously)* You're asking for trouble, big boy!
*(coyly)* Oh, really? But I just love dancing with you, too.
*(nervously)* I didn't do it . . . honest, I didn't . . . just ask my mother . . . she'll tell you.
*(hysterically happy)* I've won it! I've won the prize! Did you hear . . . I won it!
*(hysterical with grief)* Save me! Save me! I didn't mean to kill him! He's my son . . . why would I kill him? Don't you hear me . . . he's my son!
*(aghast)* Oh! He's fainted!
*(sheepishly)* Well, yes, I admit that I copied off his paper, but I didn't mean to.
*(adamantly)* You have my answer.
*(querulously)* Why are you always picking on me? Can't I do anything to please you?
*(dubiously)* You say that you were at home on the night this man was slain?
*(condescending tone)* And what did you say your name is?
*(drowsily)* What did you say?
*(turning it over in his mind)* I just might be interested in buying that land.
*(with feigned surprise)* Oh! I didn't know that you would be here!
*(wistfully)* How I would like to see my home just once more!
*(pretending to be horrified)* You aren't a detective, are you?
*(in dulcet tones)* We'd love to have you stay with us.
*(dolefully)* Gumdrops! Nothing to eat all day long but gumdrops.
*(airily)* Okay, wise guy. See you around.
*(dogmatically)* The only way to meet force is with force.

2. Switch directions in the lines. For example, use first direction for sixth line and vice versa. Notice the difference in interpretation.
3. Make up a short speech (one paragraph) or find one to read. Through changes in vocal style, read the *same* speech to represent the following character types:

| | |
|---|---|
| a dignified clergyman | a kind, elderly person |
| a gruff truck driver. | an irritable, elderly person |
| a spoiled youngster | a stern parent |
| a frightened child | a grief-stricken parent |

Actors know the psychological advantage of wearing, during rehearsal, the costumes intended for their roles. *(Monkmeyer)*

***Creating illusion through style of dress.*** It is easier for an audience to believe that you are a hobo, for example, when you dress like one than when you appear in good clothes. It is also easier for you to portray a character when you dress according to type. Donning a policeman's uniform helps you psychologically to feel more authority. The outfit that you wear, therefore, helps the audience to visualize the person that you are portraying and helps you to feel more like that person.

Costumes should be selected in harmony with the type of character, the age of the person, and the period of the play, if they are to create the illusion desired. Period plays usually present the most difficult problems unless you can make, borrow, or rent costumes. You need to compare your costumes with pictures or descriptions of costumes worn during the same era as your play setting to be sure that yours are authentic.

**Learning your stage environment.** Before you can present your portrayal on stage you need to become familiar with stage terminology in order to understand directions and to communicate with the cast, crew, and director. You cannot be an outstanding actor all by yourself unless you want to give only monologues. Turn your attention now to some of the on-stage habits which will make you a good trouper.

The stage is the acting area. It may be slightly elevated above the audience as you find it in traditional theaters; it may be floor level as you think of it in classrooms or other informal places; or it may be a lower level as you find it in presentation of theater-in-the-round or arena theater. In the last type, the seating arrangement is usually elevated enabling the audience to look down upon the acting area. In the conventional proscenium stage, three boundaries encompass the acting area. The fourth boundary is an imaginary one—open toward the audience for viewing purposes.

The accompanying diagram with acting areas clearly marked will explain the first terms that an actor must add to his vocabulary.

UPSTAGE

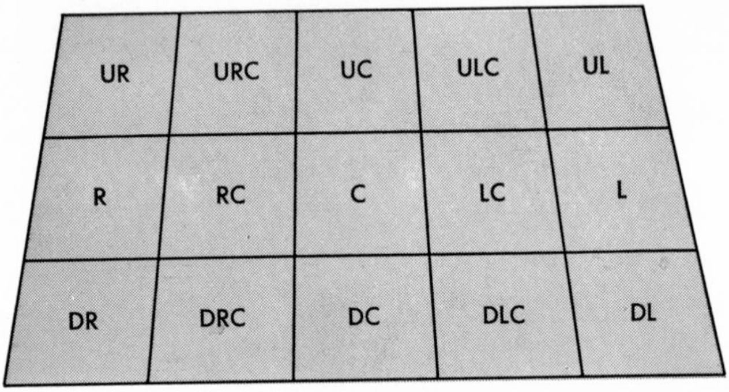


DOWNSTAGE

In the diagram you will note that UPSTAGE is the area against the back wall; DOWNSTAGE is the area closest to the audience; CENTER is the middle of the stage; and LEFT and RIGHT always refer to the *actor's* left and right *as he is facing the audience.* The abbreviations for the fifteen small acting areas are used to make it easier for you to write directions for stage movement in your play script. UR means UP RIGHT, DL means DOWN LEFT, DRC means DOWN RIGHT CENTER, and so on.

When you are given directions for movement during rehearsals, write them in your script. Use pencil so that changes can be made easily. Indicate a CROSS from one area to another with an X. Exit may be abbreviated to XIT. Often a play script calls for a cross *above* or *below* a piece of furniture or an actor. ABOVE means BEHIND and BELOW means IN FRONT OF the object or person.

## ACTIVITIES

1. Mark off an area to represent a stage with the same number of acting areas as there are in the diagram. Take turns in finding your places on the stage according to these directions:
   a. Enter UR; X to DLC; X to URC; X to DR; X to C and exit UC.
   b. Enter DR and move to different areas in the following order: RC, UR, R, DRC, DC, C, LC, L, UL, ULC, and exit UC.
   c. Work out a series of directions like the ones above.
2. In the diagram below, doorways and furniture are shown. Study the diagram closely, arrange a stage (use chairs or screens in place of large furniture), and follow the stage movement indicated. Five persons will work together. Give yourselves numbers and follow the directions indicated for your number.

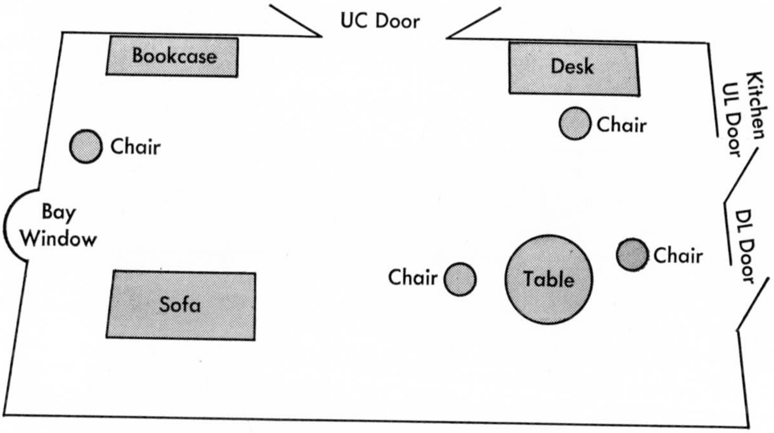


**DIRECTIONS**

No. 1. *Enter UC door, X above sofa to bay window, then sit in chair by window*
No. 2. *Enter UC door, X to chair R of table and sit*
No. 3. *Enter DL door, X below table to sofa and sit*
No. 4. *Enter UL door, sit in chair facing desk*
No. 1. *X above sofa, sit in chair L of table*
No. 5. *Enter UC door, X to bookcase, look for a book, find it and sit in chair by bay window*
No. 2. *X above sofa to bay window, look out, then talk to No. 5*
No. 3. *X below sofa to desk, talk to No. 4*
No. 4. *X below No. 3, Xit UC door*
No. 3. *Xit UL to kitchen*
No. 2. *X R of sofa and stand staring toward R*
No. 1. *X below sofa, sit on sofa, and sneeze three times*
No. 2. *Sit on sofa, offer handkerchief to No. 1*
No. 5. *X to desk and begin looking frantically for something*
No. 4. *Enter hurriedly UC door, yell "Fire!"*

*All Xit rapidly through UC door.*

**The vocabulary of the actor.** The stage has a colorful language all of its own. Many of the terms below are essential to your knowledge when you work with people of the theater; others may not be completely indispensable but are often heard.

## THE ACTOR'S GLOSSARY

**Ad lib:** To make up lines or to move without definite cue.

**Amateur:** A person who works for the theater without pay; a nonprofessional.

**Anticlimax:** An incident of less importance than the previous one—usually the climax.

**Apron:** The part of the stage between the front curtain and the footlights.

**Asbestos:** The curtain between the stage and the audience; made of asbestos or other fire-proof material.

**Baby spot:** Small spotlight.

**Backdrop:** Curtain hiding back wall which may be painted to represent skyline or any other scene supposed to be visible beyond the windows and doors in upstage area.

**Backstage:** All areas behind stage curtain such as dressing rooms, switchboard, and storage space.

**Batten:** Long strip of material, usually lumber or pipe, above the stage on which scenery is fastened.

**Black out:** To cut off all lights at once, producing total darkness.

**Blackouts:** Brief sketches with surprise endings; so named because lights are blacked out at end instead of having the curtain lowered.

**Block:** To hide a fellow-actor from view by getting in front of him; also used to describe the action of blocking yourself from view by hiding behind a person or furniture.

**Blocking a scene:** Deciding on all of the movement of the characters during a scene.

**Borderlights (borders):** Strips of individual reflectors hanging above the stage to provide overhead lighting effects; may have a variety of colors to produce desired effects.

**Building a scene:** Increasing tempo and force in a scene to reach a strong climax.

**Business:** Any action done on stage by players other than movement from one area to another; knitting, eating, smoking, reading, and playing with objects are examples.

**Byplay:** Side action used to make scenes seem natural while other actors are speaking.

**Call board:** Bulletin board containing schedule of rehearsals and notices.

**Call boy:** The person who notifies actors of their entrances.

**Cat walk:** Narrow ledge near overhead lights used by electricians.

**Character part:** Any role which requires an actor to change his natural habits of speaking or acting.

**Clip cues:** To come in with lines before the cue speech has been finished.

**Cue:** The final words of a previous speech or a bit of stage business which give you the signal to begin speaking.

**Cue sheet:** A complete list of cues for light changes, sound effects, entrances, and any other special things requiring timing.

**Cyclorama (cyc):** Similar to the backdrop except that it is larger and may be curved in shape in order to surround the sides as well as the back wall.

**Dramatis personae:** The Latin term for cast of characters.

**Feed a part:** To increase the effect of another actor's part by making it seem funnier or more tragic through your reactions.

**Flat:** A tall screen made of wood and canvas, which is a unit section of flat scenery.

**Flies:** The space above stage where scenery can be removed from sight or "flown."

**Foots:** Footlights at the front of the stage.

**Frame an entrance:** To pause in entrance in order to attract attention.

**Gallery playing:** Playing out toward the audience instead of to the actors on stage.

**Go up on lines:** To forget your lines; sometimes called "ballooning" or "blowing."

**"Hamming":** To exaggerate acting to the point of being ridiculous.

**Hand props:** Any props such as letters that the actors carry on stage themselves.

**Hold:** To remain in position; to "freeze" action; used especially in "hold for laughs" or "hold a picture" until the audience has absorbed the full effect.

**Ingenue:** Young girl, innocent and unsophisticated, who carries the romantic interest.

**Juvenile:** Actor who portrays youthful male parts up to the age of about 25.

**Light plot:** A master plan for the lighting of a play showing each change of light cued to the script for each scene.

**Muffing:** Misreading a line, reading the wrong line, or missing a cue.

**Mugging:** Overacting in a part to capture attention.

**On a line with:** Keeping *on a line* with a fellow actor, at same distance from front of stage.

**Pace:** To regulate the timing of actions and speeches.

**Places:** The signal for actors to take their places before the curtain rises.

**Plant:** A person in the audience who works with the cast on stage; a member of the cast with definite lines and business.

**Plant a line:** To say a line with such emphasis that the audience will remember it later; sometimes called "pointing a line."

**Prop plot:** A list of all props arranged according to scenes or acts and according to position on stage.

**Properties (props):** All objects except scenery which are used on stage.

**Proscenium:** The wall which separates the stage from the auditorium;

the actual opening through the wall is known as the proscenium opening.

**Set:** A group of scenery units which indicate a single locale.

**Sides:** Pages of paper containing each actor's cues and lines with space for stage business to be written.

**Spirit gum:** A glue-like substance which is applied to the skin when mustaches or beards must be worn.

**Stage directions:** List of all movements and groupings on stage; not to be confused with stage business defined earlier.

**Stage whisper:** A semi-whispered type of speech used on the stage to suggest whispering, but actually loud enough to be heard by the audience.

**Step on a line:** To start talking before the previous speech is finished. Can be applied to laughs—"step on a laugh" is talking while the audience is still laughing.

**Strike:** Term meaning remove from stage; strike during scenes means removing objects, and strike at the end means tearing down the stage set.

**Take a call:** To take a curtain call or bow to the audience.

**Teaser:** The narrow overhead drapery which conceals the top of the stage and reduces height.

**Throw a line:** To repeat a cue to a fellow actor who has forgotten lines.

**Tormentors:** Flats or drapes at the sides behind the regular curtain.

**Trouper:** An experienced actor who puts the interests of the company ahead of his own.

**Understudy:** An actor who has studied lines and actions of another and who could take that person's place in an emergency.

**Upstaging:** Moving toward the back (upstage area), forcing fellow-actors to follow—with the result that their backs are to the audience and you have the advantage of facing front; a habit in great disrepute.

**Walk-on:** A bit part either with or without lines.

**Wings:** The official term for the space behind scenes on each side of the stage.

**Behavior habits for the actor.** Here is a list of acting habits for you to develop which will make it easier for your director to work with you and more likely that you will be asked to act again!

1. Stand still unless directed to move. Avoid fidgeting and aimless moving—a nervous actor can ruin an entire scene, especially a tense one.

2. Stand so that you do not block from view any other actors and you are not blocked from view yourself. Move to one side rather than huddling in groups.

3. Hold for laughs until the audience has almost finished laughing.

4. Be ready and waiting at your entrance at least five speeches ahead of cue.

5. Make your entrances and exits *in character.* Strike your character offstage before you enter and hold it when you exit until you are completely out of the wings.

6. Avoid laughing at your own lines or those of the others on stage (unless the script calls for such reaction). "Breaking up" in the middle of a scene is ruinous to a smooth performance.

7. If you forget lines, hold until the prompter gives you your line. Never, never lose character or look frantically in the direction of the prompter. Above all, *don't prompt each other!*

8. Keep away from off-stage props after they have been arranged. Don't remove or change any unless you check with the prop manager.

9. Stay out of the way when the set is being changed between scenes or acts.

10. Remain in your assigned place offstage so that you can be found. Don't clutter entrances and exits and don't slip out into the audience to watch the play!

## Your role in production

Many theatrically-minded people have no interest in appearing in front of the footlights, but get their pleasure from planning and putting on plays. They like to "run the show" or build the scenery or sell the tickets. Luckily for all concerned, the theater needs a variety of talents. In the theater, every person from the director to the usher is an important part of a large team which must work harmoniously together in presenting a smooth performance.

**Your role as director.** The director heads the team and is directly responsible for the success or failure of a show. It can be a case of "running the show" or "ruining the show." When you assume the role of director, therefore, you must be prepared to exercise certain talents.

***Specialized talents of the director.*** Your first talent, of course, must be leadership ability. As head of the team, you must be able to get along with everybody in the cast; furthermore, you should be able to make everybody on the team get along with each other. You need a calm disposition, a tactful approach, a friendly nature, and a real liking for people to be able to keep everything moving smoothly and everybody happy.

The second talent that you need is firmness. A director must be

"He's a great one for delegating responsibility." (Drawing by D. Fredon, © 1959 The New Yorker Magazine, Inc.)

respected and must be regarded as having final authority. You must keep the confidence of the cast by using a firm rein instead of hesitating about decisions, changing your mind frequently, and asking for help. If it is apparent to the cast that you are too easily influenced by what others think, instead of having convictions of your own, they will lose respect for your judgment.

Patience is a third valuable asset. Not only do you need it to get along with people, but you need patience in working out every small detail to the point of perfection. Much of the success of plays is due to the infinite care which a painstaking director takes in adding touches of stage business here and there, working on scenes to get the correct pacing, and insisting upon such details as harmonious blending of colors in furnishings, costumes, and lighting effects.

Akin to patience is imagination, the fourth talent every director needs. A creative imagination enables a director to *think* of the unusual; his patience helps him carry it out. Whereas the actor needs imagination to interpret his own role, the director needs the imagination to interpret all of the roles not only separately but in relation to each other. Early in rehearsal he must visualize the finished production in order that he can work steadily toward transforming imagination into a true-to-life situation on the stage.

Another talent—the final one to be considered here—is the ability to organize. Organizing your time and your duties provides you with the maximum time and conserves your energy. Inexperienced directors often discover that their most difficult problem is learning how to plan ahead in order to have everything taken care of by performance time. Perhaps some of you have seen the frazzled and frantic director on the night of production urging his cast to be calm while he races back and forth making last minute changes in the scenery, asking everyone to help him remember what he has forgotten, and drafting a person at the last minute to prompt or to run the curtain. Such inefficiency is not only hard on the director but it also incites fear and panic backstage. By planning ahead, you can arrange all of your tasks according to schedule and have no worries at the last minute. Before you can organize, however, you must know what a director is supposed to do.

***Duties of a director.*** The director is responsible for the entire production of a show. His assistants are known as a production staff. In some cases, the director handles everything from the selection of a play to the striking of the set; in other cases, he delegates much of the authority to his staff.

SELECTING A PLAY. High school plays should meet certain standards, the most important of which are:

1. The theme should be appropriate, with no reference to subjects or customs unacceptable to your community.
2. The play should be within the acting range of your group.
3. The play should be of interest to both the cast and the audience.
4. The play should be one that you can stage properly. Usually one-set plays are best suited for the average high school stage. Consider costuming problems as part of the staging limitations.
5. The play should be worthwhile. Regardless of the limitation in acting ability, select a play that is challenging and worth the efforts of all concerned in its production.

CHOOSING A CAST. If you keep your available actors in mind while selecting a play, much difficulty in casting will be eliminated. Steel yourself to any pressure exerted on you to show favoritism in casting. A play poorly cast is doomed before rehearsals start.

Whenever possible, choose your cast according to type. It is much easier to train an immature, fat boy with a changing voice to play the part of an immature, fat boy than to train him to be a dignified old gentleman. A person who is naturally slow-moving, easy-going, and quiet may have difficulty in becoming a vigorous, dynamic, and exuberant personality.

ORGANIZING A PRODUCTION STAFF. Directors save energy and time by delegating all non-acting aspects of production to a crew of assistants, known as the production staff. This staff includes:

1. Assistant Director
2. Stage Manager
3. Scenic Designer
4. Property Manager
5. Costume Manager
6. Make-up Manager
7. Manager of Lights and Sound Effects
8. Publicity Manager
9. Business Manager

In organizing this staff (a) choose each member before you start rehearsals and (b) choose people who are dependable, competent, and cooperative. It is impossible to do any effective rehearsing until you have a definite idea of the size and design of your stage set. Hence, work out staging details early enough so that costly changes will not have to be made later. Conferring early in the rehearsal stage with your staff enables them to have the time necessary to do a good job. The importance of beginning all preparation early cannot be over-emphasized—it is the one sure way of finishing on schedule.

PREPARING FOR REHEARSALS. Most of the brainwork in directing should be done before the first rehearsal. An efficient director follows a systematic procedure. First, he reads the play over and over until he is sure of the main plot and the recurring situations which help in its development. Plays have a certain number of highlight scenes—scenes which are outstanding. Each one is a bit more important than the previous one in building toward the climax. He should be able to point out to the cast the highlight scenes so that all can work together in building toward each scene and in making each successive scene top the previous one. If small scenes top the main scenes, the main plot is overshadowed by a series of minor scenes. In this event, you have a weak, loosely connected series of dull moments with no apparent continuous building of dramatic action toward the climax. Choose characters capable of carrying the main scenes, make your main characters aware of the scenes which must stand out, and then see to it that every peak does stand out above the previous ones.

Second, a director before going into rehearsals needs to gain an accurate understanding of each role and the relationship of each to the other. It is quite important to be able to discuss at the first rehearsal the part each character is to play so that each actor understands his own role and has an idea of how he fits into the entire picture.

Third, the director can save time by planning major stage movements and stage business in advance. The sooner you can get your actors on stage and moving around as they say their lines, the better your final performance will be.

CONDUCTING REHEARSALS. Begin all rehearsals on time and stop within a set period, unless it interrupts a scene in action. A cast will work harder to make every minute count if the director keeps to a tight working schedule. Every minute of rehearsal time is valuable and should be spent in practicing *planned* interpretation of lines and actions. The cast and the production staff like to know at the beginning where they are going, what is expected of them, the schedule to be followed, the time permitted for memorizing lines or completing other duties, and similar points. Plan a rehearsal schedule to post at the beginning. Include dates when lines must be memorized. Mark scenes which require the entire cast and those which need only a few members. A cast appreciates such a schedule since it permits each member to organize his own plans.

The first rehearsal period is an important one. This is your first chance to demonstrate that you know your job. Actors are quick to detect whether you mean business, whether you know what you are talking about or are bluffing, and whether or not they want to work with you. Most directors use the first period for making general announcements, stipulating what they expect in the way of attending rehearsals, memorizing lines, and meeting deadlines.

In the second and third rehearsals, block business and movement for the scenes assigned. Get your actors on stage with scripts and pencils in hand and, as they read, tell them where to enter, when and where to move, whether they stand or sit, and all other movements that you have planned for them. As you dictate movement they should write it in their scripts. Any business that you have planned should also be noted early. Stage business refers to activities, mannerisms, and gestures—the things an actor *does* on stage, whereas stage movement refers to entering, crossing, exiting, and any other forms of moving about from one place to another.

As soon as you have finished blocking a scene, rehearse it several times to fix the business and movement in mind. After this, actors can rehearse anywhere by themselves, following the directions you have given them. Since lines and action should be learned together, they must be started together.

In all rehearsals, you should mark off the acting space either with chalk or chairs. Designate all entrances and windows with screens, chairs, or drawings. Use whatever is available for furniture in the first few rehearsals, but be sure that each piece of furniture is in its place. As soon as possible, rehearse on the stage which you will use for the play and use the furniture intended for the play. Have several rehearsals in which the cast can get used to opening and closing doors, moving about the complete set, and handling all props which are already on stage or must be brought on stage.

In arranging furniture, be careful to maintain balance. All large pieces on one side, for example, will give a top-heavy effect. Think of balance also when you put pieces upstage and downstage. Crowding every large piece in the front leaves a lot of bare stage in the middle and makes it difficult to play important scenes downstage. Avoid straight lines by arranging chairs, divans, and tables at slight angles—slight enough to break straightness of line, but not enough to make the actors sit in profile. Keep all entrances free by placing furniture beside them instead of in front of them. Be careful that pieces of furniture which are the center of important action are downstage rather than upstage and are not blocked from view, but furniture should not be moved downstage so far that actors are forced to play behind it.

PLANNING FOR VARIETY. A directors' downfall may be monotony—monotony of furniture arrangement, color, grouping of characters, manner of speaking, and tempo. Every skillful director aims for variety in the final production.

## ◄ POINTERS THAT PAY OFF ►

1. Use different acting areas for important scenes. Shift from one area to another as long as you use areas that are visible.
2. Avoid having actors stand in straight lines, in semicircles, or in bunches by using triangular arrangements.
3. Provide relief from monotony through elevation. Use different stage levels—stairways, balconies, risers, or steps. You can get the effect of elevation by grouping actors of different heights, having some seated while others are standing, and using floor space or the arms of chairs.
4. When large groups are on stage, try separating them into smaller groups of three, four, or five individuals.
5. Balance players on stage to avoid crowded or top-heavy effects.
6. Keep players who are sharing scenes close enough together to permit a mutual intensity of emotion. Actors standing on opposite sides of a room cannot share a love scene or a fight. It is important also to have them standing in a position so that the audience can see the facial reactions of all concerned.

7. Have actors away from entrances when it is time for someone else to appear.

8. Avoid keeping actors planted in the same spot or having them in constant motion.

Monotony of speech occurs when one character talks at the same rate and tone or when the general pattern of speaking is very much the same. A cast composed of all heavy voices, all light, or all medium voices would produce a monotonous effect. The same is true when the general rate of speaking is slow. In casting, be alert for variety in voice. In rehearsing, you must insist upon it. Certain scenes require more loudness or less loudness, more force or less force, in order to give contrast. See that your actors regulate their speaking habits to harmonize with the mood.

Variation in tempo prevents monotony. Tempo is the speed or rate of movement of a scene. When actors speak and move slowly, a scene moves slowly; when they quicken their speaking and actions, a scene moves quickly. Serious scenes reflecting deep emotion and tragic development should move slowly, whereas light, cheerful comedies move rapidly. As a director you should decide first the general tempo of a play.

Most amateur shows move too slowly, and change tempo too erratically. Many Broadway shows when produced by high school casts run at least half an hour longer than they did on Broadway. You can usually correct improper pacing by listening for those who are responsible. Being too slow in picking up cues can cause a whole scene to drop. Often only a moment's pause before a cue is picked up will make a scene drag and seem boring. If all of the cast is guilty, a scene might easily last five minutes longer than it should. By discovering the one or ones who are slow, you can quickly get the scene moving.

A few final tips will help you in getting your cast ready for a smooth performance:

1. Give your actors definite movements and insist that they follow them accurately; otherwise, stage pictures will be ruined.

2. Movement should be motivated to seem natural. Find reasons for actors to cross from one place to another, to sit, or to rise.

3. Movement should be free from awkwardness.

4. Movement should be timed with the lines and adapted to the tempo of the scene.

5. Encourage actors to use their own imagination in developing stage business, but have all business set before the performance.

6. Suggest interpretation of lines to actors instead of reading lines for them. Explain how the character is supposed to feel or what he must be thinking and try to get the actor to understand sufficiently to think

and feel for himself. You don't want actors to talk like you; you want them to talk like the characters they are portraying.

7. Insist upon enough voice projection for everyone to be heard in the last row.

8. Explain that the play is on stage and that everyone in the cast must be deeply involved with what is going on there and should not even be aware of the audience. When an audience can feel as if it is eavesdropping, the cast is giving a superb performance!

9. Give your cast at least four rehearsals complete with props and at least one dress rehearsal with make-up. It is advisable to have more than one rehearsal in which they wear their stage clothing, but make-up is needed only for testing under lights.

10. Train actors to use their upstage arm in gesturing and to refrain from covering their faces while speaking: to make turns toward the audience rather than away from it; and to ease into position instead of turning sharply.

Every director knows the importance of getting along with his production staff, especially those who run the show backstage. If you have had complete cooperation during rehearsal time with your crew, you will be able to sit in the audience and enjoy the show on the night of performance. When everyone on the crew understands his duties and carries them out satisfactorily, you can feel sure that you have fulfilled your duties as a director on stage and off stage.

**Your role on the production staff.** Do you like to build scenery, write news items, or work with make-up? Are you interested in art, in electricity, or in making costumes? If so, the world of the theater has a place for you. If you are dependable and experienced, you can probably act as manager; if you have had little experience but are eager to work and have talent, you should be able to work on the crew which each manager chooses to assist him.

***Assistant director.*** This position calls for a person who is regular in attending rehearsals and who is not afraid of work. In some cases, the assistant is primarily a prompter who has all stage movement recorded in his prompt book and all cues marked for entrances, lights, sound effects, and curtain. During rehearsals and the nights of performance, he can take the place of the director backstage.

A director may use assistants to conduct rehearsals in case he must be absent or wishes to work with a small group in a certain scene. Assistants often double for missing actors during rehearsal; also, some of them have learned lines so well that they can actually go on for an actor in case of emergency.

***Stage manager.*** Ordinarily, the stage manager's duties are limited to setting the stage. That includes arranging all furniture, hanging pictures, putting up any special decorations, and dressing the stage. It also involves removing pieces from the set between scenes and checking before each curtain to see whether everything is exactly in place. Every efficient manager has a chart with each piece of furniture marked according to scenes. He also assigns his crew of helpers to specific jobs before the final rehearsals in order that furniture can be shifted rapidly and correctly.

In small groups, the stage manager often is assigned other duties such as preparing and running all sound effects and even building the stage set.

***Scenic designer.*** In large professional productions, the designer usually makes a drawing of the set, plans color combinations, and works as a combined artist and architect. Although the title of scenic designer is frequently used in amateur productions, don't let it mislead you—you should still be prepared to use a hammer and a paint brush!

Consult the director to find out what kind of set he has in mind. Sometimes, a director wants to design his own set and will give you a rough sketch to follow. Others may expect you to use your own

If you have an artistic flair for scenic design, you may prefer to work from atop a stepladder rather than from a spot before the footlights. *(Monkmeyer)*

artistic ability and submit a drawing made to scale before rehearsals start. A setting should always be in keeping with the place, time, and mood of the play. Regardless of expenditure, your planning should be interesting, attractive, and in good taste, as one of the first things an audience notices is the stage set. If this shows artistic workmanship and if it blends well with the central idea and the characters of the play, it will be admired.

Certain colors help to create atmosphere. Warmth and cheerfulness are reflected by such colors as red, orange, yellow, and certain shades of brown. Coldness and tragic situations call for cool colors such as green, gray, blue, and purple. Beige and gray are neutral shades which are generally safe to use as background. You can also add warm or cold colors in the furnishings, costumes, and in the lighting effects. By using different colors in lighting, you can indicate many changes in time, setting, and mood.

If you are limited to drapes and screens, settle for black, gray, or neutral shades. Use heavy material such as duvetyn or velour rather than a lightweight, flimsy material. Cotton fabrics and unbleached muslin can be used, but they should be lined to give body and shape.

Backing is necessary in any set. Backing is an incomplete bit of scenery placed behind openings—doors and windows—in the regular set to give the illusion of additional rooms, gardens, buildings, and so on, beyond the set. Backing gives added proportions to the stage and keeps the audience from seeing bare walls through openings. You may draw an outdoor scene, the wall of a neighboring house, a street with a lamp post, a skyline, or anything else appropriate to the setting of the play. Flats, screens, curtains or a cyclorama can be used for backing.

If you have the money and a crew of carpenters and painters, the most durable and satisfactory set is made of flats. Flats are light but sturdy frames of lumber covered with canvas or heavy muslin tacked on one side. White pine, spruce and fir are the best kinds of framing wood. The usual frame is made of 1 by 3 inch strips of lumber; the usual size is 12 feet high and 5 feet 9 inches wide. The height is important because the flat should hide the great expanse of ceiling and should rise above the heads of the actors. The average set of flats contains, in addition to straight wall flats, two door flats, two window flats, and a fireplace flat.

***Property manager.*** If you like scavenger hunts, you should enjoy being a property manager because your main job is hunting for objects which are often difficult to find. As soon as you are appointed "prop" manager, pick a crew of helpers and make a list of properties needed. Properly prepared scripts contain such lists arranged according to scenes and acts. Be sure to check later on with the director to see if he has added or cut any.

The actors can usually be responsible for personal props such as canes, glasses, or luggage. You will have to confer with the stage manager and the scenic designer to be sure which they list as furnishings and intend to supply. All other items are your responsibility.

You can avoid confusion and possible disaster by organizing your props and having them at a definite place at the right time. The easiest method is to have a small table at each entrance containing all props which are carried in through that entrance. Station one of your crew at the table with a list of the articles and the names of the actors who will need them. At the end of each scene, have the designated crew member remove all not needed any more and check to be sure that he has everything needed for the next scene. Your final responsibility is to return all borrowed articles in good condition to their original owners. If you take care of props, you will keep your borrowing credit for future productions.

***Costume manager.*** In many plays, special costumes have to be assembled—either borrowed, rented, or made. Western plays, folk plays, or plays set in a particular period or locale require special attention.

Costumes help in establishing character types. Costumes should fit the personality as well as the body. Select costumes, therefore, with the characters in mind. They can and should reveal social position, age, occupation, and disposition, as well as historic era, geographic location, and even the time of day or year.

Generally speaking, costumes should be becoming. Avoid choosing colors that clash with actors' complexions, with pieces of furniture on which they may sit, or with the costumes of other actors who appear in the same scene. This applies to the fit and style of an outfit as well as to its color. Nothing adds to the self-consciousness and discomfort of an actor more than unbecoming and ill-fitting clothes.

The costume manager is responsible for having costumes look neat and well-pressed for every performance, for storing them between performances, and for returning in good condition any that have been borrowed or rented.

***Make-up manager.*** This might seem like an easy, fun-type position, but there is much more to the art of theatrical make-up

The artistry of make-up requires imagination, exactness, and patience to create a successful illusion of characterization. *(Faris/Black Star)*

than dabbing on some powder and paint. Make-up requires exact knowledge which you acquire through experience or from a special course in school.

Make-up serves two functions: (1) to accentuate features so that they can be seen easily even under strong lights and (2) to change features in order to heighten characterization. Make-up should always be tested under the actual lighting effects before a performance.

Every make-up that you do is an individual problem because of differences in facial characteristics. It is impossible to give you instructions for applying make-up for all types of roles. Any cosmetic supply firm will send directions and pictures to help you with difficult roles. Libraries also have books dealing with this subject in which you can find instructions for your individual problems.

In general, you should observe these principles: Avoid the usual mistake of applying too much make-up, especially rouge and lipstick. All make-up must be blended to avoid splotches of red and white. Avoid having all of the cast made up so that they appear to be of the same age. Grease paint, powder, rouge, lipstick, and liners (for eyebrows) come in different shades. Boys should have ruddy complexions varying in degree of ruddiness; girls should have lighter complexions except for those who have olive or very dark complexions; older men and women should have less color than young people. Match age, type, and special features with special shades of make-up. Remember that you are using make-up to create characters, not caricatures. It is better to have too little make-up on a cast than too much.

***Manager of lights and sound effects.*** As manager of lighting effects, you have the opportunity of displaying unlimited artistic ability. The artistry of lighting has created some memorable scenes in the theater. Through the right blending of colors, you can create a romantic moonlight scene, a night of horror, or a touching scene of death. When you control the switch, you control the mood on stage and the emotions of the audience. If you consider yourself in that capacity, you will do a much better job than if you think of yourself as merely an electrician.

You will be working with the director and the scenic designer, but you can still use your own ingenuity to show during rehearsals any special lighting of your own creation. All that you need in the

How can you miss with a lighting panel like this and a list of cues! *(Monkmeyer)*

way of equipment is a series of different kinds of lights with different colors of gelatin sheets. With imagination and plenty of artistic ability, you can perform wonders.

Important facts for you to remember include having a light plot for every scene in a play, and having all pieces of lighting equipment manned by reliable and trained people. Be alert for all cues marked on your light plot. A second's delay in dimming or increasing light can be crucial. Keep everybody away from all electrical equipment as a matter of safety and as a precaution against inattentiveness by the crew.

If you are in charge of special effects, enlarge your crew to include people who can devise the sound effects and run them. Many sounds can easily be simulated. Metal sheets can be shaken to sound like thunder; a vacuum sweeper sounds like wind or a running motor; bags containing rocks or glass can produce loud crashes; dropping beads on a drum or shaking them in a box will sound like rain; and your own crew can often imitate birdcalls, crowd noises, and other off stage effects. Moreover, theatrical firms advertise records containing every sound imaginable. If you have a backstage record player, mark the platter with chalk or tape at the spot you want and have somebody who can turn it on according to cue. Radio stations can supply information and may even lend equipment for any unusual sounds.

***Publicity manager.*** This is one of the most necessary positions in play production. Why put on a play without an audience? Furthermore, small audiences are disheartening to a cast that has worked hard to put on a good show. As publicity manager (or press agent), your duty is to fill every seat in the house.

You need a resourceful and an energetic crew to assist you. Some should have writing ability to prepare articles for local newspapers. Some should have artistic ability to draw posters or to design pictorial displays. All must be wide-awake and full of clever ideas which will attract attention and draw crowds.

***Business manager.*** The business manager handles all details of finance. Your duties as business manager include keeping all invoices and paying bills; having tickets printed and distributed; taking care of the printing and distribution of programs; running the box-office; and, in some cases, taking care of the ushers for the play.

**Production summary.** You can easily see that there is much more to producing a play than the average audience realizes. There are many important and responsible positions open to everybody

A typical backstage scene on the opening night of a school play reveals the tenseness and responsibility felt by *all* members of the production staff. (*Monkmeyer*)

who is interested in the theater. Don't think that you have to act or direct to get all of the glory. No matter how small your task may be, it is important to the total success. If you only press the buzzer button, the entire cast and director must depend upon you to be on cue, or a scene is ruined. So it is all down the line. Everyone is dependent upon somebody else for a successful, smooth performance. Who is to say who is the most important—the director who trains his cast and crew to carry out his every detail, the cast who shows off their talent and skillful direction, or the larger unseen group backstage and off stage which made the play move perfectly for an audience attracted by the publicity staff?

## Your role as a writer

Behind all of this array of talent is still another important person: the author. Without him there could be no play. Perhaps this is the role for you above all others of the theater, creating the plots and characters so that they can be brought to life on the stage. There is a great demand for playwrights with fresh, distinctive material.

Learning the techniques of writing for the theater is as involved as learning to write anything else. If you do enjoy making up plays and if you have any aspirations to become a playwright, there are many play-writing courses available. With the demand for plays on radio and television as well as in the theater, you can be sure of plenty of outlets if you can write good plays.

**The monologue.** Why not begin with the simplest activity of all—preparing a monologue? A monologue is a one-person speech in which one person does all of the talking to one or more imaginary characters on stage or to an audience. In a monologue, you need only two ingredients—a specific type of character and an interesting situation. When you decide upon these two, then make up lines which would be typical of the character and which would develop your situation.

Start with thinking about familiar situations. Life is full of humorous and serious experiences which can be developed into short episodes—an airplane trip, attending a World Series game, a slumber party, and many other incidents. Next invent a character to go with the situation. Perhaps you want to represent yourself in the situation, or you may prefer to impersonate a member of your family, a policeman, a socialite, an old maid, a country bumpkin, or a shy student. Whatever character type you choose, be sure to write copy that would be typical.

In a play, characters should be believable and the plot should have complications and unexpected developments to hold interest. The same is true in making up characters of your own and in developing situations. Monologues should be considerably shorter than plays, but like plays they need unexpected developments to maintain interest. Begin with a novel approach—try for a line that will capture attention immediately and which will establish your character and setting. You can't waste time explaining background to your audience, and they have no way of knowing who you are, where you are, and what the scene is about unless you let them in on the secret at once. A monologue should begin as if you had already been talking or thinking aloud and somebody started listening in. Plan some sequence of interest. It does not have to be a long, involved plot but it should have a planned progression that would keep the audience wondering about the outcome. A catchy conclusion which is totally unexpected is a good way to sign off.

Many monologues fail to interest an audience because they ramble on about nothing of interest and because they are too long. You will be wise to limit yourself to an incident or situation that can be developed in three to five minutes. You are also wise to limit yourself to one setting; otherwise arrange to have somebody announce a change of scene for you. Trying to represent a girl going on a shopping trip from the time she leaves the house until she comes home may be confusing, for example. Cut out unnecessary incidentals and get down to one episode which you can do well. You must be as careful in setting the stage for a monologue as you were in preparing pantomimes. Although the setting is imaginary, the audience must imagine the same things that you do.

One of the easiest monologues to prepare is a telephone conversation with an imaginary person at the other end. Try working out any one of the impersonations suggested below. Be especially careful to write just as the person would talk and to represent the character through speech, facial expression, and bodily movement.

## ACTIVITY

Write out and enact one of the scenes below:

- Your brother talking to his girl friend
- Your sister talking to her boy friend
- Your mother talking to a relative she doesn't like
- Your father taking an involved message for you
- A salesgirl taking a telephone order
- A bride calling in a grocery order
- Your school principal calling a student's home
- A gossip talking to her closest friend
- Yourself in any one of the following situations:
  - Talking to your girl friend (or boy friend) about your new romance
  - Explaining to one of the school authorities why you are not at school
  - Asking somebody to go to a formal dance

Other typical monologue situations occur when you meet a friend in the hall or on the street, when you ride downtown on a bus, when you meet somebody on a trip, when you are working in a store or shopping in one, when you are trying to teach a group, when you go to a restaurant, or when you are called on in class. You can think of dozens of interesting subjects for a monologue, once you get started.

The following monologue was composed by a high school student based on the simple but familiar problem of homework. This student approached the situation from a parent's angle and created an interesting episode. Notice how you get a definite impression of the mother and also the boys, how natural the humor is, and how the action moves quickly and enjoyably toward a catchy conclusion. You can do as well after reading other monologues and listening to the ones given in your class.

## ORIGINAL MONOLOGUE

What do you *mean*—you hope the school burns down or that old lady Stinkbomb gets the itch?—And I do wish you'd stop calling her that vile name—her name is Stinchcomb! Suppose she hears you sometime! Well, I care! James, quit muttering to yourself and stop doing your arithmetic on my clean table cloth! Now suppose you bring your book over to Mother and let me help you? What do you mean? Of course I can do it.

Three boys, A, B, C, were playing at marbles.

A remarked if B gave him one of his marbles B would have twice as many as A.

B remarked if C gave him three of his marbles C would have twice as many as B.

A remarked if C gave him seven of his marbles A would lack three of having half as many as C would have left.

How many marbles did each boy have?

Why that's simple. I'm surprised you can't do it by yourself. Now first imagine three little boys. One of them is called A—stupid name for a growing boy—the others B and C. Each one has so many marbles. Don't ask me how many. That's what we have to find out. Now reach over on that little sewing table and get that box of buttons. We'll substitute buttons for marbles, dear. Now put a little pile of buttons here—one here—and one over here. Fine. Now we'll start. A remarked if B gave him one of his marbles. Ah, I see. B gives one of his marbles—all right, buttons—to A. Now move one from B to A. Now B has twice as many as A. He doesn't? Well, he should have. James, don't screw your mouth up like that! You always do that when you're thinking. Next, C gives B three marbles—I mean buttons. Take three buttons and put them—no, dear, that's A, B is over here. Now C has twice as many as B. No, well the whole trouble is we started out with too many buttons. Let's use only half as many. That's right, James, put those back in the box. Don't screw up your mouth like that, James! Who is that outside? Your boy friends? No, you can't go out and play until you finish your homework. Tell them to come back later. No, I have a better idea. Tell them to come in. We'll all work on this problem together. Go ask them in. Hello boys, come in. James is having quite a time with his problems. You can help, if you will. By having real boys instead of letters, I can probably explain it better to James. Now your name is—A, let's see—Andrew. Yes, I know, Johnny, but just for one afternoon you can be Andrew. And your name is—B—Boris. Yes, Boris, Boris Karloff if you like. And yours is Conrad. Andrew, you sit here and take these buttons. Boris, you sit here and Conrad there. All right now we'll play marbles. I know you don't play marbles with buttons, but you can pretend, can't you? Boris, you give Andrew one of your buttons. No, it doesn't matter which one. The big pearl one will do. All right, the little red one. Now, Boris, you have twice as many as Andrew. I know it really isn't fair but that's what the problem says. Now, Conrad—yes, you. Your name is Conrad, isn't it? Well, never mind. Give three of your buttons to Boris. Don't be difficult now, Conrad. Now then, Conrad, you have twice as many as Boris. No, well, we'll come back to that part later. Now wait until I look at the problem. Andrew, you take seven of Conrad's buttons and—what, Conrad, you've only got six? But you must have more than that! Look under your chair. You must have dropped some. It should have worked out this time. I can't understand what went wrong. Sometimes I don't think I have all my buttons either. In fact, I'm slowly losing my sanity. We'll start all over. And this time there will be no mistakes. I think it would be better to use something bigger—maybe eggs. Yes, eggs would be fine. You can work with them better. James, run out and ask Annie for two dozen eggs. And be careful with them. They are expensive. That's a dear. What did you say, Andrew—I mean Johnny? Equations? Nonsense. When I was in school, we didn't fool with those. It just takes good common sense to work a problem like this. Now you wait. Ah, here, James, give them to me. Once again—A remarked to B that if B gave him one of his marbles B would have twice as many as A. How many have you to start with, Andrew—eleven? Well, that seems like a decent number. Now, Boris, give Andrew one and make it an even dozen. Careful, Andrew, that's seventy-five cents you're juggling! Next, B remarked if C gave him three—Conrad, give Boris three. Pl-e-a-se, don't toss them! Now, A remarked if B gave him three marbles, A would lack seven—no—three of having half as many of—wait, Boris, give Andrew three, no, seven of your eggs. There, I think that's right. Now, Andrew, you have half as many as Conrad. Conrad, how many do you have? One? That's impossible. You can't have half an egg, Conrad. Maybe if I separated the yolk from the wh— no, of course not. I think you naughty children are deliberately confusing me. And another thing, Conrad, this is no time for an Easter egg hunt. What did you do with those eggs? If you were hungry, why didn't you tell me? You gave them to Boris? Well, take them back. Now, A, have you got half as many as Con—oh, a lovely egg on my Persian rug! Oh, well, it makes it come out even! Boris, how many have you? Sixteen? That's way too many eggs for a boy your size. Well, something's wrong someplace, but I'll be darned if I can figure it out. I suggest we scramble them. Oh, the phone! Hello. Yes, dear, I'm having quite a time with James' homework. Now here's the problem (reads problem). See if you can figure it out, will you, dear? Have you a pencil and paper there? James, don't screw up your mouth like that! Yes, "A remarked if B gave him one of his marbles B would have twice as many as A." What do you mean, X? There are no X's in it. Just A, B, and C. All right, dear, I'll wait. James, run out and ask Annie for a rag to clean up that soufflé on the rug. Yes, dear, eleven. A has eleven! Why that's what we started out with! Didn't we, boys? There was really no point working it out. I got that answer long ago!

## ACTIVITIES

In the preparation of the monologues which follow, prepare a drawing of a stage set and write stage directions into your script.

1. Develop a humorous monologue based upon a typical situation.
2. Prepare a serious monologue to act out in class.

**The dialogue.** After preparing a monologue, you will find it comparatively easy to expand that situation into a dialogue or into a scene including even more characters. Bring to life the imaginary characters to whom you spoke in the monologue and let them do part of the talking. Try it first with the telephone conversations and then with the next situations involving more people.

## ACTIVITIES

Draw a stage set and prepare stage directions in the following scenes:

1. Select any one of the telephone conversations suggested in an earlier activity and write out the dialogue for both persons. With a classmate, carry on the two-way conversation.
2. Write out a dialogue between two strangers riding on a bus and act it out in class.
3. Carry on a conversation in the hall with a friend of yours.
4. Develop a scene between you and your younger sister or brother.
5. Select any of the pantomimic situations given earlier in the chapter and arrange group scenes complete with conversation and action.

Rex Harrison as the original "Professor Higgins" in *My Fair Lady* teaches "Liza Doolittle" (Julie Andrews) to sound her *h's* by blowing out the candle. *(Friedman-Abeles)*

**Adaptations.** You can learn much about the style of dramatic writing by preparing adaptations of poems, short stories, and novels that have dramatic possibilities for the stage. Scenario writers often make hit shows from adaptations of this type. The plot and characters are already provided in the original form of the work. All that you need to do in adapting it to play form is to plan the setting, work out the dialogue, and provide stage business. This gives you a pattern to follow which may eventually inspire you to work out your own plots. One of the most successful adaptations in recent years was the musical hit, *My Fair Lady,* based upon George Bernard Shaw's *Pygmalian.*

If you select literature that contains an abundance of conversation, you may use the conversation as it appears with a narrator to fill in any description. This method was used in the dramatized selection below. Or, if you prefer, you can follow the general plot and make up your own lines.

As you enact the roles of the characters in the dramatized selection, be sure to give an interpretation suitable for the roles and the theme. Notice how *The Spider and the Fly* resembles a melodrama with the spider in the villain's role and the fly as the poor heroine. By using appropriate voice and bodily expression, you can convert this well-known poem into a short, lively melodrama.

Children's stories which contain a large amount of conversation are easy to convert into dramatic form. *The Little Engine That Could* on page 446 is an example of preserving the original lines and using a narrator for descriptive sections.

Now try reading aloud in character the dramatization below. Produce it in class after selecting a cast.

## THE SPIDER AND THE FLY

SPIDER: Will you walk into my parlor?

NARRATOR: Said the spider to the fly.

SPIDER: 'Tis the prettiest little parlor that ever you did spy. The way into my parlor is up a winding stair, and I have many pretty things to show when you are there!

FLY: Oh, no, no! To ask me is in vain; for who goes up your winding stair can ne'er come down again.

SPIDER: I'm sure you must be weary, dear, with soaring up so high; will you rest upon my little bed?

NARRATOR: Said the spider to the fly.

SPIDER: There are pretty curtains drawn around, the sheets are fine and thin; and if you like to rest awhile, I'll snugly tuck you in.

FLY: Oh, no, no! For I've often heard it said, they never, never wake again, who sleep upon your bed.

NARRATOR: Said the cunning spider to the fly.

SPIDER: Dear friend, what shall I do to prove the warm affection I've always felt for you? I have within my pantry, good store of all that's nice; I'm sure you're very welcome; will you please to take a slice?

FLY: Oh, no, no! kind sir, that cannot be; I've heard what's in your pantry and I do not wish to see!

SPIDER: Sweet creature, you're witty and you're wise; how handsome are your gauzy wings, how brilliant are your eyes! I have a little looking-glass upon my parlor shelf; if you'll step in one moment, dear, you shall behold yourself.

FLY: I thank you, gentle sir, for what you're pleased to say, and bidding you good morning, now, I'll call another day.

NARRATOR: The spider turned him round about, and went into his den, for well he knew the silly fly would soon be back again; so he wove a subtle web in a little corner sly, and set his table ready to dine upon the fly. He went out to his door again, and merrily did sing.

SPIDER: Come hither, hither, pretty fly, with the pearl and silver wing; your robes are green and purple, there's a crest upon your head; your eyes are like the diamond bright, but mine are dull as lead.

NARRATOR: Alas, alas! how very soon this silly little fly, hearing his wily, flattering words, came slowly flitting by. With buzzing wings she hung aloft, then near and nearer drew—thought only of her brilliant eyes, and green and purple hue; thought only of her crested head—poor foolish thing! At last up jumped the cunning spider, and fiercely held her fast.

He dragged her up his winding stair, into his dismal den within his little parlor—but she ne'er came out again!

And now, dear little children who may this story read, to idle, silly, flattering words, I pray you, ne'er give heed; unto an evil counselor close heart and ear and eye, and learn a lesson from the tale of the spider and the fly.

—Mary Howitt

## ACTIVITIES

1. Prepare a dramatization of a short story.
2. Dramatize a short story using the plot and making up your own lines.
3. Dramatize a children's story using the original lines or your own.
4. Dramatize a poem modeled after the sample given or make up your own lines.

**Original plays.** The alert writer watches news items or reads literary selections for the purpose of finding suggestions for plots. As you read your newspaper, you can discover many ready-made plots complete with setting and characters. All that you need to do is disguise the names of the characters, change the setting slightly, and build a play around the circumstances.

Perhaps one of your favorite plays is the suspense type. Watch for news items that could be used as the nucleus of a suspense drama. You can also read about the trials that are in progress, in order to get a true-to-life situation and exact details. Still another source is any part or all of a literary selection that you have read. There is, of course, the chance to use your own imagination to make up a plot of your own.

## ACTIVITIES

1. Find a news item that can be used as a nucleus of a suspense drama. Write out the play, cast it, and produce it in class.
2. Select a trial that is in progress in your community or elsewhere or one that has aroused considerable interest in the past. Prepare two or three scenes involving star witnesses to present in class.
3. A literary selection packed with tenseness is *Joy Ride* by Edith List. It contains three accounts of a tragic accident. The first is given by the traffic officer, the second by the suspension bridge attendant, and the third by a witness waiting to cross the bridge. Develop these three accounts into a dramatization.

### JOY RIDE

About 2 A.M. it was—and black as pitch! I was parked just off the highway, with my motor runnin', waiting for some of those fool speeders on their way back from the shore, when that carload of singing kids whizzed by.

"Drunk!" I says, and stepping on the gas, set out after them. A tough time I had shortening the space between me an' them. Seventy-five miles per hour I was goin' before I made any headway and even then I couldn't close in on 'em.

"Trying to skip a ticket," I says, "by getting across the borough line before I nab 'em. I'll show them a thing or two."

I gave 'er more gas. Gradually I crept up on that car 'til I was only a thousand feet behind it. Couldn't get closer. They sure flew, them kids, an' a powerful machine they had.

We both got onto that flat half-mile stretch just this side of the bay, and all of a sudden I remembered the narrow bridge. Not a light on it. Seventy-five is no speed to travel over that wooden contraption. I blew my siren to warn them fools to slow down, and turned my own gas down. A lot of good that siren did, they kept right on at the same pace. But they was so near that bridge and goin' so fast, nothin' could have helped 'em anyway.

Then I saw their headlights on the uplifted section of the bridge and knew it was open and that they couldn't stop.

* * *

Waal, that night I was settin' in my booth on the bridge tryin' to keep awake by countin' the autos that passed by. Around about midnight they got so scarce I fell asleep between times. A couple of hours of this, and I was just dozin' off when a boat sounded her horn for me to open the bridge. Sort of startled me, being 'roused like that. While I set the gears to lift 'er, I looked out the window and sized up the boat. Pretty far apart the red and green lights seemed and I wondered if she was too wide to get through the small gap this thing can make. I figgered she could just about make it.

As she came on, another horn blew—this time a siren from somewhere inland. Through the other window I looked along the bridge towards shore, and saw, far away, three lights—two in front and one a good distance behind. I turned and saw the boat slidin' through and payin' no heed to the headlights on the highway, and then looked towards the lights again. They kept comin'. One, that in back, slowed, the other came right at me. I grabbed my whistle, ran out the front door, and blew for all I was worth—to stop that car. But it had already touched the bridge—nothin' could save it now. I jumped into the doorway. In a flash that machine crashed the gate, and was goin' so fast it looked like it would jump the gap—but it didn't quite. The top of the car hit the other side of the bridge and was ripped clean off before she struck the water.

* * *

I had just taken a young lady home from the dance at the Yacht Club and was parked at the other end of the bridge waiting to get through. From my position behind the raised portion of it I could see nothing but the dark water on either side and the lights of an approaching boat. As those lights disappeared beneath the bridge, somewhere in the distance a police siren screamed. Almost immediately a whistle split the darkness of the night. Then the lights of the boat slowly emerged from the other side. At the same instant came a crash of wood splintering—followed by an impact. The whole bridge trembled. Jumping from my car I ran to the railing and focused my eyes to pierce the black. Dimly I saw the boat's outline, its lights still shining cheerily. "Must have struck something . . . No," I said, recalling the impact, "No, it was clear when the crash came." I wheeled about. The bridge was lowering with slow, even pace. It sank, revealing two figures silhouetted by a single headlight; one was going through queer contortions.

I jumped into my car, started it, and pulled up beside them. "What happened?" I asked the officer who was removing his shoes. "Can you swim?" he shouted. "Yes." "Well, get in and pull them kids out." Upon that his stocking-footed body disappeared over the railing.

I jumped from my car, ripped off my coat, tie, and shoes, climbed the rail, and dove in. A cold shock swept through my body as it struck the black water. I groped around, my eyes being blinded by the darkness. My hand touched something hard. Hopefully I tried to grasp it—nothing but the bridge pilings. I swam to the surface for air and dove down again. A dozen times I repeated this action, once ramming headlong into the stomach of the cop, but had no success. The next attempt was fruitful. In groping around I grabbed an arm. I pulled—a body came along with it. Encircling the form with one arm, I used the other to sweep the water past me and reached the surface breathless. Someone took the body from me and slung it into the bottom of the boat. I clung to the side and rested for several minutes. The policeman came up for air. "Nothin' doin'," he panted. I slipped down again.

For hours this horrible procedure continued. Just before the night lifted I brought up the fifth body. My lungs were aching with emptiness; I strained to drag it to the surface. When my face felt the air and my hands were free of their burden, I clutched the side of the boat. Just as a more complete darkness enveloped me with unconsciousness, someone grabbed my arm.

I came to shortly afterwards at the filling station on shore. Several people stood about the bench on which I lay.

"Where are they?" I asked.

"What?"

"The bodies—I haven't seen them yet." I had that strange desire to look at the dead.

I swung my feet to the floor and stood up. Several yards away from me lay a low mound of dripping blankets, Five pairs of feet, toes up, protruded from beneath.

I walked over, grabbed a corner of the blanket, and pulled. There, beneath me in a row, were two young girls in evening dress, and three young men in tuxedos—and every body was minus the head.

—Edith List

Instead of spending all of your time in writing your own plays to work on in class, you may prefer to combine your efforts and talents in producing some short scenes from the plays of well-known playwrights. You can start by choosing a director, a cast, and a complete production staff to work out the interpretation of characters, costuming, and staging details for the scenes suggested in the following activities. After you have produced them in class or for a public performance, you will probably enjoy working together on a complete one-act or three-act play.

Although writing and staging your own scenes gives you opportunity to use your imagination and originality to the fullest extent, you will find satisfaction in using your creative ability to interpret scenes from some of the world's greatest dramatic literature.

In the activities which follow, you can work alone in monologues and you can work together in staging scenes from one-act and three-act plays. Follow directions closely and prove what a good trouper you can be.

## ACTIVITIES

### FOR ONE PERSON

1. Look in the library for collections of monologues. After making your selections, design a stage set for each, plan definite stage business, and memorize your selections. You should be able to impersonate at least *three* different types of personalities.

2. Find a play that you like which contains an important scene for one person. Prepare an introduction which will enable the class to understand your role and the situation. Design a stage set, plan stage business, and then memorize the scene to present to the class.
3. Portray a one-person scene from Shakespeare.

### FOR TWO OR MORE PERSONS

Follow the same general directions given for preparing stage sets and choosing a director, cast, and production staff in the following:

1. Choose a short scene from any one-act play or three-act play that you enjoy and present it to the class.
2. Choose a one-act play to present in its entirety to the class or for an assembly program.
3. Select a three-act play that you feel capable of producing before an audience and present it with student direction.

The world of the theater has a magic appeal for many types of people. Whether you work behind the scenes or in front of the footlights, you play an important role in creating entertainment. As you take your place with the great actors, directors, producers, and playwrights, you will always find an appreciative audience eager to applaud your talents.

The culmination of all the weeks of hard work in rehearsal is the thrill actors experience when they take the spotlight on stage. *(Philip Gendreau, N.Y.)*

## PRONUNCIATION PROBLEMS

Be careful in pronouncing the "er" (ûr) sound in words like "girl." Do not confuse it with the "oi" sound such as you use in "oil." The tongue should be raised halfway to the hard palate and the tip of the tongue should be poised behind the front teeth. Do not round the lips or curl the tongue. Practice saying the following:

| | | | | |
|---|---|---|---|---|
| turn | term | absurd | unfurl | research |
| earn | work | observe | perfect | squirm |
| curb | pearl | word | gird | learn |
| earl | purr | curt | hurt | shirt |
| earth | worth | world | whirl | worse |
| birth | purse | heard | third | worm |
| mirth | myrtle | stirred | thirsty | firm |

## READING CHECK-UP

Read aloud the nonsense sentences below to check your pronunciation of any problem words.

The girl with the curly hair heard the words of the pearl diver as he turned over the urn on the curb.

Washing oily shirts is hard work even for experts who toil to whirl out the dirty oil stains. The amount they earn is hardly worth the toil.

The thirty little girls squirmed when they learned that Myrtle, the nurse, was going to use a hypodermic needle that might hurt.

When the flag was unfurled at the morning church services, all of the church members observed the unfurling in perfect quiet except one girl who dropped her purse. Her mother turned and spoke to her curtly before she gave way to mirth.

Skirts and shirts are on sale on Thirty-first Street at absurdly low prices.

## VOCABULARY BUILD-UP

Use the italicized words in short paragraphs to show that you understand their meanings.

*hybrid* seed corn
a feeling of *empathy*
*disparaging* comments
a well-chosen *excerpt*
the *resonance* of his voice
a *condescending* attitude

a *rhetorical* question
*paradoxical* statements
*tantamount* to victory
holding *clandestine* meetings
unlikely to *acquiesce*
a *sagacious* answer

CHAPTER

# 22 Speaking on Radio and Television

*Shakespeare's Preview of TV:* "But for your company, I would have been abed an hour ago" (*Romeo and Juliet,* Act 3, Sc. 4) . . . "Are you crept hither to see the wrestling?" (*As You Like it,* Act 1, Sc. 2) . . . "I'll look no more, lest my brain turn . . . " (*King Lear,* Act 4, Sc. 6)

—*Credit Executive*

THERE'S an old Irish proverb that goes: "If you want to get the news about in a hurry, tell it to a woman as a secret." That might have been the best way a long time ago, but that was before the days of radio and television. Today, through the marvels of electronics, an important piece of news can be flashed all over the world within minutes of its happening. You may even see or hear the event actually taking place!

## Broadcasting: What Is It?

What, then, is this process known as "broadcasting"? Basically, so far as radio is concerned, broadcasting means transmitting a program through the air from its source to the set of anyone who elects to listen to it. The program itself can be any of a number of things: a speech; a dramatic show; music; a sports event; crises or trivia; anything that the broadcaster feels may interest his listening audience. Telecasting is very much the same; it's the transmission of a sound and a picture through the air to a receiver.

This may all sound simple, but actually it's a highly complex process that is still being improved every year. Let's take a closer look at some of the technical aspects of radio and television.

## How sound and pictures travel

If you take a piece of paper and hold it lightly in front of your mouth with both hands and then speak, you'll be able to feel vibrations from the paper. As you speak, the sound coming from your mouth causes the air and thus the paper to vibrate. When you hear a sound, your eardrum is picking up these vibrations in the air and changing them into nervous impulses which travel to your brain. Now this is a very much oversimplified version of what actually happens, but it will do for your present purposes. Sound is transmitted electronically in much the same way. As the sound causes the air to vibrate, a sensitive microphone translates these vibrations into electrical impulses. These electrical impulses are then amplified, modified, and transmitted through the air as electronic waves. When they reach your radio, the various electronic waves are changed back to vibrations which can be picked up by your ear. (Fig. No. 1). What else travels in waves and vibrations?

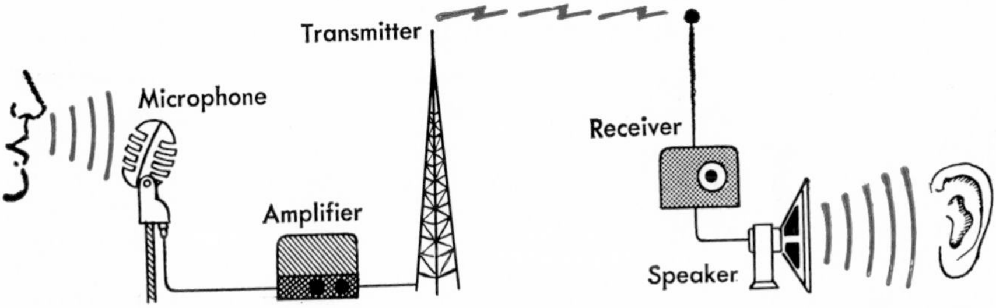


FIG. 1

Because both light and color, like sound, travel through the air in waves, we can have television. The principle is the same. The light pattern is translated by the television camera into electrical impulses which are transmitted through the air until they reach a receiver which re-translates them into light patterns. (Fig. No. 2.) The same principle holds true for color television, although color is more difficult and expensive to transmit than black and white. The audio part of television is produced just as it is for radio.

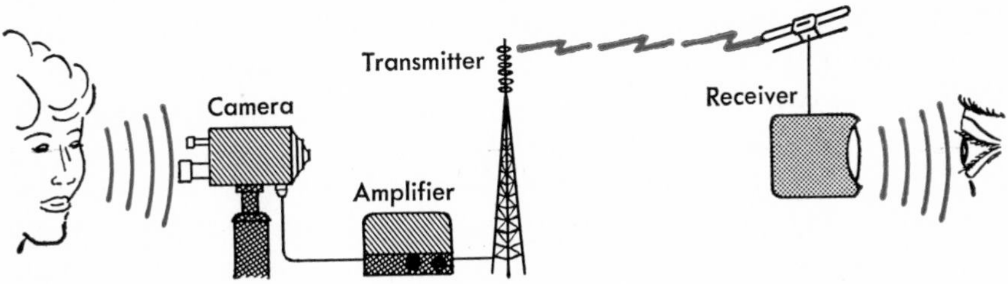


FIG. 2

## How important are radio and television?

When was the last whole day you spent without listening to the radio or watching television at least once? An amazingly high proportion of the people of our country listen to the radio at least once every day; and television producers of some of the big network shows can claim audiences of forty to fifty million people every time their particular show comes on the air. A politician can make a speech, a writer can tell a story, a pianist can perform before the largest audiences ever recorded. It's easy to see why radio and television are considered two of the most important factors in our lives today.

## Unique features of broadcast speaking

Good broadcasting or telecasting has a great deal in common with other types of good speaking. However, the broadcast situation differs enough from other kinds of speaking to justify some specific comments and tips.

**Features of broadcast speaking that affect the speaker.** Probably the greatest single difference that you will note in broadcast speaking is that you have no audience. The more accustomed you have become to live audiences, the more this lack of audience will bother you. In fact, if you have learned to adjust your speaking to your audience, you may miss this response so much in radio that you will feel ill at ease. It's important, therefore, to prepare yourself for this effect.

You may also be bothered by the fact that you usually cannot move around freely in a studio situation. Even with a lapel or other attached microphone, the dangling cord gives difficulty at first. With a microphone on a stand or boom, it is best to keep at a relatively constant distance from the microphone. This is frequently very difficult for the beginner to do.

Radio speaking, you will find, offers one problem that is almost entirely its own. You will note as you talk over radio that you are suddenly strongly conscious of the ineffectiveness of your facial expressions, gestures, and movements. You will discover for yourself that radio is truly a listening medium; the only appeal in radio is through the ear. This sudden and complete dependence upon your speech and voice can be troublesome.

**Differences that affect the audience.** Despite the fact that the entire listening audience of a program may be in the millions, most of the individual listeners will either be alone or in small groups. This means that members of a radio or television audience do not have the same influence on each other that members of a large, in-person audience have. One exception should be noted. The reaction of a studio audience, if picked up by the microphone or camera, may reach and influence the listening audience.

Broadcast audiences are not uniform. They are not all of one political party, of one religious faith, of one sex, of one age, or of one occupation. Radio and television audiences tend to be random audiences to a degree seldom encountered in the in-person speaking situation.

Not only does the broadcast audience lack the essential uniformity of many live audiences, but even its random characteristics may vary from day to day. Thus mid-morning and early afternoon weekday audiences are likely to be mostly women. Evening, Sunday, and holiday audiences are likely to have a high percentage of men listeners. Children are most likely to be listening in the late afternoon and very early evening. This lack of uniformity greatly complicates your understanding of your audience; but this complication is what gives broadcasting its challenge and interest.

Broadcast audiences find it very easy to stop listening. They are under no obligation to listen to you. It is easier to flick a dial than to get up, put on one's hat and coat, and work one's way out of a crowded auditorium or meeting room. Furthermore, your broadcast audience is not isolated from other attractions and may be listening to you with only half an ear. You are competing not only with other programs but also with books and hobbies, with neighbors who drop in, with the family dog, with a sick child, and with the double feature at the neighborhood theater.

These differences between broadcast and in-person speaking situations mean that your job is to present programs that, through sheer program content, will make your audience want to follow, and will make them a little disappointed that there isn't more.

### ACTIVITY

Prepare a list of the 10 things in commercial radio and television that irritate you most. Make a comparison of all the lists in your class. Is there general agreement among them? Is there disagreement? Why?

## Types of broadcasts

Radio and television offer many types of broadcasts and, as you will see, most of them are centered around some type of speech activity. Perhaps the best way to classify these broadcasts is to use the method that has grown up with the industry itself. Broadcast classifications usually recognized in both radio and television are: (a) news (including sports); (b) interviews; (c) speeches or lectures; (d) discussions; (e) debates; (f) drama; (g) variety shows; (h) disc jockey shows; (i) quiz shows; and (j) commercials. In addition, television has built up a type of broadcast that features movies.

**News.** Radio and television are excellent media for presenting news. They can broadcast, almost at once, world-wide news on a world-wide scale. You will recognize most of the following types of news programs:

The ***spot news announcement*** briefly notes the occurrence of an event. If a report of an event is extremely important, regularly scheduled programs may be interrupted in order to permit the announcement.

In the ***news summary,*** the news is offered, usually at a regular time, on a straight report basis with almost no editorial comment or analysis. This type of program may range in length from just a few minutes to a quarter-hour or more. Even in a 15-minute program, the amount of time actually devoted to the news is only a little better than 12 minutes. Occasionally, you may hear certain types of news summaries dealing with specific subjects such as the weather, the theater, religion, or politics.

A good play-by-play broadcast of a football game provides top entertainment for countless ardent fans. *(Philip Gendreau, N.Y.)*

In the ***news commentary***, the goal is not so much to report the events themselves as to explain the *meaning* of these events. Sometimes a distinction is made in programming between the news analyst, who explains without a particular "slant," and the news commentator, who interprets from a certain point of view.

The ***roundup*** is still another type of news program. Roundups usually cover a specified period of time: a day, a week, a month, or occasionally a year. Roundups review the most significant events during that period and place these events in perspective.

The ***special events*** program attempts to give a complete coverage of some event in which there is high interest. Elections, conventions, inaugurations, and certain sports events are examples of the special events program.

The ***sports broadcast*** falls into four major types: the play-by-play made during the game or contest; the summary of results, or the "scoreboard" type of program; the inside story, background, and prediction type of program; or a combination of these.

## ACTIVITIES

1. Prepare a spot news announcement concerning a high school, city, state, national, or international event of importance. Content may be real or imaginary. Time limit one minute.
2. Prepare a *local* news summary exactly three minutes and thirty seconds in length. Present it either as a radio or television broadcast.
3. Prepare a news summary covering local, national, and international happenings. Time limit twelve minutes and twenty seconds. Divide the remaining two minutes and forty seconds between the weather report and a commercial.
4. Work together in preparing a fifteen-minute television news summary from a local station following this plan:
   Person No. 1 act as announcer to sign the program on and off
   Person No. 2 present the national and international news
   Person No. 3 present the local news
   Person No. 4 give the sport news
   Person No. 5 give the weather report
   Person No. 6 give the commercials
5. Work together in preparing a fifteen-minute summary from a network studio in which the cameras switch to different points of interest to hear special reports from announcers. Follow the same plan as in No. 4 for Persons No. 1, 5, and 6. Let Person No. 2 be the main reporter to give all of the news and to call on at least three other reporters during his broadcast.
6. Prepare any one of these three types of newscasts: a special events program, a sports broadcast, a roundup. You may work together, if you wish.
7. Who is your favorite newscaster? Give six reasons *why* he is.

People prominent in public life or authorities on some topic of public interest are always in demand for interview programs. *(CBS Television Network)*

**The interview.** This is a highly specialized type of program, and is popular in many different forms. One of the more common is the interview with an *authority* on some subject which is of interest or importance. In this type of interview, attention is usually not on the individual, as such, but rather on what he is able to say about his subject. But in the interview with a *celebrity*, another type, the interest is on the personality of the individual, on his likes, dislikes, and hobbies, rather than on the impact of what he may be able to say on current problems. The interview with the strictly *average American*, the so-called "man-in-the-street" program, is still different. This form seeks to reflect current thinking on topics of immediate, and sometimes somewhat casual, interest. In addition, primarily for entertainment purposes, the interview with *random members of an audience* or with *specially chosen participants*—as an All-American football team—has also appeared.

**Straight speeches or lectures.** As in other types of speeches, radio and television speakers may seek to inform, to entertain, and to persuade. Usually, particularly in commercial as opposed to educational broadcasts, speakers seek to entertain or to persuade. In some instances, but particularly in educational broadcasts, the speech to inform is also common. An example is the broadcast of a lecture from a college classroom.

**Discussion programs.** Although these take various forms, the common element in discussion programs is cooperative thinking on a particular topic. In the program known as a panel, a few people with special information or talents, and usually with some degree of direction from a leader, think out loud about the subject being discussed. The function of the leader will vary from relatively active participation to relatively passive observation. The group does not necessarily reach a conclusion; indeed, it may only explore the problem. The symposium is more formal than the panel in that each member of the symposium gives a prepared speech. The participants may also answer questions from the leader, from other members of the symposium, or from the audience. When a discussion program features audience participation, it is usually known as a forum. It might be well to review the discussion material in Chapter 17 before attempting to put a program on the air.

**Debates.** Though not particularly popular or common on either radio or television, debates have still been quite successful on subjects of high public interest; for example, a debate between two

A speech to inform is being given by this teacher demonstrating an algebra lesson on an educational broadcast. *(Continental Classroom, NBC-TV)*

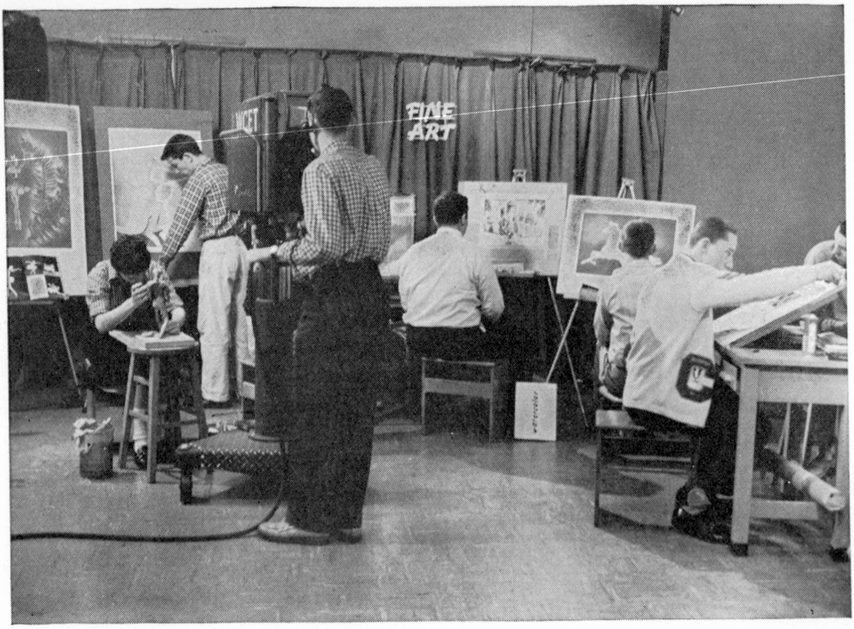


An art class is being filmed for an educational television program. *(Courtesy of Station WCET, Cincinnati, Ohio)*

men running for the same political office. The goal of each speaker or team in a broadcast debate is to present a *particular* point of view.

**Drama.** Many types of dramatic programs have been developed for radio and television. Each play may be completely separate, or it may be one of a series of related plays. If it is part of a series, the same characters or the same themes appear each time, but each play is complete in, and of, itself. There is also the serial or soap opera (so named because this form has been widely sponsored by leading soap manufacturers), in which each day's activities only serve to complicate the next.

In addition, the dramatic technique is often employed as a means of presenting news, of re-creating events, of setting the stage for a discussion, of drawing attention to social and national problems, and of presenting commercials.

**The variety show.** As the name suggests, this program wraps up in one package many types of entertainment. Among its stock ingredients are humor, vocal and instrumental music, and humorous and serious drama. These may be mixed together in different ways and with different degrees of success.

**The disc jockey show.** Although more popular on radio than on television, disc jockeys have operated successfully in both media.

In essence, these shows consist of a mixture of the personality of the host, a series of recordings that reflects either his choice or those of some poll, and frequent commercials.

**The quiz show.** This is basically a question and answer type of situation to which a large sprinkling of prize money is frequently added.

**The commercial.** The financial backbone of American broadcasting is the commercial. Whether it is straight, humorous, dramatized, singing, or novelty, it pays the bill for most of the other forms of broadcast that we receive in our homes.

## ACTIVITIES

1. Select a partner or partners and present one of the following programs:
    a. An interview with an authority on any subject of interest
    b. An interview with a celebrity . . . sports, movies, television, theater, dancing, music, exploration, or any other field of interest
    c. An interview with someone chosen at random—"man-on-the-street" type of program
    d. An interview with several members of a football team, a hockey team, the World Series winners, or any other group of outstanding importance

A disc jockey on a radio program must be able to project his personality to his unseen audience. *(Courtesy of WKRC-Radio, Cincinnati, Ohio)*

2. Present a lecture or speech on a subject that would be suitable for an educational television program. Use illustrative devices.
3. Using whatever talent is available, work together in planning a variety show similar to your favorite one on television. Include a master of ceremonies, vocal and instrumental musicians, a comedian, a couple of novelty acts, and some visiting celebrities. Include commercials of any of the types explained in the text.
4. Pretend that you are a disc jockey. Select at least five records and introduce them in some unique manner. You need not play the records—simply introduce them. Intersperse commercials with your remarks. Model your program after your favorite disc jockey show.
5. Work together in planning a quiz program based on any current one that you enjoy. You may wish to use a panel to guess the identity of contestants.

# Learning About Radio

## Participating in radio

It is usually possible for high school students to get radio experience. The most exciting way is for you to organize a radio group under the supervision of the proper faculty member. In time, such a group may be able to participate in actual broadcasts over local stations. Another very valuable method is to create radio-like conditions in your school and to hold practice broadcasts. If these practice broadcasts can be recorded so that you can listen to your programs being played back, you can easily become aware of your own technical weaknesses and strong points. Broadcast participation today can be an important part of your education.

### ACTIVITY

Prepare a list of programs available in your area that should make a well-balanced, worthwhile schedule for a high school student. Present your list to the class and be prepared to explain why you have chosen these programs.

### A GLOSSARY OF RADIO TERMS

The glossary below will help you to learn the language of professional radio.

**Across the board:** on the air every day same time
**Ad lib:** speaking lines not in script or talking without a script
**B.G.:** background; sound below normal level
**Blasting:** too much volume which results in voice distortion
**Board:** control panel in control room
**Bridge:** music or sound used in transition
**Clambake:** unrehearsed or poor show

**Commercial:** a sponsored program or a paid announcement

**Continuity:** copy prepared by continuity writers commenting on music or events

**Control room:** room from which program is directed by production director and where engineer balances various elements of speech, sound, and music

**Cross fade:** blending of music, sound, or speech, increasing volume of one of these while decreasing another

**Cushion:** a portion of a speech or music held in reserve in the event that the show runs short

**Disc:** a record, also called platter

**Dress:** dress rehearsal

**Dry grooves:** grooves at beginning of record which contain no music or sound; record is set up in advance by placing needle in dry grooves and stopping turntable

**Echo effect:** produced in echo chamber—hollow effect; reverberation

**Fade in:** gradual increase in volume of sound, speech, or music

**Fade out:** gradual decrease

**Faders:** volume controls on control panel

**Filter:** remove frequencies from speaker's voice so that it sounds "thin"; e.g. used in telephone conversations, man's conscience, eerie effects

**Fluff:** missed cue; mistake

**Level:** program balance of voice, music, etc.

**Live mike:** one that's turned on—ready to be used

**Mix:** combining input of two or more sources and balancing them

**Monitor speaker:** loudspeaker in control room; director listens to finished product or mixing here

**Montage:** a series of short scenes indicating time passage; a series of events, or ideas, serving as a bridge from one scene to another

**Muddy:** voice not clear; may be distorted

**Off mike:** position away from microphone

**P.A.:** public address system

**Pickup:** phonograph arm

**Playback:** playing record or tape for audition purposes

**Punctuate:** a musical chord which emphasizes a speech to heighten dramatic intensity; also called "stab," or "sting"

**Read level:** check the balance; also called "reading"—"take a reading"

**Remote:** a program originating in a place other than the studio

**Ride gain:** manipulate faders so that desired balance is maintained

**Salt shaker:** pressure-type mike

**Segue:** indicates change in mood of music; provides a mood transition; loosely, a transition

**Setup:** placement of mikes, sound, music, et cetera in studio

**Sneak:** to fade in a sound at an initially low level

**Sound man:** technician who produces sound effects

**Stand by:** a warning that program is ready to go on air

**Sustaining:** a program whose costs are borne by the originating station or network

**Tape:** magnetic sound tape; used for preparing programs in advance, or preserving and re-broadcasting programs

**Theme:** a signature which identifies program; may be music, sound, or talk

**Transcription:** a recording made for express purpose of broadcasting; not available for home use

**Transition:** music, sound, silence, or combinations which change the mood or direction of the program

**Under:** music or sound under speech; also "B.G."

**V.I.:** volume indicator—V.I. meter

**Velocity:** ribbon mike

**Washboard weepers:** soap operas or daily serials depicting life's woes

**Wow:** sound heard when volume is brought up before record has attained proper speed

## ACTIVITIES

1. Have a "glossary-bee," with two equal sides. Let a caller present the above descriptions alternately to the two teams; the correct answer is the name.
2. Find at least ten more terms and definitions to add to the above list.

**Simulated broadcasts.** Whether you have the opportunity to go on the air at your local station or not, you should get as much

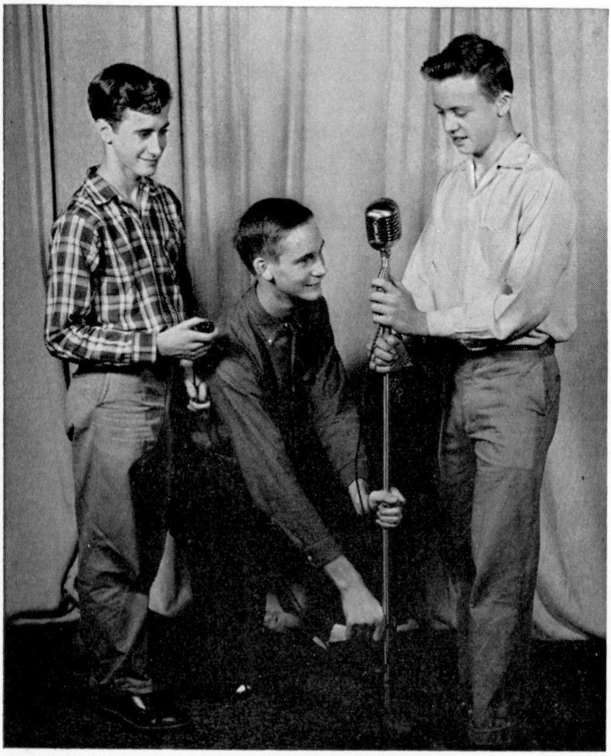

In preparing for an assembly program, a stage crew learns a great deal about the mechanical aspects of broadcasting equipment. *(Monkmeyer)*

microphone experience as you can right at your own school. Try using a microphone, amplifier, and loudspeaker for practice broadcasts. Your school may have these available either as a public address system or as a tape recorder. Prepare your programs in advance, and present them over whatever facilities are available. Your classmates can then hear your program under circumstances that will closely approximate those of actual radio.

Radio broadcasting techniques are not easy to learn, but by careful preparation and rehearsal you can become familiar with microphone techniques, sound effects, studio signs, studio behavior, and most of the other features of an actual broadcast. Indeed, you will find such a set-up to be an almost perfect way to prepare for an actual broadcast.

Incidentally, if your school happens to be equipped with some form of centralized sound system, you will find it technically possible to present radio programs that will be of service to your entire school community.

If you cannot arrange to use a microphone, amplifier, speaker set-up, or a tape recorder, you can still practice putting on radio

Your first public appearance before a microphone will show the benefit of simulated broadcasting experience. *(Pogue's Portrait Studio)*

shows. Separate your listening group from your broadcasting group by the use of a screen. Or, even more simply, group your listeners so that they face away from the performers. Even this small amount of separation will help to gain the illusion of an actual broadcast.

Many schools use the simulated broadcast for practice purposes. The signals below will prove helpful to you in your broadcast practice.

## SIGNALS FREQUENTLY EMPLOYED IN RADIO STUDIOS

**Cue:** director "throws" index finger, arm stretched out, at performer, indicating that he is to start speaking, playing, or doing sound effects

**Cut:** index finger drawn across throat as if cutting it

**Decrease volume:** palms facing downward, lower hands

**Fade down:** oblique motion downward, starting shoulder high, hand with palm down, sweeping downward

**Fade up:** oblique motion upward with hand and arm, palm up

**Faster:** index finger extended and whole hand rotated in circular motion (drawing a circle in air)

**Get on mike:** palm downward, action similar to turning valve

**Hold:** after fades when desired volume reached, other hand extended with fist clenched

**Louder:** lifting hands, palms upward, a couple of times; both hands used

**Move back:** palms of hands facing each other and moved away from each other, or back of hand to mouth and moved away from mouth

**Move up to mike:** palms of hands facing each other and moved toward each other, or palm of hand moved toward mouth

**O.K.:** thumb and first finger form circle, indicating everything fine

**On the nose:** finger pointing to nose indicates program is running on time

**Slow down:** draw hands apart slowly as if pulling heavy rubber band

**Stand by:** arm extended upward with palm open to let participants know program is about to begin

**Station break:** action with clenched fists as though breaking thin slab of wood

**Theme:** index finger of right hand across end of index finger of left hand forming a T

**Time signals:** one minute, one finger extended; two, two fingers, et cetera; index finger of one hand across index finger of other hand signifies one-half minute

## ACTIVITIES

1. Practice the hand signals with your classmates until you are able to identify each of them.
2. Prepare a reading of approximately three minutes. Read your script while taking and reacting to the signals given to you by an appointed director.

The signals, "on the nose" and "cut," are properly demonstrated here by two studio technicians. *(Cincinnati Enquirer)*

## Writing radio scripts

**General suggestions.** Now, let's consider certain techniques that help you to write good radio scripts. Note these points closely:

1. Make the appeal of your script broad. Make it interest as many listeners as possible.
2. Use an ear-catching first sentence.
3. Use freely such elements as terseness, vitality, directness, simplicity, suspense, concreteness, and economy of plot development.
4. Try to make your main points instantaneously understandable.
5. Use informal but unmistakable transitions. Your transitions will depend on sound alone; they cannot be suggested by movement or gesture.
6. Use an informal, conversational style. Think of yourself as talking to groups of two or three rather than to an auditorium full of people.
7. Make each sentence clear and reasonably short; 20 words in a sentence is about the limit for radio.

8. Plan the length of your script to fit your time. There is no ideal single rate for radio speaking, but something like 140 words per minute is fairly typical. This figure will serve as a rough guide until you begin the actual timing of your script.

9. Avoid sibilant sounds like *s* and *z* so far as possible. Microphones tend to exaggerate these sounds.

10. Use simple words. Avoid technical words as much as possible.

11. Always keep in mind that your listener is not a reader; he cannot re-read what has gone before. Make your points in 1-2-3 order, and avoid at all costs anything that may tend to confuse your listener.

**Character identification.** The above suggestions apply rather generally in writing for radio. But, in writing for radio drama, a

These interpreters, like radio listeners, must concentrate solely on a speaker's words and voice. A good script gets the best translation. *(United Nations)*

particular problem is that of easy recognition by the listening audience of the characters as they speak. Remember that your radio audience must identify each actor by his voice and speech alone.

There are several techniques in writing your script that will help your audience with identification. One is to include in the dialogue the name of the person addressed and who will respond next. Another technique is to develop characters who would be likely to speak in different ways. Thus one character might naturally speak very slowly, another might have an exceptionally nasal voice, a third might speak with a foreign accent, and a fourth might be characterized by a straight male voice. Both of these techniques, although common and reasonably effective, quickly become artificial if carried to extremes. The best method of all is to work identification subtly into the dialogue and cast *different* voices for the parts. In addition to helping in the identification of the characters, the dialogue in a radio script must also help the audience to visualize the action and the locale. In some instances, of course, a narrator may help to introduce the characters and "set the stage" for the action.

**Preparing the manuscript.** Almost without exception, you will read your radio program from manuscript, not recite it from memory. You must, therefore, take certain precautions and mark your script for radio presentation. First write the script itself; observe the special composition hints noted above. Then read it aloud several times. Note particularly those places in which you sound forced, and then rework these places. Keep trying until you can read the entire script in a fresh, spontaneous manner.

Now, having written your script word by word in the way that you want to say it, prepare for microphone reading. Type it, if at all possible, using bond paper of standard, 8½″ x 11″ size and double spacing between lines. This gives you room to make additions, changes, or corrections. Using heavy paper avoids rustling noises which are greatly amplified by microphones. Try to get a copy of a complete script from your local station, or from a book on radio in your library.

Finally, it is usually desirable toward the end of your script to include material that can be either added or cut as needed in the actual speaking situation. This makes it possible for you to time your speech "right on the nose." Remember, the sole purpose of this type of script preparation is to enable you to perform as easily and efficiently as possible within the limits of the radio speaking situation. The better your script is written, the better your performance should be.

Timing is so important in broadcasting that an announcer must begin exactly on signal and close "on the nose." *(Courtesy of Station WCET, Cincinnati, Ohio)*

### ACTIVITY

*(You have two characters—*John *and* Mary. *The scene begins with a sound cue.)*

| | |
|---|---|
| SOUND: | DOOR OPENS: |
| Mary: | Is that you, John? |

Now, continue the scene in any way you wish for a playing time of three minutes. You'll be quite surprised, when you compare what you have written with that of your classmates, to see how many different things can happen to Mary and John—if it is John—just because a door happens to open.

## Speaking on radio

**Microphone technique.** Because microphone techniques vary with studios, speech purposes, and types of microphones, statements about such techniques must be fairly general.

You must first place yourself within the pickup areas of the type of microphone that you are using. So far as pickup is concerned, there are three basic types of microphones: non-directional, uni-directional, and cardioid. A non-directional microphone picks up sound from all sides almost equally well; a uni-directional microphone picks up sound better from one side only; and the cardioid picks up in a figure 8 pattern.

Your best speaking distance will vary. In general, something like 12 to 15 inches is the best distance. Once you find your best distance for any particular situation, keep it constant. There are a few exceptions to this rule. If you want to sound as if you're speaking to a very large audience, back away from the microphone and talk rather loudly. Again, if you want to sound very personal, come close to the microphone and talk softly; or, you may want to fade your voice in or out of a scene. To do either, simply talk and walk at the same time; to fade in, walk toward the microphone; to fade out, back away.

Learn to avoid the unwanted noises that a microphone will pick up. A modern, sensitive microphone will not only pick up your speech, it will also pick up other noises in the room. Among the incidental activities that can produce unwanted noises are such things as breathing into a microphone, touching the microphone, rustling papers, moving furniture or other studio equipment, and even whispering instructions or comments.

The members of this high school panel have been well instructed in microphone technique. *(Courtesy of Station WCET, Cincinnati, Ohio)*

**Conversational style.** Because most microphones will not tolerate great changes in intensity, and because most of your audience is listening in small groups, you should speak informally. Radio professionals sometimes say that they read their lines as if there were only one person in the room with them, and that person at a distance of only four feet. A conversational style means, of course, a variety in pitch, in quality, and in timing. It does not imply sudden and large changes in intensity. Remember that broadcast equipment will not tolerate great changes in loudness. Such changes will only blast the ears of your listeners.

**Diction and pronunciation.** The microphone, being close to your mouth, will pick up the tiniest sounds in your speech. You must be very careful of your articulation. In particular, you should watch such sounds as *s, th, f, sh,* and their voiced equivalents such as *z* and *zh.* Microphones exaggerate the hissing quality of these sounds. Practice making them as softly and with as little hissing as possible. (See problems on pages 164-5, 186-7, and 230-1.)

When a broadcaster conquers the sensitivity of a microphone, the audience has the illusion of sharing the same room with the speaker. *(NBC)*

As has already been stressed in Chapter 6, *Improving Pronunciation,* it is very difficult to select any one style of pronunciation, and to say that this is right and that all others are wrong. This statement is just as true of radio speaking as of general speaking. Nevertheless, you should note certain pronunciation trends in radio. First, in straight radio speaking or announcing, try to avoid highly unusual, dialectal pronunciations such as you might find in the Deep South, in Eastern New England, or in Metropolitan New York. These are usually not recommended for radio. Of course, in some purely local programs, you may find it well to use local pronunciation. Or you may assume an accent for deliberate effect. But with these exceptions the present trend in radio is toward a more general style of pronunciation. This style probably resembles General American Speech more than any other dialect, but is not identical with it. You should be very careful to check the pronunciations of all questionable words that appear in your script. Some helpful guides are Kenyon and Knott's *A Pronouncing Dictionary of American English,* Webster's *New World Dictionary, The American College Dictionary,* Bender's *The NBC Handbook of Pronunciation,* and *The Winston Dictionary.*

It is very important that as you look up words and attempt to pronounce them correctly, you do not fall into the error of stressing every syllable. This gives a stilted, unnatural effect.

**Bodily action.** The amount of bodily action is always limited in radio because you must maintain a fixed distance from the microphone. But don't let this keep you from making use of any gestures and facial expressions that seem helpful. Your audience won't be able to see them, but such actions may make you feel more relaxed and so influence your oral style. Use your gestures and facial expressions for their effects upon you and your speech; ignore their lack of effect on your radio audience.

**Practice.** Since most radio work will be from manuscript, practice reading the script until you acquire the ability to do so in a style that suggests easy, spontaneous conversation. Always, as you practice, remember that your voice and language must carry your entire message.

## Acting for radio

You should now be familiar with the essential differences between in-person speaking and radio speaking both in composition and presentation. It is also important to be familiar with the major differences between radio drama and in-person drama. In general, the preceding remarks about pronunciation, microphone technique, and delivery are applicable to radio drama. But in the selection of plays for radio production, or in the writing of radio scripts for dramatic presentation, certain characteristics of radio drama should be noted.

For example, the plot development of a radio play should be straightforward rather than complex. The typical radio play is limited to about 26 minutes of playing time; there is simply not time, then, for subtle plot elaboration. As a result there is a tendency for radio drama to move at a slightly faster pace than does the conventional stage play. This faster pace is reflected in the acting.

You will find it easier to act in plays that require only a small cast. As you have learned earlier in this chapter, it is difficult for the listening audience to identify the various members of a large cast each time they speak, since they cannot see the actors. Since identification must be made by ear alone, you may be tempted to do strange things to your manner of speaking in order to become

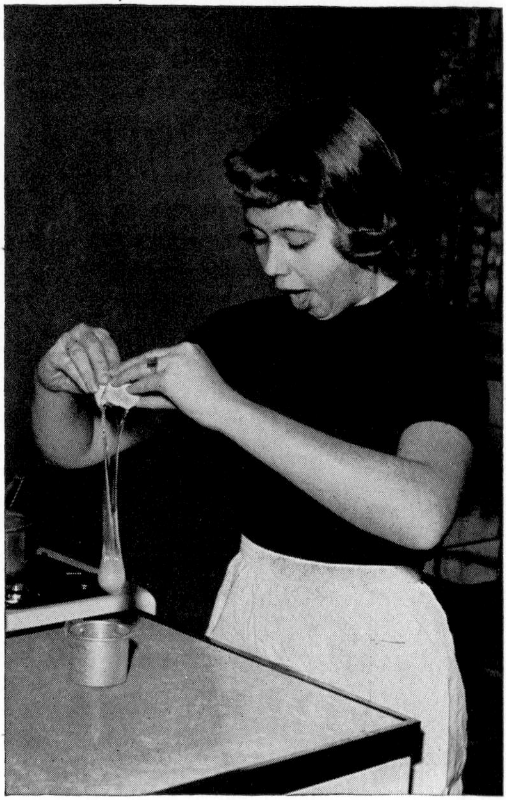

When the unexpected happens on a radio Home Ec demonstration, a good actress can ad lib her way along without the audience being any the wiser. *(Pogue's Portrait Studio)*

Entertainers, used to the spotlight and audience reaction, expend more effort to project their personalities via radio. *(Jules Alexander)*

instantly recognizable. Within limits there is some virtue to this practice, but unless you control it carefully, a simple conversation among a group of friends can become an unbelievable hodgepodge of non-authentic foreign accents, immature falsettos and sepulchral voices, Eastern New England and other regional dialects, and stylized inflection patterns that drive the meaning out of words.

It is sometimes tempting, because you read your lines instead of memorizing them, to assume that *acting* for radio is easier than acting on the stage. This is far from being true; radio acting presents many problems of its own. These suggestions may help you in meeting the problems of radio acting:

1. Rehearse your material to the extent that (a) you are able to read freely, and (b) you become familiar with all changes in microphone position as planned by the director.

2. Be alert for your cues. The strange silence of the radio studio may make listening to your fellow players more difficult than on the stage.

3. Understand your part and portray it with all of the skill and technique at your command.

## ACTIVITY

Prepare the following radio play, Lucille Fletcher's *The Hitch-Hiker*, for class production. Cast all parts, arrange for sound effects, and practice the play before producing it in class. Alfred Hitchcock's recording, *Music to be Murdered By*, (Imperial Record) provides good background music for the play.

## THE HITCH-HIKER



[MUSIC: *Opening chords, dark and ominous. A piano may be used, or a brief passage from some orchestral record. The selection will depend on the* DIRECTOR's *individual taste, but its major effect should consist of a strong, terrifying opening, followed by a kind of monotonous eeriness. The eerie part of the music continues throughout the following speech, but faded down so that the words are audible.*]

RONALD ADAMS: I am in an auto camp on Route Sixty-six just west of Gallup, New Mexico. If I tell it, perhaps it will help me. It will keep me from going mad. But I must tell this quickly. I am not mad now. I feel perfectly well, except that I am running a slight temperature. My name is Ronald Adams. I am thirty-six years of age, unmarried, tall, dark, with a black mustache. I drive a Buick, license number 6Y-175-189. I was born in Brooklyn. All this I know. I know that I am at this moment perfectly sane. That it is not me who has gone mad—but something else—something utterly beyond my control. But I must speak quickly. At any moment the link may break. This may be the last thing I ever tell on earth . . . the last night I ever see the stars. . . .

[*Pause. Music fades out.*]

Six days ago I left Brooklyn, to drive to California.

MRS. ADAMS: Good-bye, Son. Good luck to you, my boy.

ADAMS: Good-bye, Mother. Here—give me a kiss, and then I'll go.

MRS. A.: I'll come out with you to the car.

ADAMS: No. It's raining. Stay here at the door. Hey—what's this? Tears? I thought you promised me you wouldn't cry?

MRS. A.: I know, dear, I'm sorry. But I—do hate to see you go.

ADAMS: I'll be back. I'll only be on the Coast three months.

MRS. A.: Oh—it isn't that. It's just—the trip. Ronald—I wish you weren't driving.

ADAMS: Oh, Mother. There you go again. People do it every day.

MRS. A.: I know. But you'll be careful, won't you? Promise me you'll be extra careful. Don't fall asleep—or drive fast—or pick up any strangers on the road.

ADAMS: Gosh—no. You'd think I was still seventeen to hear you talk.

MRS. A.: And wire me as soon as you get to Hollywood, won't you, Son?

ADAMS: Of course I will. Now, don't you worry. There isn't anything going to happen. It's just eight days of perfectly simple driving on smooth civilized roads.

[MANUAL SOUND: *Slam of car door.* SOUND RECORDING: *Car starts. Sound of car motor running.*]

With a hot dog or hamburger stand every ten miles. . . . *(He chuckles slightly.)*

[SOUND RECORDING: *Automobile in motion full.*]

*(Calling.)* G'bye, Mom—

[*Sound recording of automobile continues behind following:*]

I was in excellent spirits. The drive ahead of me, even the loneliness, seemed like a lark. But I reckoned—without—*him.*

[MUSIC: *Dark opening chords, followed by theme of eerie quality. Continue faded down as before, mingling with sound of car motor running.*]

Crossing Brooklyn Bridge that morning in the rain, I saw a man leaning against the cables. He seemed to be waiting for a lift. There were spots of fresh rain on his shoulders. He was carrying a cheap overnight bag in one hand. He was thin, nondescript, with a cap pulled down over his eyes. . . .

[*Music fades out. Sound of auto continues.*]

I would have forgotten him completely, except that just an hour later, while crossing the Pulaski Skyway over the Jersey flats, I saw him again. At least he looked like the same person. He was standing now, with one thumb pointing west. I couldn't figure out how he'd got there, but I thought probably one of those fast trucks had picked him up, beaten me to the Skyway, and let him off. I didn't stop for him. Then—late that night—I saw him again.

[MUSIC: *Dark ominous chords, followed by eerie theme. Continue through following speech.*]

It was on the new Pennsylvania Turnpike between Harrisburg and Pittsburgh. It's two hundred and sixty-five miles long with a very high speed limit. I was just slowing down for one of the tunnels, when I saw him—standing under an arc light by the side of the road. I could see him quite distinctly. The bag, the cap, even the spots of fresh rain spattered over his shoulders.

[*Music stops.*]

He hailed me this time.

HITCH-HIKER *(off-stage, through megaphone, hollowly):* Hallooo. . . . *(Slightly closer.) Hall . . . llooo. . . .*

[SOUND RECORDING: *Automobile running faster.*]

ADAMS: I stepped on the gas like a shot. That's lonely country through the Alleghenies, and I had no intention of stopping. Besides, the coincidence, or whatever it was, gave me the willies.

[SOUND RECORDING: *Automobile out.*]

I stopped at the next gas station.

[MANUAL SOUND: *Nervous honking of horn.*]

FILLING STATION MAN: Yes, sir.

ADAMS: Fill her up.

F.S.M.: Certainly sir. Check your oil, sir?

ADAMS: No, thanks.

[MANUAL SOUND: *Clank of hose. Sound of insertion into gas tank. Tinkle of bell at regular intervals as though from filling station pump. This continues behind following conversation.*]

F.S.M.: Nice night, isn't it?

ADAMS: Yes. It hasn't been raining here recently, has it?

F.S.M.: Not a drop of rain all week.

ADAMS: H'm. I suppose that hasn't done your business any harm?

F.S.M.: Oh—people drive through here all kinds of weather. Mostly business, you know. There aren't many pleasure cars out on the Turnpike this season of the year.

ADAMS: I suppose not. *(Casually.)* What about hitch-hikers?

F.S.M.: Hitch-hikers—*here?*

[MANUAL SOUND: *Tinkling bell stops. Sound of hose being detached.*]

ADAMS: What's the matter? Don't you ever see any?

F.S.M.: Not much. If we did, it'd be a sight for sore eyes.

[*Manual sound stops.*]

ADAMS: Why?

F.S.M.: A guy'd be a fool who started out to hitch rides on this road. Look at it.

ADAMS: Then you've never seen anybody?

F.S.M. Nope. Mebbe they get the lift before the Turnpike starts—I mean—you know—just before the tollhouse—but then it'd be a mighty long ride. Most cars wouldn't want to pick up a guy for that long a ride. This is pretty lonesome country here—mountains and woods. . . . You ain't seen anybody like that, have you?

ADAMS: No. *(Quickly.)* Oh, no, not at all. It was—just a technical question.

F.S.M.: I see. Well—that'll be just a dollar forty-nine—with the tax. . . .

[*Sound recording fades in automobile starting, motor hum. Continue through following:*]

ADAMS: The thing gradually passed from my mind, as sheer coincidence. I had a good night's sleep in Pittsburgh. I didn't think about the man all next day—until just outside of Zanesville, Ohio, I saw him again.

[MUSIC: *Dark chords, followed by eeriness. Continue through following: Sound recording of auto motor fade down behind music and words, but continue quietly.*]

It was a bright sunshiny afternoon. The peaceful Ohio fields, brown with the autumn stubble, lay dreaming in the golden light. I was driving slowly, drinking it in, when the road suddenly ended in a detour. In front of the barrier—*he* was standing.

[SOUND RECORDING: *Motor hum fades out.*

*Music continues.*]

Let me explain about his appearance before I go on. I repeat. There was nothing sinister about him. He was as drab as a mud fence. Nor was his attitude menacing. He merely stood there, waiting, almost drooping a little, the cheap overnight bag in his hand. He looked as though he had been waiting there for hours. Then he looked up—

[*Music stops.*]

He hailed me. He started to walk forward. . . .

HITCH-HIKER *(Off-stage, through megaphone, hollowly).* Hallooo. . . . Hallo . . . ooo. . . .

[MANUAL SOUND: *Starter button. Sound of gears jamming.*]

*(Through megaphone off-stage, closer.)* Hall-ooo. . . .

[*Manual sound continues. Clash of gears. Dead starter.*]

ADAMS *(panicky)*: No—not just now. Sorry. . . .

HITCH-HIKER *(through megaphone off-stage).* Going to Cal-i-for-nia . . . a . . . ?

ADAMS *(panicky):* No. Not today. The other way. Going to New York. Sorry. . . .

[SOUND RECORDING: *Automobile starts noisily.*]

*(Wildly.) Sorry . . . !*

[SOUND RECORDING: *Automobile hum continuing through following:*]

After I got the car back onto the road again, I felt like a fool. Yet the thought of picking him up, of having him sit beside me was somehow unbearable. Yet at the same time, I felt more than ever, unspeakably alone. . . .

[MUSIC: *Just the eerie section fades in above the sound of automobile hum. It continues through following:*]

Hour after hour went by. The fields, the towns, ticked off one by one. The light changed. I knew now that I was going to see him again. And though I dreaded the sight, I caught myself searching the side of the road, waiting for him to appear. . . .

[*Music and sound recording out.*

MANUAL RECORDING: *Honk horn two or three times. Pause. Nervous honk again.*

MANUAL SOUND TWO: *Creak of squeaky door.*]

PROPRIETOR *(querulous, mountain voice):* Yep? What is it? What do you want?

ADAMS *(breathless):* You sell sandwiches and pop here, don't you?

PROPRIETOR *(cranky):* Yep. We do. In the daytime. But we're closed up now for the night.

ADAMS: I know. But—I was wondering if you could possibly let me have a cup of coffee—black coffee.

PROPRIETOR: Not at this time of night, mister. My wife's the cook, and she's in bed. Mebbe further down the road, at the Honeysuckle Rest.

[MANUAL SOUND: *Creak of door closing.*]

ADAMS: No—no—don't shut the door. Listen—just a minute ago, there was a man standing here—right beside this stand—a suspicious looking man. . . .

PROPRIETOR'S WIFE *(a quavery, whiny voice):* Hen-ry? Who is it, Henry?

PROPRIETOR: It's nobuddy, Mother. Just a feller thinks he wants a cup of coffee. Go back into bed.

ADAMS: I don't mean to disturb you. But you see, I was driving along—when I just happened to look—and there he was. . . .

PROPRIETOR: What was he doing?

ADAMS: Nothing. He ran off—when I stopped the car.

PROPRIETOR: Then what of it? That's nothing to wake a man in the middle of his sleep about. . . .

WIFE: Mebbee he's been drinkin', Henry. . . . *(Calling.)*

PROPRIETOR *(sternly):* Young man, I've got a good mind to turn you over to the sheriff—

ADAMS: But—I—

PROPRIETOR: You've been taking a nip, that's what you've been doing. And you haven't got anything better to do than to wake decent folk out of their hard-earned sleep. Get going. Go on.

WIFE *(calling):* Jes' shet the door on him, Henry—

ADAMS: But he looked as though he were going to rob you.

HENRY: I ain't got nothin' in this stand to lose.

[MANUAL SOUND: *Door creaking closed.*]

Now—on your way before I call out Sheriff Oakes.

[*Door slams shut. Bolted.*

SOUND RECORDING: *Auto starting, motor running.*]

ADAMS: I got into the car again, and drove on slowly. I was beginning to hate the car. If I could have found a place to stop . . . to rest a little. But I was in the Ozark Mountains of Missouri now. The few resort places there were closed. Only an occasional log cabin, seemingly deserted, broke the monotony of the wild wooded landscape. I *had* seen him at that roadside stand. I knew I would see him again—perhaps at the next turn of the road. I knew that when I saw him next—I would run him down.

[MUSIC: *Dark chords, followed by eerie melody.*]

But I did not see him again until late next afternoon.

[*Music continues eerily.*

MANUAL SOUND: *The tinkling of signal bell at railroad crossroads. Continue through following:*]

I had stopped the car at a sleepy little junction just across the border into Oklahoma—to let a train pass by—when he appeared across the tracks, leaning against a telephone pole. . . .

[*Music and manual sound continuing. Very tense.*]

It was a perfectly airless, dry day. The red clay of Oklahoma was baking under the southwestern sun. Yet there were spots of fresh rain on his shoulders. . . .

[*Music stops.*]

I couldn't stand that. Without thinking, blindly, I started the car across the tracks.

[SOUND RECORDING: *Distant, very faint cry of train whistle approaching. Manual sound of bell continuing.*]

He didn't even look up at me. He was staring at the ground. I stepped on the gas hard, veering the wheel sharply toward him.

[SOUND RECORDING: *Train whistle closer. Chugging of wheels fading in.*]

I could hear the train in the distance now. But I didn't care.

[MANUAL SOUND ONE *continues signal bell.*

MANUAL SOUND TWO: *Jamming of gears. Clash of metal.*]

Then—something went wrong with the car.

[MANUAL SOUND TWO: *Gears jamming. Starter button dead.*

SOUND RECORDING: *Train chugging up, louder.*]

The train was coming closer. I could hear the cry of its whistle.

[SOUND RECORDING: *Train chugging. Cry of whistle closer.*

*All this should be a cacophony of sound blended together, almost overriding Adams' voice, which tries to rise above it, almost hysterical with panic.*]

Still he stood there. And now—I knew that he was beckoning—beckoning me to my death. . . .

[SOUND RECORDING: *Full train chugging topped by wild cry of train whistle overpowering all other sound, full, then dying away slowly to silence.*

*Music fades in with the eerie part of the theme. We hear this a second or two, then* ADAMS *says breathlessly, quietly:*]

Well—I frustrated him that time. The starter worked at last. I managed to back up. But when the train passed, he was gone. I was all alone, in the hot dry afternoon.

[*Music continuing.*

SOUND RECORDING: *Fade in auto hum.*]

After that, I knew I had to do something. I didn't know who this man was, or what he wanted of me. I only knew that from now on, I must not let myself be alone on the road for one moment.

[*Music and sound recording of auto out.*

MANUAL RECORDING: *Honk of horn.*]

Hello, there. Like a ride?

GIRL: What do you think? How far you going?

ADAMS: Where do you want to go?

GIRL: Amarillo, Texas.

[MANUAL SOUND: *Car door opening.*]

ADAMS: I'll drive you there.

GIRL: Gee!

[MANUAL SOUND: *Car door slams.*

SOUND RECORDING: *Auto starting up, hum. It continues through following:*]

Mind if I take off my shoes? My dogs are killing me.

ADAMS: Go right ahead.

GIRL: Gee, what a break this is. A swell car, a decent guy, and driving all the way to Amarillo. All I been getting so far is trucks.

ADAMS: Hitch-hike much?

GIRL: Sure. Only it's tough sometimes, in these great open spaces, to get the breaks.

ADAMS: I should think it would be. Though I'll bet if you get a good pick-up in a fast car, you can get to places faster than, say, another person in another car.

GIRL: I don't get you?

ADAMS: Well, take me, for instance. Suppose I'm driving across the country, say, at a nice steady clip of about forty-five miles an hour. Couldn't a girl like you, just standing beside the road, waiting for lifts, beat me to town after town—provided she got picked up every time in a car doing from sixty-five to seventy miles an hour?

GIRL: I dunno. What difference does it make?

ADAMS: Oh—no difference. It's just a—crazy idea I had sitting here in the car.

GIRL *(laughing)*: Imagine spending your time in a swell car, and thinking of things like that.

ADAMS: What would you do instead?

GIRL *(admiringly)*: What would I do? If I was a good-looking fellow like yourself? Why—I'd just *enjoy* myself—every minute of the time. I'd sit back and relax, and if I saw a good-looking girl along the side of the road . . . *(Sharply.)* Hey—look out!

[SOUND RECORDING: *Auto hum continuing.*]

ADAMS *(breathlessly)*: Did you see him, too?

GIRL: See who?

ADAMS: That man. Standing beside the barbed-wire fence.

GIRL: I didn't see—nobody. There wasn't nothing but a bunch of steer and the wire fence. What did you think you was doing? Trying to run into the barbed-wire fence?

[SOUND RECORDING: *Auto motor continuing.*]

ADAMS: There was a man there, I tell you . . . a thin gray man, with an overnight bag in his hand. And I was trying to run him down.

GIRL: Run him down? You mean—kill him?

ADAMS: But—*(desperately)* you say you didn't see him back there? You're sure?

GIRL *(queerly)*: I didn't see a soul. And as far as I'm concerned, mister . . .

ADAMS: Watch for him the next time then. Keep watching. Keep your eyes peeled on the road. He'll turn up again—maybe any minute now. *(excitedly.)* There! look there. . . .

[MANUAL RECORDING: *Car skidding. Screech. A crash of metal as of car going into barbed-wire fence.*

GIRL *screams.*

MANUAL RECORDING: *A bump.*

MANUAL RECORDING TWO: *Sound of door handle of car turning.*]

GIRL: How does this door work? I—I'm gettin' out of here.

ADAMS: Did you see him that time?

GIRL *(sharply, choked)*: No. I didn't see him that time. And personally, mister, I don't expect never to see him. All I want to do is go on living—and I don't see how I will very long, driving with you.

ADAMS: I'm sorry. I—I don't know what came over me. *(Frightened.)* Please—don't go. . . .

GIRL: So if you'll excuse me, mister.

ADAMS: You can't go. Listen, how would you like to go to California? I'll drive you to California.

GIRL: Seeing pink elephants all the way? No, thanks.

[MANUAL SOUND: *Door handle turning.*]

ADAMS: Listen. Please. For just one moment—

GIRL: You know what I think you need, big boy? Not a girl friend. Just a dose of good sleep. There. I got it now. . . .

[MANUAL SOUND: *Door opens. Slams. Metallic.*]

ADAMS: No. You can't go.

GIRL *(wildly):* Leave your hands offa me, do you hear? Leave your—

[MANUAL SOUND: *Sharp slap.*

MANUAL SOUND TWO: *Footsteps over gravel, running. They die away. A pause.*]

ADAMS: She ran from me, as though I were a monster. A few minutes later, I saw a passing truck pick her up. I knew then that I was utterly alone.

[MANUAL SOUND: *Imitation of low mooing of steer, or sound recording of same.*]

I was in the heart of the great Texas prairies. There wasn't a car on the road after the truck went by. I tried to figure out what to do, how to get hold of myself. If I could find a place to rest. Or even if I could sleep right there in the car for a few hours, along the side of the road.

[MUSIC: *The eerie theme stealing in softly.*]

I was getting my winter overcoat out of the back seat to use as a blanket, when I saw him coming toward me, emerging from the herd of moving steer. . . .

[SOUND: *Mooing of steer, low. Out of it emerges voice of:*]

HITCH-HIKER *(hollowly off-stage through megaphone):* Hall . . . ooo. . . . Hall . . . oo. . . .

[SOUND RECORDING: *Auto starting. Auto hum steady up. Music continuing.*]

ADAMS: Perhaps I should have spoken to him then, fought it out then and there. For now he began to be everywhere. Wherever I stopped, even for a moment—for gas, for oil, for a drink of pop, a cup of coffee, a sandwich—he was there.

[*Music continuing. Auto sound continuing. More tense and rapid.*]

I saw him standing outside the auto camp in Amarillo, that night, when I dared to slow down. He was sitting near the drinking fountain in a little camping spot just inside the border of New Mexico. . . .

[*Music steady. Rapid, more breathless.*]

He was waiting for me outside the Navajo Reservation where I stopped to check my tires. I saw him in Albuquerque, where I bought twenty gallons of gas. I was afraid now, afraid to stop. I began to drive faster and faster. I was in lunar landscape now—

the great arid mesa country of New Mexico. I drove through it with the indifference of a fly crawling over the face of the moon. . . .

[*Auto hum up. Music more and more eerie. More desperately.*] But now he didn't even wait for me to stop. Unless I drove at eighty-five miles an hour over those endless roads, he waited for me at every other mile. I would see his figure, shadowless, flitting before me, still in its same attitude, over the cold lifeless ground, flitting over dried-up rivers, over broken stones cast up by old glacial upheavals, flitting in the pure and cloudless air. . . .

[*Music reaches eerie climax. Stops. Sound recording of auto hum stops. A low voice in the silence.*]

I was beside myself when I finally reached Gallup, New Mexico, this morning. There is an auto camp here—cold, almost deserted at this time of year. I went inside and asked if there was a telephone. . . .

[MANUAL RECORDING: *Sound of footsteps on wood, heavy, echoing.*]

I had the feeling that if only I could speak to someone familiar, someone I loved, I could pull myself together.

[MANUAL SOUND: *Nickel put into phone.*]

OPERATOR: Number, please?

ADAMS: Long distance.

OPERATOR: Thank you.

[MANUAL SOUND: *Return of nickel.* Buzz.]

LONG DISTANCE: This is Long Distance.

ADAMS: I'd like to put in a call to my home in Brooklyn, New York. I'm Ronald Adams. The number is Beechwood 2-0828.

LONG DISTANCE: Thank you. What is your number? [A mechanical tone.]

ADAMS: My number . . . 312.

[MANUAL SOUND: *A buzz.*]

THIRD OPERATOR *(from distance):* Albuquerque. . .

LONG DISTANCE OPERATOR: New York for Gallup.

FOURTH OPERATOR: New York.

LONG DISTANCE: Gallup, New Mexico, calling Beechwood 2-0828.

ADAMS: I had read somewhere that love could banish demons. It was the middle of the morning. I knew Mother would be home. I pictured her tall, white-haired, in her crisp house dress, going about her tasks. It would be enough, I thought, merely to hear the even calmness of her voice.

LONG DISTANCE: Will you please deposit three dollars and eighty-five cents for the first three minutes. When you have deposited a dollar and a half will you wait until I have collected the money?

[MANUAL SOUND: *Clunk of six quarters as through a telephone.*]

All right, deposit another dollar and a half.

[MANUAL SOUND: *Clunk of six quarters as through a telephone.*]

Will you please deposit the remaining eighty-five cents?

[SOUND: *Clunk of three quarters and one dime as through*

*telephone.]*

Ready with Brooklyn—go ahead, please.

ADAMS: Hello.

MRS. WHITNEY: Mrs. Adams' residence.

ADAMS: Hello. Hello—Mother?

MRS. WHITNEY *(very flat and proper):* This is Mrs. Adams' residence. Who is it you wished to speak to, please?

ADAMS: Why—who's this?

MRS. WHITNEY: This is Mrs. Whitney.

ADAMS: Mrs. Whitney? I don't know any Mrs. Whitney. Is this Beechwood 2-0828?

MRS. WHITNEY: Yes.

ADAMS: Where's my mother? Where's Mrs. Adams?

MRS. WHITNEY: Mrs. Adams is not at home. She is still in the hospital.

ADAMS: The hospital?

MRS. WHITNEY: Yes. Who is this calling, please? Is it a member of the family?

ADAMS: What's she in the hospital for?

MRS. WHITNEY: She's been prostrated for five days. Nervous breakdown. But who is this calling?

ADAMS: Nervous breakdown? But—my mother was never nervous.

MRS. WHITNEY: It's all taken place since the death of her oldest son, Ronald.

ADAMS: Death of her oldest son, Ronald . . . ? Hey—what is this? What number is this?

MRS. WHITNEY: This is Beechwood 2-0828. It's all been very sudden. He was killed just six days ago in an automobile accident on the Brooklyn Bridge.

LONG DISTANCE: Your three minutes are up, sir. *(Pause.)* Your three minutes are up, sir. . . . Sir—your three minutes are up, sir. . . .

[*Softly. A pause.*

MUSIC: *Fade in eerie theme softly.*]

ADAMS *(a strange voice):* And so, I am sitting here in this deserted auto camp in Gallup, New Mexico. I am trying to think. I am trying to get hold of myself. Otherwise I shall go mad. . . . Outside it is night—the vast, soulless night of New Mexico. A million stars are in the sky. Ahead of me stretch a thousand miles of empty mesa, mountains, prairies, desert. Somewhere, among them, he is waiting for me. . . . Somewhere I shall know who he is—and who . . . I am. . . .

[*Music continues to an eerie climax.*]

## ACTIVITIES

1. Using the above script as an example, prepare an adaptation of a short story for radio. Develop a script complete with sound effects and directions for vocal interpretation.
2. Prepare a soap opera type of radio drama for class production.
3. Locate another play written especially for radio and produce it in class. Your library or literature books will have such plays.

# Learning About Television

## Television defined

There are some people who have the somewhat mistaken notion that television is radio with pictures. Let's take a look at some ideas on what television is *not,* and perhaps we can discover what it *is.*

First of all, television is not like the movies, even though a large part of original television programming is done on film and many movies are shown on television. The average television show has neither the time nor the budget to afford a several months' shooting schedule with an army of technicians as the movie industry does. Moreover, television is intended for individual and small group viewing; the movies for large audiences. A film made for television use must be put together in a way quite different from those films prepared for your neighborhood theater.

A director shows how to read from a prompter above the camera lens while seeming to be looking into the lens—the viewer's eye! *(The New York Times)*

Automation equipment now puts television films together starting with the tape reader shown on the left feeding in information, then switching on projectors, cameras and microphones in announcers' booths. *(WKRC-TV, Cincinnati, Ohio)*

Television is not like reading a book, either. Many books have provided a tremendous volume of material for use on television, but reading a book and watching television, although both use the eyes, are as different as skiing and skating, both of which use the feet.

Nor is watching television an activity that can easily be combined with other activities; that is, you can't watch television while doing the many things you can do while listening to the radio. Many states, in fact, have laws against having television sets in automobiles. Watching television requires a much more concentrated use of your eyes, ears, mind, and imagination than does radio.

Finally, neither television nor radio is complete in itself. That is, both television and radio are techniques—*and only techniques.* Television and radio programs are essentially adaptations of long established communication forms. The essentials of any good radio or television program could be presented before a live audience without a microphone or camera anywhere around. The fundamental advantage to the microphone and camera is that they make the program available to a larger audience on a more intimate basis and with a minimum of distraction.

With this in mind, it's easy to see that the types of programs popular on television are much the same as those on radio. The technique used is what makes the difference. The technique of television offers a greater variety of ways to get your point across.

The Chinese say that a picture is worth a thousand words. Television is a picture *and* a thousand words—together with a few electronic devices that make both picture and words unusual and interesting. Television, as content, has not yet lived up to its potential as a medium.

## TV words and phrases

Just as in radio, television has been developing a behind-the-scenes language all its own. A good many radio terms hold true in television, and practically all the hand signals are the same, except that in television they are given by the floor manager, for the director is completely out of sight of the talent, or performers. The following is a list of terms peculiar to television.

A floor manager, with his microphone tuned in to the director's booth, and a camera man are shown in action. *(CBS Television Network)*

## A GLOSSARY OF TV TERMS

**Animations:** mechanical devices including cartoon-type films which give seeming movement to inanimate subjects

**Background:** any set, drape, drop, et cetera, used at back of scene

**Boom:** long metal arm for suspending a microphone, usually mounted on a dolly

**CU:** close-up shot; narrow-angle picture; head only, et cetera

**Contrast:** degree-of-brightness relationships between various elements in a picture

**Cutting:** the elimination of undesirable motion, film, or action

**Dissolve:** the momentary overlapping of an image produced by one camera with that of another and the gradual elimination of the first

**Dolly** (noun): a four-wheeled framework on which a camera or microphone is mounted

**Dolly** (verb): to move the camera to the proper position

**Dry run:** rehearsals previous to camera rehearsals where business, lines, sets, et cetera, are perfected

**Fade:** to bring up or black out the television image

**Flood:** single klieg light or scoop used to illuminate wide areas

**Full shot:** a full-length view of actors or talent

**Hard shadow:** a single definite shadow, as opposed to multiple shadows

**Head room:** area between the actor's head and the actual top of set

**Hot light:** a concentrated light to emphasize features or bring out contours

**Kill:** to strike out or remove

**LS:** long shot, full view of total scene; useful in scene-setting

**Lens turret:** circular base attached to camera with several lens mountings so changes can be made quickly and easily

**MCU:** medium close-up shot that cuts off actors just above the waist

**MS:** medium shot, halfway between a CU and an LS

**One shot:** a camera shot in which only one person is framed, that is, visible on the screen

**Pan:** to turn the camera right or left

**Properties:** all physical materials used in a scene: furnishings, decorations, or stage properties

**Roll it:** a cue to start the camera or film projector

**Slide:** a title or picture on a single frame of 35 mm. film that is projected into the camera, usually sealed between pieces of glass

**Superimposition:** the overlapping of an image produced by one camera with the image from another, both pictures being visible at the same time

**Tilt:** slow camera movement up or down

**Titles:** any titles used on a program; can be motion picture film, cards, slides, et cetera

**Truck** (verb): to dolly in parallel motion with a moving figure; to follow a person walking down the street

**Two shot:** a camera shot in which only two persons are framed on the screen. (May be used in higher numerical combinations.)

## Job categories in television

As you can see from Figures 3 and 4, a great number of people are needed to put a big network television show on the air.

Still, in even the smallest of stations, it takes quite a few people to put on a program. In the following charts, those job classifications outlined in heavy red are the absolute minimum for putting on a *live* show. Those outlined with a dotted line are the bare minimum for a *film* or *network-fed* show.

*TV PRODUCTION*

*Program Department*

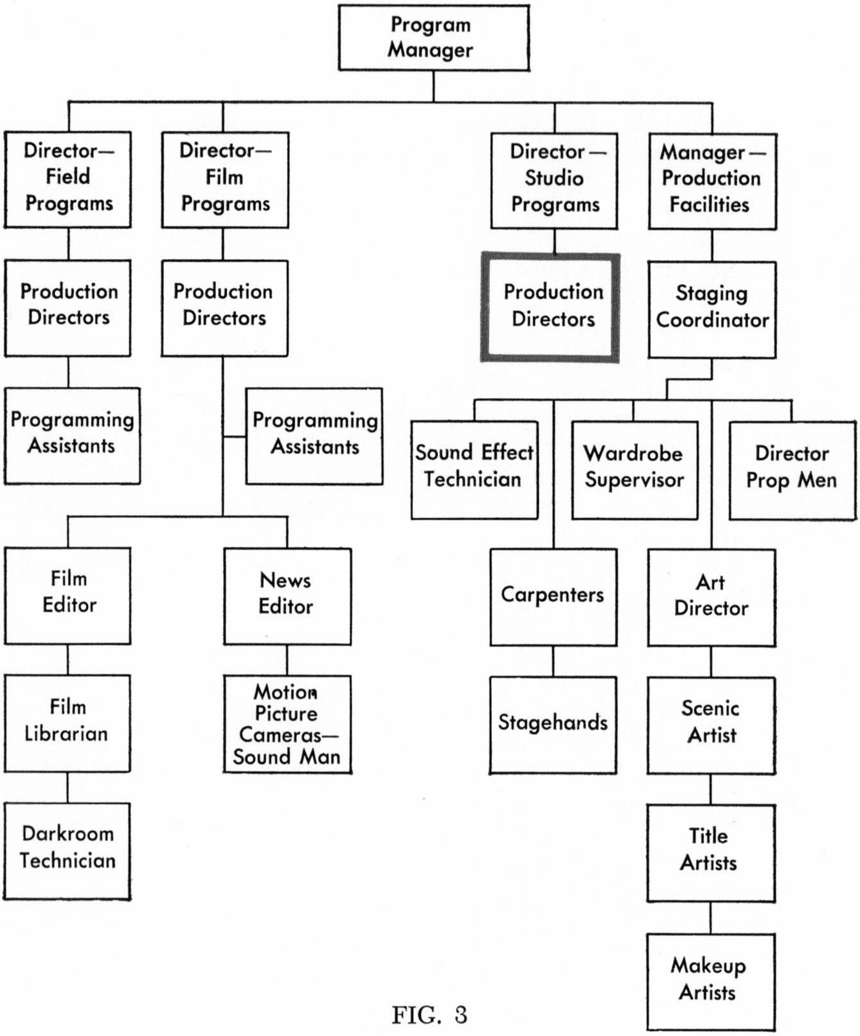


FIG. 3

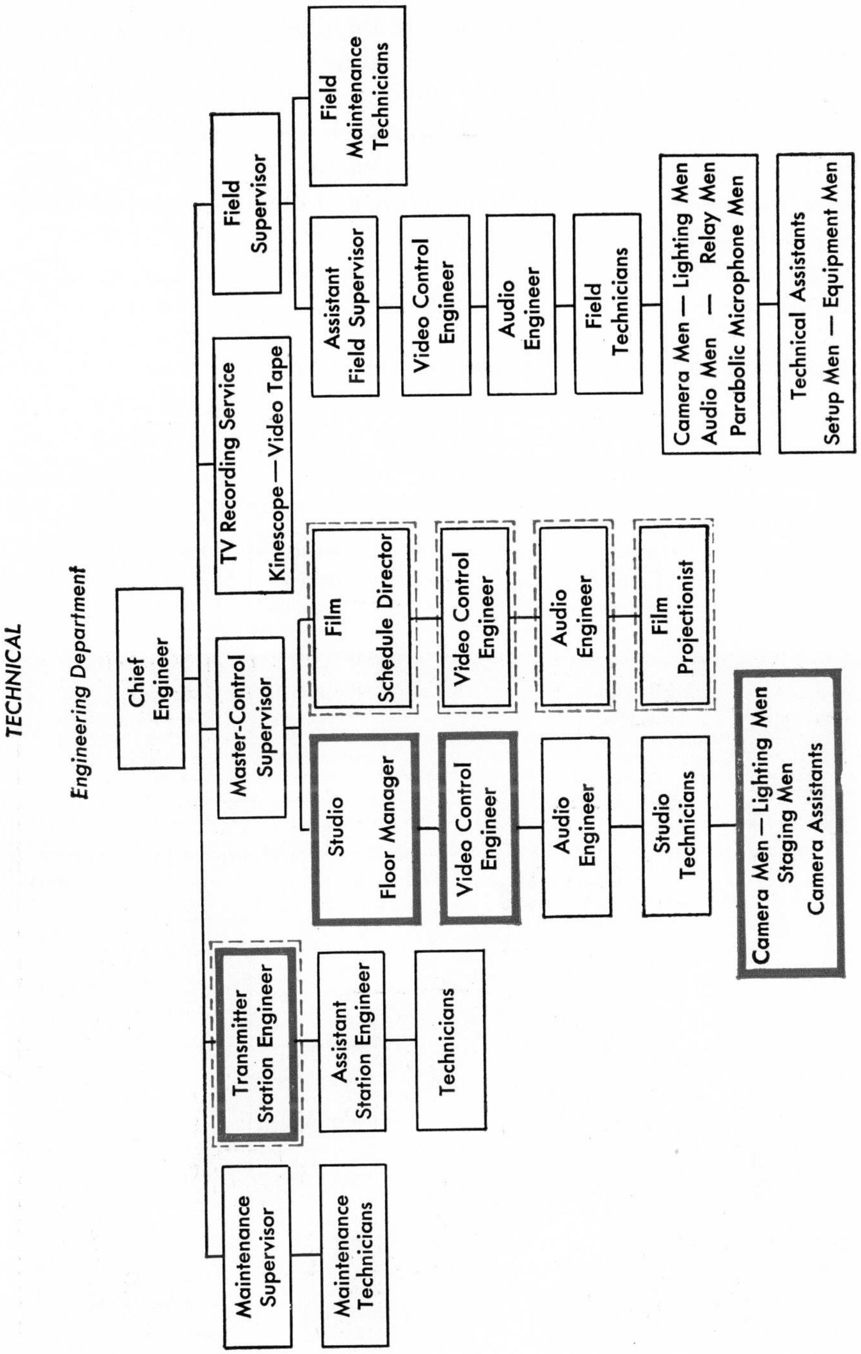
TECHNICAL
Engineering Department
Chief Engineer
Maintenance Supervisor
Maintenance Technicians
Transmitter Station Engineer
Assistant Station Engineer
Technicians
Master-Control Supervisor
Studio Floor Manager
Video Control Engineer
Audio Engineer
Studio Technicians
Camera Men—Lighting Men
Staging Men
Camera Assistants
Film Schedule Director
Video Control Engineer
Audio Engineer
Film Projectionist
TV Recording Service
Kinescope—Video Tape
Field Supervisor
Field Maintenance Technicians
Assistant Field Supervisor
Video Control Engineer
Audio Engineer
Field Technicians
Camera Men — Lighting Men
Audio Men — Relay Men
Parabolic Microphone Men
Technical Assistants
Setup Men — Equipment Men

FIG. 4

A careful study of these charts will be helpful. These charts, however, are more on the ideal side than the real, particularly so far as smaller stations are concerned. It is true, of course, that each of these job categories may be filled by a large number of people when it comes to the big networks in New York or Hollywood, but in most other cities, although the various jobs still exist, one person usually handles two or more assignments. One man, for instance, may handle the writing, production, continuity, and direction of a program—and he may even sell the show to a sponsor in his spare time.

## Problems of television techniques

With so many people concerned with the production of a television show, it's easy to see that the biggest problem to be faced in television is the human element. Let's say that only nine people are concerned with a live telecast: an actor (or talent); two cameramen; a floor manager; a director; an audio engineer; a video engineer; an announcer; and a transmitter operator. Each has an

With an ear to the director and an eye to the script, he dubs in the selected music on cue. *(Official Photograph, Board of Education, City of New York)*

If you are seriously interested in a career in television work, does this spot in a control room attract you? *(CBS Television Network)*

extremely important job to perform, and if *one* of them makes a mistake, it is reflected on the home television receiver. Fortunately, a great many "human errors" are missed by the viewing audience. It is to the credit of television people, though, that when an error is made, the person who makes it constantly tries to improve himself and his abilities so that his chances of making mistakes become fewer and fewer.

## Unique characteristics of television acting

The basic role of the actor as an interpreter does not vary whether on the stage, the screen, or television. The techniques that the actor will employ, however, must be adapted to the needs of the various media.

Television, then, like any other medium, imposes its particular requirements on the techniques of the actor. Perhaps the greatest difference between acting on the stage and for television is in the increased importance of the face. The intensity of the television close-up emphasizes the significance of facial expression. The effect is the same as that produced by a movie camera close-up.

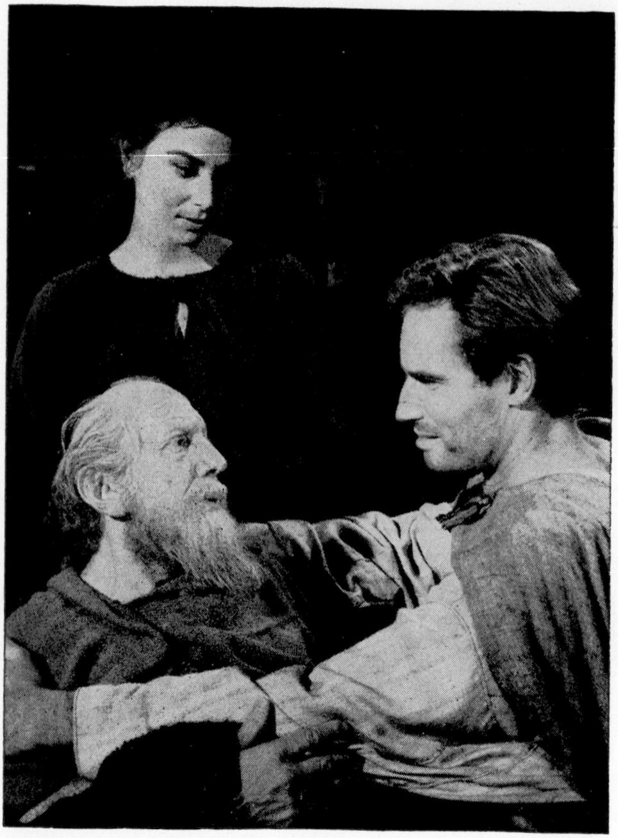

A depth of emotion is skillfully revealed by this camera close-up study in a poignant *Ben Hur* scene. *(Courtesy of Metro-Goldwyn-Mayer, Inc.)*

Other differences in technique may be noted. Because of the fact that television productions are ordinarily not rehearsed as completely as stage productions, the television actor must be a quick study. Not only must he learn his lines quickly and perfectly, but he must also learn to move precisely as is necessary for a production. Because of the small area over which the television camera is effective, precision of movement becomes extremely important. The television actor plays more to the camera and less to his fellow actors than does the stage performer. Finally, because of the use of microphones for pickup, the television actor usually need not project as much as he would were he on a stage. Indeed, the entire style of television acting tends to be reduced in its dynamic range.

## Conclusion

The techniques of radio and television cannot be learned from a book. You can learn them best by doing—by writing scripts, rehearsing shows, and trying out program ideas as suggested in this text.

Whatever experience you gain now from your speech class will help you in case you ever appear on a real radio or television show.

Like the stage, the field of broadcasting requires a large variety of creative skills and offers you many opportunities to become a part of the vast network of talent needed every day. If you should choose broadcasting as your career, you are certain of being an integral part of the amazing and exciting advancement that is being made in spoken communication. How significant your role will be will depend, of course, upon your talent. You may only push an important button, assemble props, or hold the "prompt sheet" for a famous star. Then again you may *be* the famous star. Regardless of your role, you will be participating in the great drama of bringing the world closer together through oral communication.

## PRONUNCIATION PROBLEMS

Words in which the letters "n" and "g" appear together in the spelling, as for example *song* or *finger*, create many pronunciation difficulties. Chiefly, the problem is whether the word should be pronounced with only the "ng" sound or with the "ng plus g" sound.

If the basic or root word ends in the letters "ng" or "ngue," the word is typically pronounced with the "ng" sound. Examples are words like *ring*, *sing*, and *tongue*. On the other hand, if the basic or root form of the word contains the letters "ng" in the middle of the word, the word is typically pronounced with the "ng plus g" sound. Examples are words like *finger*, *linger*, and *hunger*. Words in which the letters "ng" are followed by the letters "th," however, as in the word *strength* are pronounced with only the "ng" sound; that is, there is no hard "g" sound.

If comparative or superlative adjectival forms are created from root words that end in the spelling "ng," as *stronger*, or *longest*, the "ng plus g" pronunciation is used. But if the spelling "er" is added to a root form that ends in "ng," so that the word means "one who does," as in *singer*, the "ng" pronunciation is used.

Usually, in words in which an unstressed prefix ending in the letter "n" is added to a root form beginning with the letter "g," as in *ungrateful* or *inglorious*, the words are pronounced with "n" plus the hard "g" sound. If, under the same circumstances, the prefix is stressed, as in *congress*, the pronunciation is frequently "ng plus g," although there are many exceptions to this principle.

The suffix "ing" is typically pronounced with the "ng" sound and does not alter the pronunciation of the root word. *Singing* and *fingering* are examples.

## READING CHECK-UP

Read aloud the nonsense sentences below to check your pronunciation of any problem words.

Lingering over the tea cups, they were thinking of finding the answer and learning every single rule of spelling.

The King of England was going to Hong Kong and Bangor after returning from Bingham and Birmingham where he was engrossed watching the making of gingham.

Bring Eva, the youngest sister, to hear the ding-dong of the ringing bells.

The single singer sang songs of love long, long ago to the jingle, jangle of the tango.

The fishmonger's language was growing angrier as the hungry singers lingered longer.

The strength of the English was strengthened after rowing the length of the stream.

The stronger, younger singers sang the strongest and loudest and longest of all.

Elongate the diphthongal sounds and prolongate the "ings" in your word endings.

The youngster's coat was hanging on the hanger lengthwise while he rang the bell.

Flinging his coat the length of the bungalow, the hungry, angry gangster bungled.

Suggested additional practice reading: "The Cataract of Ladore" by Southey.

## VOCABULARY BUILD-UP

Use the italicized words in short paragraphs to show that you understand their meanings.

a few *desultory* pickets
several *contemporary* writers
of *diminutive* stature
an *overt* response
a *phlegmatic* type
displaying a *truculent* attitude
an *integral* part
to *expedite* proceedings
of a *sadistic* nature
*scurrilous* attacks

blessed with *equanimity*
a *querulous* disposition
*circumspect* behavior
*pedantic* style of speaking
a display of *opulence*
*banal* conversation
a complete *enigma*
*unrequited* love
*requisites* for college entrance
*nebulous* plans

# Acknowledgments

The authors wish to express their grateful appreciation to Mr. John D. Davies, Teacher of Speech, Kenosha High School, Kenosha, Wisconsin; Mr. Ralph G. McGee, Director of Forensics, New Trier Township High School, Winnetka, Illinois; and Miss Helen M. Ryan, Teacher of Speech, Newton High School, Newtonville, Massachusetts; for their inestimable help in reading the entire manuscript and making many excellent suggestions for its improvement.

Special thanks are also due to the following professors from the University of Wisconsin who have read portions of the manuscript: Kenneth E. Andersen, Knapp Fellow; Arnold E. Aronson, Assistant Professor of Speech; Winston L. Brembeck, Professor of Speech; James W. Cleary, Assistant Professor of Speech; Edward F. Crawley, Instructor in Photography, Extension Division; Ordean G. Ness, Associate Professor of Speech; Raymond Stanley, Program Director, TV Laboratory; and to Thorrel A. Fest, Professor of Speech, University of Colorado; and Wesley D. Hervey, Assistant Professor of Speech, University of Hawaii.

To Mrs. Lulubelle Lincks and Mrs. Jessie McDaniel of the Withrow High School Library, Cincinnati, Ohio, for their excellent research assistance; and to Mrs. Mildred Ladley, Mr. Jack Mueller, and Mr. Ray Viering, Withrow High School *Annual* Advisors, for their fine cooperation in providing all the pictures from Pogue's Portrait Studio—the authors express their sincere gratitude.

The authors also wish to gratefully acknowledge the help of the following individuals and organizations whose cooperation in supplying illustrative material for this book has been of great value: (The numbers indicate the pages on which the illustrations appear.)

| | |
|---|---|
| Abrahamsen, Inger | 239 |
| Alexander, Jules | Cover and Title Page, Unit Opening I<br>43, 79, 531 |
| Anderson, Brad | 367 |
| Barnes, Bob | 283 |
| Bell Telephone Laboratories | 60, 61 |
| Bernhardt | 41 |
| Black Star | Cover<br>111, 120, 128, 178, 253, 406, 427 |
| *The Cincinnati Enquirer* | 523 |
| Columbia Broadcasting System | Unit Opening V (Howard K. Smith)<br>83, 327, 341, 445, 514, 544, 549 |
| Cornell University–ACIR | 200 |
| Currens, Al | 192, 243 |
| Day, Chon | 320 |
| Dirks, John | 297 |
| Dunaway, Don Carlos | 146, 182, 195, 250, 261, 364, 389 |
| Eastman Kodak Co. | 29, 115 |
| Faris/Black Star | 492 |
| *Field & Stream* Magazine | 41 |
| Fredon, D. | 482 |
| Friedman-Abeles | 470, 500 |
| Fuller/Rapho Guillumette | 467 |
| Galloway, Ewing | Unit Opening IV<br>20, 46, 161, 171, 281, 288, 325, 342, 346 |
| Garrel, Leo | 36 |
| Gendreau, Philip | 168, 506, 512 |
| German Tourist Office | 454 |
| Graphic House, Inc. | 398, 405, 428 |
| Harbutt, Charles/Scope | 33 |
| Henderson, Tom | 245 |
| Irwin, John V. | 184, 236, 248 |
| Johnson, Esther | 452 |
| Langdon, David | 75 |
| Lepper, Edwin | 199 |
| Lewis, Frederic | 330 |
| Marcus, Jerry | 11, 113 |
| Metro-Goldwyn-Mayer, Inc. | 453, 461, 550 |
| Modell, F. B. | 26 |
| Monkmeyer Press Photo Service | 18, 31, 103, 132, 134, 139, 144, 152, 153, 158, 169, 189, 222, 226, 229, 255, 293, 300, 310, 313, 335, 351, 359, 366, 375, 392, 434, 475, 489, 493, 495, 520 |
| National Broadcasting Company | 381, 528, 515 |
| The National Hospital for Speech Disorders | 67, 72 |
| New York City Board of Education | 429, 548 |

| | |
|---|---|
| *The New York Times* | 542 |
| The *New Yorker* Magazine | 26, 75, 482 |
| Peck, Stephen Rogers | 53, ff. 54, 57, 58, 59 |
| Pogue's Portrait Studio | Unit Opening III<br>3, 13, 49, 68, 137, 323, 383, 521, 530 |
| Rubendunst, A. M. | Unit Opening II<br>63, 90, 23, 191 |
| *The Saturday Evening Post* | 11, 36, 113, 199, 206, 211, 234, 245, 283, 305, 320, 367 |
| Shirvanian, Vahan | 305 |
| United Nations | 524 |
| United Press International | 4, 10, 65, 98, 216, 225 |
| WCET–Educational TV, Cincinnati, Ohio | 516, 526, 527 |
| WKRC–Radio, Cincinnati, Ohio | 517 |
| WKRC–TV, Cincinnati, Ohio | 23, 543 |
| Wertheimer, Alfred/Scope | 100, 101, 431 |
| Williamsburg–*The Story of a Patriot* | 462 |
| Yates, Bill | 211 |
| Zeiss, Joseph | 206 |

# Index

R. Crockett